'HE WAR

A Tour of the Southern States

1865-1866

hARpER ✦ ɛoRChBooks

*A reference-list of Harper Torchbooks, classified
by subjects, is printed at the end of this volume.*

AMERICAN PERSPECTIVES

EDITED BY BERNARD WISHY AND

WILLIAM E. LEUCHTENBURG

Ray Stannard Baker: FOLLOWING THE COLOR LINE: *American Negro Citizenship in the Progressive Era*, edited by Dewey W. Grantham, Jr. TB/3053

George Bancroft: *THE ORIGIN OF THE AMERICAN REVOLUTION, from "The History of the United States," edited by Edmund S. Morgan.

Hyman Berman (ed.): *THE RISE OF AMERICAN LABOR: *A Reader.*

Randolph S. Bourne: WAR AND THE INTELLECTUALS: *Collected Essays, 1915-1919*, edited by Carl Resek. TB/3043

Louis D. Brandeis: *OTHER PEOPLE'S MONEY, edited by Richard M. Abrams.

Edmund Burke: *EDMUND BURKE AND THE AMERICAN REVOLUTION, edited by Elliott Robert Barkan.

Dixon Ryan Fox: THE DECLINE OF ARISTOCRACY IN THE POLITICS OF NEW YORK, 1801-1840, edited by Robert V. Remini. TB/3064

Charlotte Perkins Gilman: *WOMEN AND ECONOMICS: *A Study of the Economic Relation Between Men and Women as a Factor in Social Evolution*, edited by Carl N. Degler.

Alexander Hamilton: THE REPORTS OF ALEXANDER HAMILTON, edited by Jacob E. Cooke. TB/3060

Daniel R. Hundley: SOCIAL RELATIONS IN OUR SOUTHERN STATES, edited by William R. Taylor. TB/3058

Robert Hunter: POVERTY: *Social Conscience in the Progressive Era*, edited by Peter d'A. Jones. TB/3065

Helen Hunt Jackson: A CENTURY OF DISHONOR: *The Early Crusade for Indian Reform*, edited by Andrew F. Rolle. TB/3063

Thomas Jefferson: NOTES ON THE STATE OF VIRGINIA, edited by Thomas P. Abernethy. TB/3052

O. G. Libby: *THE GEOGRAPHICAL DISTRIBUTION OF THE VOTE OF THE THIRTEEN STATES ON THE FEDERAL CONSTITUTION: 1787-1788, edited by Lee Benson.

William G. McLoughlin (ed.): *THE AMERICAN EVANGELICALS: *A Reader.*

Alfred T. Mahan: *AMERICA'S ROLE IN WORLD AFFAIRS: *Collected Essays*, edited by Ernest R. May.

S. Walter Poulshock *and* Robert A. Skotheim, (eds.): *THE BUSINESSMAN AND MODERN AMERICA: *A Reader.*

Walter Rauschenbusch: CHRISTIANITY AND THE SOCIAL CRISIS, edited by Robert D. Cross. TB/3059

Whitelaw Reid: *AFTER THE WAR, edited by C. Vann Woodward.

James Ford Rhodes: *THE COMING OF THE CIVIL WAR (Vol. I); THE CIVIL WAR (Vol. II): an abridgment of "The History of the United States from the Compromise of 1850," edited by Grady McWhiney.

Jacob Riis: *THE MAKING OF AN AMERICAN, edited by Roy Lubove.

Charles Howard Shinn: MINING CAMPS: *A Study in American Frontier Government*, edited by Rodman Paul. TB/3062

Ida M. Tarbell: *THE HISTORY OF THE STANDARD OIL COMPANY: *abridged ed.*, edited by David M. Chalmers.

George B. Tindall (ed.): *A POPULIST READER.

Walter E. Weyl: THE NEW DEMOCRACY: *An Essay on Certain Political and Economic Tendencies in the United States*, edited by Charles B. Forcey. TB/3042

* *in preparation*

AFTER THE WAR

A Tour of the Southern States

1865-1866

WHITELAW REID

EDITED WITH AN INTRODUCTION
AND NOTES BY
C. VANN WOODWARD

HARPER TORCHBOOKS ❦ *The University Library*
Harper & Row, Publishers, New York

AFTER THE WAR

Introduction and Notes to the Torchbook edition
copyright © 1965 by C. Vann Woodward

Printed in the United States of America.

This book was originally published in 1866 by
Moore, Wilstach & Baldwin, Cincinnati and New York.

First HARPER TORCHBOOK edition published 1965 by
Harper & Row, Publishers, Incorporated
49 East 33rd Street
New York, N.Y. 10016.

CONTENTS.

INTRODUCTION TO
THE TORCHBOOK EDITION

Whitelaw Reid: Radical Pro Tem

BY C. VANN WOODWARD

THE long colloquy between North and South has
been enriched and enlivened by an enormous library
of travel books. In this literature the regional roles
have remained fixed for a long time: the North is the
traveler, the South is traveled; the North is investi-
gator, the South investigated; the North is questioner,
the South is witness. The roles are rarely reversed,
though the players have varied widely in capacity,
attitude, and compatibility. The basic theme of the
dialogue is usually *The Issue* between the regions, and
the court of opinion addressed, North or South, depends on the sympathies and predilections of the
traveler. The tradition was established early in the
slavery controversy and continues to flourish down to
our own day.

No period in our history was so productive of this
type of literature as Reconstruction, and in no other
period did travel books have quite so much impact
upon opinion and policy. The leading bibliography
lists 245 books of writers who traveled in the South
between 1865 and 1880—from that of Abzac, Paul
d', Vicomte, to Zinke, F. Barham.[1] Many of the

[1] Thomas D. Clark (ed.), *Travels in the New South: A Bibliography,* (Norman, Oklahoma, 1962), vol. I, 8-125.

authors, as the two names mentioned suggest, were foreigners, but the great bulk of them were Americans —Northerners, whose writings generally conform to the traditional pattern described above. Like their predecessors and successors, they usually concentrated on *The Issue* of their time. The difference was that *The Issue* was more sharply focused. Conditions in the South were the main concern of federal policy debate and the storm center of national politics throughout this period. Questions of constant debate were the loyalty of the ex-Confederates, their treatment of freedmen, their attitude toward Northerners, their right to amnesty, to the franchise, to confiscated property, their readiness for self-government, for responsible office, for readmission to Congress. Quite as controversial were questions about the emancipated slaves: their intelligence, their health, their morals; their readiness for education, for citizenship, for the franchise, for civil rights; their willingness to work without compulsion, to make contracts and fulfill them, to acquire property and hold on to it.

The critical year for formation of public opinion on these questions and the time when curiosity was keenest not only about them but about all matters relating to the defeated South was the year following the war. Journalists raced South to satisfy this curiosity and among the first to appear in print, all published in 1866, were three books of special interest. These were Sidney Andrews, *The South Since the War . . . ;* John T. Trowbridge, *The South: A Tour of Its Battlefields and Ruined Cities . . . ;* and Whitelaw Reid, *After the War: A Southern Tour, May 1, 1865, to May 1, 1866.* All these works had their merits and still compete, as they did then, for the attention of those interested in their common subject.

For various reasons, however, Reid's work enjoyed an advantage over its competitors. Andrews confined his tour to three states and a brief sojourn. Trowbridge stayed longer and covered more territory, but was a less sensitive observer than his rivals. All three were "radical" Republican in their point of view, favoring stern measures toward ex-rebels, but Reid possessed the detachment required to see and report evidence that did not always sustain his partisan bias and a greater flexibility and breadth of sympathies. More important, in spite of his youth—he was only 29 when his book was published—Reid was better informed and prepared for his task.

Born near Xenia, Ohio, on October 27, 1837, Whitelaw Reid was the son of devoutly Presbyterian parents, a farmer family with some cultural tradition. Young Reid was writing for newspapers before he finished his degree at Miami University, and became the editor and proprietor of the Xenia *News* before he was 21. He took to politics from the start as a passionately partisan Republican. He spoke for Fremont in the campaign of 1856 and two years later attached himself to the rising star of Lincoln.

Reid was anti-slavery and anti-South, but like many Republicans of his region combined these sentiments with a measure of anti-Negro bias. According to his biographer, "Reid laid it down as an axiom that the more or less intimate association of the two races was only productive of continual evil." The population of Xenia was about 20 per cent Negro, and the young editor reflected the feeling of the majority race when he wrote: "Where negroes reside in any great numbers, among the whites, in the existing state of things, both parties are the worse for it, and it is to the interest of both that a separation should be made as soon as practicable." Such racial views did not prevent Reid from thinking of himself as an abolitionist nor from expressing strong sympathy for John Brown after the raid on Harper's Ferry. At Frank Bird's Radical Club in Boston he was "welcomed as one of themselves by such men as Sumner, Boutwell, and John Murray Forbes," but in private he referred to them as "the New England come-outers." The rhetoric of Garrison set his teeth on edge.[2]

Early in 1861 Reid gave up the *News* and became a correspondent of several Ohio papers including the radical Cincinnati *Gazette*, of which in a few months he became city editor. He was soon off to the front as a war correspondent, making his headquarters in Washington and covering political as well as military news. His vivid and independent dispatches signed "Agate" earned the author wide acclaim. His stories of the battles of Shiloh and Gettysburg, the former in 10 columns, the latter in 14, were considered models of clarity and vigor by combat officers. In the intervals between duty in the field he reported political news at the Capital and cultivated close acquaintance with such Republican politicians as Salmon P. Chase, Charles Sumner, Henry Winter Davis, and young contemporaries such as Lincoln's secretary, John Hay. These connections not only furthered his newspaper work but helped account for his appointment as librarian of the House of Representatives from 1863 to 1866 and as clerk for a time of its military committee. His writing won the admiration of Horace Greeley, who laid plans for attracting him to the New York *Tribune*. He completed his war correspondent career

[2] Royal Cortissoz, *The Life of Whitelaw Reid* (London, 1921), I, 40-41, 138-39.

as one of the first three newspapermen to enter the fallen city of Richmond.

In less than a month, on May 1, he returned South to begin the travels that were to provide materials for his book, *After the War*. William Dean Howells knew him about this time and later recalled his appearance: "I remember him a tall, graceful youth with an enviable black moustache and imperial, wearing his hair long in the Southern fashion, and carrying himself with the native grace which availed him in a worldly progress scarcely interrupted to the end."[3] The hair style and what Reid himself called his "rebel look" stood him in good stead for his new assignment, for more than once he was taken by Rebels to be one of themselves and admitted to confidences denied other Yankees.

Reid made his first tour of the South in company with Chief Justice Chase and other dignitaries in a ship provided by President Andrew Johnson's orders and with a special pass signed by the President. This tour lasted two months, during which their ship proceeded down the Atlantic coast, around Florida, through the Gulf and up the Mississippi. In the course of it the party visited Norfolk, New Bern, Wilmington, Charleston, Port Royal, Savannah, Fernandina, St. Augustine, Jacksonville, Key West, Mobile, New Orleans, Baton Rouge, Natchez, Vicksburg, and Memphis. The presence of the Chief Justice in the party naturally brought out Southerners of official status who were inclined to be on guard. Reid wanted to see rebels "out of company dress," and after a few months at Washington he set forth in the fall for a tour of the interior on his

[3] *Ibid.*, 63.

own. Postmaster General William Dennison, however, had made him special agent of his department to give him some official status, and Secretary of the Treasury Hugh McCulloch had provided ingratiating letters of introduction to provisional governors. Returning to Washington to witness the convening of Congress in December, Reid set forth for his third reconnoiter below the Potomac early in January, 1866. This time he traveled from Washington to New Orleans entirely by land, ''taking the trip leisurely, with frequent stoppages and constant intercourse with the people.'' After this tour he brought his notes back to Washington in May and, writing furiously in the library of the House, he rapidly put together his material for *After the War*. The book was published simultaneously in New York and London later the same year.

The timing of Reid's tours is significant in relating his findings to the development of Presidential and Congressonal policy toward the South, for his book sets forth a striking thesis regarding the impact of the President's Proclamation of Amnesty in May and the Congress' exclusion of Southern representatives and senators in December. Reid's first trip began a month before Johnson's Proclamation of May 29, 1865, which revealed the lenient policy of pardon and restoration he was to pursue, and continued for a month afterward. His second tour started in the fall and lasted until the meeting of Congress in December, and his third followed hard upon the decision of Congress in December to take an independent and tougher line toward the Southern states. Whatever the validity of his conclusions, Reid had an opportunity to explore and compare the mind of the South before and after each of these momentous developments. His conclusions in all instances were unfavorable to Johnson and favorable to Congress, and his findings on these matters together with the evidence presented to support them constitute the political meat of his book.

Up to the time of the Proclamation of May 29, Reid said that he "found the South like clay," submissive, compliant, eager only to be told what to do, and he believed that at that time "the Washington potters could mold it to their liking":

> Here was the opportunity for a statesman to grasp. I speak advisedly, and after a careful review of our whole experiences through the months of May and June, in all the leading centers of Southern influence, when I say that the National Government could at that time have prescribed no conditions for the return of the Rebel States which they would not have promptly accepted. They expected nothing; were prepared for the worst; would have been thankful for anything. . . . They asked no terms, made no conditions. They were defeated and helpless—they submitted. Would the victors be pleased to tel! them what was to be done? Point out any way for a return to an established order of things and they would walk it. . . . Fully believing the debts of their Rebel Government legal and just, they were prepared to repudiate them at a hint from Washington. Filled with the hatred to the negroes, nearly always inspired in any ruling class by the loss of accustomed power over inferiors, they nevertheless yielded to the Freedmen's Bureau, and acquiesced in the necessity for according civil rights to their slaves. They were stung by the disgrace of being guarded by negro soldiers; but they made no complaints, for they felt that they had forfeited their right of complaint. They were shocked at the suggestion of negro suffrage; but if the Government require it, they were ready to submit. The whole body politic was as wax. It needed but a firm hand to apply the seal. Whatever the device were chosen, the community would at once be molded to its impress. But if the plastic moment were suffered to pass——![4]

[4] *After the War*, 219, 296-97.

Reid was not entirely sure that the proclamation marked the passing of the golden moment. "But the moment they heard of that proclamation," he observed, "the late Rebels began to take courage on the question of suffrage, and to suspect that they were not so helpless as they had imagined."

> On the Gulf we caught the first responsive notes given to that proclamation by the revived Southern temper. By the time we reached New Orleans the change was complete; the reaction had set in. Men now began to talk of their rights, and to argue constitutional points; as if traitors had rights, or treason were entitled to constitutional protection. They had discovered that, having laid down their arms, they were no longer Rebels, and could no longer be punished; as the thief who is forced to abandon his booty is no longer a thief, and may laugh at penitentiaries.[5]

Then after the December rebuff from Congress to the newly-elected Southern congressmen came the second striking change that Reid remarked in the tone of Southern sentiment. "In November," he wrote, "I had found it buoyant and defiant. In January it was revengeful, but cowed." Thereafter, he wrote,

> Prominent public men were much more cautious in their expressions. They talked less of their demands; were more disposed to make elaborate arguments on their rights. There were few boasts as to what the South would do, or how heartily that true Southern man, the President, would sustain them; there was more tendency to complain that they had been whipped for trying to go out, and that now the door was shut in their faces when they tried to come in.[6]

Reid probably overestimated the plasticity of the Southern mind and the latitude of Radical oppor-

[5] *Ibid.*, 220, 297.
[6] *Ibid.*, 440.

tunity in the spring of 1865, and his tacit assumption of a Radical consensus on Southern policy by that time is not supported by the record. But his judgment against President Johnson's statesmanship, particularly its responsibility for misleading the South about Northern expectations and encouraging its hopes of resisting reform and defying change, is quite in agreement with the findings of recent scholarship.[7] All of Johnson's political opponents naturally found comfort and support in Reid's conclusions and his charges of intransigence, disloyalty, and bad faith among Southerners. "Question them as to everything for which the war was fought, the doctrine of secession, the rightfulness of slavery, the wrongs of the South, and they are found as full of the sentiments that made the rebellion as ever," he declared. These conclusions were soon to be echoed in the report of the Joint Committee on Reconstruction after extensive hearings on conditions in the South, a report that prepared the way for Radical Reconstruction.

But Whitelaw Reid was a skilled journalist as well as a political partisan, and his book catered to the old romantic interest in the South as well as Northern curiosity about other aspects of the fallen foe. He wrote of glamorous octoroon belles of New Orleans, "beautiful with a beauty beside which that of the North is wax-work; with great swimming, lustrous eyes, half veiled behind long, pendent lashes . . ."

[7] For example, Eric McKitrick, *Andrew Johnson and Reconstruction* (Chicago, 1960); William R. Brock, *An American Crisis: Congress and Reconstruction, 1865-67* (London, 1963); and LaWanda and John H. Cox, *Politics, Principle, and Prejudice, 1865-66: Dilemma of Reconstruction America* (Glencoe, 1963).

He could forget his fierce partisanship long enough to find "his own eyes growing dim" as he watched the warmth and emotion with which crowds of women greeted "the ragged fellows in gray . . . from whom for four years they had been parted." He could even sympathize at times with the spectacular poverty of the Rebels and their bewilderment over defeat and the chaos it brought upon them.

Almost everything he had to say of the Negroes—and that was a great deal—inevitably carried some political connotation. His first encounter with freedmen in large numbers was at Port Royal and the sea islands of South Carolina, where Northern missionaries had been at work since the invasion by federal forces in 1861. Reid's account glowed with optimism for the industry, frugality, and prosperity of the Negroes and their apparent success in adjusting to freedom. His eye failed to penetrate to some of the ironies and frustrations below the surface of the famous "Port Royal Experiment."[8] But he did register some skepticism about the towering hopes for the Negroes which he attributed to "enthusiasts." And he could report with candor a scene quite uncongenial to his convictions—the reunion of Dr. Richard Fuller and his former slaves: "They pushed up against him, kissed his hands, passed their fingers over his hair, crowded about, eager to get a word of recognition." Generalizing about "the great masses of negroes whom we did see in May and June," he observed that, "they were as orderly, quiet, and industrious as any other class of the population."

[8] See chapter entitled "Plantation Bitters" in Willie Lee Rose, *Rehearsal for Reconstruction: The Port Royal Experiment* (Indianapolis, 1964).

In his later trips Reid tended to be less and less confident about the Negro's native endowments and preparation for freedom. He seemed to turn up more and more evidence of stupidity, irresponsibility, and shiftlessness among the freedmen. A distressing number had "a passion for whiskey," and among plantation hands of Louisiana and Mississippi "virtue was absolutely unknown."

The deterioration in Reid's esteem for the Negro coincided with his unfortunate adventure as a cotton planter. From his first tour he became fascinated with the stories he heard of fabulous profits to be made in cotton growing and included several such stories in his book. Toward the end of 1865 he invested heavily in three plantations in Concordia Parish, Louisiana, across the river from Natchez. Flood waters and army worms disspelled his dream of riches and brought him close to financial disaster. In June, 1866, before his book appeared, he revealed in a private letter the impact of the experience on his estimate of the Negroes. "I have now about 300 of these beings under my control," he wrote. "They work well; but life among them is a fearful thing for one's rose-colored ideas. The present generation is bad material to develop. We shall do better with the next." He had been an ardent champion of Negro suffrage in his book and earlier, but by the time his book was published he was writing: "I am fearful more than ever, since my experience here—of negro suffrage as a sufficient remedy for our troubles. I would rather see the South governed territorily by militia and wait several years yet."[9]

[9] Whitelaw Reid to Anna E. Dickinson, June 18, and November 25, 1866, in Dickinson Papers, Library of Congress.

It was another variation on the old story of the young radical who turned conservative. If Reid approached this transition at the tender age of 29, it was but another instance of his remarkable precocity. By the time he was 31 he was managing editor of the most powerful newspaper in America, the New York *Tribune,* and at 35 he was its head. Whitelaw Reid was a success, a sensational success—as nobody could deny. And life for the erstwhile young radical very quickly became a succession of after-dinner speeches, pressing engagements, and very important people.

In his own party the famous editor of the famous paper shaped rather than followed opinion. And in no trend was he quicker to take the lead and point the way than in the Republican shift to the right on the Negro, civil rights, and Reconstruction policy, particularly in the respectable Liberal Republican wing of the party. In less than four years after his book appeared he was deploring the rash efforts of radicals in behalf of the Negro and sympathizing deeply with the bitter Southern resentment. This sentiment, said an editorial he printed on February 4, 1870, was

in some measure due to the conduct of Northern settlers since the war. They have gone in too many instances into Virginia as into a conquered province, seeing no good in any but the blacks, and burning to avenge the old wrongs of the negro by their actions and words. . . . But while it is worth their while to remember this, it is worth ours to consider that there was something inherently good and worth saving in that much laughed at chivalry. The Northern new comers may bring capital, intelligence, and enterprise into Virginia, but they should beware lest they ignore and destroy something which is there as valuable as any of these. . . . Let them . . . be willing to recognize among their foes men 'who bear without abuse the grand old name of gentleman.'

This brought a hot rebuke from that most militant of abolitionist crusaders, Colonel Thomas Wentworth Higginson: "That even the war should not have ended that miserable myth of Southern chivalry, 'pure domestic morality' (faugh!), and all the distinction of 'the high-toned gentleman!'" Reid took a firm tone in reply: "Let us have done with this miserable spirit of carping at the South. . . . I repudiate and abhor the doctrine that a minority composed of negroes and disreputable carpet baggers can permanently and safely govern a large majority in any American state."[10] And in a very short time the militant Colonel Higginson was taking much the same view of the situation. So was a whole generation of onetime militants and radicals.

In the busy years that followed, Whitelaw Reid kept firm hold upon his powerful paper. He also grew ever more powerful in the inner councils of the Republican party. He served his party as minister to France, minister to Britain, and candidate for Vice President. He continued to mold opinion and advise the mighty. But having despaired of the first generation of freedmen in 1866 with the promise that "We shall do better with the next," he never seems to have had time in his busy schedule to devote any attention to that second generation after it put in its appearance.

[10] Reid to Higginson, February 7, 1870, in *Cortissoz*, Reid, I, 295-96.

EDITOR'S NOTE

The text of the original edition of Whitelaw Reid's *After the War: A Southern Tour, May 1, 1865 to May 1, 1866,* has not been altered save for the correction of a few typographical errors and misspellings and the addition of a few footnotes of identification or explanation.

C. V. W.

PREFACE.

WITH the exception of the unhealthy summer months, I spent the greater part of the year following the close of the Rebellion, in traveling through the late Rebel States, passing first around their entire coast line; and, on subsequent trips, crossing by various routes through the interior.

I have sought, in the following pages, to show something of the condition in which the war left the South, the feelings of the late insurgents, the situation and capacities of the liberated slaves, and the openings offered, under the changed condition of affairs, to capital and industry from without.

A couple of months, this spring, spent on the great cotton plantations of the Mississippi Valley, enabled me to make a closer study of the character of the average plantation negro than tourists have ordinarily found practicable; and the concluding chapters are mainly devoted to these observations.

A further word of explanation may be needed as to the part of the volume describing the journey of Mr. Chief-Justice Chase After the inauguration of President Johnson, Mr. Chase determined to visit the Southern cities, to learn as much as possible, from actual observation, of the true condition of the country. The Secretary of the Treasury was then about to send a revenue cutter to the New Orleans station, and on board of her a special agent, charged with the duty of examining the agencies, and carrying into effect the directions of the Department in the several South Atlantic and Gulf ports. He tendered the use of this vessel to the Chief-Justice, and orders were issued by the President and the Secretaries of War and of the Navy, to the officers in the naval, military, and civil services to afford him all facilities that their respective duties would allow.

It was under these circumstances that the Chief-Justice made his Southern journey. He had the best opportunities of information, and communicated his views, from time to time, to the President. As a member of the party on board the cutter, I thus enjoyed considerable, though, in some respects, more limited opportunities of observation.

A small portion of the material in the following pages has previously appeared in the journal with which I was connected, but it has all been rewritten.

W. R.

LIBRARY OF THE HOUSE,
    Washington, May, 1866.

AFTER THE WAR.

CHAPTER I.

Why, and How the Trip was Made.

THE most interesting records of the great revolution just ending have seemed to me to be those portraying the spirit and bearing of the people throughout the South, just before and at the outbreak of the war. Stories of battles, and sieges, and retreats, are kaleidoscopic repetitions of deeds with which all history is crowded; but with what temper great communities plunged into this war, which has overwhelmed them, for what fancied causes, to what end, in what boundless self-confidence and overwhelming contempt of their antagonists, with what exuberance of frenzied joy at the prospect of bloodshed, with what wild dreams of conquest, and assurance of ill-defined but very grand honors, and orders, and social dignities—-all this, as faithfully set down by the few who had opportunities to observe it, constitutes the strangest and most absorbing contribution to the literature of the Rebellion.

So I have thought that what men now most want to know, is something of the temper and condition in which these same communities come out from the struggle.

By the side of the daguerreotypes of the South entering upon the war, even the hastiest pencil sketch of the South emerging from the war may possess an interest and attraction of its own.

Therefore, when early in the month of April I was invited to accompany a small party, bound on a voyage of official inspection and observation, from Fortress Monroe around the whole Atlantic and Gulf Coast to New Orleans, and thence up the Mississippi, I congratulated myself upon the opportunity thus afforded of seeing, under the most favorable circumstances, the Southern centers which had nursed and fed the rebellion. Means of communication through the interior of the South are so thoroughly destroyed, and Southern society is so completely disorganized, that it is only in the cities one can hope for any satisfactory view of the people. Even there the overshadowing military authority, and the absence of all accustomed or recognized modes of expressing public sentiment, as through the press, the bar, public meetings, the pulpit, or unrestrained social intercourse, combine to render the task of observation infinitely more difficult than at any previous period.

But all the more, on these accounts, the Southern cities are the places to which we must first look for any satisfactory idea of the Southern condition; and a trip which embraces visits to Norfolk, Newbern, Beaufort, Wilmington, Charleston, Port Royal, Savannah, Fernandina, St. Augustine, Jacksonville, Key West, Mobile, New Orleans, Baton Rouge, Natchez, Vicksburg, and Memphis, with visits to plantations all along the route, and occasional trips into the interior, ought not to fail in furnishing a good view of the gradual beginnings to crystallize again out of the chaos to which the war had reduced one-third of the nation.

The trip would have been begun some weeks earlier, but for the deed of horror in Ford's Theater.[1] But, as Secretary McCulloch[2] well said, the wheels of Government moved on without a perceptible jar; and the arrangements of President Lincoln were only temporarily delayed by the accession of President Johnson. An ocean-going revenue cutter was ordered around from New York to Fortress Monroe for the party, and early on the morning of the first of May, the cutter "Northerner" was announced as in readiness to convey us to the Fortress.

In the afternoon an officer was good enough to bring me the following:

EXECUTIVE MANSION, WASHINGTON, May 1, 1865.

Permission is granted Whitelaw Reid, Esq., to proceed by sea to New Orleans, Louisana, and return by sea or inland to Washington, District of Columbia, and to visit any port or place *en route* in the lines of national military occupation.

[Signed,]   ANDREW JOHNSON,
President of the United States.

I had not supposed a pass necessary; but as the rest of the party went on official business, it had been thought best to cover my case with a document, about the scope and authority of which no question could be raised. At that time passes to visit many of the Southern points were still eagerly sought and procured with difficulty. The War Department was the place to which, in general, application was to be made, and the speculative gentry who mostly wanted such favors, stood in wholesome awe of the downright Secretary.[3] A pass so nearly unlimited as mine was an unheard of rarity, and before the afternoon was over, two or three who had in some way found out that I had it, were anxious to know if "five hundred or even a thousand dollars would be any inducement" to me to part with it!

[1] The assassination of President Lincoln. [Ed.]

[2] Hugh McCulloch, Secretary of Treasury, 1865-1869. [Ed.]

[3] Edwin McMasters Stanton, Secretary of War, 1862-1868. [Ed.]

By nine in the evening the last of the little party had entered the cozy cabin of the "Northerner." There were the usual good-byes to the friends who had driven down to the Navy Yard wharf to see us off; playful injunctions from young officers about laying in supplies of cigars at Havana, and from fair ladies about bringing back for them parrots and monkeys, pine apples and bananas; some consultations among the officials of the party; some final messages and instructions sent down at the last moment by the Government: then fresh good-byes; the plank was pulled in, and we steamed out into the darkness.

Everybody compared supplies with everybody else; it was found that there were books enough in the party to set up a circulating library, and paper enough for writing a three-volume novel; the latest dates of newspapers had been laid in; the last issues of the magazines, and even a fresh number of the old *North American* were forthcoming; while Napoleon's *Cæsar*, in all the glory of tinted paper and superb letter-press, formed the *piece de résistance* that bade fair to master us all—as Horace Greeley used maliciously to say the old *National Intelligencer* mastered him, when he couldn't get asleep in any other way!

CHAPTER II.

A School of Unadulterated Negroes—An Ancient Virginia Town
under the Dispensation of Sutlers.

OUR steamer for the voyage was to be the revenue
cutter " Wayanda," a trim, beautifully-modeled, ocean-
going propeller, carrying six guns, and manned with
a capital crew. While Captain Merryman was making
his final preparation for a cruise, much longer than he
had expected when the telegraph hurried his vessel
around from New York, we retained the little " Northerner" for a trip up to Norfolk—only delaying long
enough at the Fortress to drive out and see a great
negro school, established by General Butler.

The wharves were crowded by the usual curious
throng of idle spectators, laborers taking care of supplies, soldiers on duty, and a very sparse sprinkling of
ladies. Rebel soldiers by scores were mixed in the
groups, or could be seen trudging along the sidewalks
toward the Commissary's.

Everywhere were negroes—on the sidewalks—driving the wagons—in the huts that lined the road. All
the slaves of the adjoining counties seem to have established themselves at the Fortress. As we crossed the
long, narrow isthmus, contracting at last to an atten-
uated causeway, which separates the Fortress from
the main land, and came out into the ancient village
of Hampton, the negro huts thickened into swarms,
and fairly covered the sites of the old aristocratic

residences which the Rebels fired early in the war
when compelled to evacuate the place. Bricks, two
centuries old, imported by the early colonists from
Great Britain, for the mansions of the first families,
were built up into little outside chimneys for these
cabins of the Freedmen; and here and there one
noticed an antique Elizabethan chair, of like age and
origin, converted to the uses of a portly negress.

To our right, down on the water's edge, rose a high,
narrow residence—the former home of John Tyler;[4]
near it was another, somewhat less pretentious, as well
as less uncouth, which had formerly been occupied by
S. R. Mallory. Both find loyal and benevolent uses
now at the hands of the Government. Near them was
a long colonnade, with spacious piazzas, fronting a
many-windowed brick hospital, which one of our party
was observed closely scrutinizing. " Upon my word,"
he exclaimed, after a moment's reflection, "that is the
old Chesapeake Female College, of which I have been,
from the foundation, one of the Trustees." Pale-faced
men in blue occupied the chambers of the boarding-
school misses; and sentries, pacing to and fro, kept a
stricter guard than strictest duenna of boarding-school
ever achieved.

To our left extended a stretch of marshy meadows
and half-cultivated fields. In their midst was one
little field cultivated above all the rest. White boards,
with a trifle of modest lettering on each, dotted its surface, and the grass grew greenest over long, carefully-
smoothed hillocks. A file of slow-paced soldiers, with
arms reversed, was entering the inclosure; behind them
followed an army wagon, with five rude pine boxes piled
upon it; beyond, quietly, and, as one loved to think,
even sadly, regarding the scene, was a group of paroled

4 President of the United States, 1841-1845. [Ed.]

Rebel soldiers; while, as we turned, in passing, to catch a last glimpse of the mourners in blue by the open graves, there was seen away behind us, rippling in the breeze above the fort, the old flag for which these dead had died, and against which these Rebels had fought.

We found the school-house (a barn-like frame structure), a little removed from the cluster of negro huts, and took the school fairly by surprise. Passing up a long hall, wide enough for double rows of desks, in the center, with seats for about ten or twelve boys in each, and an aisle on either side, with benches for the class recitations against the walls, we came to an elevated platform, from which led off, in opposite directions, two other precisely similar halls. The fourth, completing the cross, was designed for girls, and was yet unfinished. Down these three long halls were ranged row after row of cleanly-clad negro boys, from the ages of six and seven up to sixteen or seventeen.

All seemed attentive; and though the teachers complained that the sudden entrance of visitors always led to more confusion than usual, there was certainly no more than one would expect from any school of equal extent anywhere, or under any management. The rolls contained the names of three hundred and seventy-four pupils, of whom about two hundred were present. The Superintendent, who seemed an earnest, simple-minded man, enthusiastically convinced that he had a "mission" here, spoke of this as about the average attendance. The parents, he said, were themselves so uncertain, and so little accustomed, as yet, to habits of regularity, that they could not well bring up this average to a better point. It seemed to me surely not so far behind our ordinary public schools at the North as to suggest any unfavorable contrasts.

These children had all been slaves, and nearly all had accompanied their parents on their escape from the plantations of the Peninsula, and of the upper counties of North Carolina, to the Fortress. The parents had generally been field hands, and one noticed among the children very few faces not of pure African descent. Such masses of little woolly heads, such rows of shining ivories, and flat noses and blubber lips, I had never seen collected before, unless in a state of filth utterly unbearable. The teachers were all convalescent soldiers from the hospitals, moving noiselessly about among the benches in their hospital slippers and cheap calico wrappers—as they themselves had often seen moving about among their hospital cots the angels of mercy from the North. Who shall say they were not doing as beneficent a work, or that the little negroes might not well follow them with as longing and affectionate a gaze?

Several classes were called up to exhibit their proficiency. Doubtless the teachers selected their best scholars for the test—I think even Northern schools sometimes do that—but there can be little opportunity for deception in the reading of an unlearned lesson in a book, or in answers to questions in mental arithmetic, propounded by the visitors themselves. It was strange to see boys of fourteen or fifteen reading in the First Reader; but stranger to observe how intelligently scholars in the First Reader went about their work, and with what comparative rapidity they learned. I passed among the forms and conversed with a good many of the soldier-teachers. They all united in saying that on an average the raw negro boys admitted to the school would learn their letters and be able to read well in the

First Reader in three months; while some of them, who were originally bright, and who were kept in regular attendance, made considerably more rapid progress.

An advanced class, composed of the little negro "monitors" who had been longest in the school, was summoned to the platform to read a lesson in the Fourth Reader. One or two of them read very badly; one or two quite well, and with an evident understanding of what was said. The best reader in the class was the smallest boy, an ebony-faced urchin, whose head looked as a six-pound round shot, coated with curled hair from a mattress, might. The Superintendent exhibited his manner of calling out the classes through the whole school to recite, the military style in which the boys were required to march to their places at the word of command, and the general adherence to military forms, even in such minutiæ as distributing slates, removing the stools for the monitors, returning books to their places, and the like.

Then came a little address from the Dominie of our party, a former South Carolina lawyer and heavy slaveholder; and we finally took our leave, the little urchins eagerly handing up their slates, as we passed, to have us see their penmanship; and laboriously tracing out, in school-boy characters, their oddly-sounding names, to show us how readily they could write.

This school is kept up at little or no expense to the Government, save the original cost of erecting the rough board structure in which it is held. The parents of the children have been, to a considerable extent, employed by the Government as laborers in the Quartermaster's Department; and, meantime, the convalescents from the hospitals have prepared the sons, in some measure, for the new order of things. Still there is more dependence on charity than could be desired, especially among the parents. Negroes need to be taught—just as slaves of any race or color would need to be taught— that liberty means, not idleness, but merely work for themselves instead of work for others; and that, in any event, it means always work. To teach them this, do not gather them in colonies at military posts, and feed them on Government rations; but throw them in the water and have them learn to swim by finding the necessity of swimming. For the present, these collections of negroes are an inevitable result of the war; and that would be a barbarous Government indeed which would not help in time of distress the men whose friendship to it has brought them into distress; but it must be the first care of the authorities to diminish the charity, and leave the negroes, just as it would leave the white men—to take care of themselves.

On arriving at Norfolk, we were met, at the shabby-looking old wharf, by General Gordon, commanding the post. Carriages were in waiting, and we were rapidly whirled past the tumble-down warehouses, through streets of stores from which every former proprietor had gone, by the old English brick church, whence the former pastor had departed, past elegant residences of prominent rebels, in whose parlors sat the wives of Yankee officers, and through whose superb gardens we were invited to wander, and pluck at will great bending bunches of flowers that, at Washington, were still scarce in the hot-houses.

From the gardens we turned toward the country to see the old line of fortifications (planned, curiously enough, by a nephew of one of our party), by which the Virginians, in the first months of the war, had been confident they could hold Norfolk forever against the Yankee scum. Negro soldiers manned the lines the rebel engineer had traced; but wild flowers covered the embankments, and we plucked azalias of exquisite fragrance from the crumbling embrasures. It was not less strange that another member of our party, then foremost in the Cabinet, had undertaken the search hereabouts for a landing for our troops, after the officers had given it up; and had actually chosen the point where they were safely debarked, and whence they had turned these long lines, and reduced Norfolk—"Merrimac" and all—without a blow.

The wild flowers filled the moist evening air with their perfume as we drove back through the negro quarter. Every hut exhibited the tender tokens of mourning for the good, dead President, which were missing on many aristocratic residences. There were no evidences of suffering or destitution among these people; and it was not from their windows that the lowering glances were turned upon the General, and the well-known features of the anti-slavery leader by his side.

Norfolk ought to do, and will do a fine business— whenever it has any country to do business for. It must always be the great shipping point for the Virginia and North Carolina coast; the heaviest vessels can lie by its wharves, and between it and Hampton Roads is room for the navies of the world. But, thus far, there is scarcely any business, save what the army has brought, and what the impoverished inhabitants who remain are themselves able to support. Sutlers have sat in the high places until they have amassed fortunes; but the merchants whose deserted store rooms they are occupying are paroled and ruined Rebel officers. No trade comes or can come from the interior. The people have no produce to spare, and no money with which to buy. And the very number of able-bodied men in the country has been sadly reduced.*

Everything is controlled by the military authority; and while there may be a genuine Union sentiment that warranted the attempted elections of Congressmen, one may still be permitted a quiet suspicion of the independent and disinterested patriotism of the voters. Just as we were pushing off, Mr. Chandler, a nervous, restless, black-haired Virginian, came hobbling out from his carriage. He was a claimant for a seat in the last House, which was refused; and was the leader of the Virginia delegation to the Baltimore Convention, whose admission to that body his fluent and impassioned rhetoric secured. Naturally he is a warm supporter of the Pierpoint State Government,[5] believes that "the loyal men of the State constitute the State," and doesn't see why the fact that they are few in numbers should prevent their exercising all the powers of the State. Just now he and the few really loyal men, like him, are very bitter against the Rebels, whom they wish to have excluded from any participation in the ready-made State Government, which they hope soon to have transferred from Alexandria to Richmond, and extended over the State. But they frankly admit themselves to be in a very small minority; and it remains to be seen how long a minority, however loyal, can govern, in a republican country.

*Calculations, seemingly accurate, have placed the number of dead and disabled Virginia soldiers at 105,000, or nearly one-tenth of the entire free population of the State.

[5] Recognized as the government of Virginia by Lincoln. [Ed.]

CHAPTER III.

"Beauties of the Sea"—First Views of Cracker Unionism.

ON our return to the Fortress, the "Wayanda" was ready; there was a hurried transhipment in the dark; not a little dismay at the straitened proportions of the cabin; an assignment of state-rooms, which gave me the D. D. of the party as chum; and so—amid the Doctor's loud groans and lamentations over confining a rational human being in a straight jacket of a bed like that—to sleep.

There was a very hasty toilette next morning, and a very undignified rush for the fresh air on deck. We had started in the night, were well out on the ocean, a pretty heavy sea was running, and the mettlesome little "Wayanda" was giving us a taste of her qualities. Nothing could exceed the beauty of her plunges fore and aft, and lurches from port to starboard; but the party were sadly lacking in enthusiasm. Presently breakfast was announced, and we all went below very bravely and ranged ourselves about the table. Before the meal was half over, the Captain and the Doctor's were left in solitary state to finish it alone. For myself—although seasoned, as I had vainly imagined, by some experiences in tolerably heavy storms—I freely confess to the double enjoyment of the single cup of tea I managed to swallow. "For," said the Dominie, argumentatively, "you have the pleasure of enjoying it first as it goes down, and then a second time as it comes up."

To keep one another in countenance as we held our uncertain positions on the rolling and plunging deck, we combined to rehearse all the old jokes about sea sickness. One gave a definition of it, which, like many another indifferent thing, has been unwarrantably fathered on the late President. "Sea sickness is a disorder which for the first hour makes you afraid you'll die, but by the second hour makes you afraid you won't!" Another recited Artemus Ward's groaning lamentation over Point Judith, to the effect that he "never before saw a place where it was so hard to keep inside one's clothes and outside one's breakfast!" "Sure, it isn't say sick yez are," pleasantly suggested an Irish engineer, among the officers, who looked provokingly happy amid all the pitching—"it isn't say sick yez are; but yez mighty sick of the say!" "O *si sic omnes!*" punned the Chief Justice.[6] How the rest stood it I don't know; but that was the last straw, and drove one unfortunate of the party to his stateroom, and a basin and towel.

Toward evening the sea calmed down, and one after another emerged on deck. The air was delightfully bracing; the moon sent its broad streams of light, shaking across the waters; the revolving light of Hatteras shone out—guide and safeguard to a hundred eyes besides our own—and so with calmest weather, and a delicious beauty of scene that no words need be vainly employed in efforts to describe, we spent half the night in watching the passage of the ship by the most dangerous part of the Atlantic coast. Next morning, at breakfast, we were steaming under the guns of Fort Macon into the harbor where Butler and Porter rendezvoused for Fort Fisher.

As a boat's crew slowly pulled some of our party

[6] Salmon Portland Chase, Chief Justice of the Supreme Court, 1864-1873. [Ed.]

through the tortuous channel by which even the lightest gigs have to approach the single landing of Beaufort, the guns of the naval force began to thunder out a salute for the Chief Justice. "How many guns does a Chief Justice receive?" inquired one, as he counted the successive discharges. "You'd a great deal better ask," reprovingly hinted the Doctor, "how many guns a Baptist minister receives!" "Well, how many, Doctor!" "Oh, just count these up, and then you'll know!" With which church-militant suggestion, we rounded to at a crazy old wharf, climbed up a pair of rickety steps that gave the Doctor premonitions of more immersion than even he had bargained for, and stood in the town of Beaufort, North Carolina. In front of us was the Custom House—a square, one-story frame building, perched upon six or eight posts—occupied now by a Deputy Treasury Agent. A narrow strip of sand, plowed up by a few cart wheels, and flanked by shabby-looking old frame houses, extended along the water front, and constituted the main business street of a place that, however dilapidated and insignificant, must live in the history of the struggle just ended. Near the water's edge was a small turpentine distillery, the only manufacturing establishment of the place.

The landing of a boat's crew, with an officer in charge and a flag fluttering at the stern, seemed to be an event in Beaufort, and we were soon surrounded by the notabilities. A large, heavily and coarsely-built man, of unmistakable North Carolina origin, with the inevitable bilious look, ragged clothes and dirty shirt, was introduced, with no little *eclat*, as "the Senator from this District." "Of what Senate?" some one inquired. "The North Caroliner Senate, Sir," "Umph, Rebel Senate of

North Carolina," growled the Captain, *sotto voce;* "you make a devil of a fuss about your dignity! North Carolina Rebel Senate be hanged! A New York constable outranks you." But the Senator didn't hear; and his manner showed plainly enough that no doubts of his importance ever disturbed the serene workings of his own mind. The Clerk of the Court, the Postmaster, the doctor, the preacher and other functionaries were speedily added to the group that gathered in the sand bank called a pavement.

"How are your people feeling?" some one asked. "Oh, well, sir; we all went out unwillingly, you know," responded the legislator, fresh from the meetings of the Rebel Senate at Raleigh, "and most of us are very glad to get back." "Have you no violent Rebels yet?" "Yes, quite a good many, among the young bloods; but even they all feel as if they had been badly whipped, and want to give in." "Then they really feel themselves whipped?" "Yes, you 've subjugated us at last," with a smile which showed that the politician thought it not the worst kind of a joke after all.

"And, of course, then you have only to submit to any terms the conquerors may impose?" "No, sir—oh, ah—yes, any terms that could be honorably offered to a proud, high-minded people!" The rest of the dignitaries nodded their heads approvingly at this becoming intimation of the terms the "subjugated" State could be induced to accept. It was easy to see that the old politi cal tricks were not forgotten, and that the first inch of wrong concession would be expected to lead the way to many an ell.

"What terms do you think would be right?" The County Clerk, a functionary of near thirty years' service, took up the conversation, and promptly replied, "Let

Governor Vance call together the North Caroliner Legislater. We only lacked a few votes of a Union majority in it before, and we'd be sure to have enough
now." "What then?" "Why, the Legislater would,
of course, repeal the ordinance of secession, and order
a convention to amend the Constitution. I think that
convention would accept your constitutional amendment."

"But can you trust your Governor Vance? Did not
he betray the Union party after his last election ?"

"Yes, he sold us out clean and clear."

"He did nothing of the sort. North Caroliner has not
got a purer patriot than Governor Vance." And so they
fell to disputing among themselves.

I asked one of the party what this Legislature, if thus
called together, would do with the negroes?"

" Take 'em under the control of the Legislater, as free
niggers always have been in this State. Let it have
authority to fix their wages, and prevent vagrancy. It
always got along with 'em well enough before."

" Are you not mistaken about its always having had
this power ?"

"What!" exclaimed the astonished functionary.
"Why, I was born and raised hyar, and lived hyar all
my life ! Do you suppose I don't know ?"

" Apparently not, sir ; for you seem to be ignorant of
the fact that *free negroes in North Carolina were voters
from the formation of the State Government* down to 1835."

"It isn't so, stranger."

"Excuse me ; but your own State records will show
it ;* and, if I must say so, he is a very ignorant citizen

---

* North Carolina, by her Constitution of 1776, prescribed three
bases of suffrage :

1. All FREEMEN twenty-one years old, who have lived in the

to be talking about ways and means of re-organization, who doesn't know so simple and recent a fact in the history of his State."

The Cracker scratched his head in great bewilderment. "Well, stranger, you don't mean to say that the Government at Washington is going to make us let niggers vote?"

"I mean to say that it is at least possible."

"Well, why not have the decency to let us have a vote on it ourselves, and say whether *we'll* let niggers vote?"

"In other words, you mean this: Less than a generation ago you held a convention, which robbed certain classes of your citizens of rights they had enjoyed, undisputed, from the organization of your State down to that hour. Now, you propose to let the robbers hold

county twelve months, and have had a freehold of fifty acres for six months, may vote for a member of the Senate.

2. All FREEMEN, of like age and residence, who have paid public taxes, may vote for members of the House of Commons for the county.

3. The above two classes may, if residing or owning a freehold in a town, vote for members of the House of Commons for such town: provided, they shall not already have voted for a member for the county, and *vice versa*.

By the Constitution, as amended in 1835, all freemen, twenty-one years of age, living twelve months in the State, and owning a freehold of fifty acres for six months, should vote, except that

"No free negro, free mulatto, or free person of mixed blood, descended from negro ancestors to the fourth generation inclusive (though one ancestor of each generation may have been a white person), shall vote for members of the Senate or House of Commons."

The last clause would seem to have looked to amalgamation as a pretty steady practice, for such zealous abolition and negro-haters. Under the Constitution of 1776, free negroes, having the requisite qualifications, voted as freely as any other portion of the voting population.

an election to decide whether they will return the stolen property or not."

"Stranger," exclaimed another of the group, with great emphasis, "is the Government at Washington, because it has whipped us, going to make us let niggers vote?"

"Possibly it will. At any rate a strong party favors it."

"Then I wouldn't live under the Government. I'd emigrate, sir. Yes, sir, I'd leave this Government *and go north!*"

And the man, true to his States'-Rights training, seemed to imagine that going north was going under another Government, and spoke of it as one might speak of emigrating to China.

Meantime, the younger citizens of Beaufort (of Caucasian descent) had found better amusement than talking to the strangers in the sand bank of a street. One of them wagered a quarter (fractional currency) that he could whip another. The party thus challenged evinced his faith in his own muscle by risking a corresponding quarter on it. The set-to was at once arranged, in the back-yard of the house in front of which we were standing, and several side bets, ranging from five to as high as fifteen cents, were speedily put up by spectators.

One of our party, who joined the crowd at the amusement, reported that half-a-dozen rounds were fought—a few "niggers" gravely looking on from the outskirts of the throng—that several eyes were blacked, and both noses bruised; that there was a fall, and a little choking and eye-gouging, and a cry of "give it up;" that then the belligerents rose and shook hands, and stakes were delivered, and the victor was being challenged to another trial, with a fresh hand, as we left the scene of combat; and so closed our first visit to a North Carolina town.

CHAPTER IV.

Newbern and Beaufort—Black and White.

SHORTLY after our arrival in the harbor, the military authorities had provided a special train for us—that is to say, a train composed of a wheezy little locomotive and an old mail agent's car, with all the windows smashed out and half the seats gone. By this means we were enabled, an hour after our visit to Beaufort, to be whirling over the military railroad from the little collection of Government warehouses on the opposite side of the harbor, called Morehead City, to Newbern.

The whole way led through the exhausted turpentine forests of North-eastern North Carolina, which the turpentine growers have for many years been abandoning for the more productive forests of upper South Carolina. Here and there were swamps which Yankee drainage would soon convert into splendid corn land; and it is possible that Yankee skill might make the exhausted pineries very profitable; but, for the present, this country is not likely to present such inducements as to attract a large Northern emigration.

The poorer people seem to be quietly living in their old places. Where the paroled rebel soldiers have returned, they have sought their former homes, and evince a very decided disposition to stay there. Throughout this region there is, as we learned, comparatively little destitution. The ocean is a near and never-failing resource; and from Newbern and Beaufort (both of which have been in our possession during the greater part of the war) supplies have gone through the lines by a sort of insensible and invisible perspiration, which it would be unkind, to the disinterested traders who follow in the wake of an army, to call smuggling.

Passing the traces of the works thrown up at the point where Burnside had his fight, we entered the remarkable city of log cabins, outside the city limits, which now really forms the most interesting part of the ancient town of Newbern. Before the war, it had between five and six thousand inhabitants; now, these newly-built cabins on the outskirts, alone, contain over ten thousand souls.* Yet, withal, there are few old residents here. The city proper is, to a considerable extent, deserted by its former inhabitants, and filled by Union refugees from all parts of the State; while these squares of crowded cabins contain solely Union refugees—of another color, but not less loyal.

Within a few days back, however, men, whose faces have not been seen in Newbern for nearly four years, are beginning to appear again, with many an anxious inquiry about property, which they think ought to have been carefully preserved for them during their hostile absence. Sometimes they have kept an aged mother, or an aunt, or a widowed sister, in the property, to retain a claim upon it; and in these cases they seem to find little difficulty in quietly resuming possession. But, in more instances, they are forced to see others in an occupancy they can not conveniently dispute, and

---

* The census of 1860 gave the population of Newbern at, whites, 2,360; blacks, 3,072; aggregate, 5,432. The Newbern people are now setting forth, as a reason for inducing emigration, that the city is the largest in the State, and has a population of between twenty and thirty thousand. The increase is mainly made up of negroes.

to learn of fortunes made from the property they abandoned.

The hotel keeper, for example, has returned. He finds here a Yankee, who, seeing the house deserted when we occupied the city, and being told by the officers that they wanted a hotel, determined to keep it. The Yankee has paid no rent; he has been at no expense, and he has made a sum reckoned at over a hundred thousand dollars, by his hotel keeping and a little cotton planting which he was able to combine with it. Naturally, he is in no haste to give up his rent-free establishment, and the Rebel owner has the satisfaction of contemplating the Yankee in possession, and calculating the profits which might have gone into his own pockets but for the frantic determination, four years ago, never to submit to the tyrannical rule of the Illinois gorilla. Returning merchants find sutlers behind their counters, reckoning up gains such as the old business men of Newbern never dreamed of; all branches of trade are in the hands of Northern speculators, who followed the army; half the residences are filled with army officers, or occupied by Government civil officials, or used for negro schools, or rented out as "abandoned property."

Yankee enterprise even made money out of what had been thrown away long before the war. In the distillation of turpentine a large residuum of the resin used to be carted away as rubbish, not worth the cost of its transportation to market. The mass thus thrown out from some of the Newbern distilleries, had gradually been buried under a covering of sand and dirt. A couple of Yankee adventurers, digging for something on the bank of the river, happened to strike down upon this resin, quietly had it mined and shipped to a Northern market. I am afraid to tell how many thousands of dollars they are said to have made by the lucky discovery.

The negro quarter has been swelled to a size greater than that of almost any city on the coast, by accessions from all parts of the State. They came in entirely destitute. The Government furnished them rations, and gave the men axes, with which they cut down the pine trees and erected their own cabins, arranging them regularly in streets, and "policing" them as carefully as a regiment of veteran soldiers would do. Every effort was then made to give them work in the Quartermaster's Department, to keep them from being simply an expense to the Government; but the close of the war necessarily cuts off this source of employment, and the General commanding is now looking with no little uneasiness to the disposition to be made of this great collection of negroes, for scarcely a tithe of whom can the natural wants of the town itself supply employment.

Some have rented a large rice plantation in the vicinity—contrary to the currently-received theory that no human being, white or black, will work on rice grounds except when driven to it—and they are doing exceedingly well. Others could go further into the interior and do the same, if they were sure of protection; but till some understanding with the planters is reached, and the *status* of the Rebel planters themselves is defined, this is almost impracticable. Something, however, must be done to disperse this unwholesome gathering at Newbern, or the tumor, thus neglected, may do serious injury.

A dispatch from General Sherman (on his way north from Savannah, and forced by bad weather to put in at

Beaufort) had reached Newbern, while we were there, expressing a very earnest desire to see Chief Justice Chase; and on the return of the party, General Sherman's vessel was lying at the wharf, opposite the railroad terminus, awaiting us. Nervous and restless as ever, the General looked changed (and improved) since the old campaigns in the South-west. He was boiling over with pride at the performances of his army through the winter, and all the more indignant, by consequence, at the insults and injustice he imagined himself to have received, in consequence of his arrangement with Johnston. "I fancied the country wanted peace," he exclaimed. "If they don't, let them raise more soldiers."

The General complained, and, doubtless, with some truth, if not justice, that the Government had never distinctly explained to him what policy it desired to have pursued. "I asked Mr. Lincoln explicitly, when I went up to City Point, whether he wanted me to capture Jeff. Davis, or let him escape, and in reply he told me a story."

That "story" may now have a historical value, and I give it, therefore, as General Sherman said Mr. Lincoln told it—only premising that it was a favorite story with Mr. Lincoln, which he told many times, and in illustration of many points of public policy.

"I'll tell you, General," Mr. Lincoln was said to have begun, "I'll tell you what I think about taking Jeff. Davis. Out in Sangamon county there was an old temperance lecturer, who was very strict in the doctrine and practice of total abstinence. One day, after a long ride in the hot sun, he stopped at the house of a friend, who proposed making him a lemonade. As the mild beverage was being mixed, the friend insinuatingly asked if he wouldn't like just the least drop of something stronger, to brace up his nerves after the exhausting heat and exercise. 'No,' replied the lecturer, I couldn't think of it; I am opposed to it on principle. But,' he added, with a longing glance at the black bottle that stood conveniently at hand, 'if you could manage to put in a drop *unbeknownst* to me, I guess it wouldn't hurt me much!' Now, General," Mr. Lincoln concluded, "I'm bound to oppose the escape of Jeff. Davis; but if you could manage to let him slip out unbeknownst-like, I guess it wouldn't hurt me much!"

"And that," exclaimed General Sherman, "is all I could get out of the Government as to what its policy was, concerning the Rebel leaders, till Stanton assailed me for Davis' escape!"

A heavy gale blew on the coast all day Friday, Saturday and Sunday, and neither General Sherman's Captain nor our own thought it wise to venture out. Meanwhile, delegations of the Beaufort people came off in little sail-boats to visit the "Wyanda," bring us flowers and strawberries, and talk politics. Since their last demonstrations, a few days ago, they had toned down their ideas a good deal; and the amount of their talk, stripped of its circumlocution and hesitation, was simply this: that they were very anxious to re-organize, and would submit to anything the Government might require to that end. They said less against negro suffrage than before—frankly said it would be very obnoxious to the prejudices of nearly the whole population, but added, that if the Government insisted on it, they would co-operate with the negroes in re-organization "But the poor, shiftless creatures will never be able to support themselves in freedom. We'll have half of them in poor-houses before a year!"* Nothing could overcome this rooted idea, that the negro was worthless, except under the lash. These people really believe that, in submitting to the emancipation of the slaves, they have virtually saddled themselves with an equal number of idle paupers. Naturally, they believe that to add a requirement that these paupers must share

* And yet an official report, since published in the newspapers, shows that out of three thousand whites in Beaufort last winter, between twelve and fourteen hundred were applicants for the charity of Government rations. Out of about an equal number of negroes, less than four hundred were dependent on the Government! The secret of the disparity was, that the negroes took work when they could get it; the whites were "ladies and gentlemen," and wouldn't work.

A Richmond letter, of June 30th, in the Boston *Commonwealth*, testifies to the same feeling among the Virginians. Describing the charities of the Sanitary Commission, it says:

"The most fastidious, though not too dainty to beg, were yet ludicrously exacting and impatient. They assumed, in many ways, the air of condescending patrons. 'Do you expect me to go into that dirty crowd?' 'Haven't you some private way by which I could enter?' 'I can never carry that can of soup in the world!' they whined. The sick must suffer, unless a servant was at command to 'tote' a little box of gelatine; and the family must wait till some alien hand could take home the flour. The aristocratic sometimes begged for work. Mr. Williams, of the Sanitary Commission, when asked by a mother to furnish work for her daughters, said: 'If they will serve as nurses to the suffering men in your own army hospitals, I will secure pay for them.' 'My daughters go into a hospital!' exclaimed the insulted mother. 'They are ladies, sir!' 'Our Northern ladies would rather work than beg,' quietly remarked Mr. Williams. Another mother begged Mr. Chase, of the Union Commission, to give her daughters 'something to do.' 'Anything by which they can earn something, for we have not a penny in the world.' 'They shall help me measure flour,' said Mr. Chase. 'My daughters are ladies, sir,' replied the mother."

the management of public affairs with them is piling a very Pelion upon the Ossa of their misfortunes.

My room-mate, the Doctor, appointed me a "deacon for special service"—even he had absorbed military ways of doing things from our neighbors—and I arranged for his preaching in Beaufort, Sunday morning. The people were more than glad to welcome him, and he had a big congregation, with a sprinkling of black fringe around its edges, to appreciate his really eloquent discourse; while the trees that nodded at the pulpit windows shook out strains of music, which the best-trained choristers could never execute, from the swelling throats of a whole army of mocking-birds. An old Ironsides-looking man, who had occupied an elder's seat beside the pulpit, rose at the close, and said he little expected to have ever seen a day like this. Everybody started forward, anticipating a remonstrance against the strong Unionism and anti-slavery of the Doctor's sermon, but instead there came a sweeping and enthusiastic indorsement of everything that had been said. He saw a better day at hand, the old man said, and rejoiced in the brightness of its coming. How many an old man, like him, may have been waiting through all these weary years for the same glad day!

At other times there were fishing parties which caught no fish, though General Sherman sent them over enough fine ocean trout to enable them to make a splendid show on their return; and riding parties that got no rides, but trudged through the sand on foot, to the great delectation of the artist who sketched, *con amore*, the figures of gentlemen struggling up a sandy hill, eyes and ears and mouth full, hands clapped on hat to secure its tenure, and coat tails manifesting strong tendencies to secede bodily, while in the distance, small and indistinct, could be perceived the ambulance that couldn't be made to go, and underneath was written the touching inscription, "How Captain Merryman and Mr. R. accepted Mrs. W.'s invitation, and took a ride on the beach at Fort Macon."

At last the gale subsided a little, and we got off. Another salute was fired as we steamed out; the "Wayanda" returned a single shot in acknowledgment, and all too soon we were among the breakers, pitching and writhing, fore and aft, starboard and larboard, diagonally crosswise and backward, up to the sky and down, till the waves poured over the deck, and the masts seemed inclined to give the flags and streamers at their tops a bath. But for some of us, at least, the seasickness was gone. *Io Triumpe!*

CHAPTER V.

Fort Fisher.

On the morning of the 8th of May we came in sight of a long, low line of sand banks, dotted with curious hillocks, between which the black muzzles of heavy guns could be made out, and fringed with a perfect naval *chevaux-de-frise* of wrecked blockade runners, whose broken hulls and protruding machinery gave an ill-omened look to the whole coast. As we were closely studying the bleak aspect of this entrance to the great smuggling *entrepôt* of the Southern Confederacy, the glasses began to reveal an unexpected activity along the line of the guns, which our signal shot for a pilot by no means diminished. Our ship drew too much water to cross the bar, excepting at high tide, and we were, consequently, compelled to go over in the Captain's gig to the pilot boat—a proceeding that the rough sea made very difficult and even dangerous. Leaving those who could not venture the transhipment, to roll wearily among the breakers till evening, we headed straight through the narrow and difficult channel for Fort Fisher, and learned that we had been mistaken for the Rebel pirate "Stonewall," and that the guns had been shotted ready to open fire the moment we should show signs of a disposition to run in.*

*The Stonewall seems indeed to have produced about this time an excitement along the whole coast, amounting, in some places, to

Ah! that weary day at Fort Fisher! To see a fort is naturally supposed to be not the most formidable of undertakings; but to see Fort Fisher means a ride of miles over the bleakest of sand bars; means the climbing of great heaps of sand, under the hottest of suns; means a scrambling over irregular chasms and precipices of sand, where the explosions have destroyed at once every semblance of fortification and every foot of solid earth—means all this, prolonged for hours, under the penalty of the consciousness that otherwise you would be pretending to see Fort Fisher, when you were doing nothing of the sort.

We began by climbing Battery Buchanan, near the landing, and inside the main line of works. Trenches, embrasures, casemate and barbette guns, bomb-proofs, gabions, riflemen's pits, all in sand that no rifle projectiles could breach, and bombardment could only render stronger, seemed to assure absolute impregnability to this work alone, except against regular siege operations. Yet it was but protection for one flank of the long line before which Weitzel[7] turned back, and which no soldiers but ours would ever have stormed. To this battery (so called, although a perfect and very strong fort in itself) the Rebels made their last retreat, after that long, hand-to-hand fight through the sea front of the fort, which stretched far into the night, and seemed doubtful to the last. But Battery Buchanan, though impregnable, as a flank to the sea line, is itself commanded by the last work of that sea line; and so when the Mound

panic. The naval officer at Key West, for example, issued orders to extinguish the lights in the light-houses along the coast, lest the Stonewall should run into some of the harbors and destroy the shipping.

---

[7] Godfrey Weitzel, Union general noted as a military engineer. [Ed.]

Battery fell into our hands, its guns had only to be turned, and Buchanan fell almost without a struggle.

The Mound Battery is a vast heap of sand, uplifting its guns and embrazures from a flat and desert beach against the sky, and commanding perfectly the whole northern entrance to the river. It contained one of the finest specimens of heavy ordnance ever seen in this country, the famous Armstrong rifle, presented by British sympathizers to the Confederacy.

Imagine a long line of batteries, connected by traverses in the sand, separated by huge hillocks of sand, and fronted by deep trenches in the sand, stretching away almost interminably along the coast toward the North, and ending in another strong work, which was supposed to protect that flank as perfectly as Buchanan did the other; put in magazines and bomb-proofs, at convenient points, and a very heavy armament; then conceive muzzles of the guns knocked off, guns dismounted, carriages shattered, the parapets plowed with shells, a great crater in the sand where a magazine had exploded, all shape and symmetry battered out of the works, and only their rude strength remaining; and you have Fort Fisher.

The ground was covered with showers of musket balls. Behind every traverse could be found little heaps of English-made cartridges, which the Rebel sharpshooters had laid out for the convenience of rapid firing, as they defended line after line of the successive batteries, along which they were driven. Fragments of shells lay everywhere over the works. Behind them were great heaps of shells, bayonets, broken muskets, and other fragments of iron, which were being dug out and collected to be sold for old iron. Hundreds on hundreds of acres were under negro cultivation, producing this valuable crop.

No man, I think, will ride along the coast line, which, by an inconceivable amount of labor, has been converted into one immense fort, without sympathizing with the officers who refused to assault it, and marveling at the seeming recklessness which success converted into the splendid audacity of the final attack. *

The pilot boat was again placed at the disposal of our party, after some hours spent at Fort Fisher, and we ran over to Fort Caswell, one of the main defenses of the other entrance. It was originally a regularly-built brick fortification, with casemate and barbette guns, salients, ditch and interior castle, pierced with loopholes, for a last defense with musketry. Like Fort Macon, at Beaufort (and like Sumter), this has been converted into an infinitely stronger work, by having earthen fortifications thrown up outside and against it. The Rebels blew it up after the surrender of Fort Fisher, and we shall probably be making appropriations, every Congress, for the next dozen years to rebuild it.

The labor here, as well as the vast amount involved in the construction of Fort Fisher, was all performed by slaves, impressed from time to time by the Rebel authorities. Both works were completed—Wilmington had grown rich on the profits of blockade-running;

---

* The joint Committee of Congress on the Conduct of the War, after examining Generals Grant, Butler, Weitzel and Terry, and Admiral Porter, as well as the Rebel commander of the Fort, and after a careful inspection of the fortifications themselves, have, in a report published since the above was written, reached substantially the same conclusions. They attach no blame to any one for the failure to attack, in the first movement upon the Fort.

Nassau had risen to first-class commercial importance, and the beach under these guns was strewn with the wrecks, which spoke more loudly than could any balance sheet, of the profits of a business that could afford such losses—before our Congress had done disputing whether the Constitution, and a due regard for the rights of our Southern brethren, would permit us to use negroes as teamsters!

CHAPTER VI.

GENERAL HAWLEY,[8] commanding at Wilmington, had
come down to Fort Fisher, on hearing of the arrival of
our party, accompanied by General Abbott,[9] General
Dodge,[10] and a number of prominent citizens of North
Carolina. They were all transferred to our vessel,
and, with the tide in her favor, and under sail, the
"Wayanda" astonished us all by steaming up the river
at the rate of fourteen knots an hour. Captain Merryman, however, insisted she could do as much any
time, only it wasn't always convenient to get her
best speed out of her! And, of course, we were bound
to believe the Captain. Do we not make it a point of
patriotic duty to believe all the brilliant reports of the
running capacity displayed by our iron-clads and
double-enders?

Blockade runners had been sunk for miles up the
river, and in some places the hulls and machinery still
formed a partial obstruction to navigation. Torpedoes,
fished out by the navy, lay here and there along the
banks, and a few, it was said, were still in the channel,
unless, as was hoped, the tide had washed them away.

Among the North Carolinians accompanying General
Hawley, were a couple of gentlemen from Raleigh—
Mr. Moore, a leading lawyer there, and Mr. Penning-
ton, the editor of the Raleigh *Progress*—who had come

[8] Joseph Roswell Hawley, Union general, later Governor, Congressman, and U.S. Senator from Connecticut. [Ed.]

[9] Henry Larcom Abbott, Union general and military engineer.
[Ed.]

[10] George S. Dodge, Union general who fought at Fort Fisher.
[Ed.]

down to Wilmington to see Chief Justice Chase. Another gentleman in the company, introduced as " Mr." Baker—a tall, slender man, of graceful manners, and evident culture and experience—had been through nearly the whole war as Colonel of a North Carolina Rebel regiment.

Strangely enough, Colonel Baker claimed to have been a Union man all the time, from which some idea may be had of the different phases Unionism in the South has assumed. His father had been a Unionist of unquestioned firmness; but the son, returning from Europe in the midst of the secession enthusiasm, found the social pressure of his circle too much to withstand. " I was forced," he naively said, " to raise a regiment in order to retain my influence in the community !" And, with equal *naïveté*, he added, that if he had not thus retained his influence, he could now have been of no use in aiding to compose these difficulties ! He pointed out a fine rice plantation on the bank of the river, which he had owned, but about his title to which, now, he seemed to have some doubts. He claimed, and other Wilmingtonians agreed with him, that the rice grown here is superior to that of South Carolina and Georgia, and that its culture, in spite of the latitude, is quite as profitable. *

The gentlemen from Raleigh and Colonel Baker seemed each to be a representative of a different phase of North Carolina Unionism. The editor had always opposed secession till it was accomplished. Then he was compelled to go with the current, but as soon as

---

* The farther north you can grow any grain, or other crop, and *mature it*, the better it is—according to the theory of the North Carolina planters. The rice crop is more profitable here, they claim, than on the best plantations about Savannah.

the first fury was over, and the reaction began, he became openly anti-Davis, and as much anti-war as he dared. He was an enthusiastic admirer of General Sherman; thought the censure by the Northern press, of his arrangement with Johnston, very unjust; was anxious now for the speediest possible restoration of civil authority, and believed the people stood willing to acquiesce in whatever basis of re-organization the President would prescribe. If he had his way, he would have no negro suffrage; even that would be preferable to remaining unorganized, and would be accepted by the people, though it would cause great dissatisfaction.

The lawyer, on the other hand, insisted that none would revolt, with more loathing, from the bare idea of negro suffrage, than the best Union men in the State, who had suffered the most for their devotion to the Government and opposition to the war. "It would not even be satisfactory," he insisted, "to leave the negroes, like other non-voting classes, to take care of themselves. To leave them absolutely without any control, save such as the law extends to white people, also, would be unendurable. Either you must take pity," he exclaimed, on those of us who, for four years, have endured everything for the sake of the old flag, and send the negroes out of the country altogether, or you must place them under the control of the Legislature." "What policy toward them would the Legislature be apt to adopt?" "It ought to provide against vagrancy; adopt measures to require them to fulfill their contracts for labor, and authorize their sale, for a term of years, for breaches of order. * Either do that, and so protect us against

---

* In other words, call them freedmen, but indirectly make them slaves again. The same idea seems to pervade the State, and,

an intolerable nuisance, or colonize them out of the country."

The Colonel was not so emphatic in favor of this virtual re-enslavement of the negroes, nor so peremptory in his condemnation of negro suffrage; but he thought it would be wise to conciliate as much as possible, and to avoid deep-seated prejudices. It was easy to see that he was looking to what would be the least unpopular with the people of North Carolina; and, indeed, I heard later in the evening, that he was not unwilling to ask them to send him to Congress.

Clearly enough, few Union men in the South, who have political aspirations, can be safely expected to advocate justice, much less generosity, to the negro, or severity to the Rebels. The latter are sure to be voters—many of them now, after carelessly taking oaths of allegiance—all of them some day; and politicians are not likely to make haste in doing that which they know to be odious to the men whose votes they want.

At a dinner party at General Hawley's, and subsequently at a little party, later in the evening, we saw

indeed, the entire South. Colonel Boynton, a very intelligent and trustworthy officer, writing from Danville, North Carolina, on the 21st of June, said:

"The belief is by no means general here, that slavery is dead, and a hope that, in some undefined way, they will yet control the slaves, is in many minds, amounting with some to a conviction. They look for its restoration through State action—not yet comprehending that the doctrine of State sovereignty has been somewhat shattered by the war. Here, as in Richmond, the people, instead of grappling with the fact that the war has liberated the slaves, are very busy proving the utter worthlessness of the negroes, and treating them with additional cruelty and contempt—neither offering them fair inducements to work, or working themselves."

and heard a good deal of the feelings of the people. The women are very polite to Yankee officers in particular, but very bitter against Yankees in general. Negro troops are their especial detestation; and for the monstrosity of attempting to teach negroes to read and write, they could find no words to express their scorn. A young officer told me that he had been "cut" by some ladies, with whom he had previously been on very cordial terms, because they had seen him going into one of the negro schools! The men of North Carolina may be "subjugated," but who shall subjugate the women?

Governor Vance has been very unpopular, and the people seem to take kindly enough to the idea that his authority will not be recognized. They say he was a Union man in feeling and conviction, but that Jeff. Davis, alarmed by the dissatisfaction in North Carolina, sent for him about the time of his last election, and persuaded him that he could be the next President of the Confederacy! The Presidential idea was as baneful in Rebeldom, as it has proved to so many Northern statesmen, and Vance was destroyed.

Every Northern man in Wilmington lives in the very best style the place affords, no matter how slender his visible resources. I was the guest of a civil officer whose salary can not be over two thousand dollars. His home was a spacious three-story double structure, that would have done no discredit to Fifth Avenue. You approach it through a profusion of the rarest shrubbery; it was in the most aristocratic quarter of the city, was elegantly furnished, and filled with servants— all on two thousand dollars a year, less the Government tax. But this is modest and moderate. The officer at least made the one house serve all his purposes.

Another—a Colonel on duty here—is less easily satisfied. He has no family, but he finds one of the largest
and best-furnished double houses in the town only sufficient for his bachelor wants, as a private residence.
Another house, equally spacious and eligible, is required
for the uses of his office! And, in general, our people
seem to go upon the theory that, having conquered the
country, they are entitled to the best it has, and in duty
bound to use as much of it as possible.

These houses are generally such as were shut up by
their rich Rebel owners on the approach of our troops
below the city. The proprietors have retired to adjacent country places, to be out of harm's way till they
see how Rebels are to be treated, and already they are
making their calculations about returning in the fall,
with a coolness almost disconcerting to their self-
appointed tenants. Mrs. General Hawley tells a piquant
story of a visit from the wife of a runaway Rebel,
whose showy but uncomfortable house the General has
seized for quarters and private residence. The lady
made herself as agreeable as possible, spoke of the General's occupancy and her own absence, much as people
who had gone off to the sea-shore for the summer
might speak of renting their town house till their return;
intimating that she wouldn't hurry the General commanding for the world, and hoped that he would remain
with his family until it was entirely convenient to
remove, but suggested that she and her husband
thought they would probably return in a couple or
three months, when, of course, they supposed their house
would be ready for them! Confiscation seemed to have
no terrors for her; or, if it had, they were dexter-
ously concealed under an air of smiling and absolute
assurance.

The loosest ideas prevail as to the execution of the "abandoned-property" act of the Thirty-seventh Congress. Deserted houses, not absolutely needed for military purposes, can be rented for handsome sums, and to whatever amounts can be thus realized the Government has an equitable as well as legal claim. But here, and report says everywhere throughout the South, are evidences of the old clashing betwixt War and Treasury Department officials; and between them, the revenue the Government ought to derive from the abandoned property, is sadly reduced.

The practice of regarding everything left in the country as legitimate prize to the first officer who discovers it, has led, in some cases, to performances little creditable to the national uniform. What shall be thought of the officer who, finding a fine law library, straightway packed it up and sent it to his office in the North? Or what shall be said of the taste of that other officer who, finding in an old country residence a series of family portraits, imagined that they would form very pretty parlor ornaments anywhere, and sent the entire set, embracing the ancestors of the haughty old South Carolinian for generations back, to look down from the walls of his Yankee residence?

One sees, at first, very little in the mere external appearance of Wilmington to indicate the sufferings of war. The city is finely built (for the South); the streets are lined with noble avenues of trees; many of the residences are surrounded with elegant shrubbery; there is a bewildering wealth of flowers; the streets are full, and many of the stores are open. Sutlers, however, have taken the places of the old dealers, and many of the inhabitants are inconceivably helpless and destitute. While I was riding over the city with Captain Myers, a young Ohio artillerist, a formerly wealthy citizen approached him to beg the favor of some means of taking his family three or four miles into the country. The officer could only offer the broken "Southron" a pair of mules and an army wagon; and this shabby outfit, which four years ago he would not have permitted his body servant to use, he gratefully accepted for his wife and daughter!

Struggling through the waste of sand which constitutes the streets, could be seen other and more striking illustrations of the workings of the war: a crazy cart, with wheels on the eve of a general secession, drawn generally by a single horse, to which a good meal of oats must have been unknown for months, loaded with tables, chairs, a bedstead, a stove and some frying-pans, and driven by a sallow, lank, long-haired, wiry-bearded representative of the poor white trash, who had probably perched a sun-bonneted, toothless wife, and a brace of tow-head children among the furniture; or a group, too poor even for a cart, clothed in rags, bearing bundles of rags, and, possibly, driving a half-starved cow. These were refugees from the late theater of military operations. They seemed hopeless, and, in some cases, scarcely knew where they wanted to go.

Few of the old residents of Wilmington are believed to have profited by the blockade running. It was always considered a disreputable business, in which a high-minded Rebel would not care to be thought concerned; and so it fell chiefly into the hands of foreigners, and particularly of Jews. A few prominent Richmond people were believed to be deeply engaged in it—Trenholm,[11] Governor Smith,[12] Benjamin[13] and Jeff. Davis are all named—but wherever the profits went, they did

[11] George A. Trenholm, Richmond merchant active in blockade running, Confederate Secretary of Treasury, 1864-1865. [Ed.]

[12] William ("Extra Billy") Smith, Confederate general and Governor of Virginia at the end of the war. [Ed.]

not go to a general diffusion of property among the Wilmingtonians themselves.

Jay Cooke was under the impression that there must be a great deal of gold throughout the Southern cities, and especially in this center of blockade running, that ought to be available for the 7.30 loan; but the testimony here goes to show that the wealthy people have most of their gold abroad, and that they do not have a great deal of it anywhere. Undoubtedly nothing would more tend to tie these people to the Union than such a cord as a United States bond, connecting their pockets with national permanence and prosperity, but they seem now hard enough pressed to buy the necessaries of life; and money for investments in national securities, is not likely to flow northward, for the simple reason that it is not in the country.

Negroes are already beginning to congregate here from the surrounding country. They do not wish to trust their old masters on the plantations; and, without any definite purpose or plan, they have a blind, but touching instinct, that wherever the flag is floating it is a good place for friendless negroes to go. Others are hunting up children or wives, from whom they have long been separated. Quite a number have been located on plantations, and these are working better than could be expected; but the uncertainty of their tenure of the land, the constant return of the old proprietors, and the general confusion and uncertainty as to the ownership of real estate, under the confiscation and abandoned-property laws, combine to unsettle both them and the Superintendents of Freedmen, who are trying to care for them.

The native negroes of Wilmington, however, are doing

---

[13] Judah Philip Benjamin, Confederate Secretary of War, 1861-1862, Secretary of State, 1862-1865. [Ed.]

well. They are of a much higher order of intelligence
than those from the country; are generally in comfortable circumstances, and already find time to look into
politics. They have a Union League formed among
themselves, the object of which is to stimulate to industry and education, and to secure combined effort for suffrage, without which they insist that they will soon be
practically enslaved again. A delegation of them waited
on Mr. Chase; and certainly looked as well and talked
as lucidly as any of the poor whites would have done.
There are a very few of the whites who encourage
them; but, in general, the bitterest prejudice against
these black Unionists, is still among those who have
been the only white Unionists—the often-described poor
white trash.

The Wilmington negroes have no faith in the ready
assent to the proposition that slavery is dead, which all
the old slaveholders give. They say—and the negro
refugees, all, and some of the whites bear them out in
it—that in the country slavery still practically exists.
The masters tell them that slavery is to be restored as
soon as the army is removed ; that the Government is
already mustering the army out of service; that next
year, when the State is re-organized, the State authorities will control slavery. Meantime, the negroes are
worked as hard as ever—in some cases a little harder—
and they have no more protection from the cruelty of
the whites than ever. *

---

* Numerous instances were told, while I was at Wilmington, but
the following case, related by Colonel Boynton, occurred farther in
the interior:

"Here in Salisbury, two prominent men are on trial by a military court, for killing a negro, and one of the wealthiest, most
refined and respectable young ladies in all this section, is under

"I tell you, sah" said a very intelligent negro, who had been reciting the present troubles of his people, "we ain't noways safe, 'long as dem people makes de laws we's got to be governed by. We's got to hab a voice in de 'pintin' of de law-makers. Den we knows our frens, and whose hans we's safe in."

The war, according to these negroes, had, in some respects, made slavery harder for them than before. They were naturally trusted less, and watched more. Then, when provisions became scarce, their rations, on the large plantations, were reduced. On one, for example, the field hands got no meat at all, and their allowance consisted of a peck of unsifted corn-meal and a pint of molasses per week. On another, they got two pounds of meat, a peck of meal, and a quart of molasses per week. Before the war, they had double as much meat, and a peck and a-half of meal. Thus fed, they were expected to begin work in the fields at day-break, and continue, with only the intermission of half an hour at noon, till dark.

In some cases the negroes, understanding that they are freed, have refused to work without a contract for wages. Some of them have been promised their board, and a quarter of the corn crop; others three dollars for

twenty thousand dollars bonds to appear and answer for shooting a negro woman with her own hands. Miss Temple Neeley is considered one of the belles of the State. The family is very wealthy, aristocratic, and all that, and stands at the very top in this section. Her mother was flogging a little negro child, when the mother of the child interfered to protect it. Miss Neeley stepped up, and, drawing a revolver from her pocket, shot the negro woman dead, firing a second ball into the body. She was arrested, and will be tried by a military court. The papers here are defending her, and trying to stir up the old feeling toward the slaves, and excusing her under the black laws of the State."

a season's work; others a dollar and a-half or two dollars a month. But the town negroes, especially those of the League, say they have but little faith that the contracts will be kept.

Further conversation with the people led me to think that, in the main, they might be divided into three classes. One, embracing, I think, a majority of the people, is thoroughly cowed by the crushing defeat, has the profoundest respect for the power that has whipped them so badly, and, under the belief of its necessity, will submit to anything the Government may require—negro suffrage, territorial pupilage—anything. A smaller class are Union men, if they can have the Union their way—if the negroes can be kept under, and themselves put foremost. And another class are violent and malignant Rebels, enraged at their defeat, and hardly yet willing to submit to the inevitable.

The loss of life has been frightful. Half the families are in mourning. I hear of a Danville regiment, twelve hundred strong, of whom less than fifty survive. Not less than eighty thousand arms-bearing men of the State are believed to have been killed or disabled. This, and the disorganization of the labor system, have naturally left thousands of families through the State utterly destitute. Mr. Pennington, the editor of the Raleigh *Progress*, predicts great distress next winter. In fact, the Government is already issuing rations to thousands of destitute whites.

As yet, notwithstanding their poverty and destitution, few of the large landowners have put their estates in the market. No such feeling exists here, however, as in Virginia, where the farmers are said to hold on with a death grip to their lands, and to consider it discreditable to sell to a Yankee. Many of the most violent Rebels here will sell at exceedingly low rates, in order to get out of the country, where everything reminds them of their mortifying defeat and disgrace. And of those who remain, large numbers will be forced to sell part of their lands, to get means for living comfortably on the remainder. * The new blood, likely thus to be infused

---

* On the 1st of August a single real estate firm in Raleigh advertised no less than *sixty-three* different tracts of North Carolina lands for sale at low rates, and on easy terms. Here are a couple of specimens:

" We offer for sale one of the finest rice plantations in the State of North Carolina, known as 'Lyrias,' and situated on the northwest branch of Cape Fear river, three and a-half miles above Wilmington. This plantation contains 275 acres, 250 of which are cleared, and 25 are river swamp lands. There is also an upland settlement attached, with a dwelling-house, all necessary outhouses, comfortable quarters for fifty laborers, and an excellent well of water.

"The rice lands, with the exception of about 20 acres, are of a clay soil, of unsurpassed and inexhaustible fertility, and capable of producing rice, corn, wheat, oats, peas and hay.

" It is every way susceptible of being also made a good stock farm, for cattle and hogs, and an excellent market garden.

"The entire plantation is in *good order*. It has on it two commodious barns, 100 by 40 and 75 by 60 feet, respectively. Also, a steam engine of ten-horse power, together with a powerful pump, or water elevator, worked by the engine, which throws out *two thousand gallons* of water per minute. Also, a threshing machine, in a building 25 by 35 feet."

" All that really baronial estate, known as William S. Pettigrew's 'Magnolia Plantation,' for sale cheap.—1,000 acres improved !—Over 600 acres in a high state of cultivation !—50, or over, bushels of corn per acre !—Rich alluvial soils, suitable for farms and vegetable gardens !—Only ten hours from Norfolk !—Water transporta-

into North Carolina, will be its salvation; and the capital which is now seeking openings for trade, will presently find vastly more profitable returns from investments in lands.

General Hawley, General Abbott and their wives, the Collector, the Treasury Agent, a party of staff officers and others, pursued us with kindness till our vessel had absolutely pushed off from the almost deserted wharf, which, four years ago, was crowded with the keels of a thriving commerce, and even a year ago bustled with scores of adventurous blockade runners. Trade, indeed, follows the flag; but for trade you must have money; and of this there is far too little in the exhausted country to bring back business into its old channels, as speedily as Northern speculators are imagining.

Some of the officers and their wives came down with

tion from the barn.—The far-famed 'Scuppernong' grape is a native of this county, and grows in a luxuriant abundance unsurpassed in any country. The residence, barns, out-buildings, groves, etc., etc., are *very superior*. Good well of water, etc., etc.

"This very large, and really magnificent estate, contains seven thousand acres of those rich alluvial Scuppernong river lands; one thousand acres already *drained*, and most of it in a high state of cultivation, and the whole of the rest can be easily and effectually drained; thus opening up large plantations scarcely surpassed in fertility by the Mississippi bottoms, which they greatly exceed in proximity to markets, having cheap and easy carriage, almost, if not quite, from the barn door to Norfolk, Baltimore, Philadelphia, New York, Boston and the whole world!

"Sea-going vessels can now come within a few miles of the barn door, and by deepening one canal, this desirable result can be obtained."

us in the river steamer, to the bar, whither the "Way-anda" had returned to await us; and kindly good-byes and fluttering handkerchiefs could still be heard and seen after the vessels had each begun moving. At the North we think little of loyalty; here loyal men, and especially those in the service of the Government, seem drawn toward each other, as are men who serve under the same flag in a foreign country.

CHAPTER VII.

Charleston Harbor—Could Sumter have been Stormed—Negroes
and Poor Whites.

WE steamed into Charleston Harbor early in the
morning; and one by one, Sumter, Moultrie, Pinkney,
and at last the City of Desolation itself rose from the
smooth expanse of water, as the masts of ships rise from
the ocean when you approach them. Where, four years
ago, before the fatal attack on this now shapeless heap
of sand and mortar, the flags of all nations fluttered,
and the wharves were crowded with a commerce that
successfully rivaled Savannah, Mobile and every other
Southern city save New Orleans, and even aspired to
compete with New York in the Southern markets, only
transports and Quartermasters' vessels were now to be
seen, with here and there a passenger steamer, plying
to and from New York for the accommodation of
Yankee officers and their wives! The harbor itself
was dotted with insignificant-looking iron clads, mingled with an occasional old ship of the line, and, in
ampler supply, the modern "Yankee gunboats," of
the double-ender type, which formed so potent a cause
for alarm in the councils of the privates in the Rebel
armies.

The elegant residences along the battery front
retained the aristocratic seclusion of their embowering
shrubbery, creepers and flowering plants; but even
through these gracious concealments which Nature cast

over them, the scars from the Swamp Angel could
everywhere be seen.   Pavements had been torn up
from the principal business streets, to build the batteries that lined the shore; and great embankments,
crowned with Tredegar guns, shut out the prospect from
many an aristocratic window. The unfinished Custom
House was among the most conspicuous buildings, the
white marble blocks lying scattered about it, as they
were left by the workmen four years ago. "We'll never
finish it," the fervid revolutionists said, as they began
the war. "We've paid Yankee tariffs long enough;
now, hurrah for free trade with our friends of France
and Great Britain!"   But the Custom House stands,
and next winter Mr. Fessenden will be reporting to the
Senate an item in the military appropriation bill for its
completion.

Admiral Dahlgren[14] and Fleet Captain Bradford
came alongside in the Admiral's gig, soon after our
arrival; and while our boatswain was piping his whistle
as the Admiral came over the ship's side, the guns of the
"Pawnee" began a salute for the Chief Justice. The
Treasury Agent and some other officials soon followed,
and the Admiral took the party under his charge,
transferred us to a comfortable and speedy little
harbor steamer, and started toward that first goal of
every man's curiosity—Sumter.

The rebellion has left its marks on the pale, thought-
ful features of the Admiral, not less than upon the harbor
he has been assailing. The terrible death of noble young
Ulric Dahlgren, a martyr to the barbarism of slavery,
might well grave deep traces on a father's face; but the
climate here, and the labors of the past have also been
very trying, and one can readily believe, what used to
be rather sarcastically urged by the Admiral's enemies,

[14] John Adolph Dahlgren, Union admiral, commander of the
South Atlantic Blockading Squadron. [Ed.]

that his health did not permit him to keep up in gunnery with General Gillmore.[15]

We passed a little sailing vessel manned by blacks.
The Admiral told us that they had brought it down one
of the rivers, the other day, and he had allowed them
to keep it. They earn a livelihood bringing wood to
the city. Recently there have been a number of out-
rages perpetrated on the blacks inland, by their late
masters and some of the returning Rebel soldiers.
Greatly infuriated, the blacks came to him begging for
arms. "I have never before doubted their orderly disposition," he said, "and I am not sure that anybody
would remain orderly under those circumstances."

The Charleston city negroes were represented as
unexpectedly intelligent. "Out of two hundred and
seventy-four laborers at work on the streets," said one
of the city officials who had joined us, "one hundred
and seventy-four are negroes—the rest whites. Of the
negroes, over a hundred (or over four-sevenths) can
read, while scarcely one-seventh of the whites have
made the same advancement!" * Captain Bradford
gave a significant illustration of the progress of some
ideas among the less intelligent negroes of the country.
They had again and again asked him, he said, what
good it did them to make them free, unless they were
to own the land on which they had been working, and
which they had made productive and valuable. "Gib
us our own land and we take care ourselves; but widout land, de ole massas can hire us or starve us, as dey
please."

* The ignorance of the poor whites in South Carolina is pro-
verbial. But, as a negro acutely pointed out, "Dey have n't learned,
because dey do n't care; we, because dey would n't let us." A little
before the time of this visit, James Redpath, acting as Superintend-

[15] Quincy Adams Gillmore, commander of the Department of
the South, February 9—June 28, 1865. [Ed.]

A huge mass of iron was pointed out as we passed, not unlike the plates of the famous "Merrimac," or like the gunboat "Benton," on the Mississippi. It was one of the Rebel iron clads, sunk just before the evacuation of the city. They had injured it very little, and our authorities are confident of making it one of the best iron clads in the service. Enforced self-reliance, had, indeed, gone far toward making the South a nation; for here were fine engines, worthy of our most extensive Northern shops, which had been manufactured in Georgia within a year. Before the war, such an undertaking as making engines for a great steamer, in the South, was scarcely dreamed of. Near the iron clad lay some of the cigar-shaped torpedo boats—an invention never very successful, and now, let us hope, with its occupation, wholly gone.

The obstructions in the harbor, which so long kept the iron clads under Dupont and Dahlgren at bay, still stretched in a long line, unbroken in parts, across from Sumter toward the land on either side. Plenty of torpedoes were supposed to be still in the harbor—Captain Bradford himself had been blown up not long ago by one of them, to the serious discomposure of his personal

ent of the schools, reported nine public day and five night schools, under the superintendence of his bureau, with the following average attendance:

At Normal School	620
At St. Philip School	1,100
At Morris Street School	822
At Ashley Street School	305
At King Street School (boys)	306
At Meeting Street School (boys)	256
At Chalmers Street School (girls)	161
At St. Michael's School (boys)	160
Night Schools for adults contain	500

effects, in cabin and state-room, but without actual physical injury.

But for two things, a stranger might have supposed Sumter a mere pile of mortar, stones and sand, which only culpable lack of enterprise left to block up the harbor. From the center of the rubbish rose a flag-staff, with the stars and stripes floating at the top; and near the water's edge, uninjured casements still stood among the debris, with black muzzles peeping out, as from the lower deck of an old ship of the line. Closer inspection showed, also, some little howitzers and other light pieces, placed on what was once the parapet.

The sun fairly parboiled us, and, coming into this tropical heat so suddenly—for the night before, on the deck of the "Wayanda," at sea, we were wearing over-coats—it was so oppressive as to produce a sickening faintness on some of the party; but we patiently followed everywhere, clambered over the shapeless sea wall, inspected the sand gabions, worked our way into the snugly-protected little out-looks for the sharp-shooters, ran down the inside of what had been the walls, and dived into the subteranean regions where the casemate guns stood all the time of the bombardment, uninjured, but not deigning to waste their ammunition in useless replies. The contracted but comparatively comfortable quarters here remain almost as the Rebels left them. A long, damp hall, with a few cots still standing in it, was the place for the garrison, where they slept in comparative indifference to the explosion of shells overhead; a rather more airy hall still contained the old, split-bottom arm-chairs, which the officers had collected; on another side were the hospitals, and—ghastly sight— there, on a shelf, were half a dozen coffins, which had been all ready for the reception of the next victims to Gillmore's shells !

Fresh from Fort Fisher, which had been stormed, it was natural that one should look on Fort Sumter with surprise, when told that it could not be stormed. The officers say the garrison would have retreated to the casemates, from whence they could have made the occupation of the interior area of the fort impossible; but surely the men who swarmed over that northern end of Fort Fisher, and fought through the whole afternoon and far into the night, from traverse to traverse, down to the Mound battery, would have needed little time to establish themselves here. They say, too, that the fire from the Rebel works on Morris Island would have rendered Sumter untenable, but that fire could not have been more powerful than ours had been from James Island. Yet the Rebels did not find Sumter untenable on account of our fire. Whether an assault upon Sumter—necessarily bloody beyond precedent—could have been justified by the maxims of war, is a question; but that such men as took Fort Fisher could have taken Fort Sumter, if aided by a proper naval force, seems to me clear.

It is said that the Rebels had a similar idea—long in fact before Fort Fisher had been attacked. It was one of the strange personal complications of this war, that the regular Rebel officer who had command of Sumter when our terrific bombardment began, had no faith in its defensibility, and had been replaced by a young nephew of the very Dominie of our party, who has been walking with us over the ruins. The Doctor is as glad as any of us that the fort is reduced, but his eye kindled as Admiral Dahlgren gave the tribute of honest admiration to the splendid bravery and tenacity of his Rebel nephew.

From Sumter we steamed off to Sullivan's Island, and in a few moments were clambering among the mazes of the Rebel works. Here, four years ago, the first fortifications of the war were thrown up. Here the dashing young cavaliers, the haughty Southrons who scorned the Yankee scum and were determined to have a country and a history for themselves, rushed madly into the war as into a picnic. Here the boats from Charleston landed every day cases of champagne, *pâtés* innumerable, casks of claret, thousands of Havana cigars, for the use of the luxurious young Captains and Lieutenants, and their friends among the privates. Here were the first camps of the war, inscribed, as the newspapers of those days tell us, with such names of companies as "The Live Tigers," "The Palmetto Guards," "The Marion Scorpions," "The Yankee Smashers." Here, with feasting, and dancing, and love making, with music improvised from the ball room, and enthusiasm fed to madness by well-ripened old Madeira, the free-handed, free-mannered young men who had ruled "society" at Newport and Saratoga, and whose advent North had always been waited for as the opening of the season, dashed into revolution as they would into a waltz. Not one of them doubted that, only a few months later, he should make his accustomed visit to the Northern watering places, and be received with the distinction due a hero of Southern independence. Long before these fortifications, thus begun, were abandoned, they saw their enterprise in far different lights, and conducted it in a far soberer and less luxurious way.

The works stretched along the sandy shore of Sullivan's Island almost as far as the eye can reach. They consist of huge embankments of sand, revetted with palmetto logs, and were evidently planned throughout by a skillful engineer. Coupling these with the works on the other side of the harbor, and with Sumter, one readily believes them to constitute the strongest system of harbor defenses on the coast. Strolling around one of the works, we came upon a little slab, near a palmetto tree, under the shade of the embankment, "To Osceola, Patriot and Warrior." It is the grave of one of the last of the Florida chieftains, who died here in confinement, and for whom some white enemy but admirer, had done these last tender honors. Shall the latest warriors of this island ever find similar admirers?

After our fatiguing trip, the Admiral spread out, on our return to the flag-ship, a lunch of oranges, bananas, pine-apples, and other tropical fruits, brought over from Havana. At the end of his table hung the only Union flag, or trace of anything resembling it, which the naval officers have been able to find anywhere in South Carolina or Georgia—a long, narrow strip of coarse bunting, containing two stripes, red and white, and a few stars in a ground of blue—taken from a deserted cabin near Savannah.

New York papers, only five days old, had just arrived. In the midst of the wonders which the war had wrought here, it was scarcely surprising to see even the New York *Herald* out vigorously for negro suffrage!

CHAPTER VIII.

Charleston, Now and Four Years Ago.

In the afternoon, the General commanding the post was waiting with carriages for the party, at the wharf, when Admiral Dahlgren set us ashore. The wheels cut deep into the sand, throwing it into our faces and filling the carriage with it, till we began to realize what it meant to have taken up the pavements to get stone for the fortifications.

"Shall we go first to the statue of Calhoun?" asked the General. "It is scarcely necessary—here is his monument," said some one (in imitation of the old eulogium), pointing around the destroyed parts of the city. Later in the ride we did pass an old statue to William Pitt, which the English-loving cavaliers of Carolina had erected in the old Colonial days. During the Revolutionary war, a British ball broke off one of its arms. When we entered the city it was found that the other was also gone.

A foreigner, who visited Charleston in May, 1861, spoke of these streets as "looking like Paris in the revolution—crowds of armed men singing and promenading the streets; the battle blood running through their veins; that hot oxygen, which is called 'the flush of victory,' on the cheek; restaurants full; reveling in bar rooms, club rooms crowded, orgies and carousings in taverns or private houses, in tap rooms, down narrow alleys, in the broad highways." This is the anniversary of that mad era; but the streets look widely different. There are crowds of armed men in the streets, but they move under the strictest discipline and their color is black. No battle blood mantles the faces of the haggard and listless Charlestonians one meets—it is rather blood born of low diet and water gruel. For the flush of victory we have utter despondency. The restaurants are closed and the shutters are up; the occupants of the club rooms are dead, or in prison, or in exile; there is still carousing in taverns, but it is only by the flushed and spendthrift Yankee officers who are willing to pay seventy-five cents for a cobbler.

Of the leaders of those days, scarcely one remains to receive the curses which, even in the midst of their hatred of the Yankees, the people pour out upon the men who converted their prosperity into desolation. Then they were singing—

"With mortar, paixhan and petard,
We send Old Abe our Beauregard.'

But Beauregard is a prisoner, given leave, by "Old Abe's" parole, to humbly enter his home at New Orleans, from which the loving wife, whom he deserted for secession, has gone out forever. Huger[16] is dead. Barnwell Rhett is in exile, and the very journal by which he fed and nurtured the germs of the Rebellion, has passed absolutely out of existence—no new editor daring to revive so ill-omened a thing as the Charleston *Mercury*.* Governor Pickens, who announced in one of his early proclamations that he was born insensible

* A proposition has since been made to re-establish it, as an organ of the freedmen—to be edited by negroes!

[16] Probably Daniel Elliott Huger, South Carolina politician who died in 1854. [Ed.]

to fear, has lived to learn his mistake, and has vanished into the dim unknown of "the interior." Governor Aiken, who,(like that political eunuch, Alexander H. Stephens,)weakly yielded his convictions and eased his conscience by blockade running, instead of fighting, has, for some unknown reason, been arrested and sent to Washington. Governor Manning, Porcher Miles, Senator Chesnut, Barnwell, have all vanished into thin air before the Ithuriel touch—nay, rather before the mere approach of negro bayonets. The merchants, too, whom Southern independence was to make the cotton factors of the world, have disappeared. Their direct line of steamers to Liverpool failed to get beyond the blockading fleet, and long before the politicians had given it up, these men were hopelessly ruined. Trenholm, indeed, pushed a precarious but lucrative trade in blockade running, and succeeded better in managing his own funds than he did those of the Rebel Treasury Department; but he is now an absconding member of the Jeff. Davis Cabinet, and will be fortunate if he escape arrest. Rose and Minor are gone.

One name, of all that were so prominent in Charleston four years ago, should never be taken on loyal lips save with reverent regard—that of Mr. Petigru.[17] He remained faithful to the last; but his eyes were not permitted to see the old flag waving again, and his wife is to-day in Charleston, living on Government rations! She has stated her destitution frankly, however, to General Gillmore, commanding the Department, and some small part of the nation's debt to her husband will yet, it is hoped, be paid in the tenderest care for herself.

"There are twenty thousand people here in Charleston." said the haughty representative of an ancient

[17] James Louis Petigru, South Carolina unionist to the last. [Ed.]

Carolinian name, "and only six families among them all!" Judging from what one sees on the streets, one could very readily believe the paradox which, in Carolina lips, becomes no paradox at all. There are plenty of resident Irish on the streets; the poorer class of natives, too, begin to venture out; but, in the course of the whole afternoon's driving about the city, I did not see a single one whom I should have supposed to belong to a leading family. My companion had spent the greater part of his life in Charleston, and, in his own language, knew everybody in the town; but he failed to see one whom he recognized as having ever held any position in politics or society.

The extent of the damage by the bombardment has, I imagine, been generally overrated at the North. The lower part of the city was certainly not an eligible location for a quiet residence; but it is an error to suppose that most of the houses, or any considerable number of them, have been destroyed. The shells generally failed to explode, and the marks on the houses are rather scars than serious breaches. Roofs are injured, walls are weakened, windows destroyed and floors more or less ripped up; but still the houses stand, and can, with comparatively little outlay, be repaired. The General's headquarters are established in the midst of the bombarded district; but the elegant house which he occupies shows no mark whatever. Most of the other officers who have taken houses are in the same quarter, and I observe that they have the same passion, as at Wilmington, for getting the very best establishments in a place.

The General drove us through the Arsenal grounds, and past those of the Military Academy, where, of old, the martial spirit of South Carolina had been fostered. The drives and walks had been bordered with spherical case, round shot and shell; and here and there, at the corners, little ornamental effects were produced by the erection of small pillars, made of our long rifle projectiles, flanked by a few broken bayonets. It was thus the Charlestonians amused themselves during the progress of the bombardment.

Passing through the shabby suburbs, which would hardly comport with the dignity of a first-class Northern village, we came out upon the track where, of yore, all the beauty and fashion of Charleston was wont to congregate—the Race Course. Of late years it has been used for a different purpose. Here, without shelter, without clothing, and with insufficient food, were confined the Yankee prisoners; and in a little inclosure, back of the judges' stand, may be seen their uncounted graves. Sympathizing hands have cleared away the weeds, and placed over the entrance an inscription that must bring shame to the cheek of every Southern man who passes: "The Martyrs of the Race Course." Near it was an elegant cemetery, carefully tended, glorious with superb live-oaks, and weeping with the long, pendent trails of the silvery Spanish moss; but into this consecrated ground no Yankee's body could be borne. Negro soldiers were strolling through it as we passed, and some were reading from showy tombstones, to the dusky groups around them, the virtues of the—masters from whom they had run away to enlist!

Occasional vehicles were seen on the road, bringing in black and white refugees. The country is in such confusion that many seek the safe shelter of the cities, solely from the blind instinct that where there is force there must be protection. Such wagons and such horses were surely never seen. Each rivaled the other in corners, in age, in protuberance, and shakiness, and general disposition to tumble down and dissolve. They all bring in saddening stories of destitution in the country. Still I am inclined to think that these stories are exaggerated. There is little evidence of actual suffering in the country; and in the cities none who want have any scruples in calling upon the hireling minions of the tyrannical Washington Government for rations. Next winter is the dead point of danger. There is a smaller breadth of cereals sown in the South this year than in any year since 1861, and by fall the stock on hand is likely to be exhausted. Now the suffering is only individual; then it promises to be too nearly general.

On the other hand, the reports from the North-west, or mountain region of the State, indicate little prospect of suffering. "I tell you," said a South Carolinian, from Greenville, "the South could have continued the war for ten years, if it had had your Northern gift of perseverance. We were neither exhausted of men nor of provisions; it was only that the flame of enthusiasm had burnt out. I have myself traveled, within the past month, through sections of South Carolina, from Greenville to Columbia, and thence north-east and north-west, so as to know accurately the condition of the crops in one-half the State. There is no trouble about starvation. The people are not suffering, except in such isolated cases as you will always find, and there is a larger breadth of grains planted than ever before. With reasonable care there ought to be no starvation this winter.

There was a little party in the evening, in the fine old mansion of a noted Charleston banker, but there were

few South Carolinians there, excepting the house servants who had remained to wait on the new occupants.
Admiral Dahlgren, Major-General Saxton,[18] two or three
Brigadiers and Brevet Brigadiers, and their wives, made
up the bulk of the company; and the talk was of the
army and navy and the policy of the Government. A
gentleman was introduced as the editor of the Charleston *Courier*, and I was not a little surprised to find that
redoubtable Rebel personage greeting me with the
warmth of an old acquaintance. He turned out to be a
former *attaché* of a leading New York paper, who had
often reported to me in Washington, when I had been
in temporary charge of its bureau there.

Persons writing from here in the spring of 1861, said
there was no feature of the feeling among the leaders
more marked than their scarcely disguised hostility to
the freedom of the press. I had been reading over
some of those letters, of four years ago, in the morning;
and it sounded curiously, like a continuation of the old
strain, to hear the editor's lamentations over the impossibility of making a newspaper where you could express
no opinions, and couldn't always even print the news.
"Here, yesterday, for example, was a reconstruction
meeting. The call for it was sent to me. I published
that, and then sent phonographers to make a full report
of the proceedings. There was a big row; the whites
ordered out the negroes; then the latter got re-enforced,
and came back to maintain their ground, whereupon
the whites left. The speeches on both sides were racy;
there was a good deal of excitement. I had a splendid
report of the whole thing, and it was capital news. I
had it all in type, when an order came to make no allusion whatever to the meeting. This morning every-

[18] Rufus Saxton, Union general in command at Port Royal
since 1862. [Ed.]

body thinks the *Courier* is behind the times, because
it didn't know anything about the reconstruction
meeting!"

After the party, the Dominie told me of his explorations among his old friends in Charleston.

I ought, perhaps, before this, to have explained that
my genial room mate, whom I have been rather irreverently terming the Dominie, is Rev. Dr. Fuller,[19] of
Baltimore, now a noted Baptist clergyman, formerly a
leading South Carolina lawyer and planter. He still
owns large plantations on the sea islands, and, down to
the date of the emancipation proclamation, had on them
between two hundred and two hundred and fifty slaves,
who came to him by inheritance, and whom, under the
laws of South Carolina, he was unable either to educate
or emancipate. Governor Bradford[20] said to him once:
"Mr. Lincoln's emancipation idea has been an expensive one to you, Doctor. It must have cost you over a
hundred and fifty thousand dollars." "Yes, I presume
it did; but then, Governor, it took over a hundred and
fifty thousand pounds of iron off my conscience!" So
great had been the change since he held his public discussion with President Wayland,[21] on the rightfulness
of, and Scriptural warrant for, slavery!

All the Doctor's connections were with the South, and
nearly all his relations, who have not been killed, are
living here. It was his nephew who held Fort Sumter
to the last; a near relative of his laid out the fortifications at Fort Fisher; another was the Rebel engineer
at Norfolk. Last night he found a granddaughter,
of perhaps the most prominent member of the first
Congress, living on Government rations! Another,
equally destitute, bears a historic name, and is the

[19] Richard Fuller had lived in Baltimore since 1847. [Ed.]

[20] Augustus W. Bradford, Governor of Maryland, 1862-1866.
[Ed.]

[21] Francis Wayland, fourth President of Brown University.
[Ed.]

granddaughter of one of Washington's most confidential friends and intimate advisers in the Revolutionary war.

It has been naturally supposed that the bitterest drop in all the bitter cup of humiliation for these haughty South Carolinians, must be the necessity of accepting alms from the Government they had been seeking to overthrow. But the ingenious high priestesses of secession regard the matter in no such light. The Dominie found a number of them living solely on Government rations. He hastened to offer them assistance. Their Northern relatives had already repeatedly volunteered similar offers, but they refused them all, and persisted in living on the bacon and hard bread issued by the United States Commissary. They explained that they preferred to make "the Washington Government" support them. It had robbed them of all they had, and now the very least it could do was to pay their expenses.* Every penny of cost to which they put it was so much got back from the fortunes of which it had robbed them, by waging this wicked war for their subjugation! Doesn't somebody think it a shame that these repent-

---

* The same idea prevailed among some of the Richmond Rebels. A Richmond letter to the Boston *Commonwealth*, dated 30th June, describing the scenes at the points where rations were gratuitously issued to the destitute, says:

"'We are all beggars, now!' I heard one of them say, apologetically. But most of the high-born were coarse and imperious. 'This is not begging,' one of the most inveterate beggars said. 'It is taking from the United States Government a very small portion of what it owes us.' 'As long as the Yankees have taken possession of Richmond, of course it's their place to feed us,' more than one said. To the few who gave thanks, and to the many who cursed, all the Commissions gave largely, for several weeks."

ant South Carolinians should be treated with so little magnanimity as the Government is displaying; and that Northern Abolitionists should quit watching them critically, and "mind their own business?" Already, a few of the South Carolinians talk thus; and in a few months, if freedom of expression is allowed them, we shall see much of the old vituperation of the Government and of the North.

CHAPTER IX.

"Unionism"—Black and White, in Charleston and Through South
Carolina.

A VERY few Union men could be seen. Perhaps it
would be more accurate to say, a few could be found
less treasonable than the majority of South Carolinians.

"To be frank with you," said one of these men, a
sallow-faced country lawyer, from the mountain district, "to be frank with you, we were all Rebels. The
North has never understood, and I doubt if it ever will
understand, the absolute unanimity with which, after
the war was begun, we all supported it. While there
was any use in it, we resisted secession; but after the
State seceded, our district, which was always strongly
Union, sent more and better volunteers to the war than
any other."

"You mean, then, that after secession was accomplished, the former Unionists became more violent
Rebels than the rest; and that, practically, not a soul
in the State remained true to the Union, except the
negroes?"

"Well, I suspect you're a little mistaken about the
negroes. They're very ignorant, and most of them
were, and are, governed by their masters' notions."

"What security have we, in restoring political power
to a community disposed toward us as yours was, and
still feeling as you now represent?"

"Oh, our people are impulsive, and they are always decided, one way or the other!"

"Suppose Representatives should be admitted to Congress, and South Carolina should thus be clothed with all her old power. You who, before secession, were the Union men, will be the only voters now; but in two or three years, of course, everybody will vote again. Will not you original Union men be again outnumbered by the original secessionists?"

"I don't believe we ever were outnumbered. I don't believe there ever was a majority for secession in South Carolina."

"The poll books tell a different story."

"Yes; but remember we had been fighting secession for thirty years, and had got tired of it. Men said these restless spirits will never be quiet until they have tried secession. If we don't let them try it now, they'll keep us in a constant turmoil until we do. It is bound to come some time, and we may as well spare ourselves further trouble and let it come now."

"In other words, then, men said, let the Union be destroyed, with whatever attendant horrors, rather than one should be bothered to keep up this perpetual struggle."

"Well, not exactly that. You must remember there was a tremendous pressure. I myself had my house surrounded by a hundred and fifty armed men, one night, before the election, because they thought I was a Union man. There was no making head against the current."

"By your showing, then, the rebel element was resistless before the passage of the secession ordinance, and universal after it. As you frankly say, you were all rebels. We have incurred an enormous debt in subduing you, and we know that there is a small party at the North openly, and a larger one secretly, desirous of repudiating that debt, in order to shake off the burden of heavy taxation. Now, if South Carolina, and other States occupying her position, are restored to power in the nation, what security have we that all you rebels would continue voting for heavy taxation to pay the debt incurred in whipping you? Would there not be very great danger of your uniting with this minority at the North, and thus securing a national majority in favor of repudiation?"

"Well, our attention has never been called to that subject, and we were not aware that there was likely to be any portion whatever of your people favorable to repudiation. I can't say, however, what our more violent people would do. There has been very little comparison of views; and all our efforts must first be given to getting our civil authority and power restored, without considering what questions may come up back of that."

"With what political party at the North, then, would your people be more likely to affiliate?"

"Of course with the Democratic. We have understood all along that it sympathized more with us than any other; that it was more opposed to the war, more disposed to leave us alone with our slaves, more ready for favorable terms of peace."

"And if any considerable portion of that party were to propose lightening the taxes by repudiating (in reduction of interest or otherwise) part of the debt incurred in subduing you, you would be very apt to unite with them?"

"I don't know but we would; but I can't say; for, as

yet, we are giving no attention to anything excepting re-organization!"

Recurring to his admissions concerning the bitterness of the original secessionists, I asked: "What security will we have, if political power should be fully restored to South Carolina, that the secessionists may not regain control of the State Government, and prove as pestilent as ever, if not in the field, then in Congress, and in the old expedients of obnoxious State legislation?"

"Oh, a barrel of cider never ferments twice."

I asked about the popular feeling toward Jeff. Davis, curious to see if the hatred to him, of which we have heard at the North, really exists among any class in South Carolina except the negroes. My Union man replied: "There is a very general feeling of great kindness to him, and great sympathy for his present misfortunes. One party in the South assailed his administration very bitterly; but the feeling was not, to any extent, a personal one. He is greatly admired and loved by our people."

"Was the South exhausted of men when the rebellion broke down? Was it really impossible to re-enforce Lee's army, and, if so, what citizens have you now for re-organizing State government except the rebel soldiers, unless, indeed, you reckon the negroes?"

"The South never was exhausted of men, sir; there were plenty of them everywhere. Disaffection, weariness, indisposition to the long strain of an effort that took more than four years to accomplish its purpose; that was what broke down the Confederacy. There were plenty of men all the time, but they dodged the conscripting officer, or deserted at the first chance they got. Of course, our losses by death and disabling wounds have been terribly great; but the race of arms-bearing men in South Carolina is not extinct."*

On the afternoon of our last day's stay in Charleston, a meeting, in one of the negro churches, afforded me the first opportunity of the trip to see large masses of negroes together. It was called a week or two ago by General Saxton, who stands in the light of a patron saint to all these people; but it was doubtless swelled by the hope that Chief Justice Chase, whom General Saxton had earnestly invited, might consent to be present. He had emphatically refused, the evening before, and had forbidden any announcement of his name; but had finally said that, if he could go unheralded, he would like to see the negroes together.

The church is of the largest size, and belongs exclusively to the negroes, who have their own negro pastor, occupy pews in the body of the building, and send the poor people to the galleries, very much after the fashion of their white brethren. The pavement in front was crowded, and the steps were almost impassable. A white-wooled old deacon saw my difficulty in forcing my way up the steaming aisle, and, crowding the negroes and negresses aside with little ceremony, led me to a seat almost under the pulpit, where I found, perhaps, a dozen whites, all told. Among them was Colonel Beecher—a brother of Henry Ward Beecher—and at the table sat the inevitable reporter. If the people of Timbuctoo were to have a great meeting to consider the subject of their rights, and were to give a week's notice of it, I believe some gentleman with a pocket full of sharpened lead pencils, and a phono-

* This man now holds an office under the National Government in South Carolina.

graphic red-ruled note-book under his arm, would come walking up at the last moment and announce himself as the special reporter for some enterprising American journal.

A Major-General, in full uniform, occupied the desk and was addressing the crammed audience of negroes in a plain, nervous, forcible manner. It was an odd sight, but General Saxton certainly adorns the pulpit. Ladies would call him a handsome man; and his black hair and luxurious English whiskers and mustache would be their especial admiration. He looks—to judge of his intellect by his face and head—narrow, but intense; not very profound in seeing the right, but energetic in doing it when seen; given to practice, rather than theory; and, withal, good and true. He is the first regular army officer who was found willing to undertake this work of caring for and superintending the freedmen; and he has done it faithfully, under all manner of slights and obloquy from brother officers, who thought his work unworthy of West Point. And yet he undertook it, not from any special love of the negro, but because he was ordered. "I would have preferred being in the field," he said simply, last night, "but I was ordered to do this thing, and I have tried to do it faithfully, till the Government gave me something else to do. I was educated in its school and for its service, and I thought it my business to do whatever it required." The Government has rarely been so fortunate in selecting its agents for tasks that required peculiar adaptability.

The audience was a study. Near the pulpit sat a coal-black negro, in the full uniform of a Major of the army, with an enormous regulation hat—be sure there was no lack of flowing plume, or gilt cord and knots—

disposed on the table beside him. At every emphatic sentence in the General's speech he shouted, "Hear, hear," and clapped his hands, with the unction and gravity of an old parliamentarian. Near him were two others in uniform, one a mulatto, the other scarcely more than a quadroon, and both with very intelligent faces, and very modest and graceful in their bearing. One was a First Lieutenant, the other a Major.

Around them was a group of certainly the blackest faces, with the flattest noses and the wooliest heads, I ever saw—the mouths now and then broadening into a grin or breaking out into that low, oily, chuckling gobble of a laugh which no white man can ever imitate. Beyond them ranged all colors and apparently all conditions. Some, black and stalwart, were dressed like quiet farm laborers, and had probably come in from the country, or had been field hands before the war. Others, lighter in color and slighter in build, were dressed in broadcloth, with flashy scarfs and gaudy pins, containing paste, or Cape May diamonds. Others looked like the more intelligent class of city laborers; and there were a few old patriarchs who might recollect the days of Denmark Vesey. On the other side of the church was a motley, but brilliant army of bright-colored turbans, wound around wooly heads, and tawdry bandanas, and hats of all the shapes that have prevailed within the memory of this generation, and bonnets of last year's styles, with absolutely a few of the coquettish little triangular bits of lace and flowers which the New York milliners have this year decreed. Some of them wore kid gloves, all were gaudily dressed, and, a few, barring the questionable complexion, had the air and bearing of ladies.

They were all enthusiastic, the women even more

than the men. Some of the ancient negresses sat swaying to and fro, with an air of happy resignation, only
broken now and then by an emphatic nod of the head,
and an exclamation, "Dat's true, for shore." The
younger ones laughed and giggled, and when the great
cheers went up, clapped with all their might, and looked
across to see how the young men were doing, and
whether their enthusiasm was observed. Ah, well!
Who is there who does n't want to know whether his
world, bo it a big one or a little one, is noticing him?

But the noteworthy point in all this enthusiasm was,
that it was intelligent. Bulwer makes Richelieu relent
toward a young man who applauded his play at the
proper places. General Saxton had equal occasion to be
gratified with his auditors. On taking his seat, he was
followed by the gorgeous Major (who turned out to be
the same negro about whom Lord Brougham raised that
beautiful little diplomatic muddle with United States
Minister Dallas, at a meeting of the Royal Geographical
Society in London). The Major was not happy in his
remarks, and elicited very little applause, till, suddenly,
he was astounded by a thundering burst of it. He
began acknowledging the compliment, but the tumult
burst out louder than ever; and the orator finally discovered that it was not for him, but for Major-General
Gillmore, commanding the department, who was
advancing up the aisle, escorting Chief Justice Chase.

Presently General Saxton introduced the Chief Justice,
and the whole audience rose and burst out into cheer
after cheer, that continued unintermittedly till we had
counted at least nine, and possibly one or two more.
The negroes may be very ignorant, but it is quite evident
that they know, or think they know, who their friends
are. The little "talk" that followed was like its author,

simple, straightforward and weighty, till, at the close, it rose into a strain of unaffected eloquence that almost carried the excitable audience off their feet. "'T isn't only what he says," whispered an enthusiastic negro behind me to his neighbor, "but it's de man what says it. He don't talk for nuffin, and his words hab weight."*

After more tumultuous cheering, the audience called for Gillmore, till the great artillerist absolutely blushed in his embarrassment. *His* speeches for Charleston were made from the muzzle of the Swamp Angel.[22]

I spent the evening in the Charleston *Courier* office. The old library remained, and *Congressional Globes* and arguments on the divine right of slavery stood side by side with Reports of the Confederate Congress, and official accounts of battles, while on the wall was pasted one of the most bombastic proclamations of the runaway Governor. Several of the old *attaches* of the concern remain, among them a phonographic reporter and the cashier. The circulation of this most flourishing Southern paper in the seaboard States, had dwindled down to less than a thousand. "We wrote our reports," said

---

* This was Mr. Chase's single "speech" during the entire trip. Ten minutes, or less, of familiar and fatherly talk to helpless negroes, advising them to industry, economy and good order, telling them he thought they should vote, but did n't know whether the Government would agree with him, and advising that, if the right of suffrage should be refused them, they should behave so well, educate themselves so fast, and become so orderly and prosperous, that the Government should see they deserved it; this was what subsequently became, in certain Northern newspapers, "Chief-Justice Chase's endless stump speeches, and shameless intriguing with old political leaders, in his electioneering tour through the South." The speech is given in full in the appendix (A.)

[22] A Parrott gun used briefly against Charleston from Morris Island. [Ed.]

the phonographer, "on the backs of old grocery bills,
and in blank pages torn out of old account books."
"We deserved all we got," he continued, "but you ought
not to be hard on us now. The sun never shone on a
nobler or kinder-hearted people than the South Carolinians, and this was always the nicest town to live in, in
the United States."

Encountering a so-called South Carolina Unionist,
from the interior, I asked about the relations between
the negroes and their old masters. "In the main, the
niggers are working just as they used to, not having
made contracts of any sort, because there was no competent officer accessible before whom the contracts could
be approved. A few have been hired by the day; and
some others have gone to work for a specified share in
the crops. In a great many cases the planters have told
them to work ahead, get their living out of the crops,
and what further share they were entitled to should be
determined when the officers to approve contracts came.
Then, if they couldn't agree, they could separate."

"Have there been no disturbances between the negroes
and their former masters, no refusals to recognize the
destruction of slavery?"

"In our part of the State, none. Elsewhere I have
heard of them. With us, the death of slavery is recognized, and made a basis of action by everybody.
But we don't believe that because the nigger is free he
ought to be saucy; and we don't mean to have any
such nonsense as letting him vote. He's helpless, and
ignorant, and dependent, and the old masters will still
control him. * I have never been a large slaveholder

* The disposition to "control" the negroes after the old fashion, subsequently developed itself in Eastern South Carolina, to

myself—for the last year or two I have had but twelve, little and big. Every one of them stays with me, just as before, excepting one, a carpenter. I told him he'd better go off and shift for himself. He comes back, every two or three nights, to tell me how he is getting along; and the other day he told me he hadn't been able to collect anything for his work, and I gave him a quarter's provisions to get started with."

"I had to give him," he significantly added, "a sort

such an extent that the military commandant considered the following order necessary:

"HEADQUARTERS NORTHERN DISTRICT, D. S., }
CHARLESTON, S. C., June 24. }

"General Orders, No. 62.

"It has come to the knowledge of the district commander that, in some of the contracts made between planters and freedmen, a clause has been introduced establishing a system of *peonage*—the freedman binding himself to work out any debt he may hereafter incur to his employer. All contracts, made under authority from these headquarters, will be understood as merely temporary arrangements, to insure the cultivation of the ground for the present season. Any contract made under the above authority, which contains provisions tending to *peonage*, will be considered null. The officers having charge of contracts, will examine them carefully; and when they are found to contain such a clause, will notify the planters that new contracts must be made, in which the objectionable feature will be omitted. Contracts will be simply worded. Whilst acknowledging the freedom of the colored man, such expressions as '*freed by the acts of the military forces of the United States*' will not be permitted. The attempt to introduce anything into the contract which may have the appearance of an intention, at some future day, to contest the question of the emancipation of the negroes, will be reported to the commander of the sub-district, who will examine into the antecedents of the person making the attempt, and report upon the case to district headquarters.

"By command of

"Brevet Major-General JOHN P. HATCH."

of paper—not, of course, pretending to be legal—certifying that he was working for himself, with my consent, in order to enable him to get along without trouble." There was a world of meaning in the phrase, "To enable him to get along without trouble," though he was as free as the man that gave the paper.

I asked what they would do with the negroes, if they got permission to re-organize.

"Well, we want to have them industrious and orderly, and will do all we can to bring it about."

"Will you let any of them vote?"

"That question has not been discussed. Nobody could stand up in the State who should advocate promiscuous negro suffrage. It is possible that a few might be willing to let the intelligent negroes vote—after some years, at any rate, if not now."

"I believe you let the sandhillers vote. Don't you know that these disfranchised negroes of Charleston are infinitely their superiors, in education, industry, wealth and good conduct?"

"Well, they're pretty bad, it's true—those sandhillers—but there isn't the same prejudice against them."

The moon lit up, with a softened effulgence, all the beauties, and hid all the scars of Charleston, as, late at night, I walked, through its desolate streets, and by its glorious shrubbery, to the landing, and hailed the "Wayanda." A boat shot out of the shadow for me; and before I had joined the Doctor, below deck, the anchor had been hoisted and the vessel was under way.

CHAPTER X.

Port Royal and Beaufort.

AT daylight we were steaming into the broad sheet of water which Du Pont[23] first made famous, and which our sailors have since come to consider the finest harbor on the Southern coast. Admiral Dahlgren had evidently prepared the naval authorities for our arrival. Within a few moments, the numerous vessels were dressed in all their colors, the sailors manned the yards, and a salute was fired from all the men of war in the harbor. A few minutes later a deluge of naval officers set in, till the quarter deck of the "Wayanda" overflowed with the dignitaries, and the indefatigable boatswain grew weary blowing his whistle as they came over the ship's side.

Everybody seemed possessed with the mania of speculation. Even these naval gentlemen were infected by it; and we saw no civilians or army officers who were not profoundly versed in the rival claims of Hilton Head, Bay Point and Beaufort. That a great city must spring up hereabouts, has been laid down as an axiom. This is the best harbor on the coast, while that of Charleston is positively bad, and that of Savannah is contracted, and not easy of access. Situated midway between the two, the speculators insist that it ought to fall legitimate heir to the trade of both. Besides, the Carolina sea-coast must have a seaport, and Charleston is so utterly ruined, they argue, and so odious to the

[23] Commodore Samuel Francis Du Pont, commander of the force that took Port Royal in 1861. [Ed.]

nation that Northern trade and capital would discrimi-
nate against it, in favor of its younger rival. And the
most flourishing part of South Carolina to-day is made
up of the sea islands, cultivated by the freedmen, all
whose trade already centers here. Therefore, for these
reasons, and many more, which your speculator will
set out in ample array before you, if you only listen, it
is necessary and fated that a great city should grow
up on the waters of Port Royal harbor.

But where?—that is the rub. Not at Hilton Head,
say some, for there are hurricanes there, every dozen
years or so, that blow everything flat, and even now, in
rough weather, shipping can hardly live at the wharf.
Not at Bay Point, rejoin the Hilton Head landholders,
for it is low and unhealthy. And not at Beaufort, some
ten or fifteen miles up Broad river from here, they both
agree, because it is so far off.

And so, while they make it quite clear that an
immense fortune is to be realized here by the purchase
of real estate, they leave one in the most provoking
uncertainty as to the precise point at which the fortune
is located. It is very clear that you can treble and
quadruple and quintuple your money here in two or
three years—if you don't lose it all by investing in the
wrong place! But, alas, what good did it do Archimedes
to know that he could move the world, when he couldn't
find the place to fix his lever?

Hilton Head has taken a start, however, and quite a
village of frame houses line the shore—wide, roomy
cottages, occupied by army officers, and mostly built for
them by the Government, under a liberal construction
of the regulations about providing the officers with
quarters, making up the street fronting on the water.
Back of these are warehouses and other Government

buildings; and a row of two-story houses, ambitiously entitled "Broadway" or some other high-sounding name, by the occupants, has received, from the unfortunates who are compelled to frequent it, the more expressive designation of "Robbers' Row." It is the street of the sutlers!

General Gillmore had arrived from Charleston in advance, and he had carriages in waiting for us when we landed. Captain James, of his staff, had provided horses for those who preferred to ride, and the delights of a gallop along the superb beach were not to be overrated. The sun was intensely hot, and the horses were in a lather, almost in a moment; but the Captain said they were used to it, and that they really seemed to stand as much fatigue and rough usage here as at the North.

Half an hour's ride brought us to an extraordinary collection of cabins, arranged in long streets, and teeming with little woolly-headed, big-stomached picaninnies, in all stages of primitive costume. This was the village of Mitchelville, so named in honor of General Ormsby M. Mitchel, who died here shortly after he had begun his work, but not until he had impressed the grateful negroes with a firm belief in his friendship. The population is made up entirely of freedmen, and is regularly organized, with a Mayor and Common Council, Marshal, Recorder and Treasurer—all black, and all, except the Mayor and Treasurer, elected by the negroes themselves.* The Common Council requires

---

* The following are the main points of the military order under which Mitchelville is organized :

"I. All lands now set apart for the colored population, near Hilton Head, are declared to constitute a village, to be known as the village of Mitchelville. Only freedmen and colored persons

every child, between the ages of six and fifteen, to attend school regularly, except in cases where their services are absolutely necessary for the support of their parents, of which the teacher is made the judge! Gen-

residing or sojourning within the territorial limits of said village, shall be deemed and considered inhabitants thereof.

"II. The village of Mitchelville shall be organized and governed as follows: Said village shall be divided into districts, as nearly equal in population as practicable, for the election of Councilmen, sanitary and police regulations, and the general government of the people residing therein.

"III. The government shall consist of a Supervisor and Treasurer, to be appointed by, and hold office during the pleasure of the Military Commander of the District, assisted by a Councilman from each council district, to be elected by the people, who shall also, at the same time, choose a Recorder and Marshal. The duties of the Marshal and Recorder shall be defined by the Council of Administration.

"IV. The Supervisor and Councilmen shall constitute the Council of Administration, with the Recorder as Secretary.

"V. The Council of Administration shall have power:

"To pass such ordinances as it shall deem best, in relation to the following subjects: To establish schools for the education of children and other persons. To prevent and punish vagrancy, idleness and crime. To punish licentiousness, drunkenness, offenses against public decency and good order, and petty violation of the rights of property and person. To require due observance of the Lord's Day. To collect fines and penalties. To punish offenses against village ordinances. To settle and determine disputes concerning claims for wages, personal property, and controversies between debtor and creditor. To levy and collect taxes to defray the expenses of the village government, and for the support of schools. To lay out, regulate, and clean the streets. To establish wholesome sanitary regulations for the prevention of disease. To appoint officers, places and times for the holding of elections. To compensate municipal officers, and to regulate all other matters affecting the well-being of citizens, and good order of society.

"VIII. Hilton Head Island will be divided into School Districts,

eral Mitchel was one of Cincinnati's contributions to the war. But is Cincinnati behind Mitchelsville?

As we passed up Broad river, in the afternoon, a straggling collection of old two-story frame houses, with faded paint and decayed boards, but with the inevitable wide halls and spacious verandahs, rose among the islands on the left. Of old, it was the very center of the aristocratic country residences of the wealthier South Carolinians; to-day, it is the capital, if I may so call it, of a new community of South Carolinians, liberated by the war, and settled on the famous sea-island plantations.

"Here," says some one, "secession was first plotted," and he points out houses which had been the residences of the Barnwells and the Barnwell Rhetts. Near here, another tells, is the plantation where the "*South-Side View*" was taken; and there are negroes in the village who tell of the rustic seat in the bough of a great live-oak tree, where Dr. Nehemiah Adams wrote the book, and of the appetizing claret cobblers they bore him to

to conform, as nearly as practicable, to the schools as established by the Freedmen's Association. In each District there shall be elected one School Commissioner, who will be charged with supplying the wants of the schools, under the direction of the teacher thereof. Every child, between the ages of six and fifteen years, residing within the limits of such School Districts, shall attend school daily, while they are in session, excepting only in case of sickness. Where children are of a suitable age to earn a livelihood, and their services are required by their parents or guardians, and on the written order of the teacher in such School District, may be exempt from attendance, for such time as said order shall specify. And the parents and guardians will be held responsible that said children so attend school, under the penalty of being punished at the discretion of the Council of Administration.

cheer him up, from time to time, in his work. Could the good Doctor return now, he would scarcely find the blacks so affectionately attentive, but he would be pleased to see that the plantation is in a much higher state of cultivation than when it elicited his eulogies.

General Saxton had carriages waiting for us at the wharf, and, after a short drive through the sandy streets, we were taken to see the dress-parade of a regiment of negroes, commanded by a brother of General Howard. The men marched from their camps, by companies, into line with as steady a tramp and as soldierly a carriage as the average of other troops, and, however lacking in beauty the individual negro may be, the bitterest negro hater would have been willing to admit a thousand of them looked handsome. Yet these men were scarcely a month from the plantations! They had made little progress in the drill beyond the manual of arms and the formation of the regimental line, but what they did know, they knew thoroughly. They were all coal black, and seemed larger and more muscular than the negro troops raised farther north.

General Saxton has, within his present district, over a hundred thousand negroes. He claims that all are now absolutely self-sustaining, save those swept in the wake of Sherman's march. Even the rations issued to these are charged to them, and the thrifty negroes make all haste to quit leaning on the Government, lest their debt should swell to too great proportions. Most of the older-settled negroes, who were originally dependent on Government support, have already repaid the advances thus made them, and many have, besides, accumulated what is, for them, a handsome competence.

The astonishment of our Doctor at the changes he witnessed, among these scenes of his earlier life, is unbounded. His old slaves have been greeting him very enthusiastically; and many a hand-kissing, or worse, has "Massa Richard" had to endure; but he sees among them manliness of bearing, and a sober cheerfulness wholly novel to his experience of negro character; and he begins to suspect that perhaps, after all, there were characteristics of the negro nature which all his former familiarity with it had not disclosed. Withal, he says, that he never saw the slaves of Beaufort so well clad, or seemingly so comfortable. General Saxton rather proudly responds that the peasantry of no country in the world is better behaved or more prosperous.

CHAPTER XI.

Among the Sea Islanders.

THE most degraded slaves in the South, it has been commonly testified by Southerners themselves, were to be found in South Carolina and on the sugar plantations of the South-west. Of the South Carolina slaves, the most ignorant and debased, beyond all question, were those on the sea islands about Port Royal. Engaged in unhealthy work, to which none but the coarsest of fiber were likely to be subjected, and steeped in the normal ignorance of the rice swamp and the cotton field, they were likewise isolated on their islands, and shut out from that mysterious transmission of intelligence, concerning their own interests, which seemed to permeate, like a magnetic current, all large communities of negroes.

They were mostly of the pure Congo type; there was no mixture of white blood; intelligent mechanics and "smart niggers" generally were too valuable to be sent here; their masters were absent a great part of the year, and they were left to the humanizing control of the overseers; their provisions were, in many instances, grown elsewhere and sent to them, so that there was not even this diversion of a different culture from the never-ending monotony of the cotton and rice fields. They received, once a week, a peck of corn, and, once a month, a quart of salt, *and on this they lived.* When the hardest work was required, they received a little molasses and salt meat in addition; and, for a part of each year, a bushel of sweet-potatoes was allowed each week, *in place of* the corn. Whatever more than this they received, they owed to the generosity of unusually kind masters. They herded together in cabins, twelve by eighteen or twenty feet, sometimes floored, but oftener floorless; they got enough of the coarse negro cloth to make, by close cutting, two suits a year, and at Christmas they had three days to themselves. The other three hundred and sixty-two were given to cotton and rice. Marriage was unknown among them; breeding was enjoined as the first of duties; purity, delicacy and education were alike impossible. If any system of compulsory labor could make brutes out of intelligent men, would not this do it? If any system could fail to make brutish men more brutish, surely it would *not* be this one!

When the "great confusion" (as they call the sudden flight of their masters on Dupont's arrival at Hilton Head) came, the house servants, who, by contact with the whites, had necessarily gained some intelligence, were all taken off to the interior. This utterly debased cotton and rice-planting community of Congoes was left; and it is this community, almost unmixed, which now cultivates the sea islands under the supervision of General Saxton. There were some five thousand of them here before the war. I am told that not five hundred of the old stock are now missing from their accustomed places.

The moral of what I have written is plain. If the "negro-elevation" effort of the Abolitionists is to fail anywhere, it would be likely to fail here. If it succeed among these degraded people, it would be likely to succeed anywhere. The experiment has been tried, amid constant uncertainties and discouragements, for three years. The results, whatever they may be, are of the first importance.

When Generals Gillmore and Saxton, therefore, proposed to take our party through Lady's and St. Helena Islands, without any previous notice to the blacks; to show us the crops, the villages, the negroes at church and on their plantations, I prepared myself for any disappointment. The morning was a beautiful one; and, although the rays of the unclouded sun were intense, a fresh breeze from the ocean made the trip by no means uncomfortable. On steaming up to Beaufort we found carriages, in waiting, on the opposite side, at the upper end of Lady's Island. Some little cabins, surrounded by unfenced fields of cotton, remarkably free from weeds, stood near the landing; and a few picaninnies watched our debarkation, while their fathers, cleanly clad and respectful, stood by the carriages.

The sandy road led off among the cotton fields down the island. On either side were old wire fences, constructed by the former proprietors, sometimes running along fine avenues of trees, in the stems of which the wires are deeply imbedded, and sometimes propped upon crazy posts. Here and there could be seen frame houses, containing three or four rooms, the old residences of the overseers, or, indeed, sometimes of the planters themselves; for Southern "mansions" were generally inferior, in every particular, save high-sounding titles, to Northern "cottages." Rude pine-log cabins, sometimes with the bark removed in a rough attempt at hewing, dotted the fields. They were, occasionally, large enough for two rooms, and were nearly always surrounded by a few growing garden vegetables, separated in no way however, from the rows of cotton that extended up to them.

Sometimes, for half a mile, the road passed through a splendid avenue of live-oaks, the pendulous Spanish moss, from the limbs, sweeping across our carriage tops, while the whistle from the mocking-bird came from the upper branches. Then the avenue faded away into a thicket of dwarf live-oaks, trespassing for several yards, each side of the road, upon the cotton fields, and mingling presently with cotton-woods, bayonet plants and other like species of the palmetto, yellow pines and a clambering growth of grape-vines and honeysuckles. Through this undergrowth could still be seen the long rows of cotton stretching along on either hand out of sight.

The fences by the roadside soon faded out, and for miles scarcely any were to be seen. Little stakes, here and there, would mark the boundaries of individual possessions ; but besides these, there would be no divisions in fields of two or three hundred acres of cotton. Then would come a tract, equally as large, lying fallow, and covered with a luxurious growth of dewberries that tempted more than one of our party to delay the progress to church while we went " berrying." In other places great tracts were observed in which the furrows of cotton, cultivated years ago, could still be plainly traced, although the ground was now covered with a dense growth of pines. Since the flight of the slave-holders, however, some of this has been reclaimed; and more land is now under cultivation, both on Lady's Island and on St. Helena, than when they fell into our hands.

The cotton was still small, but the rich sandy loam seemed to suit it well, and gentlemen familiar with the cotton culture, who accompanied us, said it could not look better. The fields were beautifully clean—it is rare that a Western corn field shows as careful culture—and the women and old men, who now do most of the work on these islands, had carefully hilled it up with the hoe, till, in places, it could hardly be distinguished from the ridges heaped for the sweet-potato plants about the cabins. We did not pass a field, in our twelve miles drive out and as many back (partly by a different road), that would not bear a favorable comparison with the average of Northern farming.* Since the Government has been offering large bounties for volunteers, most of the young men from these islands have gone into the

---

*I subsequently, however, saw several badly-neglected cotton fields. The very intelligent correspondent of the Boston *Advertiser* (Mr. Sidney Andrews,) writing from Beaufort, in July, likewise found ill-tilled plantations. He says:

"Some of the cotton and corn fields, through which we passed, were in a decidedly bad state of cultivation, others better, but hardly any quite satisfactory, until we reached the plantation to which our journey was directed. Then the appearance of the crops suddenly changed; the fields were free from weeds, the cotton plants healthy, and the corn fields promising a heavy yield. Everything bespoke thrift and industry. We passed through a most beautiful grove of live-oaks, with its graceful festoons of gray moss—under the shadow of the trees a roomy log cabin, in which a colored preacher was addressing an audience of devout negroes, for it was Sunday—until, at last, we found the 'mansion,' surrounded with live-oaks and magnolia trees. The estate had, before the war, belonged to one of the wealthiest planters of that region, who had gone to parts unknown as soon as the blue jackets threatened their descent upon Beaufort. It struck me as singular that a man of such wealth, as he was reputed to possess, should have lived in a house so small and unpretending, as in the North would be considered as belonging to a forty-acre farm; but such was the case."

army, filling up such regiments as that of Colonel Howard, which we saw at Beaufort, and all this work has, therefore, been done by the weaker and more infirm classes of the population. General Saxton has not encouraged it, but the negro women still work freely in the fields. The withdrawal of the young men from the islands has been, in some respects, an advantage. They tell of such sights as the uncles and aunts, gathered in to tie and whip some young scapegrace who persisted in neglecting his crop, and whom they feared they would, therefore, have to support next winter. No whipping is needed now; the crops are cultivated better than before, and when young scapegrace comes back from the army, he will be found to possess a manliness that will scarcely require the further stimulus of the lash.

A long, wooden bridge, spanning one of the little estuaries that cut up these islands, led us across into St. Helena. By this time the roads were alive with a gaily-dressed throng of blacks, of both sexes and all ages, wending their way, on foot, on horseback, in carts and wagons, and even, in a few cases, in Northern trotting buggies, to the Central Church. Noticing their cheer-ful, contented air, their gay chat, their cleanly appear-ance and *repartie* among themselves, their respectful and cordial greetings to the passing Generals, and the man-ifest tokens of prosperity evinced in modes of locomo-tion, personal adornment and the like, one could clearly believe General Saxton's renewed declaration, that, in all substantial respects, considering their peculiar diffi-culties, they would contrast not discreditably with any peasantry in the world.

As we turned off from the main road, which runs the whole length of the island, and began to pass through the gates, which made a sort of private way among the cotton fields to the church, the throng increased, till the roads were alive with the church-going freedmen. Every little group stopped as we came up; every old negress gave us a droll bob of the head; the men touched their hats, soldier fashion, or lifted them altogether from their heads, and the young women made, in many cases, not ungraceful courtesies. "Dere's General Saxby," we could often hear energetically whispered among the groups, and there was no mistaking the pleased expression which the name summoned to every countenance. "Are not negroes likely hereafter, as heretofore, to be controlled by their old masters?" some one asks. "We's know our frens, massa," was the emphatic answer of a coal-black plantation hand, the other day, when I put some such question to him. Clearly, these people, on St. Helena, "know their friends."

Presently a group of negroes, with many a respectful scrape of the foot and tug at the hat, threw open the last gate, and, under a refreshing canopy of trees, we drove to the old country church, which, time out of mind, has been the central worshipping place for both whites and blacks of St. Helena. Overflowing all the church-yard, flooding the road, through which our carriages could hardly be driven, and backing up against the grave-yard, were the negroes, gay with holiday attire, many-colored kerchiefs, and the best their earnings (and the sutler's extortions) would permit them to buy. The woods, back of the church, were filled with carts and wagons; the horses were unharnessed, tied to the trees and fed; their owners were gathered in groups about the carts, discussing the condition of the cotton crop, or the price Sam had paid for "dat new mar;"

and how much "Aunt Sukie was gittin' down to Bufor' for dem dis year's pullets."

The interior of the plain, low brick church was deserted, the deacons having decided that there was not room for the throng in attendance—an event, as we afterward learned, of almost weekly occurrence. Three times in the week these people had filled the "praise meetings" on their respective plantations, and already there had been another such meeting on Sunday before they started to church; yet, here was a great throng, which the church could not contain, and still the roads, for miles in each direction, swarmed with those yet coming. We have been told that emancipated slaves would be disorderly vagrants, and, doubtless, there is ground for some apprehension, but this Sabbath scene does not tend to increase it.

Within the church were traces of the slaveholding era, as one finds in the Silurian stratification fossils that tell the story of a past age. The doors were on each side, near the middle of the building, and connected by a broad aisle. Above this, toward the pulpit, were the square, high-backed pews for the planters of the island—when they chose to occupy them. Back of the aisle were rude benches, which the poor whites, or, in their absence, the negroes, were privileged to take; and in the long galleries on either side (approached by stairs that were built for the steps of giants), were benches exclusively devoted to the negro population. The pews still stand with open doors, nearest the pulpit; but the men that filled them come no more. Some are North, many fill unknown graves, or trenches on battle-fields, the rest are in that unexplored region, whence come no sounds but those of sorrow, "the interior." And to the right of the pulpit, in a shady little inclosure, still carefully preserved, are the moss-grown marble monuments, which no filial hands come now to garnish or adorn. The graves of their fathers have passed under the guardianship of the alien race.

While our party stood looking about this scene of the past, a white-wooled deacon came, with the politeness, if not the grace, of an old-world master of ceremonies, to summon us to one of the present. "De people is gathered, sah, and was ready for de suvvices to begin." There was a not unnatural sensation as the Major-Generals, the Chief Justice and the ladies of the party, were led through the crowd to a little platform under the live-oaks; but it was when Rev. Dr. Fuller—"ole massa Richard"—made his appearance, that the wondering stare brightened and eyes grew moist, and ancient negresses could be heard vehemently whispering "Bress de Lod, bress de Lod!" "Hebenly Marster!" "Gra-a-ate King!" No word had been sent of our coming, and it was but within the last half hour that the old slaves of Dr. Fuller had heard that he was to address them. There was no way of estimating the number of these "Fuller slaves" in attendance—he had owned between two and three hundred, but probably half of them were now at Beaufort. Every adult negro in the assemblage, however, seemed to know him.

The scene was a striking one. In front of us was the old church; behind, the new school-house. Half a dozen superb live-oaks spread their gnarled branches over us, the silvery, pendulous streamers of Spanish moss floating down and flecking with the sunlight the upturned faces of the great congregation of negroes, while the breezes made mournful music among the leaves, and the mocking-birds sent back a livelier refrain. The little valley between the platform and

the church was densely packed with negroes, all standing, and, as the Deacon told us, "eagah fur de Wud."
They clustered, too, about the platform, leaned over the
railing, behind, and at the sides, and spread away in all
directions, among the carts and wagons, that formed a
sort of outer line of works, shutting in the scene. The
coats were of every color, and cut, and age. There
were a few straw hats on the heads of the younger
females, and cotton gloves, gaudy calico dresses and
crinolines were abundant; but the older ones clung to
the many-colored handkerchiefs, wound turban-wise
about the head, and affected gowns that clung closely
to their *not* graceful figures. Altogether they were
dressed as well as the average of day-laborers' families
at the North would be, but in a taste that even such
Northern families would pronounce barbarous.

A quaint old African, clad in cotton checks, and bowed
with many years of cotton hoeing, stepped out on the
platform, when all the party had been seated. Leaning,
like a patriarch, on his cane, and gently swaying his
body to and fro over it, as if to keep time, he struck up,
in a shrill, cracked voice, a curiously monotonous melody,
in which, in a moment, the whole congregation were energetically joining. For the first time I observed, what had
often been told me (though I had never before realized it),
that the language of these sea islanders (and I am told
that, to some extent, the same is true of the majority of
plantation hands in South Carolina), is an almost unintelligible *patois*. Listening carefully to the swaying old
leader, I found it impossible, for a time, to make out his
meaning; and the vocal contortions to which the simplest
words seemed to subject him, was a study that would
have amazed a phonetic lecturer. The words were

those of an old song, which our soldiers found them
singing shortly after the fall of Bay Point:

> "Ma-a-a-assa Fullah a sittin' on de tree ob life;
> Ma-a-a-assa Fullah a sittin' on de tree ob life,
>   Roll, Jordan, roll.
> Ma-a-a-assa Fullah a sittin' on de tree ob life,
>   Roll, Jordan, roll.
> Ma-a-a-assa Fullah a sittin' on de tree ob life,
>   Ro-o-oll, Jordan, roll,
>   Ro-o-oll, Jordan, roll,
>   Ro-o-oll, Jordan, roll."

And so on, with repetitions that promised to be endless. The grateful negroes had cherished the memory
of Dr. Fuller, who had abandoned his lucrative legal
practice to preach to them; and, long after his departure
to the North, had still kept his name green among
them, by thus associating it with their ideas of heaven.
But, as freedom came, and no Dr. Fuller with it, they
gradually forgot the old benefactor, and substituted the
name of the new one. To them, General Saxton was
law, and order, and right; he secured their plantations;
he got them rations till they were able to support themselves; he decided disputes, defended privileges, maintained quiet, and was the embodiment of justice; and
so it gradually came to pass that "General Saxby," as,
with a ludicrous persistence, they still call him, took the
place of "Ma-a-a-assa Fullah" in the song. The presence of the good Doctor recalled their old love, and
they gave him the first place; but they could not depose
their later favorite and greater benefactor; and so, after
interminable repetitions, we came to the second stanza:

> "Gen-e-ul Sa-a-axby a sittin' on de tree ob life,
> Gen-e-ul Sa-a-axby a sittin' on de tree ob life;
>   Roll, Jordan, roll.

> Gen-e-ul Sa-a-axby a sittin' on de tree ob life;
>> Roll, Jordan, roll,
> Gen-e-ul Sa-a-axby a sittin' on de tree ob life;
>> Ro-o-oll, Jordan, roll,
>> Ro-o-oll, Jordan, roll,
>> Ro-o-oll, Jordan, ro-o-oll!"

The patriarchal old African, swaying on his cane before the congregation, threw the whole power of his lungs into the harsh tones with which the concluding "ro-o-o-oll" was given, and then followed the great feat of the African reception to the visitors. Wherever we had been, the negroes seemed to know something of Mr. Chase. Their ideas were very vague, but they thought that, in some way, he was a great, large friend of theirs, who had done something or another for them, what, they scarcely knew, and was to be held beside "Linkum" in their esteem. So now, with a droll look of intelligence toward the crowd, and particularly toward a group of open-faced, enthusiastic young fellows, who seemed to be the main dependence for promptly supplying the volume of sound, the antique leader struck out in harsher tones, and more indescribably bewildering difficulties of pronunciation than ever:

> "Me-is-ta-ah Che-a-ase a sittin' on de tree ob life,
> Me-is-ta-ah Che-a-ase a sittin' on de tree ob life,
>> Roll, Jordan, roll;
> Me-is-ta-ah Che-a-ase a sittin' on de tree ob life,
>> Roll, Jordan, roll.
> Me-is-ta-ah Che-a-ase a sittin' on de tree ob life,
>> Roll, Jordan, roll,
>> Roll, Jordan, roll,
>> Ro-o-oll, Jordan, ro-o-oll."

The chorus was sung with a vehemence that pierced the ears, and swayed the leaflets of the live-oaks above our heads; while picaninnies crowed, and their mothers smiled, and there was a general bustle in the crowd, and all fixed beaming eyes—who has not admired the deep, liquid ox-eye of the Southern negro?—upon the embarrassed Chief Justice, whom they were establishing, in all his avoirdupois, on the identical limb where Doctor Fuller and General "Saxby" were already perched. And then a plain, bald-headed, middle-aged, black preacher, who had, doubtless, a few years back, been at least "a twelve-hundred-dollar nigger," came reverently forward and commenced a prayer. The congregation devoutly bowed their heads, a few interrupted with an occasional "Amen," or "Glory," but the most kept respectful silence. The prayer was simple, full of repetitions, abounding in Scripture language, not always appropriately used; and, on the whole, I was in doubt whether either speaker or congregation understood all of it. There was no mistaking the sincerity of the devotion; but it seemed to be mainly emotional, rather than intellectual, and might, therefore, well give rise to inquiries as to what effect this abounding religion had on the matter of stealing sweet-potatoes, or taking care of their wives and children, during the week.*

* The correspondent of the Boston *Advertiser* gives the following Sea Island incident, which occurred in July:

"While we were conversing with the lessee, we observed a negro woman, with two children, leaning against the railing of the Verandah. Her countenance wore so sad a look that we asked for the cause. The story was mournful enough. She had been sick. Another woman had come into her house to attend to her work. Her husband, Tony, had taken a fancy to the other woman. After awhile, he had gone away and 'married her.' She had insisted upon his remaining with her. He had done so, for some time, and then gone off again to live with the other wife. Where was her husband? 'He was in the meeting-house, yonder, praying.' Of

When Doctor Fuller came to speak to them, there was less cause for doubt on this subject. They evidently understood him, and undoubtedly meant to obey his instructions. When, for example, he told them that at the North their enemies were declaring that they would be idle and dissolute, and asked if they were going thus to bring shame upon those who had befriended them, there was an emphasis of response, and an earnestness in the looks men and women gave each other, that spoke both for their understanding and their intentions. "I know that new machinery will work a little roughly," said the Doctor, "I am not surprised that, at first, there were some blunders and faults; but it is time you had got over that. If a man who has been shut up for a long time, in a dark room, is suddenly brought into the light, it dazzles his eyes, and he is apt to stumble. Well, then, what will you do? Put him back in the dark again?" "No, no," energetically exclaimed the crowd, with many an earnest shake of the head. "What then?" "Tell him what to do," suggested some. "Lead him a little while," whispered others. "GIVE HIM MORE LIGHT!" at last exclaimed the Doctor; and it was curious to watch the pleased noddings of the woolly heads, the shaking of the turbans, the sensation, exchange of smiles, and other indications that the Doctor's solution of the difficulty was thoroughly understood, in its application to their own condition.

course, they had been slaves, had but recently left the 'old plantation,' where such things were little more than matters of course. The vices of the negro are the vices of the slave. When 'Tony' will know what it is to be a freeman, he will know, also, that it will not do to have two wives, and to go praying, while one of his wives, with her and his children, are standing by the side of the meeting-house, weeping over his inconstancy."

Mr. Chase followed, in a few words of calm advice, as to the necessity of industry, economy, study and the like. When he added that, for his own part, he believed, too, that the best way to teach them to swim in the ocean of suffrage, was to throw them in and let them take care of themselves, the emphatic nods and smiles, and cries of "yes," "yees," showed that the figure was not thrown away upon them.

More singing followed, in which they were led by a white teacher, from one of the schools, and the ordinary hymns of the church were used. The great volumes of sound rang like organ peals through the arches of the oaks. Once the teacher asked to have the children gathered in front of the platform, that they might sing "My country, 'tis of thee, sweet land of liberty," etc., Mothers passed up their little four-year olds, decked in all the cheap finery they could command; fathers pressed forward and made room for sons and daughters, whom they followed with eyes of paternal pride; and there was a general smiling, and bustling, and eagerness to show off the shiny-faced, large-eyed little creatures. When they were once collected, it was just about as difficult to keep them still as it would be to silence so many parrots.

Presently one of the Northern ministers, who have devoted themselves to working among these freedmen, made them such a sermonizing talk as seems to be the common mode of instruction. There was something too much, perhaps, of glorification over the fact that at last the slaves were free from the clutches of the wicked and tyrannical slaveholders; but, in the main, the address was judicious, and seemed to be in a vein to which the negroes were accustomed. At the request of different members of the party, he asked several questions, such as :

"You all seem to be better dressed than when your masters ran away. Now tell us if you are able to afford these clothes, and how you get them?"

"Yes," "Bought 'em wid our own money," "Bought 'em down to Hilton Head," "Got 'em at Bufor," and a further medley of confused answers came back from the open-eyed, open-mouthed crowd.

"You bought them? Well now, you know at the North people think you are starving beggars, dependent on the Government? Is it true? How many of you support yourselves without any help from the Government? All that do, hold up their right hands."

In an instant every adult in the crowd held up a hand, and not a few of the boys and girls, supposing it to be some new play, held up their hands, too!

"Now, before your masters ran away, you all say that your wives were not as attentive as they should be to the wants of the household; that they required a great deal of beating to make them do their work; that they didn't mend your clothes and cook your meals. Perhaps freedom has made them worse. All who say it has, hold up your right hands."

There was a deal of sly chuckling among the men; the women too, affected to make light of it, though some bridled up their turbaned heads and stared defiance across at the men. Not a hand, however, was raised; and as the preacher announced the result, the women laughed their oily gobble of a laugh.

"Well, now, I'd like to have the women tell me about the men. Are they as good husbands as when they were slaves? Do you live as well in your houses? Do they work as well, and make you as comfortable?"

There was a great giggling now; the ivories that were displayed would have driven a dentist to distraction, and many a stalwart black fellow, who had no notion of being a dentist, did seem to be distracted. But every woman's hand was raised, and the good preacher proceeded to announce the result and moralize thereon.

"Then," he said, "I am asked, by our distinguished guest, to put a question that I'm afraid you'll laugh at. You know your old masters always said you were much happier in a state of slavery than you would be in freedom, and a good many people at the North don't know but it may be true. You've tried supporting yourselves now for some time, and a good many of you have found it pretty hard work sometimes. Now, I want as many of you as are tired of it, and would rather go back and have your old masters take care of you, to hold up your right hands."

It was fine to notice the start and frightened look, and then the sudden change that came over their faces. The preacher had warned them not to laugh, but they did not look as if they wanted to laugh. They were more disposed to get angry; and the "no, noes" were sufficiently emphatic to satisfy the most devoted adherents of the old system, who used to be constantly declaring that "the slaves were the happiest people on the face of the earth."

But there remained a scene that showed how, if not anxious to return to their old masters, they were still sometimes glad to have their old masters return to them. Dr. Fuller rose to pronounce the benediction, and all reverently bowed their heads—the proud mothers and their hopeful children, likely plantation hands, gray-headed and gray-bearded patriarchs, like one who stood at my elbow, and, black though he was, looked so like the busts we have of Homer, that I could hardly realize him to be merely a "worn-out nigger"—bowed all together before God, the freedmen and the Major-Generals, the turbaned young women from the plantations, and the flower of Northern schools and society, the woolly-headed urchins, who could just remember that they once "b'longed to" somebody, and the Chief Justice of the United States.

The few words of blessing were soon said; and then came a rush to the stand, "to speak to Massa Richard." Men and women pressed forward indiscriminately; the good Doctor, in a moment, found both his hands busy, and stood, like a patriarchal shepherd, amid his flock. They pushed up against him, kissed his hands, passed their fingers over his hair, crowded about, eager to get a word of recognition. "Sure, you 'member me, Massa Rich'd; I'm Tom." "Laws, Massa Rich'd, I mind ye when ye's a little 'un." "Don't ye mind, Massa Rich'd, when I used to gwine out gunnin' wid ye?" "How's ye been dis long time?" "'Pears like we's never gwine to see 'ou any more; but, bress de Lord, you'm cum." "Oh, we's gittin' on cumf'able like; but ain't 'ou gwine to cum back and preach to us sometimes?" So the string of interrogatories and salutations stretched out. "I haven't liked him much," said an officer of our cutter, standing near, whose rough-and-ready oaths had sometimes provoked the rebuke of the Dominie, "but I take back every harsh thought. I'd give all I'm worth, or ever hope to be worth, in the world, to be loved by as many people as love him."

Leaving the crowd still thronging about the Doctor,

we drove out beyond the church half a mile, to a village of cabins, which the negroes have christened "Saxtonville." It contains a single street, but that is a mile and a-half long. Each house is surrounded by its little plat of potatoes and corn. Back of the house, stretching off to the timber in the distance, is the narrow little parallelogram of land, called the plantation, averaging from thirty to forty acres, planted in cotton, and, in nearly every case, in the highest possible state of cultivation. Poultry swarmed about the cabins, but no swine were to be seen, and no fences were needed to divide one plantation from another.

Returning, we found the roads alive again with the gaily-dressed groups of freedmen, going home from the "meetin'," and full of animated talk about the great things they had seen and heard. There was constantly the most deferential courtesy. The old women seemed delighted if they could secure a recognition, and not a man of the hundreds on the road passed without lifting, or, at least, touching, his hat. Whenever we approached a gate some negro near us would run ahead to open it; but there was no servility in the air with which he did it. He seemed rather, in bearing and attitude, to say, "I'm a man, and just as good before the law as you are; but I respect you, because you are all friends of ours, and because you know more than I do." These people can never be made slaves again. They have tasted too long of freedom to submit to be driven. But, perhaps, their danger is in a not very dissimilar direction. They are grateful and confiding; and they *may* prove easily led.

An old negress, whom we passed after we had crossed back to Lady's Island, followed us wearily, on foot, through the broiling sun, many miles, down to the landing. "I want to see Massa Richard—I used to b'long to him," was her only explanation. The dumb expression of grief on her rude features, when she found him gone, and realized that she had probably missed her last chance of seeing him, haunts me yet.

Returning from St. Helena, Doctor Fuller was asked what he thought of the experiment of free labor, as exhibited among his former slaves, and how it contrasted with the old order of things. "I never saw St. Helena look so well," was his instant reply. "I never saw as much land there under cultivation—never saw the same general evidences of prosperity, and never saw the negroes themselves appearing so well or so contented." What has been said, from time time, about the improved condition of the emancipated Sea Islanders, has been said by Northern men, with limited opportunities for previous observation; but this, it must be noted, is the testimony of an old planter, re-visiting the slaves emancipation has taken from him, whose interests and prejudices would alike make him a critic hard to please.

But, it should be added, that the islands about Beaufort are in a better condition than those nearer the encampments of our soldiers. Wherever poultry could be profitably peddled in the camps, cotton has not been grown, nor have the negroes crystalized, so readily, into industrious and orderly communities. What has been done on the more secluded of these sea islands, may be taken as a fair evidence of what may be expected (when not more than the average discouragements are encountered) of the most ignorant and degraded of the Southern slaves. With such negroes as we saw at Charleston, the progress would be incomparably more rapid.

The question about the slaves being self-supporting,

is a question no longer. On St. Helena, and wherever else they have had the opportunity, the negroes have bought the titles to their little farms—or "plantations," as they still ambitiously style them. They have erected their own cabins, secured whatever cheap furniture they contain, and clothed themselves far better than their masters ever clothed them. All who have been established more than a year, have paid back to the Government the rations drawn in their first destitution. They have stocked their plantations, paying the highest prices, and often bidding against white men, at the auction sales of condemned Government property. I saw one man who had paid three hundred dollars in cash for a condemned Government horse, and plenty who had paid prices ranging from a hundred and fifty to two hundred dollars. A single horse only, is needed to cultivate one of their little places; and the instances have been rare in which, after a year or two of work, the negro was not able to command enough money to secure it. Their purchases at the trade stores have been so liberal that the military authorities have occasionally been compelled to interfere, to prevent what they thought extravagance. Cloth they sometimes buy, in their new-born thrift, by the piece, to secure a lower price; flour they are able to get by the barrel, as an industrious Northern mechanic does. In the houses, chairs have made their appearance; dishes and knives and forks are no longer the rarities they were when our troops arrived. And, for whatever they have thus bought, be sure they have paid twice or thrice the New York price.

To some extent this prosperity is delusive; as for the matter of that, the prosperity of the whole country, during the same period, has been delusive. The soldiers paid them three or four prices for their vegetables, eggs and poultry; and when their cotton was ready for market it brought, in some cases, nearly ten times the old price. Naturally they are prosperous. It is more important to observe that they exhibit the industry which deserves prosperity, and, in most cases, the thrift which insures its continuance. Their money has been spent for articles they needed for stocking their farms, clothing their families, or, in some way, bettering their condition. It has not always been spent economically, but they may learn to make better bargains with the Yankee traders, by-and-by; and, for the present, it is sufficient to know that they have enough left to establish a National Bank with their savings, and that in this Bank *one hundred and fifty thousand dollars worth of United States bonds have been bought by the freedmen!* This last statement seemed to me utterly incredible; but General Saxton vouches for it, and explains that when the young negroes from the islands volunteered to enter the military service, they each received (precisely like other volunteers) three hundred dollars bounty, of which, in nearly all cases, at least two hundred were, of their own motion, given to their families, used in stocking the farms, or invested in Government bonds.

Withal, they work less, and have more time for self-improvement, or for society, than when slaves. It is the common testimony, on those islands where white men have bought the plantations, and employed the negroes as laborers, that the old task, which the slave worked at from sunrise to sunset, is now readily performed by the freedman in six or seven hours. Still, the exports from the sea islands will not be as great as during the existence of slavery. Then, they were mere machines, run with as little consumption as possible, to the single end of making money for their masters. Now, as it was in the West Indies, emancipation has enlarged the negro's wants, and, instead of producing solely to export, he now produces also to consume. Then he ate with his fingers from the hominy pot, in the fire-place; now he must have plates, knives and forks, with a table on which to spread them. Then he wore the scant summer and winter suits of negro cloth; now he must have working suits and Sunday suits, and each must be cut with some vague reference to prevailing fashions, and made up by hands that, under the old *regime*, would have been busy beside his own in the cotton field.

These are undeniable evidences of progress in phys-ical well-being. When it comes to mental culture, less can be said. Of the crowd at the St. Helena church, not one in twenty of the adults can read, though they have had three years of partial and interrupted oppor-tunities. But, on the other hand, not one in twenty of the boys and girls was unable to read. They do not seem so anxious themselves to get "white folks' larnin" as at Charleston and other points to the northward; but every parent is painfully desirous that his children should learn; and many of them are known to take private lessons at home from their children. The latter learn rapidly; they tell the same story everywhere here, just as it has been told down the whole coast from Fortress Monroe. Experienced teachers say they can see no difference in the facility with which these and ordinary white children at the North learn to read. But this is comparatively valueless as a test of negro intellectual capacity. Reading, writing, memorizing, whatever is imitative, or may be learned by rote, will be rapidly acquired; and no schools have yet advanced far enough to show what the average negro mind will do when it grapples with higher branches that require original thought.

Nearly thirty thousand negroes have been settled by General Saxton, (as he informed us over his hospitable dinner table, on our return from St. Helena,) on these islands and adjacent plantations of the main land. Of these, seventeen thousand are now self-supporting. Between twelve and thirteen thousand of those who have come in latest from the interior still draw rations, but all do it with the distinct understanding that they and their farms will be held responsible for the re-payment; and the experience of the Government with the others shows that this debt may be reckoned a safe and short one. None have been forced to come, and the locations upon the plantations have all been made to the satisfaction of the negroes themslves.

General Saxton found a charming wife among the bright Yankee teachers sent down to these schools, and he has established himself in the house of a runaway slaveholder, condemned by the Government authorities, and legally sold to the highest bidder. Two thousand dollars thus gave the General a home among these people, and put him in possession of a fine, airy, large-windowed, many-porched Southern residence, stripped of furniture (which has been sold by the Treasury Agent as abandoned property), and, like the lands on which the negroes are located, with still a worrying doubt about the security of the title. Rebels, who have abandoned their houses, may, some of these days, return, get pardon, and propose to take possession. Barnwell Rhett's house, for example, is next door; suppose he should profess repentance, for the sake of getting back his property, precisely what is there to prevent this

fervently-loyal Major-General from having the prince
of all fire eaters for a neighbor? In Beaufort, as at
Hilton Head, there are wonderful efforts to create a
flame of speculation; but capital is timid, and looks
sharply to the guarantees of title deeds.

In the evening, there was another immense meeting
of negroes in the outskirts of Beaufort. It was again
found that no church would hold them, and so God's
first temples—it must have been live-oak groves Bryant
thought of, when he wrote the well-known lines—were
again sought. Crowding through the throng that
obstructed all the approaches, and ascending the platform, one was struck with the impressiveness of a scene
as peculiar as that in the morning on St. Helena, and
yet widely differing from it. Great live-oaks again
reared their stately pillars of gray, and spread their
glorious canopy of green, beside and above the platform; negroes, old and young, again spread out in a sea
of black humanity before us; but for the rows of carts,
and the old meeting-house, and the moss-grown grave-
stones that shut in the view on St. Helena, we had here
the serried ranks of two full regiments of negroes.
Black urchins clambered up into the live-oak boughs,
above our heads; black girls adjusted their scarfs, and
fidgeted about the front of the platform; white-wooled,
but black-faced, old men leaned against the railing; the
mass of the congregation in front were women, and, as
for the young men, they were clad in blue, and they
stood in ranks outside the rest.

The faces seemed somewhat more intelligent than
those on St. Helena. There were more house-servants,
and all had been brightened by the contact with business in the town. A keen-eyed lady on the platform

called my attention to the owner of a particularly showy turban, and lo! beneath its dazzling colors looked forth, in befitting black, the very face of Mrs. Gummidge, the "lone, lorn creetur'" of David Copperfield's early acquaintance. To the very whimper of the mouth, and watery expression of the eyes, and last particular of desolate and disconsolate appearance, it was Mrs. Gummidge's self, as Dickens has made her immortal. But this was not a common expression. Chubby-faced, glittering-eyed youngsters, of the Topsy type, and comfortable, good-natured Aunties, at peace with themselves and the world, were the prevailing characters. Beaufort was more stylish than St. Helena, and many a ludicrous effort was made in willow crinoline, tawdry calico and cotton gloves, to ape the high-born mulattoes whom the traveled ones had seen in Charleston, and occasionally at Hilton Head.

The sermonizing, singing and speech-making, need hardly be described. Given the occasion and the circumstances, and what weary reader of the papers can not tell, to the very turn of the climax and the polish of the peroration, the nature of the speeches? But it was worthy of note that the orators found the audience to their liking; and, on the point of intelligence, your popular orator is exacting. "I have been in the habit of addressing all sorts of people," said Doctor Fuller, "but never felt so intensely the inspiration of a deeply-sympathizing audience" Two or three humorous little sallies were caught with a quickness and zest that showed how understandingly they were following the speaker; and, at times, the great audience—greater than Cooper Institute could hold—was swaying to and fro, now weeping, then laughing, in the agitation of a common passion the orator had evoked. They seemed to know all about the Chief Justice, and clamored for him, till, as he stood up for a moment, the thunder of the cheers swayed the Spanish moss that hung in pendent streamers above our heads, and made the leaves of the live-oaks quiver as if a gale were blowing through the branches. "If I had only known you were coming," whispered a superintendent, "we might have had two or three marriages here, under the live-oaks, to conclude the exercises of the day!"

But it was when the "exercises" were over, that the real interest of the occasion was brought out. Not less than a hundred of Doctor Fuller's former slaves were in the audience. The moment the benediction was pronounced, they made a rush for the platform, and the good Doctor found his path blocked up at the steps. "Lod bress ye, Massa Rich'd; was afeard 'ud never see ye agin." "Don't you know me, Massa Rich'd? I'm Aunt Chloe." "'Pears like ye wa'n't never comin', no more!" And all the while a vigorous hand-shaking and hand-kissing went on, the former master standing on the steps, and looking benevolently down into upturned faces that fairly shone with joy and excitement.

Presently one of the Aunties, whose happiness was altogether too exuberant for words, struck up a wild chant, and in a moment half a hundred voices had joined her. She stood with clasped hands and beaming face, balancing from one foot to the other in a sort of measured dance, sometimes stopping a moment to shout "glory," and then resuming with yet more enthusiasm; while the former slaves still kept crowding up, feeling the Doctor's hair, passing their hands over his shoulders, clustering lingeringly about him, and joining with deep-throated emphasis in the chant. Soon other women had approached the swaying leader, two or three clasped hands, there was the same animal, half-hysteric excitement, the same intoxication of the affections, which we had witnessed in the morning on St. Helena; while, meantime, a few middle-aged negroes, who gave no other marks of excitement than a perfectly gratified expression of countenance, quietly engaged the Doctor in conversation, told him something of their life since they had become freemen, their hardships and their final prosperity. The women kept up the singing; more and more negroes were joining the circle about the former planter, as we pushed through and left them to themselves. Long lines of soldiers were marching away, their glistening bayonets setting the red rays of the sinking sun to flickering in grotesque lights and shades over the shouting and dancing slaves. Under the trees on the outskirts stood a group of interested spectators, officers, traders, agents of different departments of the Government; a few ladies wonderingly looked on; the breeze was fluttering the flags over the platform; and the late slaves were still singing and kissing their former master's hand. It was our last sight of Beaufort.

A lead-colored little steamer lay at the wharf to take us down to Hilton Head; a short, heavy-set, modest-speaking, substantial negro, a little past middle-age, came to say that the vessel was ready, and awaited our orders. It was the "Planter," and the negro was her Captain, Robert Small—lionized over much, but not spoilt yet. The breeze over the island was delicious; not a film of mist flecked the sky; and down to the very meeting of sky and water, we caught the sparkle of the stars, brilliant with all the effulgence of tropic night.

CHAPTER XII.

Business, Speculation and Progress Among the Sea Island Negroes.

WHATEVER may be the end of the wars for the "great city," which everybody assures us is to be built here-abouts—at Hilton Head, *or* at Bay Point, *or* up the river, at Beaufort—it is certain that, thus far, Hilton Head has the start in business. Wading through the sand here, one finds, at the distance of a square or two from the landing, a row of ambitious-fronted one and two-story frame houses, blooming out in the most extravagant display of fancy-lettered signs. The sut-lers and keepers of trade stores, who do here abound, style their street Merchants' Row. The luckless staff officers, who have made their purchases there, preferred to call it "Robbers' Row," and there was the inherent fitness in the title which makes names stick.

The counters in Robbers' Row are piled with heavy stocks of ready-made clothing, pieces of coarse goods, hats and the like; and the show-cases are filled with cheap jewelry, and the thousand knick-knacks which captivate the negro eye. It was a busy season for the negroes, but still a number were in the stores making purchases. "There, my fine fellow, that fits you exactly. Now, when you get one of those cheap cravats, and an elegant hat, together with a pair of new boots, which you *must* have, and this elegant pair of check pants to match your coat, you'll look like a gentleman, won't he,

Auntie?" The uncouth, coarse-limbed plantation black eyed the trader suspiciously, however, and felt the coarse check coat, with which he had been furnished, as if he were afraid so fine a fabric would fall to pieces at his touch. But "Auntie's" pleasure in contemplating her husband thus gorgeously arrayed, in something becoming his style of beauty, was unbounded; and the reduction in the family purse, that day wrought, must be set to her account. Substitute straight hair for wool, and change the complexion somewhat, and the scenes here become reproductions of others, familiar long ago. They, however, were witnessed far above the head of navigation, on the Mississippi, at a lonely trading post, among the Chippewas, kept by a thrifty half-breed. Of the two races, the Sea-Island negroes evince decidedly the superior judgment in selecting articles, with some reference to their usefulness.

Of course, at all these stores, just as at the Indian trading posts, the customers are swindled; but there is the consolation that the swindle is regulated and limited by law. A military order has been found necessary to curtail the extravagant profits of the traders, and protect the negroes; and, in most cases, they do not now probably pay over two prices for what they buy Kid gloves, I found, were only five dollars a pair, and a very good lady's riding guantlet could be had for six dollars. From these, the average scale of prices may be guessed.

This, however, is only of late date. The prices that were charged, and the profits realized, here in the earlier months, and even years, of the occupation, seem fabulous. One man, for example, has accumulated what would be regarded a handsome fortune, even in New York, who had to work his passage down here as a deck

hand. He was a bankrupt merchant, honest, but penniless. He believed the fall of these islands would open
a field for handsome trade, and came down, as a sailor,
to see for himself. Returning, he told his creditors
what he had seen; and they had faith enough in him
to make up for him a stock of goods, which he sold out
immediately, at such profit as to enable him to make
subsequent purchases on his own account. He has paid
off every dollar of his indebtedness, and is a wealthy
man. Numerous stories of the kind are told; and it
may be safely concluded that whoever would endure the
dirty work involved in following the army as trader,
has had almost unlimited opportunities before him.

Speculation now busies itself about something more
permanent. In spite of the fact that vessels find it
hard to ride at anchor near Hilton Head during a
storm, every effort is to be made to stimulate on its site
the growth of a city. A newspaper is already published,
which dilates on the magnificence of its future, and
rebukes everybody who doesn't call the place Port
Royal (the name generally given to the great sheet of
water constituting at once its harbor, that of Bay Point,
and of one or two other places farther in), rather than
Hilton Head. An immense wooden hotel is up, and
nearly ready for the furniture, which is all stored here
in advance, ready for the shoal of visitors expected with
the return of cool weather. A railroad is projected
nearly due north to Branchville, a distance of seventy
to eighty miles, where it would connect with the whole
railroad system of the South, and make Beaufort and
Hilton Head absolutely independent of Charleston and
Savannah. "Charleston can never have the trade of
this coast again, you know; the North hates it too
much, and, in fact, the port never ought to be opened

again; and if we can only get this railroad connection, our harbor is so much finer than any other on the coast, that we will inevitably have the greatest city south of Baltimore." Boston capitalists are said to stand ready to advance the money for the railroad, but where, in the absence of State Government, to get the authority to build it, is the question; and General Gillmore tells me he was appealed to, the other day, to know if he couldn't declare it a military necessity.

That these glowing anticipations of Port Royal greatness will be realized, at least in part, is unquestionable. The harbor is one of the very finest on the coast—incomparably superior to either Charleston or Savannah. The Sea Island soil produces the best cotton in the world, and the negroes already have it in a state of more thorough cultivation than was ever before known. The increased wants of the freedmen will stimulate trade, and small farmers will not be able, as the planters were in old times, to go to Savannah or Charleston and buy supplies at wholesale. Whatever the fortune of South Carolina, the Sea Islands must henceforth be flourishing. Whether negroes will not, by and by, prefer to trade with persons of their own color, remains to be seen. Real estate ventures must be further complicated, also, with the probabilities that the whole sea-coast of South Carolina (if not the entire State), will speedily become one vast negro colony. Already, the only inhabitants on the Sea Islands are negroes, and the same race is in a majority for many miles inland. Compulsory colonization has always been a failure; but is it not probable that there will be a natural tendency of negroes to places where flourishing negro communities are already established, and the local government is mainly in their own hands?

Some of our party, who remained at Beaufort after the meeting, gave amusing accounts of a negro wedding. It seems that the good superintendent's remark—if he had only known we were coming he would have had two or three weddings for us—was no idle boast. Scarcely a Sunday passes without a marriage, and the young volunteers, who imagine their monthly pay a pretty good "start" for a family, are especially given to matrimonial ventures.

Many of the Sea Islanders, while in slavery, came well up to the description of Brigham Young, whom Artemus Ward pronounced the "most married man" he ever saw. But polygamy is a practice not permitted by the beneficent Government to the poor negroes now— only white people, in distant localities, can be indulged in so doubtful a luxury—and herewith arises one of General Saxton's chief embarrassments. It would often happen that, in the course of being transferred from one plantation to another, a negro would have successively three or four, or even half a dozen wives. Now that he is restricted to one, which should it be? Moralists and theorists would answer, "the first;" General Saxton, with the instinct of a sound political economist, says "the one that has the most children." As for the rest, they must hunt up other husbands.

The negroes really seem to appreciate the dignity and solemnity of the marriage institution; and they have a great anxiety to enter its bonds fashionably. At the Beaufort wedding, just referred to, the bride wore a calico dress whose colors were as glowing as her own was swarthy; her hands were covered with white cotton gloves; and as for her head, neck and shoulders, a true history will be forever at a loss to tell how they *were* clad, for over her head was cast, in flowing folds of

portentous thickness, a gauzy sheet, supposed to represent a white veil. It shrouded the features in unnatural pallor; it suggested no hint of neck, and but the
remotest suspicion of shoulders, and it was only gathered into terminal folds somewhere in the region of what
should have been the waist.

From beneath this effectual concealment, the bride
made haste to give her responses. The poor girl had
been cheated out of her marriage, a week before, by
some unexpected order to the regiment which claimed
the services of her soldier-intended, and she was deter
mined to have " de ting trou wid, dis time." When the
minister asked if he would have this woman to be his
wife, *she* hastily exclaimed, " Oh ! yes, massa, I 'll be his
wife;" and when the irrevocable words were said, the
huge veil disappeared with wondrous rapidity before
the ardor of the kiss. But they got, on their marriage
certificate, the signatures of a couple of witnesses which
the highest born in the land would be proud to possess.

It has been seen that, among the Sea Islanders, the
course of true love runs very much as it does elsewhere. The course of justice seems to be sometimes as
tortuous. Take, for example, the story of a stolen hen
in Mitchelville, and what came of the theft.

Mitchelville, it must be remembered, is the negro village on Hilton Head Island, regularly organized with
negro officers, and enjoying its Councilmen and Supervisor, whom their constituents insist on styling Aldermen and Mayor. The "Aldermen" are enjoined, among
other things, to settle disputes concerning claims for
personal property and the like. Before one of these
Aldermen came a disconsolate negress. Her hen had
been stolen, and Gawky Sam was the boy who did it.
The boy was summoned, the evidence heard, the case

clearly made out, and two dollars fine imposed. But here stepped in another Alderman, who, re-hearing the case, added another dollar to the fine. Before the money was paid, still another managed to get the case before him, and he imposed a fine of five dollars. By this time, the Supervisor ("Mayor") heard the story, and summoning all the parties before him, inquired: "Uncle Ben, why did you fine de boy two dollars?"

"Well, sah, de case was clar; de hen was a mity fine, fat un, and I reckon she worf about a dollar. Den, sir, nobody oughtub be 'lowed to steal for less dan a dollah, nohow. So I made him pay de wuf of de hen to the owner, and a dollah for stealin beside."

"Well, 'Cl'erklis (*Anglice*, Uncle Hercules), why did you make de fine tree dollah?"

"Well, de hen war wuf a dollar, easy. Den de boy ought to pay a dollah for stealin', anyhow. But den, sah, dat hen war a layin' eggs, and if dat Gawky Sam hadn't done stole her, de eggs she'd a laid 'ud a been wuf 't least 'nuther dollar by this time!"

And the third Alderman, it was found, had proceeded upon the same basis, but had reckoned the hen more fertile of eggs, or allowed for her having a longer time in which to produce them; and he had made the boy pay for three dollars' worth of eggs that the hen would have laid for the owner, if she hadn't been stolen!

What new versions of law and justice the Mayor would have given, alas! were lost to the jurisprudence of the Sea Islands, and the case came to an ignoble ending; for Gawky Sam's father had grown frightened at these successive additions to the fine, and the hen had been hastily carried back to the coop whence she was originally stolen. The Mayor, accordingly, imposed a fine of a dollar for the crime of the theft, and peace reigned again among the Aunties of Mitchelville.

Ludicrous as was the solemnity of these proceedings, they were, nevertheless, of value, as showing inherent ideas of justice. In the days of slavery every negro believed it right to steal, for was he not stolen, bodily, from himself? And from taking "Massa's" property, it was no very hard step to taking that of other people. But with freedom have come better practices, and already we are assured that theft is comparatively rare.

Whoever has read what I have written about the cotton fields of St. Helena will need no assurance that another cardinal sin of the slave, his laziness—"inborn and ineradicable," as we were always told by his masters—is likewise disappearing under the stimulus of freedom and necessity. Dishonesty and indolence, then, were the creation of slavery, not the necessary and constitutional faults of the negro character. May it not be reasonably hoped that the other great sin of the slave, his licentiousness, will yet be found to have its origin in the same system, and its end in the responsibilities of educated freedom?

Mrs. Stowe, in one of the most striking passages of *Uncle Tom's Cabin*, suggests a comparison between Eva and Topsy, the one, the child of refined and educated parents, and coming of a race in which refinement and education had bettered the blood from generation to generation; the other, born of ages of oppression, barbarism, bestial ignorance and sin. The comparison might be pushed to a conclusion Mrs. Stowe does not draw. How *can* the brain, thus cramped and debased from father to son, at one bound, rise to the hight of the Anglo-Saxon mind, which these generations of culture have been broadening and strengthening? Enthusiasts tell us that the negro mind is to-day as good as that of the white; but I doubt if ten or fifteen years of education on these Sea Islands will prove it. They seem to me, in some cases, to have *as much* intellect as the whites; but it is in the rough, is torpid, needs to be vitalized and quickened, and brought under control. Things which require no strong or complex intellectual effort—how to read, how to manage their farms, or bargain for the sale of watermelons—they learn quickly and well. An average negro child will learn its letters, and read cleverly in the First Reader, in three months. The average of white children do little, if any, better. But the negroes who are to make rapid progress in the higher branches, or who are to be proficients in skilled labor, have not yet been found abundantly on the Sea Islands.

So their moral faculties seem to me to be torpid, like their minds. Their religion seems rather a paroxysm of the affections than an intelligent conviction; and it is only beginning to lay hold upon the realities of their daily lives. Their affections, whether toward God or toward their neighbors, are unquestionably lively, but of doubtful depth. One sees, however, scarcely a trace of revengeful feeling toward their old masters. If good passions are shallow, so, too, are bad ones. Nor do I see any element whatever out of which a negro insurrection could now, or ever could have been, evolved. The enterprise which risks present pains and dangers for future good is not now a characteristic of the Sea-Island negroes. If it come at all, it must come—as it has *not* yet, to some of the most cultivated peoples in the world—with the education and aspirations of comparative freedom.

CHAPTER XIII.

Pulaski—Savannah—Bonaventure.

From Hilton Head to Savannah, an inner passage among the Sea Islands is practicable for all vessels of light draught. General Gillmore, who accompanied us to Savannah with his staff, took our whole party on board his headquarters' boat, a spacious side-wheel river steamer; and, about the middle of the afternoon we pushed off from the Hilton Head wharf, and were soon steaming rapidly along Scull Creek. On either side was the lush vegetation and low, flat scenery of the islands. Cultivated plantations were nearly always in sight; but they were mainly given over to the negroes, and but few of the former residences of the planters could now be seen. A magnificent beach on our left extended, apparently, half way from Fort Pulaski to Hilton Head; and the staff officers talked appetizingly of gallops along its entire length. During the whole afternoon we did not see one white man on the plantations; nor, probably, would we if we had searched them carefully. They have all fled to the misty, undefined "interior," and abandoned the islands to the "niggers."

It was something to be shown over Fort Pulaski, by the one who had revolutionized gunnery in reducing it. General Gillmore pointed out —— by the way, I have neglected to tell what the hero of Pulaski is like. Fancy a fine, wholesome-looking, solid six-footer, with

big head, broad, good-humored face, and a high forehead, faintly elongated by a suspicion of baldness, curly
brown hair and beard, and a frank, open face, and you
have him. A quick-speaking, quick-moving, soldierly
man he is, an accomplished engineer, one of the finest
practical artillerists in the world, and, withal, a man
whose ideas are not limited by the range of his profession, wherein he forms a notable contrast to some other
regular officers one might name.

The garrison of Pulaski—apparently a company,
with, I believe, a young artillery Captain in command
of the post—were on the look-out for the party, and a
salute was firing from the barbette guns of the fort
before our vessel had rounded to, at the rickety and
almost inaccessible wharf. The low, flat ground on
which the fort is situated, is grassy and firm as a well-
kept lawn; and as the sinking sun, lit up with sloping
rays the distant woods and the rippling river, gilded the
burst columbiad (which had been set upright over the
graves of the soldiers killed in the bombardment, and
with its terse inscription, constituted a monument as
beautiful as unique,) flashed from the bayonets of the
slow-pacing guard on the parapet wall, and brought
dimly out beyond the wood the spires of Savannah,
one could readily credit the declaration of an engineer
officer on General Gillmore's staff, who had been sta-
tioned there for a month or two, that it was the pleasantest place he had found on the whole South Atlantic
coast: An hour's conflict with the mosquitoes, however, would be apt to cause a hasty retraction (and
retreat.)

The General led us first around the outer moat to
the face fronting Tybee Island, from which he had
bombarded it. The breaches have all been thoroughly

repaired, but with a different-colored brick; and the pock-marked appearance of the casemates sufficiently attested the efficiency of the fire. Inside the fort there was nothing to see, save that with mosquito-nets, instead of doors and windows, with ample supplies of ice, and by the aid of the thick walls of the fort, our Yankee officers have learned to make garrison duty in the South quite endurable. Beside Sumter and Fisher, Fort Pulaski is contemptible; and the main interest now attaching to the place is, that it taught us, as General Gillmore tersely expresses it, "how any brick or stone fort can be rapidly breached at 1,650 yards distance," and that, "with guns of my own selection, I would undertake to breach a brick scarp at 2,000 yards." The fort is now stronger and better every way than when seized by the Rebels; but, as a protection to the harbor of Savannah, against an attack of iron-clads, or the advance of an army, with rifled artillery, it is nearly valueless. Like our other brick and stone forts on the coast, however, it may be made the basis of a powerful defense. Heap up earthworks on the outside, and, so long as its garrison could be provisioned, it would be impregnable.

A sunken vessel lay in the channel, off the fort, and the narrowness of the passage showed how utterly impossible the fall of Pulaski had made blockade running for Savannah. Realizing the fact, its defenders had taken little pains to keep the river open; and their cribs of logs, firmly bolted together and filled with stones to obstruct the passage of our iron-clads up the stream, had so nearly destroyed the navigation that, even at the time of our visit, after weeks of work in removing them, since the city fell into our hands, our Captain was afraid to attempt the passage in the dark, and we had to lie at anchor, half a mile above Pulaski, all night.

Everybody was awakened, next morning, by the announcement that Jeff. Davis was alongside. If the officer who came hurrying through the cabin to tell it, had said the Prince of Darkness was alongside, in the bodily presence, no one would have been more surprised. Admiral Dahlgren had told us of close watch kept along the west coast of Florida for the fallen Chief, and General Gillmore had, only the day before, been expressing rather faint hopes that, possibly, the vigilance of the land and naval forces in that distant quarter might be rewarded with success. That, in the midst of these expectations, Jeff. Davis should be quietly brought up and lashed alongside our boat, before anybody but the crew was awake, and while we were peacefully steaming up to Savannah, was quite enough to move our special wonder.

The Colonel in charge of the prisoner had been directed to report to General Gillmore, and await orders, which were promptly given. It was thought best, under all the circumstances, that there should be no other intercourse between the boats. The story of the capture, in a semi-female disguise, was fully told by the captor; and so, fresh from this final illustration of the absolute collapse of the rebellion, we landed, in the gray morning, at the Savannah wharves. To our left, across a narrow and rather turbid stream, stretched away to the sea a level marsh, flat as a Western prairie, and green with the lush vegetation of the rice swamp; on the right were rows of fine warehouses, that for four years had known neither paint nor'repairs; wharves, through the broken planks of which a careless walker might readily make an unwelcome plunge into not over-cleanly water; and, back of the warehouses, high stone walls, up which, at infrequent intervals, rude staircases conduct the pedestrian to the level of the city proper.

To the Northern reader, Savannah, Charleston, Wilmington, Richmond, have always seemed important names; and while never unconscious that none of them were New York, or Boston, or even Baltimore, yet he has nearly always associated with them the idea of large population, fine architecture and general metropolitan appearance. Nothing better illustrates the pretentious policy of this latitude, which has been always successful in being accepted at its own valuation. Savannah, for example, which is a scattered, tolerably well-built town of twenty thousand inhabitants, about the size of Oswego or Utica, in New York, or Dayton or Columbus, in Ohio, has aspired to be the "metropolis of the South Atlantic coast;" and by dint of their perpetual boasts, Georgians had actually succeeded in making us all regard it very nearly as we do Cincinnati, or Chicago, or St. Louis. A Savannah shopkeeper was indignant, beyond description, at a careless remark of mine. I had asked the population of the place, and, on being told, had answered wonderingly, "Why, that isn't more than a thousand ahead of Lynn, the little town in Massachusetts, where they make shoes and send Henry Wilson to the United States Senate." The shopkeeper swept off the counter the articles he had been showing me, and, with an air of disdain, said he would like to count profits on goods by the arithmetic Yankees used in estimating the population of their nasty little manufacturing holes.

But the people in general were exceedingly polite, though one could now and then detect the sullen air which showed how hard it was to bear the presence of the Yankees. It was evident that they felt conquered, and stood in silent and submissive apprehension, awaiting whatever course the victors might see fit to pursue, and ready to acquiesce, with such grace as they might, in whatever policy the Government should adopt. Surely, now is the golden opportunity for a statesman to shape and mold these Southern institutions as he will. Shall it not be improved?

The little squares at the intersection of the principal streets, with their glimpse of sward, their fountains, live-oaks, magnolias and pride-of-India trees, make up, in part, for the absence of the elegant residences, embowered in luxurious shrubbery, which form so attractive a feature of Charleston. One strolls from square to square, seeing here children and their nurses playing under the trees, and there groups of negroes idly enjoying the shade; and scarcely realizes, till he sets foot again in the unpaved streets, and sinks in the burning sand, that he is in the heart of a "great Southern metropolis," the chief city of "the Empire State of the South." A little shopping for some members of our party showed that the old merchants still had certain lines of goods in abundance. Jewelry stores had large remnants of the stocks laid in during the winter of 1860-'61; coarse dry goods were plenty, and so were what, I believe, are technically called "wet groceries." Execrable soda water gurgled at almost every corner; large and gay-looking drug stores seemed to laugh at our impotent blockade on calomel; and what the native traders could not supply in the way of the fashions for the last four years, a dozen sutlers' establishments, already in full blast, were ready to furnish. Rebel currency had wholly vanished; and small pieces of gold and silver were gradually

The Talk at Dr. Fuller's Plantation.—Page 102.

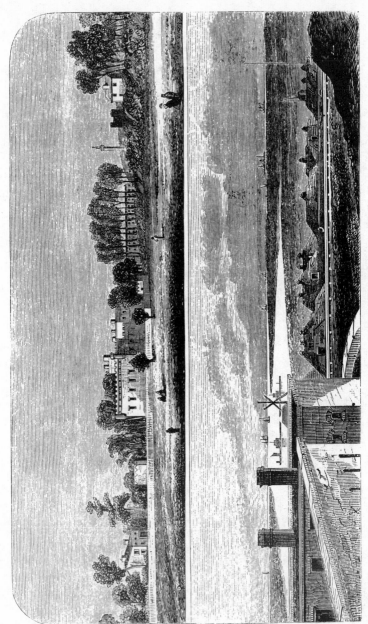

Forts at Savannah.—Page 131.

W G Jackman.

UNCLE SANDIE.

Engraved expressly for this Work

MOORE WILSTACH & BALDWIN PUBLISHERS

Negro Schools of New Orleans.—Page 246.

Trash, Log and Plow Gangs at work.—Page 496.

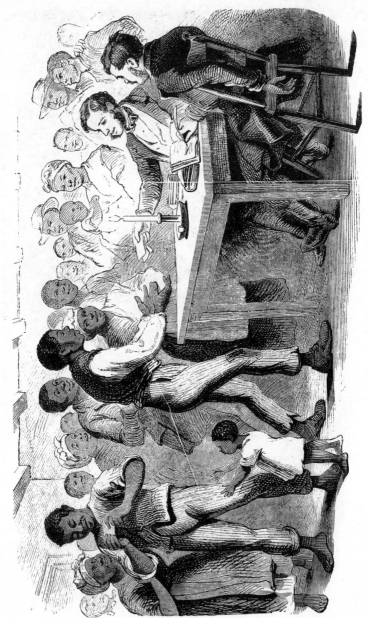

Paying Off.—Page 525.

making their appearance, particularly in the hands of persons from the interior.

The streets of Savannah present the most striking contrast to those of Charleston. There, scarcely a white inhabitant of the city was to be seen. The merchants, the small shopkeepers, the *restaurateurs* were all gone, and, where the soldiers had not taken possession, shutters, barred and bolted, closed in their establishments. Here, on the contrary, the town had been taken, inhabitants and all. The difference is about that between having a watch and a watch case. As a smart sailor from the Wayanda said, "this town isn't dead; it's wound up and running." The stores were all open; business of every sort progressed precisely as usual. Save that the schools were filled with negroes, and the rebel newspapers had been succeeded by loyal ones, and guards in blue, instead of gray, stood here and there, it was the rebel Savannah unchanged. The streets were filled with the inhabitants, dressed somewhat antiquely, but giving no signs of suffering; little knots gathered in the public squares, or around the saloons and shops, to discuss the news and their prospects; and curious eyes followed us at every corner, as if to say, "There go some more of the Yankees." Every house was occupied; the front windows were open as usual; and the ladies seemed to have no particular prejudice against being seen—old clothes and all.

Some of us went to the hotel, nearly opposite the plain, square shaft erected in honor of Pulaski, and, as an experiment, tried their breakfast. As an experiment it was quite successful; as a breakfast, very poor; but we had a dozen rebel officers as neighbors, and passed salt and broke bread with them as indifferently as though they were not yet wearing the very uniform and side arms that proclaimed their treason. The furniture of the hotel had grown shabby with four years' use; dishes had been broken and forks stolen, and there had been no means of supplying the loss; even napkins were scarce, but negro waiters were abundant, and as polite as ever. The bar was doing a thriving business; swarthy and ringleted cavaliers in gray were pledging each other in bumpers of liquors altogether too strong for the climate, and old acquintances were producing their hoarded rolls of greenbacks to "treat" the returning braves. "Well, Colonel, you don't come back victorious, but I'm d—d glad to see you, any way. Your old friends are proud of you. Come and have a drink." "Sorry about that ugly wound, Captain. A hand is a bad thing to lose, but it wont hurt you among the ladies of Savannah. There are plenty that you can persuade to give you one. What'll you drink?"

Whoever goes to Savannah must see the city cemetery. There is nothing else to show; so we all made the most of what there was, and drove heroically through the sand to Bunoaventua. From a street of well-built frame houses we plunged square off into the squalid country. Elegant suburbs and fine country residences seem a thing unknown. The shell road was once the pride of Savannah, but its glory, too, was departed; and our carriage wheels powdered us with sand, till, chameleon like, we had taken the hue of our surroundings, and seemed clad in Confederate gray. The few houses to be seen were forlorn-looking shanties, belonging to the poor white trash, with rotten steps and doors awry, and foul passages and oozy back yards. Here and there we met a creaking cart, drawn by an ox or a broken-down horse, laden with rickety pine furniture, and guided by the lank, lantern-jawed, stubby-bearded, long-haired owner. He was "toting" his goods in from some house which Sherman's "bummers" had burned or plundered. If his "woman" trudged on foot behind him, be sure she assuaged the fatigues of the journey with great quids of tobacco and profuse expectoration; while the ragged, frowzy children were kept busy with the vagaries of the cow. The Yankee soldiers "had taken his corn, and spiled his crop, and he'd heern that the Government was a givin' out rations in Savannah."

But our drivers presently left the main road, for one which led through sandy barrens, covered with a stunted undergrowth, and seemed to be better in that the sand was a little firmer. Here and there a brilliant flower enlivened the barren scene; but the expected profusion of glowing colors we had all been led to look for about Savannah was wanting. At last, after a ride, which, in the melting sun and abounding sand, entitled one to a sight of something beautiful, we reached a rustic gate, and decayed lodge by its side; and, passing through, were at once in a scene for the possession of which New York might well offer a large fraction of what she has expended on her Central Park.

The finest live-oak trees I have yet seen in the South, stretched away in long avenues on either hand, intersected by cross avenues, and arched with interlacing branches, till the roof over our heads seemed, in living green, a graining, after the pattern of Gothic arches, in some magnificent old cathedral. It is the finest material in the country for the elaboration of the most beautiful cemetery. But, as in most places in the South, everything has stopped where nature stopped. One of the Tatnalls, probably an ancestor of the Commodore of our navy, of Chinese and Rebel note, long ago selected this site for his residence, builded his house, and laid out the grounds in these stately avenues. The house was burned down during some holiday rejoicings. An idea that the place was unhealthy possessed the owners, and, with a curious taste, what was too dangerous for men to live in was straightway selected for dead men to be buried in. We would hardly choose a malarious bottom, or a Northern tamarack swamp for a burying ground, beautiful as either might be, but what matters it? After life's fitful fever, the few interred here sleep, doubtless, as sweetly beneath the gigantic oaks in the solemn avenues, as if on breeziest upland of mountain heather.

Even into this secluded gloom have come the traces of our civil wars. The only large monument in the cemetery is that bearing the simple inscription of "Clinch," and within it lie, I am told, the bones of the father-in-law of "Sumter Anderson," as in all our history he is henceforth to be known. Some vandal has broken down the marble slab that closed the tomb, and exposed the coffins within.

This very barbarism, with the absence of the rows of carefully-tended graves, and the headstones with affectionate inscriptions that mark all other cemeteries, increases the impressive gloom of the lonely place. The sun struggles in vain to penetrate the Gothic arches overhead. Here and again a stray beam struggles through, only to light up with a ghostly silver radiance, the long, downward-pointing spear point of the Tillandsia or Spanish Moss. The coolness is marvelous; the silence profound—or only broken by the gentle ripplings of the little stream by which the farther side of the cemetery is bounded. Everywhere the arches are hung—draped, perhaps, I should better say—with the deathly festoons of the Spanish Moss, slowly stealing sap and vigor—fit funeral work—from these giant oaks, and fattening on their decay. Drive where you will, the moss still flutters in your face, and waves over your head, and, lit with the accidental ray from above, points its warning, silvery light toward the graves beneath your feet; while still it clings, in the embrace of death, to the sturdy oaks on which it has fastened, and preaches and practices destruction together. Noble and lusty oaks are these; glorious in spreading boughs, and lofty arches, and fluttering foliage, but dying in the soft embrace of the parasite that clings and droops, and makes yet more picturesque and beautiful in decay—dying, even as Georgia was dying in the embrace of another parasite, having a phase not less picturesque, and a poisonous progress not less subtly gentle.

Some day, when Georgia has fully recovered, this spot too, will feel the returning tide of her generous, healthy blood. The rank undergrowth will be cleared away, walks will be laid out among the tombs where now are only tangled and serpent-infested paths; shafts will rise up to the green arches to commemorate the names of those most deserving in the State, and the Tillandsia, still waving its witchery of silver, will then seem only like myriad drooping plumes of white, for-ever tremulously pendant over graves at which the State is weeping.

CHAPTER XIV.

White and Black Georgians—The Savannah Standard of Unionism.

THE difference between Savannah and Port Royal negroes is the difference between the child and the man. Young men, fresh from Massachusetts common schools, do not surpass raw Cornish miners more; average Yankees do not surpass average Mexicans as much. Naturally, in listening to the negro delegations that called on Mr. Chase and General Gillmore, I heard the best talkers they have; but there is a general air of intelligence and independence among them, here, which comes only of education and knowledge of the ways of the world. Train the children of the present Port Royal negroes steadily in common schools, and let them mingle, till middle age, with their superiors in life, learning to see for themselves and take care of their own interests, and you will then have about what the Savannah negroes are now. There are eight thousand five hundred of them, who belong to the city proper; and, of these, about a thousand have been free since long before the war, while many of the rest, being sons and daughters of their masters, or, otherwise, house servants, have had advantages not possessed by ordinary slaves. Besides these, there are large numbers here who have escaped from their masters in the interior, and these may always be set down as the most intelligent and enterprising on their respective plantations.

A delegation, headed by one or two preachers and a school-teacher, called on Mr. Chase, by appointment previously sought by one of their number. Some of them were jet black; none of them were lighter than mulattoes. The spokesman was a mulatto preacher, of more than usually intelligent features, and with the quiet bearing of a gentleman. The courtesy with which they approached and addressed the Chief Justice could hardly have been surpassed by any of the accomplished counselors of the Supreme Court; indeed, politeness seems to be a speciality of all negroes, and, among the cultivated ones, it takes on a deferential grace which no Anglo-Saxon may hope to exceed.

The spokesman said they had called partly to pay their respects and express their gratitude to one whom they recognized as foremost and most potential among the living in their deliverance; but mainly to inquire what the Government was likely to do with them, and what they themselves ought to be doing to secure the rights of which they thought they had been unjustly deprived. Especially they desired to know what their prospect was for being permitted to exercise, in common with all other native freemen, the elective franchise.

"Suppose you *were* permitted to vote," said the Chief Justice, "what guarantee would the Government have that you would know how to vote, or that your influence would not be cast on the side of bad morals and bad politics?"

"Oh, Mr. Judge," ejaculated a little black fellow, "we know who our friends are!"

"I am not so sure about that. You don't know the positions of many of the leading men here, and some of them, by professing to be your friends, might easily deceive you."

"No, sir; I 'sure you we knows our friends," responded the same coal-black speaker.

"Perhaps you in the cities may. I am not disposed, myself, to doubt it. But here is a great mass of ignorant field hands from the plantations. They are scattered all over Georgia, and they don't have the advantages or the opportunities of learning which you have. What is to prevent them from voting just as their old masters may tell them?"

"Oh, we'll tell them how to vote, sir; we have means of reaching them; and *they'll follow us sooner than they will their old masters or any white man.*"

"Possibly; perhaps even probably. But neither they, nor even you, are familiar with political history, the organization of parties, the antecedents of parties or of leaders; and you are very liable to be deceived. How do we know that, in your ignorance, you will not be tricked into voting the slavery ticket, under some pleasant and deceptive name, rather than the freedom ticket?"

"Mr. Judge, we always knows who's our friends and who isn't. We knows the difference between the Union ticket and the Rebel ticket. We may not know all about all the men that's on it; but we knows the difference between the Union and the Rebel parties. Yes, sir; we knows that much better than you do! Because, sir, some of our people stand behind these men at the table, and hear 'em talk; we see 'em in the house and by the wayside; and we *know* 'em from skin to core, better than you do or can do, till you live among 'em as long, and see as much of 'em as we have."

"I have no doubt of your competency to take care of yourselves in Savannah," said the Chief Justice; "but what your friends at the North are afraid of, is, that your people in the interior will not know how to tell whom to vote for, for the present at least, and that in their bewilderment they will vote just as their old masters tell them they ought."

"I tell you, Mr. Judge," said the preacher, "we can reach every colored man in the State; and they would rather trust intelligent men of their own color than any white man. They'll vote the ticket we tell them is the ticket of our friends; and, as fast as they can, they'll learn to read and judge for themselves."

"Sir," he continued, "the white population of Georgia is five hundred thousand, and, of that number, fifty thousand, or one in ten, can't read and write. Give *us* three years to work in, and, among our younger adults, the proportion who can not read and write will be no greater. But, sir, these whites don't read and write because they don't want to; our people don't, because the law and public feeling were against it. The ignorant whites had every chance to learn, but didn't; we had every chance to remain ignorant, and many of us learned in spite of them."

Another delegation consisted of blacks from the country, wearing coarse negro clothes instead of broadcloth, less graceful in their bearing, and less cultivated in their talk. Their old masters were abusing them, were whipping those who said they thought they were free, and were doing all they could to retain them in a state of actual, if not also nominal, slavery. Some were endeavoring to earn a living by hauling wood to the country towns, and they complained that their old masters went with cunning stories to the military authorities and contrived to have them stopped. Others had tales of atrocities to tell, whippings and cutting off of ears and the like, for the crimes of going where they pleased and assuming to act as freemen. All the negroes knew that the North had triumphed in the war, and that they were by consequence free; but the white masters did n't yet seem to understand it. Some of these men appeared patient enough under their wrongs; others bore themselves angrily, and were full of revengeful thoughts. A slave insurrection is not probable; but where whites and negroes are alike unarmed, and the negroes are nearly or quite equal to the white population, there may be such a thing as goading the patient bearer of burdens into revolt. If so, let the masters beware. On the levees of the Mississippi any man can loose the floods of half a continent; but it takes many men to confine them again.

Few of the negroes, and, indeed, few of the whites, spoke of any settled arrangements between the late slaves and the late masters, on the basis of the freedom of the blacks, and their consequent right to wages. Wherever any bargains had been made, they seemed to be such as would virtually establish the Mexican peonage instead of Southern slavery. Negroes were hired at nominal monthly wages, "with board;" and whatever debts they incurred in getting their clothing were to be subsequently "worked out" at the same rates. The result was, of course, certain to be that the masters would encourage the negroes to run in debt; and, this done, would hold them forever by a constantly strengthening chain.*

I saw none of the negroes, either residing in Savannah or from the country, who had any desire to be colonized away from their present homes. Ask them if

---

* General Carl Schurz, who subsequently examined these contracts critically, said they substantially renewed the slavery of the freedmen who entered into them.

they would like to live by themselves, and they would generally say "Yes" (as they did to Secretary Stanton); but further inquiry would always develope the fact that their idea of "living by themselves" was to have the whites removed from what they consider their own country. Admiral Dahlgren's observation at Charleston (that the negroes couldn't see what good it did them to make them free, unless they were to have the land to which their slave labor had given all its value), is confirmed here, as it was at Port Royal. The more intelligent negroes generally think it would be better for their people to be freed from contact with the whites; but their idea of accomplishing it is, not to remove the blacks, but to have the whites remove from them. They believe in colonization; but it is in colonization on the lands they have been working. From the bare idea of enforced, or even voluntary, removal to other sections, they utterly revolt.

No one, who saw or conversed with the leading Savannah negroes, would doubt their entire capacity to support themselves. They were all well-dressed, in clothes bought by their own earnings; many of them were living in large and well-furnished houses; some owned their own residences, and not a few had quite handsome incomes. In short, the negro has shown in Savannah, just as in more northern cities, that in proportion as he advanced in intelligence, he advanced also in the arts of money getting, and gathered about him those substantial evidences of prosperity which all governments regard as the best guarantee for the good behavior of the citizen.

The negroes have been holding meetings here, marked, apparently, by more than their usual discretion, and,

indeed, so wisely conducted as to elicit from one of the
Savannah papers this eulogium:

A more orderly, decorous audience never assembled within
the walls of an edifice, than these enthusiastic people, whose sincere gratitude was depicted in every emotion. We rejoice that
these people understand, perfectly, that freedom does not mean idleness, but perseverance and industry.

A correspondent of one of the newspapers is reminded,
by their bearing, of certain passages of Scripture, and
copies out, and the paper gravely quotes, in its editorial
columns, as follows:

For the Lord our God, He it is that brought us up, and our fathers, out of the land of Egypt, from the house of bondage, and which
did those great signs in our sight, and preserved us in all the way
wherein we went, and among all the people through whom we
passed. (Joshua xxiv: 17.)

And when thy sons asketh thee, in time to come, saying, what
mean the testimonies, and the statues, and the judgments, which
the Lord our God hath commanded you?

Then thou shalt say unto the son: We were Pharaoh's bondmen
in Egypt; and the Lord brought us out of Egypt with a mighty
hand.

And the Lord shewed signs and wonders, great and sore, upon
Egypt, upon Pharaoh, and upon all his household before our eyes.

And He brought us out from thence, that He might bring us in,
to give us the land which He sware unto our fathers. (Deut. vi:
20, 21, 22 and 23.)

The newspapers which make these Scriptural applications, however, it must be remembered, are the productions of the Northern editors who have come down
in the wake of the army, or of Southern journalists
who have stood ready to change with the tide.

This evening several of these gentlemen called on me,
on board the boat. One, of unkempt hair and clothes,

and glittering eye, that even opium could have made
no brighter, and air at once of the gentleman and the
seedy Southerner, has already a wide Northern acquaintance. Who has not read of "Doesticks," — his
adventures at Niagara, and his multifarious encounters
with a single glass of ale? "Doesticks" turns up in
the flesh in Savannah; and Mr. Mortimer Thompson
assures us that he finds it pay down here very well, if it
"were not for this cursed blockhead of a Commanding
General!" Alas! how that ghost still stands in the way
of the enterprising journalist! Even Punch, with all
his gibes, is overawed before our conquering Northern
Mars; and Doesticks groans under the oppression of
the uniform of the "Commanding General." His
circulation is good, he avers (and there lurks no fun,
for a wonder, beneath the word), every Rebel takes the
paper, because every Rebel wants to know the news
from the Yankees; and there is a better chance than
ever before, to spread Yankee notions among this people, *if* it weren't for that cursed Commanding General!
Advertising is good; Savannah merchants and Northern
sutlers compete for the trade of the army and the city;
news is plenty; there is no trouble about selling papers
and coining money; *if* it weren't for the perpetual
interference of that blockhead of a Commanding General! Northern men could succeed, even better as journalists here than Southerners, because they have more
industry, know more about their business, and could
make better papers, *if* it weren't for that Commanding
General! I believe, from a hint Gillmore has given,
that the Commanding General is about to be changed;
and, from the bottom of my heart, I congratulate Doesticks on it.

Communication with the interior is yet very uncer-

tain. The mails are all stopped; the railroads broken
up; the highways blockaded by sentries that imitate the
fly-trap—let you in but won't let you out. There is no
scarcity of news here from the interior, but Savannah
is, as yet, a focus which receives all these diverse rays of
intelligence and reflects none back again. The town
is full of black and white refugees from all parts of
Georgia; both races are daily coming in large numbers,
some for supplies, some to find what the policy of the
Government is likely to be, some to go North. What
the negroes tell, in the way of trouble with their masters, and petty persecutions that seem designed, since
their freedom can't be taken away, to make freedom
very unpleasant for them, has already been partly
recited. The whites are, of course, discreetly silent on
such subjects, though I have heard one or two refer
rather significantly to the "uncommon amount of whipping it takes now to keep the plantation niggers in
order." But they are full of complaints of their own,
telling how lazy and worthless the negroes are, how
Sherman's soldiers desolated the country, and how
unsettled every one feels.

There is apparently no apprehension among them of
guerrilla warfare; in fact, they scout at the idea. Question them as to everything for which the war was
fought, the doctrine of secession, the rightfulness of
slavery, the wrongs of the South, and they are found as
full of the sentiments that made the rebellion as ever;
but every man has apparently schooled himself into
saying, with an air of utter frankness: "We're whipped,
and we give it up. There will be no more fighting of
any sort; no guerrillas; no resistance to the Government; and we all accept the death of slavery as inevitable." Ask them what should be done with them, now

that they're subdued, and they say: "We're wholly in the hands of the Government, but would like to have our State Governments restored as soon as possible." Ask them what should be done with the negroes, now that they're free, and the bolder ones answer, "Put them under the care of the State Legislature;" while all seem to insist upon some sort of apprenticeship, or other legal restriction that will practically keep them as much slaves as ever. I have found no Georgian who, now that his slaves can no longer be made to work for him, expects to work for himself. In fact, working for themselves does not seem to be, in any event, of success or of failure, of loyalty or of rebellion, a part of their philosophy of life. Work is for "niggers"—not for white men.

Nor do they seem to entertain any idea of selling off part of their lands, in order to get money to stock and till properly the remainder. Some of them think selling their lands, inherited from their fathers, would be dishonorable; others affect to believe that nobody would buy; while it is quite evident that, as long as they can help it, none of them mean to sell.

"What would be the sense of my selling?" asked one. "Suppose I did; what then could I do for a livelihood? I don't know how to do anything to make money, and I wouldn't go at it if I did. I'm no book-keeper or counter-jumper. I never learned a trade; I have no profession. I own these lands, and, if the niggers can be made to work, they'll support me; but there's nothing else that I know anything about, except managing a plantation."

By-and-by, however, necessity will begin to pinch them more and more. Then, unless they succeed, in some way, in cheating the Government and making emancipation a sham, many of them will throw their lands into the market, rather than honestly attempt to work them with free labor. When that time comes, Northern capital will have such an opening as rarely coffers twice in one capitalist's lifetime.

A large number of leading citizens of Savannah, and gentlemen gathered here from different parts of the State, waited on the Chief Justice and General Gillmore during our visit. One, a fine-looking old gentleman, of rubicund visage and silvery hair, with two sons holding high rank in the Rebel army, wanted to remonstrate against the admission of the negroes to the public schools. He was painfully polite, but, in spite of his calmness, the deep feeling under which he labored could not be wholly concealed. "Sir, we accept the death of slavery; but, sir, surely there are some things that are not tolerable. Our people have not been brought up to associate with negroes. They don't think it decent; and the negroes will be none the better for being thrust thus into the places of white men's sons."

Accompanying this old gentleman, and one or two of the other Savannah magnates, was Mr. Charles Green, a noted British merchant, of many years' residence here. Mr. Green is among the wealthiest inhabitants; has made more money out of the war than any one else, unless Savannah rumor greatly belies him; lives in one of the finest houses; was the first man to greet General Sherman and offer him the hospitalities of his residence—in short, is at once a British and a Savannah institution, and is, withal, a gentleman of culture and refinement. His cordial courtesies had to be declined; but it was interesting to see, in the short interview in which he tendered them, how completely the old prejudices of the section retained their influence. Mr. Green was Doctor Russell's[24] host during the much-abused *Times'* correspondent's stay in Savannah, and in those days it does not appear that he differed very widely from other secession-loving Britons in the South. But it is amazing what difference success or failure makes in the soundness of a principle!

Mingling freely with a crowd of fifteen or twenty gentlemen, who called a little later, all Georgians, and all but two or three residents of Savannah, I made some effort, by comparison of their various views, to get at the nature and standard of Savannah Unionism. Some of them, indeed, made no profession of being Union men, and said they only called to indicate their entire disposition to submit, without opposition, to whatever the Government might do, and to pay their respects to the man whom they recognized as the ablest in our public life, and, by virtue of his management of the finances, their real conqueror. But the most were all desirous of being considered now warm Union men. They were all ready to submit to anything. They were helpless, they said, but surely the Government would be magnanimous. They knew slavery was gone; but the Government ought not to permit the slaves to become vagabonds. If they must have the negroes living among them, they ought to have some power to make them work. The Rebel soldiers and officers were always spoken of with warm kindness; and it was evidently only in exceptional cases that active service for the Rebellion had made any of them think less of a returning Rebel neighbor. They hoped civil government would be re-established as soon as possible, and the military restraints removed. Of course, confiscation would be abandoned, now that all had submitted; and it would

[24] William Howard Russell, war correspondent of the London *Times.* [Ed.]

be very hard if the majority of the old voters were not still permitted to vote. Judge Wayne, of the Supreme Court of the United States, had returned within a few days, and settled down in his old house, among his old neighbors. They were glad to welcome him back, and hoped his coming was a token of the kindly feeling of the Judiciary toward them. They knew they would not be betrayed in returning like repentant children, and asking for protection in their rights.

This last phrase was reiterated so often that at last I exclaimed to one of them: "But what rights have you?"

"Our rights as a sovereign State under the Constitution."

"Your people, then, do not realize that, having rebelled from the Constitution, and abjured all rights under it, they can not, with a very good grace, after failing to destroy it, come back and demand the right to enjoy it."

"Why, of course, the Constitution stands. We only went out from under it. It would be strange, if, when we come back under it, we should find its protecting power gone."

"You do not regard any of your rights, then, as destroyed or imperiled by your rebellion?"

"Why should they be? The right to hold slaves has been destroyed by the military authorities; but, unless the Constitution is destroyed, we have all the powers under it we ever had."

And, in short, they consider that they have the absolute right to State Governments, the old suffrage, and, in a word, the old *status* on everything, slavery only excepted. Yet, withal, there is a curious submissiveness about them, whenever there is talk of the power of the conquerors. The simple truth is, they stand ready to claim everything, if permitted, and to accept anything, if required.

In the evening a stroll through the streets gave some other phases of the city life. As has been said, the place was full of returning rebel soldiers. At every corner their friends, and particularly their female acquaintances, were greeting them with a warmth that seemed in nowise tempered by contempt for their lack of success. Many a stalwart fellow, in coarse gray, was fairly surrounded on the sidewalk by a bevy of his fair friends; and if without an arm or a leg, so much the better—the compliments would rain upon him till the blushes would show upon his embrowned cheeks, and he was fairly convinced that he had taken the most gallant and manly course in the world.

Very pretty it was, nevertheless, if one could only forget what these men had been doing, to see the warmth of their welcome home; to watch little children clinging to the knees of papas they had almost forgotten; to observe wives promenading proudly with husbands they had not seen for years; to notice the delighted gathering of family groups around some chair in the piazza, long vacant, but filled again by a crippled soldier, home from the wars, with only his wounds and his glory for his pay.

The bearing of the rebel soldiers was unexceptionable. My companion was a staff officer, in undress uniform, and without arms. At times, for squares, there would be no sentry in sight; so that it was not the mere vulgar fear of immediate arrest that made them respectful. Occasionally I observed them look curiously and rather admiringly at the elegant texture and easy fit of the uniform, so unlike their own; often they straightened up to a thorough soldierly bearing, and even sometimes respectfully saluted as they passed.

Indeed, nothing was more touching, in all that I saw in Savannah, than the almost painful effort of the rebels, from Generals down to privates, to conduct themselves so as to evince respect for our soldiers, and to bring no severer punishment upon the city than it had already received. There was a brutal scene at the hotel, where a drunken sergeant, with a pair of tailors' shears, insisted on cutting the buttons from the uniform of an elegant gray-headed old Brigadier, who had just come in from Johnston's army; but he bore himself modestly and very handsomely through it. His staff was composed of fine-looking, stalwart fellows, evidently gentlemen, who appeared intensely mortified at such treatment—wholly unmerited, by the way, since they had no clothes save their Rebel uniforms, and had, as yet, had no time to procure others—but they avoided disturbance, and submitted to what they might, with some propriety, and with the general approval of our officers, have resented. What these men may become, under a lax rein, can not be said; but, supposing themselves under a tight rein, they are now behaving, in the main, with very marked propriety.

Half a dozen pretty women were keeping up a busy chatter, all to themselves, in an ice-cream saloon, where we sat down for a few moments. "I'm going North, in a few days," said one, "to buy some clothes." "But, Laura, you musn't do that; you'll have to take the oath to get a pass; and, you know, you're just as much of a Rebel as ever you were." "Yes, of course," with a pretty shrug of the aforesaid Laura's pretty shoulders, "but, then, one must have clothes, you know!" Of old, it was discovered that sermons might be found in running brooks. May not Generals and higher authorities, who believe in hard swearing as a means of grace, take a lesson in statesmanship from an ice-cream saloon?

CHAPTER XV.

Florida Towns and Country—A Florida Senator.

On our return from Savannah to Hilton Head, a few hours were spent in sending letters home, and preparing finally to cut loose from any Northern communications till we should reach New Orleans. General Gillmore decided to accompany the party through the whole of his Department. There was a final plunge in the bracing surf; a good-bye to the Dominie, who declared he couldn't stay longer away from his congregation, and so went back on the "Arago;" a parting dinner, at which we were regaled with the sayings, doings and endurings of Jeff. Davis and party. It seems that the Sea Island negroes heard of General Gillmore's dispatch, which mentioned Mr. Davis' capture and coming, and so were prepared for his arrival. They lined the shore in vast numbers, and, as soon as his vessel had approached within what they supposed to be hearing distance, the affectionate creatures—otherwise known, while in slavery, as the happiest people on the face of the earth—of their own motion struck up the song—

"We'll hang Jeff. Davis on a sour apple tree,"

with such a thunderous volume of sound, that there was no possibility of Mr. Davis' remaining ignorant of their amiable intention toward the one whom they regarded as typifying the whole race of their kind and benevolent masters.

When we had all mustered on deck, next morning, the ancient town of Fernandina, Florida, was rising from the water on our right, with the quaint old fort beside it, and the new town in the distance. A medium-sized, plain frame house was pointed out as the residence of Senator Yulee, and, among the rambling, forsaken-looking wooden buildings of the place, it really had a Senatorial look. Fernandina, Florida, had always sounded in the North like a name of consequence. I find that it means a straggling village, which, in New York or Ohio, might have a post-office, but certainly could not aspire to the dignity of a county-seat.

But it has, according to the pilots and to the Coast Survey, the best harbor on the whole Atlantic coast, south of Fortress Monroe. There are over twenty feet on the bar, and the anchorage is safe and ample. Whenever the country back of it becomes anything, Fernandina must be a considerable place.

Whether Florida should ever have been a State in the Union, is a grave question; but whether it should be one now, is, as it seems to me, no question at all. The total free population of the State, at the outbreak of the war, was seventy-eight thousand—a little more than a third as much as the city of Cincinnati, and only a few thousand over the present population of Cleveland or Albany. Giving such a constituency, scattered over a peninsula of swamps and everglades, and outlying barren islands, two Senators to balance the votes of Messrs. Wade and Sherman, or Sumner and Wilson, or Morgan and Harris, is very much like erecting Cleveland and Albany into independent governments, and saying they

shall exercise equal powers in Congress with the States
of Ohio and New York. Giving these Senators now,
when their constituents have nearly all been in the
Rebel army, and when, vehemently protesting against
negro suffrage, they shut out all possibility of loyal
votes, would be putting a reward on treason that we
can hardly afford to pay.

One fails to understand how contemptibly small is the
population scattered over this great expanse of territory, till he looks at the sizes of the principal towns. I
have spoken of Fernandina as a village. Its population is less than fourteen hundred, all told; its white
population less than eight hundred; and yet it is one
of the largest towns in the State! Here is a table of
the population of all the other "principal places:"

	White.	Total.
Apalachicola	1,379	1,904
Jacksonville	1,133	2,118
Key West	2,241	2,832
Pensacola	1,789	2,876
St. Augustine	1,175	1,914
Tallahassee	997	1,932

The citizens of Fernandina had recently been having an election for Mayor, and the old ways had been
destroyed by the participation of negroes in the election. The violent Rebels of the place were all away
in the Rebel army; the loyalists were very glad to be
re-enforced by the negroes, and so they had been the
first in the United States to exercise the right of suffrage. The Mayor elect, a M. Mot, was an enthusiastic
little Frenchman, devoted to the idea that Fernandina
might rival the olives of Seville, and that the olive oil
of Florida might yet be fully equal to that of old Spain.
He had not been sworn in, and so the Chief-Justice

performed the ceremony in the little wooden building at the water's edge—used for the custom house—in the presence of half a dozen witnesses. The little French-man may not make a fortune from his olive oil, but he enjoys the pre-eminence of being the first officer elected in the United States by universal loyal suffrage, and of having his election recognized by the highest judicial authority of the nation. The chances of the olive, how-ever, seem to be also good. M. Mot came on board with a little bottle of oil, which he displayed in great triumph. "Bettare oleeve oil dare vas nevare." And he seemed quite right. The old inhabitants say that every few years the frosts are likely to nip his olives; but we saw orchards of them growing beautifully in the open air, which had never been injured. If he should succeed, he will have added no inconsiderable element to the productive industry of Florida.

Fernandina has been held by our troops for a long time, but for over a year the Rebels were just across the Bay, and the pickets of the opposing forces were often separated by only this narrow sheet of water. Mr. Hallett Kilbourn, the Government purchasing agent, has thus found his area greatly circumscribed. He boasts that he has bought enough to pay the expenses of his office, but beyond this his operations are not likely to extend. Rebels are beginning to return, and disputes as to property are already common. Men who find that the Government, while they have been fighting to over-throw it, has used their property, complain bitterly of the injustice with which they are treated; and through the very importunity of their complaints, they are not unlikely to carry some of their claims.

A little negro school here, displayed the same rapid progress in the lower branches which has been observed all along the coast. Here, too, the negroes seemed deficient in love for the old masters, to whom we have been told that they were so much attached; and when informed of Jeff. Davis' capture, spontaneously struck up the same song as at Hilton Head—

"We'll hang Jeff. Davis on a sour apple tree."

Leaving Fernandina, and steaming up the St. Johns' river, we saw something of the cracker "plantations." The native forests generally ran down to the water's edge, but here and there, little lawn-like inclosures, extended back to clumps of trees, in the midst of which shabby frame houses could be seen—the "mansions" of the Floridian planters. Cultivated fields were rare, and the country seemed rather used for grazing than for any more strictly agricultural purposes. Pelicans were seen occasionally in the water, quite near the boat, and immense stories were told of the alligators one did not see. Scarcely a white man appeared along the whole route, and even the negroes were seen infrequently.

Starting from Fernandina at noon, we were at Jacksonville an hour before sundown. A few brick warehouses and stores make up the street fronting on the water, and a huge billiard saloon seems as much of an institution as the stores. Everywhere the sand was almost bottomless, and walking, for even a square or two, was exceedingly uncomfortable. A negro guard paced along the wharf; negroes in uniform were scattered about the streets, interspersed with a few Rebel soldiers, and a very neatly-policed negro camp occupied one of the vacant squares. These negroes are fine, stalwart men, better in physique than those at Savannah, and, in fact, rather superior to the lusty fellows at Port Royal. They seemed to speak a worse patois than the

Sea Islanders, and words of Spanish, in the mouths of some of them, testified to their being genuine sons of the soil, with a lineage running back in a straight line to the days of the Spanish occupation. There was scarcely a mulatto among them.

Within a few moments after our boat touched the wharf, a Tax Commissioner of Florida, and a curious, squatty military officer, with certainly the most extraordinary squeaking voice ever heard on a parade ground, came on board. The officer was General Israel.Vogdes, an old West Pointer, standing high in the technical points of his profession, and more than fair in its practice. He commanded the post, and proved as agreable in all other respects as he was vocally atrocious. He had established his headquarters in the best house in town; and the staff whiled away their leisure hours in the runaway Rebel's billiard room, or over his books.

Here, in the evening, came ex-Senator Yulee[25]—a Hebrew, who, like Belmont, has changed his name. When he represented the Territory of Florida in the House, he was known as Mr. Levy. When Florida was admitted as a State, and he had married into the family of old "Duke Wickliffe," of Kentucky, he turned up as Senator, under the name of Yulee, and remained in that body till, in 1861, he resigned to enter the Rebellion. Now, with his property in Fernandina confiscated, his office, influence, means of livelihood all gone, the ex-Senator comes out of the Rebellion, and out of the interior, where he has been hiding, to have an interview with the Chief Justice, whom, as fellow-member of the Senate, he had treated as "outside of any healthy political organization."

Mr. Yulee was, of course, polite and plausible, but it

[25] David Levy Yulee, U. S. Senator from Florida at the time of Secession. [Ed.]

was amusing to see how ignorant he was that during the last four years anything had happened! Slavery was dead—that much was hastily admitted—but what other change the causeless Rebellion could have, or ought to have wrought, he didn't see. That there was any modification of the old order of things—that Southern men were not to be heeded whenever they stamped their feet—that every Rebel had not the same rights under the Constitution with every loyal man—were things which, in his seclusion in the interior, had never occurred to him. He had been appointed a Commissioner to see whether the Administration would not permit the Governor and Legislature to resume control of the State, and dispense with further military interference! While we were at Hilton Head, General Gillmore had issued an order overturning the effort of the fugitive South Carolina Governor to continue *his* control of his State; and Senator Yulee had just heard of it. He was greatly disturbed, and begged Mr. Chase to tell him whether it could be possible that the Administration would sustain Gen. Gillmore, and thus, by refusing to recognize the only constitutional authorities of the State, plunge them all into anarchy again!

But worse horrors remained for the sanguine Senator to encounter. He had not recovered from the shock of learning that, instead of being again clothed with the authority of the State, he and his fellow conspirators stood a better chance of being dealt with for treason, when the negro question came up. He was desirous that the State officials should control the freedmen. It was suggested that the freedmen, being in some sections in the majority, and in all having the advantage of loyalty, might better control the State officials. "Why, they'll all starve. They are shiftless, improvident, idle, and incapable of taking care of themselves." The experiences of Port Royal were recited. He was incredulous. He did n't know what the Port Royal negroes were like; but it was exceedingly strange if any negroes could save enough during the summer to support them through the winter.

His desire to be polite, and to avoid committing himself to any unpleasant declarations, made the ex-Senator very cautious; and toward the close he seemed too much surprised and bewildered, by what he heard, to have much to say. He came down to Jacksonville, seeing no reason why he should not run up to Tallahassee, help the Governor engineer the State back into the Union, and, through the elections, patch up some policy for "taking care of the negroes," and then prepare to resume his seat in the United States Senate at the beginning of the next session. He returns to the country, assured that neither he nor the Governor will be recognized as State officials, and somewhat alarmed lest they may be recognized as traitors.*

Meanwhile, one of our party, who had been strolling about the town, came in with a curious case. A returned Rebel soldier had found a pretty little cracker girl, scarcely fourteen years old, and not yet emancipated from short dresses and pantalets, to whom he had taken a violent liking, and whom, by promises of toys and a new dress, he had induced clandestinely to marry him. The poor girl's mother was distressed, took the girl away, and refused to recognize the marriage. The

---

* Senator Yulee was arrested, a few days after this interview (under orders forwarded before the authorities knew anything of his meeting with Mr. Chase), and was confined in Fort Pulaski, to await the process of Floridian re-organization, in which the Government did not propose that he should share.

Rebel soldier came into town, found the girl and her mother here, and seized upon the child, vowing that she must straightway come home with him, or he would kill her. The people of the town did not seem to think the affair unusual, or requiring any attention; nobody was going to interfere, and the fellow was about to force away the child from her mother. Perhaps the incident is as good an illustration of the Florida cracker stage of civilization as could have been found.

General Vogdes procured horses, and a party, including one of the Florida ladies, went out riding, just as the sun was going down. The roads were bad; where there was no sand, there were stumps and mud holes; and the country, wherever we rode, was flat, uninteresting and unimproved. Returning, we found the straggling little town had put on new attractions. The trees that belt all its streets had hidden the omnipresent sand; the moonlight, glimmering through the foliage, concealed all the shabbiness and doubled all the beauties of the dilapidated, but shrubbery-embowered houses; the air was delightfully balmy—more than realizing all that has been said of the Florida climate; and, in short, we kept riding about for an hour, by moonlight. Then, how to get back was the question. My companion lived in the town; surely she ought to know its dozen streets, but she didn't. "There's our house, just beyond that clump of trees!" We rode up, and found it wasn't. Protracted searching ensued; then, "Oh, here it is; I know it by the piazza." But when we rode up, it was found the moonlight and shadows had been deceptive. At last she heard a familiar voice: "Beckie, is that you?" "Laws, missus, what you doin' out heah. Thort sure yous gwine home an hour ago."

"Beckie, I'm not lost, but I can't see in the shade, and have just got turned around a little. Which way is our house?" "Haw, haw," in chorus from half a dozen African females. "Laws, Missus, to think of yous a gittin' lost in Jacksonville! Why, chile, deres de house right round de cohnah, whar it allus was!"

"Right round de cohnah" we started; but somehow we didn't get there. I've done a good deal of horse-back riding, in a good many out-of-the-way places; on prairies where there wasn't a landmark; in pine woods, where there were so many I couldn't see; through the labyrinthine mazes of roads cut in the forests by the several advancing brigade trains of a great army; through unfamiliar swamps, without a road, under heavy fire, where I was compelled to rely on my pocket compass, to know how to get out from the sweep of the batteries; but I never got lost before. That sensation was reserved for enjoyment at the village of Jacksonville, and within the corporate (and sandy) limits of the same, in the State of Florida. We rode blindly around, for about two hours, till General Vodges sent out soldiers to look for us. When, at last, we cantered up in grand style, we strenuously declared that the evening was so charming we couldn't think of coming in sooner.

CHAPTER XVI.

Orange Groves and an Ancient Village—The Oldest Town and
Fort in the United States—Northern Speculations.

FROM Jacksonville, we steamed down the coast to St.
Augustine. "The oldest town in the United States,"
managed, in the good old times, to secure handsome
gratuities from the national authorities. A long granite wall, splendidly built, by Government contractors,
lines the whole water face of the village, and gives
wharfage for a place of twenty, instead of a paltry two
thousand inhabitants. Toward the upper end of the
harbor stands the quaint Spanish fort, the oldest fortification on our sea-coast, "bastioned on the square," as
the engineers describe it, with Spanish inscription by
the old drawbridge,* and Spanish coat of arms over

* "Reynando en Espana el Fernando Sexto y Siendo Gov^{or} y
Cap^n de Es^a C^d Sa^{an} ang^n de la Florida y Sus Prov^a el mariscal
de Campo D^n Alonzo Fern^{do} Hereda Asi Concluio Este Castillo El
Anod 1756 Diri^s endo Las obras el Cap Ingru^{ro} Dn Pedro de Brazos,
y Garay."

"Don Ferdinand the Sixth, being King of Spain, and the Field
Marshal Don Alonzo Fernando Hereda being Governor and Captain General of this place, St. Augustine, of Florida, and its prov-
inces, this fort was finished in the year 1756. The works were
directed by the Captain Engineer, Don Pedro Brazos y Garay."

The Fort first erected was called San Juan de Pinos. The same
name attached to the present Fort at the commencement of its erection.
Subsequently it was called St. Mark; and finally, upon the acquisition

the gate, and rusty Spanish guns still standing on the parapets; Spanish dungeons beneath, with rings to which men were chained, and French inscriptions, penciled more than a century ago, in solitary despair, on the dungeon walls, and still telling their own story of the sufferings of the times.

Climbing the old look-out tower of concrete shells, which stands nearly perfect yet on the sea face of the fort, one sees a collection of curious little antique houses, built so closely together that the streets between them can hardly be made out, a widening circle of orchard-like spots of green in the midst of seemingly waste expanse, a tumble-down collection of old grave stones, and beyond all, the dark-green line of the forests. This is St Augustine, with its Spanish streets, and orange groves, and relics of three hundred years of growth and decay.

Even to this quaint old Sleepy Hollow of the extreme South the war has penetrated with its changes. On the Plaza del Armas, where, of old, Spanish soldiers, in cumbrous accouterments, had trained their firelocks, and marched beneath the Red and Orange, with the arms of Spain, and where, later, Spanish monks, to the tolling of the bell, that still remains, had formed their long processions, and solemnly moved out in stately show, to pronounce the doom of God alike upon sacriligious invaders and the pagan infidels, who inhabited the country; this very Plaza was surrounded by long

of Florida by the United States, Fort Marion. Don Juan Marquez Cabera commenced the construction of the present Fort in 1681. The Apalachian Indians were employed upon it for more than sixty years. The first Fort was built by Don Pedro Melendez de Avila, in 1565. In the same year, the foundation of St. Augustine was laid. It is thus, by more than forty years, the oldest town in the United States.

rows of stalwart negroes, black as ebony, splendidly armed, and drawn up in handsome regimental lines for dress parade. There is an island, not far off the coast of Florida, where the Spanish colors still float, and where this spectacle of soldiers made from slaves might prove suggestive.

When St. Augustine was laid out, the theory of those days was that, without excessively narrow streets, it was impossible to have a cool town in these low latitudes. The narrower the streets, they argued, the more perfect the draught through them; and so it comes that, from the projecting second-story balconies on the one side, in the main street of St. Augustine, you can almost step to the similar balconies on the other side. In the street itself there is no room for sidewalks, and I am not even sure that carts can pass each other.* Behind each house is a luxuriant garden; great masses of flowers hang over the walls or depend from the trellises; and, through the open doors, one gets glimpses of hammocks, swinging under vine-clad trees, and huge, but airy, Sleepy-Hollow chairs. Curious little piazzas jut into the narrrow streets, and dark Spanish faces, with coal-black brows and liquid eyes, look out from the windows.

One such, a pretty Madame Oliveras, whose husband has gone to the Rebel army, and concerning whose fate, on his (now daily expected) return, his fond wife is prettily anxious, displays a tempting array of palmetto

---

*This is a specimen of Spanish sanitary precautions, but those of Anglo-Saxon origin in the South were little better. Till within a very recent period, Southern physicians have held that it was unhealthy, in low latitudes, to pave the streets of a city, because the dust and sand were needed to absorb the unhealthy moisture! And to this day New Orleans is the only Southern city that can be said to be paved at all.

work in her rag-carpeted little parlor—toy baskets, hats, napkin rings, fans and the whole catalogue of palmetto fancy work—drawing numerous greenbacks from the Yankees, and evoking, in consequence, much warm politeness from the grateful grass widow. There are not many Rebels here, she thinks; but the fact that any number of wives, like her, are expecting returning husbands, "now that paroles have been given," remains unexplained. Of course the Government will never think of interfering with their little plantations; surely, they meant no harm, and knew no better than to fight for their State, as they were told!

Passing through an old cemetery, where obelisks of granite, without a word of inscription, have stood for nearly three hundred years; where old tombs have fallen to pieces in the lapse of time, and human bones protrude amid the decaying masonry; while, over all, the rich vegetation of the semi-tropical climate throws a kindly concealing veil of beauty, we come out into groves of exquisite fragrance. The ground is covered with oranges, and the fruit is still clinging to the trees in bunches that bend down and almost break the branches. The oranges are of a size, and especially of a flavor, never found at the North; and the deliciously dreamy, luxuriously indolent retreats one finds amid these orange groves, and in the pleasant cottages of the owners, make St. Augustine seem a town of another continent and century.

One of the orange groves was pointed out as that purchased by Major John Hay, late the President's private secretary. It had been sold for unpaid taxes by the Land Commissioner—the taxes having remained unpaid for the sufficient reason that the owner was away in the Rebel army—and Major Hay had secured it by an investment of some five hundred dollars. Last year, as an enthusiastic Floridian explained, the orange crop was worth two thousand five hundred dollars! But, unfortunately for my dormant enthusiasm, Hay had told me of his financial success in Florida before I left Washington. "Incidental expenses" had required him to advance another sum about equal to the original purchase money, and while the orange crop might, for all he knew, have been a very fine one, he had never seen an orange or received a penny from it! The Floridian pointed out beautiful little groves that were soon to be sold, and dilated on their advantages; but the party produced no purchasers.

There is great uncertainty, of course, about the titles in these tax sales, and many people find it dificult to regard the transactions as very creditable to the Government. There is no doubt, however, that, if the titles stand, investments made in the lands about St. Augustine must be profitable. The exquisite climate will always make the place a resort for debilitated people, and particularly consumptives from the North; and the orange crop, although occasionally injured by the frost, is so nearly certain that, for those who can have it properly attended to, it must, at the present prices for investments, prove unusually profitable. At the rates now ruling, the gross returns of a single year's crop will nearly pay for the land. Whoever purchases, however, will here, as elsewhere through the South, have to bear the odium among the returning Rebels, who will soon make up again the bulk of the population, of having taken advantage of their misfortunes and helplessness to get possession of their property for nothing. Under such circumstances, let the climate be never so delightful, and the profits never so inviting, a sensitive man might still find residence in St. Augustine unpleasant.

The negroes here seem to have a vague idea that they are free; but little change in their relations to their old masters is perceptible. In the back country they remain, as usual, on the little cracker plantations, and neither masters nor negroes succeed in more than making a rude living.

Little boys were "playing marbles" in the streets with green oranges, as we returned to the wharf, and a crowd of people, who had seen no other opportunity for months to get North, were begging permission to go on board our boat, and return with us to Fernandina.

CHAPTER XVII.

Dungeness, and the "Greatest of the Lees"—Cultivation of the Olive—Criminations of the Officers.

WHEN Nathaniel Greene, one of the best and most trusted of Washington's Generals, retired to civil life, it was with an estate seriously embarrassed by his patriotic sacrifices. During his brilliant campaign in the Southern Department, the battles of the Cowpens, Guilford Court-House and Eutaw Springs, destroyed the British power in Georgia and the Carolinas. At its close there was only left to Washington the easier task of concentrating all his forces upon Cornwallis in Virginia, and so ending the war. But in carrying on this campaign, General Greene had been compelled to exhaust his private means in his efforts to clothe and feed his army. Congress voted him thanks and medals; North and South Carolina and Georgia voted him waste lands. He died in Georgia. Congress, enlarging its bounty, then voted him a monument. The grateful people whom he saved, had actually forgotten where they buried him; the monument was never built; and to this day "no man knoweth the place of his burial."

His wife removed to one of the Georgia land grants, a little island on the extreme Southern border of the State, but a few miles from Fernandina. Here she married again, builded, planted olive trees and died; and when they came to put a head-stone to her grave, they inscribed it to the memory of "Catharine Miller, widow of the late Major-General Nathaniel Greene. Poor Miller was never mentioned, and General Greene, whose grave was not worth a head-stone, had a name good enough to lend special honor to the monument of his re-married and then wealthy wife.

Our last trip along the upper coast of Forida was to steam over to this little island, given by Georgia to Greene, and passed subsequently into the hands of Rebels, who have now deserted it to the negroes.

Landing at a tumble-down dock, and climbing the bluff, we came to a corn-field, cleanly cultivated by the negroes, skirted a little wood, giving wide berth to a black-snake in the path, and then, through some tangled shrubbery, suddenly came out in front of what had been intended for a fine mansion. It was built of shell concrete, and but partly finished, when the family deserted it at the approach of the national forces. Since then the negroes have been too busy supporting themselves to give much thought to house building, and now the mansion of their "masters" is likely to remain unbuilt forever.

But no neglect could destroy the magnificent shrubbery. Beneath the few spreading live-oaks, were superb oleanders, as large as Northern apple-trees, and in full bloom. Great bayonet plants reminded us that we were still in the spiteful land of the Palmetto. Cactus reached above our heads, cloth of gold roses, mimosa and a score of Southern flowering shrubs, to which our Northern amateur florists could give no names, made up a tangled mass of luxuriant loveliness all about the house. Beyond these stretched the rows of olive trees. "Here you can make *beaucoup de l' argent*," exclaims our enthusiastic little French Mayor

of Fernandina; and straightway whips you out a bottle
of oil from his vest pocket to prove it. The happy
dreamer imagines olive oil the Philosopher's stone, and
is sure that now, with these olive trees of Dungeness,
and the young ones he is planting at Fernandina, the
future of Florida is secure. And, indeed, so far as being
able to grow olives and make oil is concerned, it is.
The orchard here has received no attention since the
flight of the Rebel owners, but the olive crop this year,
in spite of the neglect, will be good. and the trees look
vigorous and hardy.

Through a wilderness of forest trees and dense undergrowth, a blind path led to a little cleared eminence,
shut in by a wall of the same shell concrete—the family
grave-yard. Conspicuous among the dozen moss-cov-
ered monuments is that of Mrs. General Greene, already
referred to. Near it is another, inscribed to the foremost of Greene's Generals, beside whose grave we may
well stop thoughtfully and long:

> " Sacred to the memory of
> GENERAL HENRY LEE,
> of Virginia,
> Obiit 25 Mar.
> 1818,
> Ætat 63."

It is the grave of Henry Lee—"Light-Horse Harry,"
of the Revolution—greatest of the partisan leaders of
those days, Governor of Virginia, inmate of Spottsylvania jail, and noblest of the "Virginia Lees." Four
years after the wife of his old commander had died here,
he returned from the West Indies, poverty stricken, neglected and dying, sought this island, the former home of
his chief, and was buried in the burying ground of the

Greenes. One gratefully remembers that the injuries of which he is believed to have finally died, were received in a gallant defense of the freedom of the press, against the assault of a Baltimore mob upon a Liberal newspaper office.

Long, coarse grass grows rank over these historic graves; lizards play about the chinks of the dilapidated tombs; the outer wall is partly broken down; but the peaceful solitude of the graves is not disturbed, and the spot is controlled, if by an alien, at least by a loyal people.

While a few of us lingered beside the slab, above the remains of "Legion Harry," the rest of the party had completed their explorations of the lonely little island; and the boat was whistling loudly for our return. The "last of the Lees" had done nothing to honor the neglected grave of the greatest of them; but Yankee hands still delayed the steamer to arrange lovingly a chaplet of flowers on the rude tombstone.

At Fernandina there was talk among the traders of a large quantity of resin, eighteen hundred barrels, some of them said, which had been bought by a well-known *attaché* of the State Department, and out of which, if their stories were true, he was likely to make a fortune. He had paid 42 cents a barrel for it, they said, and could sell it in New York for twenty-five dollars. I fancy this must be grossly exaggerated, although a Government official was my informant; but these irregular bargains, made by persons having special facilities, with the distressed holders of produce in the interior, have often disclosed marvelous profits, and the most unscrupulous use, by the buyers, of the advantages of their positions. To drive as hard bargains as the Yankees, is likely to be thought henceforth, in these regions, something more than a good figure of speech.

On the other hand, there are constant dissentions here, and charges against each other of improper practices among the Government officers themselves. The military men abuse the Treasury agents roundly, accuse them of enormous speculations on their own account, and the most unwarranted system of spying into the operations of others.*

*The tax Commissioners, and other civil functionaries, fare little better; while the military men, accord-

---

*An account in the Port Royal *New South* of an April-fool performance at Fernandina (said to be a literal record of an actual occurrence), is greatly gloated over by the military authorities, as a specimen of what they call the meanness and imbecility of the civil officials. It illustrates, at least, the state of feeling between the services. The account sets forth that a Mr. Goodrich had brought into Fernandina, from Nassau, a small schooner, in ballast. The Collector had suspicions of intended contraband trade. He was stimulated by pretended disclosures, to the point of bringing Mr. Goodrich before the Provost Marshal for an examination. The *New South* proceeds:

"Mr. Wells testified that Mr. Goodrich had, in a season of friendly confidence, exhibited to him, at his house, a pipe of whisky, which he admitted having brought on shore from his schooner, after dark, and without the knowledge of the Collector of the Customs, the said pipe of whisky being ignored in the vessel's manifest; and that Goodrich further disclosed that he had two more pipes in the house, that would be brought into requisition when this was exhausted.

"Mr. Goodrich admitted that he had no witnesses to examine, and very little to say in his defense, but he would like to interrogate the witnesses who had testified against him. Permission being granted, the following conversation ensued:

"*Mr. Goodrich*—Do you swear positively, Mr. Wells, that you saw the pipe of whisky?

"*Mr. Wells*—I do, solemnly.

ing to the stories of the civilians, believe the modern substitute for glory to be—"loot."

All accounts, both here, at Jacksonville and at St. Augustine, agree that the country contains little more than is needed for the sustenance of the inhabitants. Trade may come by and by, when Florida begins to be used again as a grand national sanatarium; but for a year or two, the openings for business with the Floridians are likely to require very little of the capital now looking for Southern investments.

There was a parting tune from the band as we left General Gillmore's boat, kindly good-byes with General and staff officers. Altogether the pleasantest party met, thus far, on the trip. The "Wayanda" fired a gun as she began hoisting her anchor, and we were off for a sail of five hundred miles, along what used to be considered the most dangerous coast of the United States.

"*Collector*—That's conclusive—I don't think it worth while to waste time; I've decided to seize the vessel.

"*Mr. Goodrich*—I insist on my right. Were you permitted to satisfy yourselves that the pipe contained whisky?

"*Witnesses*—We were,

"*Collector*—I think, Mr. Provost Marshal, this case is a clear one.

"*Mr. Goodrich*—I'll make it clearer, sir. Gentlemen, would you recognize that pipe of whisky if you saw it again, so as to be able to swear to it.?

"*Witnesses*—We should.

"*Mr. Goodrich*—(taking an old Briar Wood from his pocket). Was that the pipe?

"*Witnesses*—(emphatically)—*That's the identical pipe.*

"*Collector*—(with very long face and very large eyes)—What do you say?

"*Witnesses*—That's the pipe that Mr. Goodrich had whisky in.

"*Collector*—(rushing out of the office)—Go to——. The rest of the sentence was lost in the distance.

CHAPTER XVIII.

The Southern "Ultima Thule" of the United States.

ALONG the Florida coast there were occasional glimpses of solitary light-houses and barren beaches; once we got aground where there ought to have been deep water, and were pleasantly assured that, if we had to take to the land, we would be among the everglades, with no chance of finding any inhabitants but moccasin snakes, and possibly a stray Seminole; for the rest, we had schools of porpoises plunging about our feet, the superb phosphorescence of the waters, and fine fishing—each haul of a dolphin or a Spanish mackerel from our stern line creating as much sensation on deck as one would have expected from the *Stonewall*. And so, with favoring breezes and the most delicious weather, we coasted among the keys, and finally steamed into the harbor of Key West.

The United States District Attorney, pleasantly known in Washington, where he occupied a responsible position in the Treasury Department, during the dark days of the war, as "Plantz, of Florida," came aboard the "Wayanda" as soon as she touched the wharf. He was full of the glories of Florida, and the hopes of the re-organizing State; but, in this climate, there were things more important than politics. "It's your sacred duty, you know, to take care of your health in this tropical country; and there's nothing so good to begin

with as our acclimatizing drink, which is the greatest
of all the institutions of Key West." "Champerou,"
it appeared, was the name of this acclimatizer. Its con-
coction appeared a miracle of the powers of combination. Curacoa was taken as the base; Absinthe, Maras-
chino and other *liqueurs* were added, with sugar and
eggs thrown in, till an analytical chemist would have
been hopelessly puzzled by the compound. But it proved
acclimatizing; and I observed that even the natives
still thought it wise to take prudent precautions—such
as a glass of Champerou—against the effects of the
climate.

As a coaling station at the entrance of the Gulf, and
the location of the United States civil officers for the
Southern District of Florida, Key West had attained
such importance before the war as to have attracted,
according to the census of 1860, a population of two
thousand eight hundred and thirty-two. Notwithstanding the departure of many rebels, the town has
increased during the war to a population of about three
thousand five hundred. It is neatly built, and better
paved than most Southern places of like size. There is
a street of good-looking frame business houses; a large
hotel offers naval officers and others, who happen in
port, a variation from ship fare; and a club house, sustained by the civil, military and naval services, supplies many of the comforts that would hardly be expected
on this last desolate sand bank of Florida, and extreme
Southern possession of the United States. Yet it took
all the familiar sights and conveniences to enable one
to realize that it was an American town. Bananas were
for sale in the shops nearly four months earlier than we
expect at the North the unripe, leathery fruit, which is
all Northern people can get for the banana; limes, and

sapadillos, and "sour sops," were the common fruits of
the season; the houses were here and there hedged in,
not with arbor vitæ, or box, or even Cherokee rose, but
with great, branching, luxuriant cactus, as high as a
man's head; for shade trees in the front yards, they had
the palm-like cocoa.

The Spanish Consul sent down his carriage, and the
supply of other vehicles in the little island was pretty
well exhausted in providing conveyances for the party.
Our drive took us around the whole island. Spots of
dark green constantly dotted the water near the beach—
the uninhabited "keys." Some of them did not seem
to be more than half an acre in extent; others would
make nice little farms, but for snakes, and sharks, and
storms, in which the Atlantic Ocean and Gulf of Mexico
would combine in washing over the crops. The stunted
shrubbery (which, my fair campanion in the ride told
me she had learned, after a year's residence, to call the
"Forests of Key West"), was, apparently, no where
more than ten or twelve feet high. Wild cocoas were
abundant. Gigantic, and not attractive looking, cactus
covered the rocks, and forbade strolls out of the beaten
track. Tamarinds, hibiscus, sugar-apples, pawpaws,
(totally different from the Northern tree of that name,)
sapadillos, lime trees, buttonwoods, mastics, with lignum
vitæ, gum elemi and sal soda plant, made up a vegetation as varied as it was novel to Northern eyes.

Old salt vats, where, before the war, the slaves, in the
rude, shiftless way which slavery perpetuated, made salt
enough for the consumption of Key West, by letting in
sea water and evaporating it, lined the coast for perhaps a mile.

Elsewhere there was nothing but the dwarfed veg-

etation to be seen, till we came to what had been spoken
of at the outset as the main feature of the ride around
the island—"Old Sandie's farm." A rude fence separated this from the surrounding waste land, but the soil
was equally stony, and apparently sterile; and it was
hard to see how any exertions could make it productive.
So everybody in Key West had always thought, and till
"Sandie" came the islanders did'nt grow their own vegetables.

The carriages drew up at a little hut with two rooms,
which was announced as "Sandie's house," and "Auntie"
(his wife), who came to the door, led us to a little, open
"lean-to," which she called a piazza.

Presently there came hurrying up a stalwart negro,
with the *physique* of a prize fighter; body round as a
barrel, arms knotted with muscles that might have
belonged to a race-horse's leg, chest broad and deep,
with room inside for the play of an ox's lungs. So
magnificent a physical development I have never seen,
before or since. The head was large, but the broad
forehead was very low. Above it rose the crisp, grizzled
wool, almost perpendicularly, for a hight quite as great
as that of the exposed part of the forehead; and the
bumps above the ears and at the back of the head were
of a corresponding magnitude. The face was unmis-
takably African, glossy black, with widely-distended
nostrils, thick lips and a liquid but gleaming eye. This
was Sandie himself, an old man—"now in my sebenty-
tree yeah, sah," he said—yet the strongest man on the
island, the richest of the negroes, the best farmer here,
and with a history as romantic as that of any Indian
whom song and story have combined to make famous.

He was a native of Maryland; had bought himself
for three thousand two hundred dollars from his master,

and had earned and paid over the money; had removed to Florida, and been engaged at work on a railroad, where he had already accumulated what for him was a handsome competence, when his little house burned down, and his free papers were lost in the fire. A gang of unprincipled vagabonds at once determined, there being no accessible evidence of his freedom to be produced against them, to seize him, sell him in the New Orleans market and pocket the proceeds. He frustrated their attempt by whipping the whole party of six; then hearing that they were to be re-enforced and were to try it again, he deliberately proceeded to the public square, accompanied by his wife, cut the muscles of his ankle joint, plunged a knife into the hip joint on the other side, and then, sinking down on a wheel-barrow, finished the work by chopping off with a hatchet the fingers of his left hand! Meanwhile, an awe-struck crowd of white men gathered around, but made no attempt at interference. Finally, brandishing the bloody knife, Sandie shouted to the crowd that if they persisted in their effort to sell a free man into slavery after he had once, at an extortionate price, bought himself out of it, his right arm was yet strong, and he had one blow reserved, after which they were welcome to sell him for whatever he would bring.

That the essentials of this story are true, there is unquestionable evidence. The fingers on his left hand are mutilated, and the scars on the hip and ankle are still fearfully distinct, while besides there are still white eye-witnesses to testify to the main facts. Sandie's powerful constitution brought him through; he was confined to bed six months; then he began to hobble about a little, and at the end of the year was again able to support himself.

He showed us through what he proudly called his plantation. Ripe sapadillos hung from the trees; and a particularly large "sour-sop" was pointed out as specially intended for our dinner. He had a little patch of tobacco; green cocoanuts rested at the tops of the palm-like stems, and tamarinds were abundant; the African cayenne pepper berry was hanging on little bushes, and one or two of the party who had been promiscuously experimenting on Sandie's fruit, came to grief when they reached it, and were heard complaining that their "mouths were on fire." Plucking two or three berries of another kind, Sandie handed them to the Chief Justice. "Take dem home and plant 'em in your garden, and you'll hab you own coffee aftah while." "But coffee won't grow, Sandie, where I live." "Don't know bout dat, sah. Dat's just what dey told me heah; but you see it does. I didn't know no reason why it shouldn't, and so I try. Now, you just try, too!"

Finally, he asked for a picture of his guest, and the Chief Justice handed him a one-dollar greenback. The scene that followed was curious. Old Sandie, bare-headed and with his shirt thrown loosely back from his brawny bosom, stooped down, spread the bill out on one knee, and gazed from it to Mr. Chase and back to the bill again for some moments, in perfect silence. "Now I knows you," he broke out at last, "you's Old Greenback hisself. You mout come heah fifty yeah from now and I'd know you just de same, and tell you all about sittin' in dis yeah piazza heah."

In curious contrast with such impressions as Sandie's farm and story might leave, was the talk of another old man, like Sandie, "in his sebenty-tree yeah," and, like him, hale and hearty; but white, a native of Connecticut, and, till the war, a slaveholder. He was the harbor-master; and in the intervals of shouting at the negroes to hurry up putting coal in the "Wayanda," he wiped his brow and denounced "the niggers." The ungrateful creatures he had owned, had expected to live with him and work for themselves after the emancipation, but he had told them that if, after his care of them all their lives, they didn't mean to work for him now, they could just pack out of his house at once. They were all saucy and worthless; wouldn't work a bit more than enough to keep soul and body together; charged two or three prices always, and still would rather steal than work any day; would dance all night and be good for nothing next day; were fearfully licentious; and, in short, were an unmitigated nuisance. The island was over-populated with runaways, too, from the main land, and before long there would be any amount of suffering among them. Sandie was a great liar and swindler, but managed—the black scoundrel— to make a better appearance than the rest. It might, perhaps, be true, that he had once bought himself and gone through some of the subsequent persecutions he was so fond of talking about; but, for his part, he had his private doubts about the whole story. If these worthless vagabonds were to be allowed to have a share in the future government of the State, no man could tell what a miserable future was before the whole community.

On the other hand, Judge Boynton,[26] the United States District Judge, District Attorney Plantz, and numerous other gentlemen, declared that there was no unnecessary crowding of negroes from the main land; that they were quite as industrious as could be expected, and that all

26 Thomas Boynton, originally from Ohio. [Ed.]

who were on the island could find work at remunerative prices. That they make money the village itself attests. In driving about it, we passed dozens of new frame houses, built and occupied by negroes, who had bought, with their own earnings, the lots on which their dwellings stood. As to the general character of the negroes, the common testimony seemed to be that their behavior would compare favorably with that of any other class of the laboring population.

Key West is so directly dependent upon the Government, that its public sentiment is hardly a fair reflex of the feeling of the South Floridians. Yet, as it practically manages the politics of the lower half of the peninsula, it was worth notice that a large proportion of the inhabitants seemed still to sympathize to a marked extent with the fallen Rebels. All were looking eagerly forward to re-organization, and it was plain that the contest then would lie between the new-comers and the old citizens. Ranking themselves among the former were likely to be the "Conks"—i. e., natives of the Bahama islands—who make a considerable part of the business population. All regarded slavery as dead; the old citizens thought the negroes ought to be put under State control, and thus practically re-enslaved; the new-comers wanted emancipation honestly carried out, and were willing for negro suffrage.

There were all manner of courtesies by the military and naval authorities, salutes from the fort, drives about the spacious and airy barracks, calls from Consuls and others, shells from Mr. Howe (the Collector of the Port), beautiful pressed seaweeds, Florida crabtree canes, dinners, fruits, etc. The visit was a delightful one, but it wouldn't bear repetition. It's a very pleasant thing to stand on the southernmost point of land on the continent over which the flag of the Union floats, but once is enough. And so good-bye to "Plantz, of Florida," Judge Boynton and all the rest. May my feet never again be turned to their homes, but may their's be often turned to mine! And every one of them get honors and profits from Florida

CHAPTER XIX.

A Remarkable Negro Story—One of the Strange Possibilities of Slavery.

THE story of "Uncle Sandie," given in the preceding Chapter, seemed to me one of the most remarkable exhibitions ever made public of the results which inhere, as possibilities, in the system of slavery. On a subsequent visit to Key West, Sandie was persuaded to repeat his account of his self-mutilation at length, and the following phonographic report of it was taken down from his lips. I have endeavored to preserve throughout his exact language

It is only needful to add that Sandie is at once one of the wealthiest and one of the most respected citizens of Key West. He has contributed largely to the erection of a handsome church for the negro congregation, of which he is the leading spirit; and in the management of his private affairs, even the Rebel residents admit that he displays singular prudence and skill. Since the war, his remarkable history has attracted many visitors—among whom were some of our most distinguished naval officers—and brought him many attentions that might readily have turned the head of a less judicious person; but Sandie pursues his quiet way, modest as ever, and still industrious and money-making.

When the following report of his story was made, he appeared in the village in a faultless suit of broadcloth,

with a well-brushed silk hat. But for his color, he
might have been thought a superbly-developed prize-
fighter, transformed in some way into a quiet preacher.
The production of the note-book startled him a little,
but rubbing his head a moment, as if to recall the
dates, and standing, hat in hand, under the cocoas, he
began.

"I left Maryland on de 2d day of October, '39. My
wife went wid me. She was free, and we came to Florida. I got to work at Port Leon, on de railroad. Dere
I worked nine yeahs to buy myself. I got six hundred
dollahs, and de yeah's findin'. Lily, my wife, got fifteen
dollahs a month. My massa charged me thirty-three
hundred and fifty dollahs for myself, which Lily had to
see paid.

"She made herself a slave to go wid me. After we
had paid de money, and got our papers—dat tuck us
nine yeahs—and we had sumfin over, de town cotch
fire and burnt my papers, and pretty smart money.
All de money was burnt, 'cept a little silver and gold.
Afterward, when dey found de papers was burnt, den
they come upon us to sell us to New Orleans. Dey come
one night after I'd been out fishin'.

"I was settin' stripped off, washin' my feet. Fifteen
men rapped at de do. I said, 'Cum in,' and tole 'em to
take a seat. Dey tole me a hog had been stole dat
mornin', and dat I had bought one, and dey wanted me
to go up to de Squire's, and tell him where I bought it.
I sed I had thirty-nine head Buckshire hogs, and didn't
want no more hogs, so, of cose, I hadn't got no more.
Den dey axed me if I was against goin' to see de Squar,
and let him know I didn't buy any. I tole him yes, I
wasn't against dat, and started in my shirt sleeves, and
bare head, to go and see him.

"Wen we got to de street whar it turned off to de Squire's, de fellows took me toward de jail. I tole 'em dat wasn't the way to de Squire's, and dey said de Squire would be at de Cou't House, dat was near de jail.

"Den dey ax me ef I was aginst bein' tied, and I tole 'em no. Den dey brought out a new Manilla, good tyin' rope, and placed my hands behind me, tied my hands, and lashed my arms wid de slack, clean up to de arm-pits. Den dey said, "Sandie, we got you fixed."

"I looked over my shoulder and said, 'What you about with your rascally tricks?' Dey sed, "We gwine to sell you to New Orleans; one-half goes to us, and one-half to your guardian." Dey sed dey'd take me to jail, and de next mornin' to de railroad, and would send me to New Orleans.

"Sez I, 'I ain't gwine,' and I wouldn't move for 'em. Den de man behind tuck a club and broke my head heah (showing a deep scar about three inches long, on the side of his head), and ax me again would I move. I wouldn't, and another at my side struck me till he broke my head in another place (showing another scar under the wool). De blood run down my face, and I licked it in on each side wid my tongue.

"Den I gave an Injin yell, tell dey heerd me down at ——'s plantation, five miles off. Den I straightened up, and stooped down and broke de cord into five pieces. Den I cotch one man by de breast, and made an instrument ob him, and swung him around and beat de oders ober de head and breast wid his heels. I beat dem down on de ground, and frowed him hard ober de palins.

"Den I went back to de house and tole my wife. I tole her not be accited, but just mind me. I axed her for my box ob needles, wid de crooked needles and de lances. It was about nine o'clock wen I was in de contuct. Dis was about ten.

"After she got dem, I axed her for de stickin' plaster, and she began to 'spicion, and sed I was mad. I tole her not, as she tought, not mad dat way. Den I put de needles and de stickin' plaster into a box and went to bed. Lily she cried all night. Next mornin' was Thursday. When I got up I call for her and for de box. We went togedder, and to de public squar; and I gave free yells, so dey cud be heard all ober town. Every body gathered around de squar. Wen de people was all standin' roun', but some little distance off, I tole 'em I didn't want dis (putting his hand on his right leg), nor dis (left arm), nor dis (left leg), but did want dis (right arm).

"Den I libitly run my knife froo de heelstrings and cut em out; Den I stoop down on de wheel barrow, wid my needles, and seew it up, and stuck de stickin' plaster on it.

"Den I tuck a knife and drove it into my right hip heah (showing over the hip joint a very ugly scar, nearly eight inches long), and dey sed I work de knife back and forward four times, but I don't know zactly how many times. But I cut hole ten inches long, and four inches deep, till my leg hung useless.

"My wife Lily she freaded de needles; and den held de lookin' glass, so I could see to make long stitches, and sew it up, and stick on de stickin' plaster.

"Den I set down, and chopped my hand as hard as I cud wid de hatchet, and cut one finger clean off (holding up the left hand, with the shockingly mutilated fingers). Dat little finger I tuck up and put in my mouf, and smoked it for a cigar, till de blood from it run down my lios. Dat I sewed too, and den tole 'em if that wouldn't do, I would cut open my belly, and pull out de entrals before 'em. But dat I wouldn't go down to New Orleans for a slave agin, for I was free.

"Dey den tuck me—not de whites, dey not come near me, afeared, but de brack people—and wheel me home on de wheel-barrow, wid de utensils.

"I was down sick two months. After dat could go about on crutches.

"My ole massa was Wm. Eggleston, of Cambridge, Maryland. I waited on him. I never worked in de field, not I, till I was thirty year old. Wen he die, my young massa gave me my time for $83 a yeah. Dat was about $40 more dan common people paid. I couldn't get along fast at dat in Maryland, but de Company (the Railroad Company) offered me $600 and findin', if I'd cum to Florida, and work on de Railroad. Dat look to me big as de moon. Lily and me made nuff to buy ourselves in nine yeahs, and considerable beside."

CHAPTER XX.

Among the Cubans—The Impending Downfall of Cuban Slavery.

THE absence of certain officers compelled the officials of our party to make a delay of nearly a week at Key West, which we improved by steaming across to Cuba. Looking back now over the delightful days spent in the "Ever Faithful Isle," I recall, out of all the pleasant memories, one or two only of which it seems needful here to speak. The bull fight in Havana, with which the pious Spaniards closed their celebration of Ascension Day; the witchery of dark-browned, liquid-eyed Senoritas; the fashion and beauty of the evening full-dress display on the volante-crowded drive around the Plaza del Armas, and to the Captain-General's country palace; the mysteries of shopping before breakfast, with clerks bringing out the goods into the street to your volante; the delicious absurdity of doing business in English or French with a shop-keeper who knows nothing but Spanish; the tropical scenery of the interior, the glorious palm groves, the lordly sugar plantations, the miseries of the slaves and the profits of their masters—have not all these been faithfully written down in every book about Cuba for the last dozen years?

But, after a tour of many hundred miles among emancipated slaves, it was a noteworthy sensation to be plunged again into the midst of a system of slavery as bad as the worst form which our nation ever suffered. The slaves seemed spiritless, where the emanci-

pated negro had only been purposeless. The one was
without hope, where the other had been disturbed only
by the vague universality of his hopes. Both were
polite, for courtesy seems native to the African disposition; but the courtesy of the freedman was cheerful,
while that of the slave was only patient and submissive.

In Charleston and Savannah, however, we found the
negroes in their churches. In Havana they were congregated, on a holiday, among the whites at the bull
fight, while the flag of "most christian" Spain floated
above this entertainment she had provided for her
humble subjects, and Spanish bayonets guarded the
entrance and preserved order throughout the assemblage. Our emancipated negroes had everywhere been
striving for school-houses, and eagerly seizing every
opportunity for learning to read, while the aspiration
of every parent was that his children, at least, might
acquire "white folks' larnin'; these Cuban slaves knew
so little about education that they seemed to have no
special desire for it.

And yet it was not easy to tell how much of this
apathy was reality, and how much of it was only cunning. Unless intelligent Cubans are greatly deceived,
and, indeed, unless the keen-scented Spanish police are
themselves at fault, many of the negroes are beginning
to form secret societies among themselves, with a view
to organization for a struggle for freedom. Their masters believe them to be well acquainted with the essen-
tial facts in our own great conflict, and the whole slave
community is said to be fermenting with ideas engendered by American emancipation. With slavery sum-
marily wiped out over an extent of adjacent country

equal to a dozen Cubas, it is natural that they should begin to look for their own day of jubilee.

Meanwhile, the elements of revolution exist among the people far more conspicuously than in the days of Lopez and the "fillibusteros." The antagonism between the Creoles and the Spaniards is greater than ever, and betrays itself in many unexpected ways. At Matanzas I was expressing, to a vivacious Creole lady, my surprise at the numbers of well-dressed and apparently respectable people who attended the bull fight in Havana, and cheered the matadors in a frenzy of delight at the brutal bloodshed. "You didn't see a Cuban there," she exclaimed, "unless, perhaps, some ignorant negroes, who, of course, can not be expected to be better than their masters. Such gloating over cold-blooded barbarity doesn't belong to the Creoles; you find it only among the native-born Spaniards."

The same aversion came out again and again. This municipal regulation ought to be amended. "But our Spanish masters never learn anything." That institution is far behind similar ones in the United States. "But how could you expect anything better while we have to import officers from Old Spain to govern us?" The Custom House rules are needlessly vexatious. "But we shall manage things better when Creoles control Cuba." An adjacent sugar planter wouldn't make so bad a neighbor. "But then, you know, he is a Spaniard." A certain ball would be pleasant to attend, but the Spaniards are to have the management of it; and sundry young men are quietly "cut" by their fair Creole friends for presuming to go.

Where a class, regarded with such feelings by the people, is held in power by influences from without, and exerted at a distance of thousands of miles, revolution is only a question of time. Some very intelligent Creoles now profess to believe it comparatively near. The downfall of our rebellion has given a fresh impulse to liberal ideas, and stimulated the feeling of resistance to the Spanish authorities. The swarms of secret societies among the Creoles have sprung up anew. Even on the north coast they are said to be abundant; but it is among the wealthy and isolated young planters of the south, removed from the embarrassments of commerce, and with ample leisure for intrigues, that they find their especial development. Here, the monotony of plantation life is relieved by plots against the Spaniards; and the possibility of growing sugar by free labor is set over against the necessity for the present constant importation of negroes from Africa, in defiance of the remonstrances and active efforts of Christendom.

Heretofore the Spanish authorities have had a short and simple method of quieting the rumors of rebellion. Arms were deposited under guard at various points throughout the island, and the significant declaration was made, that Spain would rather lose slavery than lose Cuba. Visions of armed negroes, drunk with their new-found liberty, and eager to please those who had conferred it by butchering their enemies, have crowded before the eyes of the Creoles and paralyzed their plans. But they have even an army of nearly two hundred thousand slaves in the United States, as orderly, as well disciplined, and, in the main, as efficient as any other troops; and they have naturally concluded that such allies are as available for their purposes as they were for ours. Convinced that their hope of success lies, therefore, in a hearty alliance with the slaves, they are said to be ready for the abolition of slavery, and anxious to encourage and hold communication with the negro secret societies.

Meantime the Spaniards, alive to the dangers which our success has brought to all slaveholding countries, and fully aware of the wishes, if not of the plottings of the Creoles, are themselves looking to the slaves as allies for the coming struggle. The Captain-General, himself, declared within the week of our visit, that the time could not now be far distant when Spain would voluntarily decree the emancipation of her slaves.

The negroes thus stand between two chances of freedom. An attempt at revolution, therefore, is certain to insure their emancipation; and that side will probably be successful, which secures their confidence, and thus their aid. Whether a rising of the Creoles, such as many of them now hope to bring about at some not very distant period, would or would not be successful, may admit of doubt; but it would seem that in either event, slavery in Cuba—the cruelest system of slavery now in existence—is henceforth doomed. Our Proclamation of Emancipation bore wider blessings than they knew who signed it. See appendix (D.)

All along the coast we had been hearing of the "Stonewall," and, truth to tell, there seemed to have been no small panic about her.* She had recently been surrendered to the Spanish authorities, and was lying in the harbor of Havanna. Our party went on board and inspected her. Captain Merryman gave it as his opinion (and the Spanish naval authorities agreed with

---

*A panic which absolutely led to the extinguishment of the lights in sundry light-houses along the South-Atlantic coast, to prevent the dreaded pirate from running in and destroying our fleets.

him), that a single one of our first-class wooden ships
of war could have sunk her. The Rebel game of brag
had been played in her case, even more conspicuously
than usual, and an abortion of wood and iron that could
neither sail, steam nor fight, and was only fit for decoy-
ing unarmed and unsuspecting merchantmen under her
guns, had been magnified into an iron-clad, before which
our whole South-Atlantic squadron was to be swept
away!

Blunders in foreign languages are the common entertainment of all travelers; but one of our party at
Matanzas achieved a success in this line, which may
fairly be considered uncommon. The Vice-Consul-
General, the Consul at Matanzas, and some Cuban
ladies, together with our own party, had gone out to
the Valley of the Yumuri. Altogether we had six or
seven volantes. Returning in the evening, mine happened to be the last in the procession. My companion
had a theory of his own about the Spanish language,
to wit: that all you had to do to make a Spaniard
understand you was to add an "*o*" to every English
word. Seeing one of the gleaming bugs, which strangers put in little cages, and carry off as curiosities, lit
on the shoulder of our volante driver, he conceived this
a good opportunity, and straightway shouted, "*Catcho
buggo.*" Some word, faintly resembling one or the
other of these, as we were afterward told, means, in
Spanish, "faster." The poor Cuban, perched on the
back of the forward horse, eight or ten feet in front of
us, looked around in astonishment, only to be met by
the renewed exclamation, "Buggo, *buggo*, I say!"
Ahead of him were six volantes, filling up the narrow
road; we were at the top of a steep, stony hill, nearly

two miles long; the road sides were precipitous, and even the track was filled with obstructions; but behind was the savage looking "Americano," shouting, "Buggo, buggo." So with a crack of the whip over the horse in the thills, and a cruel plunge of the spur into the heaving flank of the free one, away we went, past the nearest volante, and over the stones down the hill; looking back to see how his passengers appreciated his performance, the driver found one of them laughing immoderately, and the other still screaming "Buggo, buggo." Greatly encouraged he gave the horses an extra lash, and whirled by the next volante, and the next, and the next. The example was contagious, the rest whipped up, and meantime we dashed ahead, careening over the sides of the hill, bounding off the great stones in the track of the wheels, jolting and clattering along at break-neck pace, past every volante; past amazed muleteers, coming in with their burdens of forage; past groups of countrymen, lassoing their young cattle; past the sword-bearing farmers, riding out from town to their country homes; past astonished negroes, and stupidly staring coolies on the roadside; across the bridge and into the narrow streets of the town; nearly running over some of the stately Senoritas at the Plaza del armas, astounding the grave Spaniards, upsetting coolies that loitered about the crossings, raising such a racket as apparently Matanzas hadn't seen for a twelve-month, and finally drawing up, seven volantes in succession, with unprecedented clatter, and whirl of dust, at the door of the "Leon d' Oro."

The moment we stopped, my persistent companion pounced upon the poor volante-driver, exclaiming "Buggo, buggo, I say."

Of late, the cave near Matanzas has been much talked of, and all American tourists are urgently advised to visit it. They will find much that is beautiful, and some lofty passages deserving to be called grand; but whoever has seen our own great caves in the West will be apt to come away from that of Matanzas disappointed.

CHAPTER XXI.

Scenes in Mobile—The Cotton Swindles.

SPRING had ripened into fervid summer, as, after days of exquisite sailing on the Gulf, we steamed past the forts where Farragut added the latest laurels to our navy. Our pilot proposed taking us directly up the river, but presently the Wayanda's keel plowed deep into the oozy mud of the channel, and admonished us that Mobile is an inland city, to which ocean-going vessels may not always venture to ascend.

A boat's crew was sent forward, and even it had a perilous passage among the torpedoes which still lined the channel. Meantime we surveyed the greenish mud of the river from all its possible aspects, and through the long hours of a hot morning were taught the force of those early hopes which, in 1861, led the Mobilians to believe that their torrid weather and abounding mosquitoes would surely prevent the Yankees from making any successful movement against the forts.

Here, through all that braggart spring, from day to day, resounded the boasts of the young soldiers, who still thought war a sport like horse-racing or dueling.*

---

* One of the best private libraries I have ever seen in the South belongs to a wealthy young Kentuckian, who has had a handsome catalogue of it printed. The books are classified for enumeration under subjects. Under the head of "Sports" were set down, first, some works on gunning, fishing, cock-fighting, etc. Among these

The first volunteer companies, eager for Yankee scalps, and carrying pine coffins among their camp equipage, in which, they had told their wives and sweethearts, when they started, that they meant to bring back the corpses of Lincoln and his Cabinet, were hurried here to possess the forts, before "old Harvey Brown" should send over some of his regulars from Fort Pickens. Here Colonel Hardee[27] experienced the difficulty of making gallant Southerners conform to his own tactics; and here, amid their champagne, the brave fellows murmured at being kept ditch-digging, when they wanted to be led at once against the cowardly Yankees. Here John Forsyth, at once Peace Commissioner and professional inflamer of the Southern heart, (now desirous of renewing his old vocation,*) took Dr. Russell and

came others on the laws and usages of dueling! I was assured that the classification was intentional, and in accordance with Southern ideas.

* He was subsequently permitted to renew it. Shortly afterward, copying and indorsing the foolish falsehood that Chief-Justice Chase had given it as his opinion, since his Southern tour, that the negro race would speedily root out the whites throughout the Gulf States, he thought it wise and in good taste to say:

"The Judge, before he made his recent tour through the South, believed that every white man within these States was too lazy to work, and, instead of going out in the morning to get the meat that was desired for dinner, would seize a young negro and pitch it into the dinner-pot, to be served up for the post-prandial meal. By diligent inquiry he found out that this was not true; and so he agreed to make a compromise between his prepossessions and the facts he discovered in his journey. The result is announced in the telegraphic report which we reprint above. We do not eat little negroes, as he believed, but we are so lazy that he seems to be fearful that, as we do not eat them, we are bound, from our demoralized condition, to be presently eaten by them. Well, this is what he has been

27 William Joseph Hardee, Confederate general from Georgia. [Ed.]

other foreign visitors to show them model fortifications and model soldiers. By and by there was need for more serious work to the northward, and the young volunteers, their champagne and *pâtés* ruthlessly thrown out of the wagons, were taught on Virginia fields the beginnings of real war.

At last a light side-wheeler came steaming down the river for us, and presently we were joined by General Gordon Granger, and the whole array of city officials, representing the Yankee Government in the city. Among them was a keen-looking, suspiciously-elegant cotton agent, shirt and fingers ablaze with diamonds, and face wreathed in smiles, to meet the gentlemen whom he supposed all-powerful at the Treasury Department. He was enamored of the South; thought it would be best now not to irritate her, and especially that there should be no more offensive abolitionism than was absolutely necessary. He doubted very much the policy of talking about negro suffrage, and was sure he could do better for the Government in cotton by conciliating the Southern character. Besides, the negroes ought to be under some rigid control any way. If left to absolute freedom, they would not work, and the country would be ruined.

Secretary McCulloch once said: "I am sure I sent *some* honest cotton agents South; but it sometimes

teaching for many years—the right of the negro to eat the white man.

"But why should a sensible man deal with such folly? The expression of it shows with how little wisdom the world is governed, and shows, moreover, how little wisdom there is in the fanatical hosts of which Judge Chase is the most conspicuous member; and yet this man was feted and caressed in his travels through the South, by Southern men and Southern women."

seems very doubtful whether any of them remained honest very long." This man, who greeted us with such bright smiles and smooth-spoken talk, has since been fined two hundred thousand dollars and sentenced to twenty years' imprisonment for cotton stealing!

With attention about equally divided between the dangers of our tortuous, torpedo-lined passage, and the "thunders" of the salute to the Chief-Justice, we finally reached the tumble-down wharves. Planks had been torn up for squares along the levee to make fire-wood, and the bare sleepers were rotting from exposure; elsewhere the decayed planks rattled ominously under carriage-wheels, and disclosed here and there ugly holes that might prove dangerous to unwary walkers. Half the warehouses and shops along the levee seemed closed; a few transports only lay at the landing, and anchored off in the stream were portions of Farragut's famous fleet; but of the commerce that once made Mobilians dream of rivaling New Orleans, scarcely an indication remained.

When one entered the city, however, save in the universal torpor of business, and the presence of soldiers at every corner, few traces of the war were to be seen. The shrubbery was as glorious as ever—a little more luxuriant indeed, since the pruning-shears had perforce been idle for a year or two. Lovely country villas still lined the shell-road, which was once the glory of Mobile. There were hedges of Cherokee rose, and arbors of Scuppernong grapes, groves of orange-trees, and everywhere the glossy leaves of the magnolia, gleaming and shimmering in the sunlight, as the wind stirred them. A better hint that the war had wrought its changes was to be gathered when one came to pay the bill for an hour's drive. The craziest, ricketty vehicle, with a single seat, cost ten dollars.

Everywhere the Rebel soldiers clustered on the corners, or mingled in the throngs about the bar-rooms and hotels. They still wore their uniforms, for the best of reasons—they had no other clothes to wear; but nothing could have been more unexceptionable than their general conduct. "I tell you, sir," exclaimed one of our Generals, in a burst of enthusiasm, "I tell you, they are behaving splendidly. In fact, sir, these Rebel soldiers are an honor to the American name."

"You've whipped us," said one of their officers, with whom I had been carrying on a desultory conversation, "and you did the work thoroughly. I think too much of the bravery of our army and of my own honor to admit that we would have surrendered if we had *not* been thoroughly whipped. Of course, then, we've had enough of it. If we hadn't, we'd have fought on. As we had, we mean to d——n politics, try and get some clothes, and go to making money."

Nearly all the old inhabitants of Mobile were in the city when it fell, and very few had yet procured the means, even if they had the desire, to leave. Stores that had been closed for months, or even years, were being reopened, in the hope that the antiquated stocks of goods might bring in some trifle in a currency no longer worthless, to supply the wants of the family. A large furniture store was pointed out, where the owner had sold enough to supply himself with the immediate necessaries of life, and had then closed again, declaring that he wouldn't sell another article till fall. His explanation gives a curious glimpse into the condition of the people. Everybody, he said, wanted to buy, and nobody had any money. When they began

to sell their lands or their cotton, and get money, he
was ready to resume business; but till then, it would
ruin him to have his store open. If he refused credit,
he would make all his old customers enemies; if he
gave credit, he would soon be bankrupt. To save himself from destruction, there was absolutely no way but
to bolt his doors and put up his window-shutters!

Cotton was beginning to come out, but the enormous
frauds which have since made the very name of cotton
agent odious were then only in their infancy, and there
is no reason to suspect that at that time the Mobile
agent already referred to, who subsequently gained
such a disgraceful notoriety, contemplated any other
rascality than a swindle of the "Rebel holders," that
should still seem technically honest in the showings to
the Government.

But the germ of all the difficulties had already made
its appearance. There were, as the officials believed,
in Mobile itself, six thousand bales, and in the adjacent country not less than one hundred and twenty
thousand, which captured records showed to be the
property of the Rebel Government. Much of this was
soon in the hands of private parties, who professed to
have bought it from the Rebel authorities in good faith,
to have given adequate compensation for it, and therefore to be now its legitimate owners. What was to be
done in such a case? Or again: Planters had subscribed large amounts of cotton to the Rebel loan, under
the same species of coercion by public sentiment which
filled the Rebel ranks with men who had sturdily voted
against secession in all its stages. The authorities had
never removed the cotton; the former owners had been
compelled to take care of it; they had steadily kept

possession of it all the time, and they now claimed this possession to constitute ownership, arguing, plausibly enough, that their compulsory contracts (by subscription) with the Rebel Government had never been carried out, and that now it ill became the United States Government to undertake their enforcement. In other ways, and by all manner of side issues, the subject had become so inextricably complicated that the immediate representative of the Treasury Department in our party was at his wits' ends.

Naturally, Mr. Chase's opinion had great weight, and it was freely given. He thought it wiser and better for the department over which he had presided, and which was now administered by one of his own most trusted appointees, to wash its hands of the whole business. Here was a quantity of cotton promised under compulsion to the Rebel Government. They never came to take it; in most cases it was never actually in their possession; it was now in the hands of its old owners. It would better comport with the dignity of a great and successful nation to leave it among this impoverished people, rather than enter into a confused scramble against ready swearers and men who felt that they were being cheated out of their all, in order to gather up and auction off the beggarly effects of the bankrupt Confederacy. In any event, the Government would be apt to realize very little from the effort, and it would lose far more in a wasted opportunity for diffusing good feeling and promoting the revival of industry than it would gain in cotton.

Weeks, indeed, before this, while the party was at Key West, Mr. Chase had foreseen, from the indications along the Atlantic coast, the troubles in store, and ad suggested what seemed to him the wisest policy for avoiding them. He would have had the President issue a proclamation setting forth substantially:

1st. That all present holders of cotton sold or subscribed to the Confederate Government, but never delivered, should be recognized as its lawful owners, on the ground that the consideration for the stipulated transfer had failed.

2d. That a general amnesty should be accorded to all persons willing in good faith to take the required oaths, and aid in the re-establishment of civil government; and that the Executive influence should be given for the repeal of all confiscation laws.

3d. That this (which should be done, in order to show the Rebels now returning to their allegiance, that the Government was magnanimous, and not mercenary, as well as to relieve the general distress, and aid in the revival of industry and the return of prosperity,) must be accompanied or preceded by the adoption of fundamental laws in the States thus generously dealt with, which should permit no distinction of rights based merely on color; that thus the principal source of trouble in the future might be avoided.

Time will show—indeed, most men will agree that it has already shown—the wisdom and statesmanlike sagacity of the views thus early presented to the consideration of the President. That they would have been gladly accepted by the South, every man who saw the temper of the Rebel States in the May and June following the surrender is well assured. How much political embarrassment and pecuniary corruption their adoption would have saved can only be told by those who have probed to the depths the festering corruption of the cotton agency system, and who can forecast the issues of the present Congressional and Executive complications.

I speak advisedly in saying that every Rebel State would have promptly reorganized under such conditions, and that the majority in Congress would have as promptly admitted their representatives.

But, so far as the political points were concerned, they had already been adversely decided at Washington. As to the question of cotton, Mr. Mellen, in whose charge the entire matter was placed, without controverting the views above suggested, was unable to accept and act upon them. His instructions contemplated making the most out of the captured cotton. To give it away would at once be denounced as a corrupt waste of great sums of the public money. It was replied that this cotton was not the same as public money or even public property now in hand; that it was not actually captured; was scattered over hundreds of miles of territory; was only known by uncertain records to have been subscribed to the Rebel Government; could not be found without protracted search, nor without protracted examinations in each case, which opened up boundless opportunities for bribery and wholesale frauds; in short, that no effort could be made to collect this cotton which would not end with little profit and less credit to the Government.

Mr. Mellen earnestly desired to do the right thing. Much abused as he has been, I have never seen an official charged with such weighty responsibilities, and so liable to slanderous accusations, whatever course he should take, who seemed more earnestly and sincerely bent on simply finding out his duty, and then doing it with his whole mind and heart. But as to the general policy of making the most out of the effects of the Rebel Gov-

ernment, whatever might be his own opinions, his instructions left him no discretion.

The work of cotton seizure therefore began. Before
these records of Southern travel are finished, there
will be ample opportunity to tell how it ended.

Alabamians had as yet scarcely recovered from the
shock of the surrender, and few in the country adjacent to Mobile had formed any definite plans for the
future. Some thought of going to Brazil ; some wanted
to plunge into Mexican broils ; a few wanted to get
away from the " sassy free niggers " by going North.
Scarcely any seemed to regard their chance of cultivating their lands by free negro labor as hopeful, and
the most had a vague, uncertain idea that in some way
or another they would have to give up their lands.
Still there were scarcely any sales, and prices had
found no settled standard. Some would take one-tenth
of what used to be considered the value of their estates ;
others would be satisfied to sell their plantations for
the cost of the buildings which stood upon them.
Nearly all were without faith in greenbacks. If they
sold at all, they must get something for their lands.
They did n't want much, but what they did want must
be in gold.

There was general uncertainty, however, as to
whether they had any right to sell, or whether the
titles they might execute would be valid. They were
not willing to believe it possible that an attempt would
be made to enforce so absurd a piece of legislation as
the Yankee confiscation law, but still there was no
telling !

Communication with the interior was still very difficult. They could reach Selma and Montgomery by

a week's steamboating, and the Tombigbee would take them to Demopolis, but trips were rare; and though Mobile was the necessary political and business heart of the State, this heart's circulation was yet so impaired, that it neither strengthened nor was strengthened thereby. What was said at Mobile, therefore, was not, as formerly, the concentrated thought of the State, gathered there through all its converging lines of approach, but rather the thought of those who were accustomed to speak for the State, at a period when almost completely isolated from their constituents.

Railroads were not in running order, nor likely to be for some months. The war had destroyed their rolling stock. Some were left without cars; nearly all without good locomotives. Bridges were burnt; rails were torn up and twisted for miles and miles; the companies themselves were utterly impoverished; and unless they could get unlooked-for aid, most of them would have to go into liquidation.

To the courtesies of a serenade, drives, rides, dinners, and innumerable calls, the officials added a review of the entire military force in and about Mobile, in honor of the Chief Justice.

The Mobile men gathered about the corners, or sullenly contemplated the pageant from their windows, but scarcely a lady could be seen. They had neither smiles nor glances, just then, for the garrison of the conqueror. One needed indeed to be sanguine, as he watched the scene, and especially as he studied the bearing of the inhabitants, not to think of Warsaw.

General Granger, a fine, soldierly-looking person, with face browned by many a campaign, and a history through the war, from its very inception down to his

last action, at the head of the land forces co-operating
with Farragut in the attack on Mobile, that makes soldiers always ready to follow where he leads, took his
station, with the Chief Justice by his side, and a showy
staff surrounding them, at the crossing of the principal streets. Regiment after regiment marched past,
whose banners, as they drooped low in salute, showed
names of nearly every battle in the war. One came
up with swinging, steady tramp, but with ranks sadly
thinned, though often recruited. Its tattered and
stained standards were crowned with the name of the
first great conflict of the West. In their young, fresh
beauty they had waved where Lyon fell.

Infantry, artillery, and cavalry streamed by, and
then came the sight which brought curses to the mouths
of nearly all the onlookers. The negro troops marched
very handsomely, and made, perhaps, the best appearance of any regiments in the column; but every citizen seemed to consider their appearance as a personal
insult to himself. That the "miserable runaway niggers" behaved so handsomely only aggravated the
offense. "There's my Tom," muttered a plethoric old
citizen, while the natural red of his face inflamed to
purple. "How I'd like to cut the throat of the dirty,
impudent good-for-nothing!"

But no such voices reached the party surrounded by
the glittering staff. The subjugation was as yet too
fresh and real. One had to mingle with them to find
how sore they were at the degradation of being
guarded by these runaway slaves of theirs. To be
conquered by the Yankees was humiliating, but to
have their own negroes armed and set over them they
felt to be cruel and wanton insult. Yet they scarcely
dared still to speak of it above whispers, and their

combination of rage and helplessness would have been ludicrous, but for its dark suggestions of the future.

The review occurred early in the morning, and the heat did not seem oppressive to us, quietly remaining about the hotel; but a portion of our party who were out riding found it intense, and in the course of the day there were several deaths in the suburbs, chiefly among Northern men, from sun-stroke. But the general testimony of Northerners in Mobile is to the effect that they find but little difference between people from the different sections in their capacity for enduring the heat. Only its long continuance, they say, and not its intensity, makes the Southern summer dangerous to Northern men.

General Andrews,[28] three or four years ago a briefless young lawyer in a remote Minnesota village—such have been the rapid promotions the war has offered—showed us through the portions of the city destroyed, only a week or two before, by perhaps the most destructive explosion that ever devastated any American city. How it originated will be forever a mystery. Every one who might explain it perished. There were large quantities of ammunition stored near the upper end of the landing, and in the heart of the cotton warehouses. One of the concealed torpedoes left by the Rebels may have been touched; Rebels may themselves have stealthily arranged a system of wires to explode it; a percussion shell may have been dropped; some reckless dare-devil may have been smoking a cigar. However it occurred, there was a sudden roar in the midst of the busy throng of workmen and soldiers, and one common, instantaneous destruction overwhelmed them all.

Over four-fifths of the entire storage of the city was

[28] George Leonard Andrews, Union general who commanded Negro troops. [Ed.]

destroyed. A hundred mules were buried in a single corral. Days afterward corpses of here and there a hapless soldier began to be dug out by those who cared to risk exposure to the scattered shells still hourly exploding. Even when we drove down into the ruins we heard now and again a dull, heavy thud, like the stroke of some ponderous weight against the solid earth. It was a shell buried far beneath the rubbish of fallen houses, and fired by the heat that still smouldered across whole squares.

Long before we reached the scene of complete destruction, we came upon houses shattered, bottom stories bereft of superstructure, door and window-frames driven in, gable-ends standing up alone, without the roofs they were raised to bear. The streets were filled with the rubbish. Here was a little fragment of a wall, twenty bricks, perhaps, lying sidewise as they fell, still fastened by the unbroken mortar; there the whole outer course of a gable-end dropped flat, and paving the street. Other walls would still be standing; but six or eight feet from the ground the outer course of bricks had been abruptly started outward an inch or more, and thence upward the wall imitated the direction—but by no means, as we momentarily witnessed, the security—of the leaning towers of Pisa.

All this passed, we came to the scene of actual explosion. Here, for eight or ten squares, was one waste of broken brick and mortar, still smouldering and smoking, and still—horrible thought!—roasting beneath this parched debris its human victims. Solid warehouses, chimneys, cotton-presses, machinery, all had been flattened as a whirlwind might flatten a house of card-boards.

It was a sickening sequel to such a scene to listen, as

we afterward did, to the descriptions by our surgeons in the old United States hospital, of the condition in which the Rebels had left it, filthy to the last degree, full of neglected sick men, destitute of medicines, or, indeed, of the commonest hospital comforts. Several of the surviving victims of the explosion had been brought here, who all seemed to attribute it to Rebel torpedoes, fired by design.

Among the soldiers who filled the other wards, it was curious to watch the recognition of the Chief Justice, by his likeness on the one-dollar greenbacks. Finally he entered into conversation with a soldier in one of the outer hospital tents, who told him he was from Ohio. "Ah, so am I." "Are you? from what part?" asked the soldier. "Do n't you know Mr. Chase, your former Governor?" suggested General Andrews. "O yes; but, Governor, you must remember we have n't seen any of them greenbacks o' your 'n for so long, we 've kinder forgot the look o' your features!" It seemed the paymaster had neglected him.

CHAPTER XXII.

Mobile Loyalists and Reconstructionists—Black and White.

THE political situation in Mobile, in the early days of June, might be briefly summed up. They were anxious for a re-establishment of civil government that would release them from suspense about confiscation. They expected severe punishment for their rebellion, as far as civil rights were concerned, but were disposed to put the best face possible upon affairs, ask for a good deal, and take whatever they could get.

One day the Mayor called, together with his city council—a group of fine-looking gentlemen, several of them past middle age. The Mayor himself was a Northern man, who, years ago, had removed to Alabama and identified himself with her interests. Of course, therefore, he joined in the war against the Yankees, and professed no love for them now; but, say what he might, he couldn't help looking like the shrewd Yankee he was. They were all "ready to accept the new order of things." That is, they knew they had to submit, and they preferred, by putting a a good face on it, to continue in their offices. That anybody wanted "acceptance of the new order of things" to have a wider significance, I failed to discover. The negroes were free; but to expect them to work, or even to behave themselves, without coercive measures, was preposterous. Slavery being destroyed, the Mobilians awaited the lead of the United States in discovering some new mode of constraining service. The idea of service without constraint never entered their heads.

Among the callers was a fine, courteous, florid-faced old gentleman, with gray locks carefully collected behind into an antique queue, who began his talk about "this unfortunate class of our population," by going back to the foundations of things. "You know they are the descendants of Ham, sir, and that service in some form is their heritage. It would be flying in the face of Providence to attempt changing that. Now, sir, there are foolish fellows among them, who, since they have been made free, want to rise from that sphere to which they have been appointed. Of course, they'll fail; we have no uneasiness on that score; but we are the friends of these people, and we are sorry to see them expose themselves to so much misery in making attempts that we know from the outset must be abortive. Isn't it better to have the laws in some way take the matter out of their hands and make them work?"

I told the old gentleman of what we had seen at St. Helena. He utterly refused to believe that free negroes could be self-supporting. General Saxton had helped them, and stood in the place of a master to them. No negroes were going to work steadily and successfully without the aid of Anglo-Saxon organization and direction.

Negro suffrage seemed to all the most revolting of possibilities. They were not willing to think their conquerors could mean to inflict such degradation upon a gallant people. In fact, they wouldn't—no, they did n't really think their population *could* be brought to endure it!

Herein was observable a marked change of tone since our visit to the cities on the Atlantic coast. There they were just as vehement in their protestations against negro suffrage, but they ended in entreaties that the conquerors would spare the infliction of such disgrace. Here came threats. Everywhere else it was manifest that if the restoration of civil authority depended on negro suffrage, then negro suffrage would be accepted. Here, for the first time, we were told the people would not stand it! The explanation is simple. They were just beginning to get a knowledge of the North Carolina proclamation, and to imagine that the President was willing to concede to them more power than they had dared to hope. It was the old maxim illustrated once more. They had been offered an inch; they were soon to be seen clamorous for ells.

A "reconstruction meeting" was called for the evening on which we left, and men were busy consulting on plans to be pursued. The upshot of the whole matter was that they meant to resist negro suffrage just as far as they dared, and to seek a reconstruction that should let them back with as few changes as possible.

All this was natural. It required small statesmanship at Washington, or anywhere else, to comprehend it. They were powerless; they wanted to make the best arrangement they could, but were sure to take, because they must take, any they were offered. Down to the time when the terms of the North Carolina proclamation came to be understood, we had found the South like clay. The Washington potters could mold it to their liking; it was only to be hoped they knew of what fashion republican vessels should be shaped. But the moment they heard of that proclamation, the late Rebels began to take courage on the question of suffrage, and to suspect that they were not so helpless as they had imagined. Even yet, however, the golden moment was not wholly past.

Less bitterness was observed than might have been expected. The most heated manifestations were those of the returning Rebel soldiers against some who had tempted them into the ranks. Here and there one heard of a case in which returned soldiers had attacked or even hung citizens for failures to keep their promises about supporting the families of those who had volunteered. Northerners in Mobile had an idea that the presence of our soldiers alone prevented such scenes in the city itself, and they professed, on what authority I scarcely know, to enumerate at least twenty cases of the kind in adjoining counties. But proofs were not wanting of the spirit in which, to the very last, the conflict against the Government had been waged. One of our officers, whose duty led him to search for a quantity of Rebel manuscripts, by lucky accident discovered in time a torpedo planted among them, and so arranged that his movement of the papers would have been sure to explode it. The spirit of unconquerable hate, after the battle was fought and lost, could hardly go further.

"Where do you come from?" one of the party happened to ask a negro who had been employed for some trifling service. "From Charleston, sah. I b'longed to Massa Legree, uncle to the great lawyer." Massa Legree had proved worthy of the name which an Abolition pen has made immortal. He had sold this man into Alabama fifteen years ago, and the gray-wooled fellow said that since then he had neither seen nor heard from wife or child. "But I's much 'bliged to all the good gemmen and ladies as has helped us to freedom. We'll all s'port oursel's now, and I's hope soon to hab money enough to go back and look for my old 'oman and babies." The poor man seemed to have no comprehension of the fact that his babies of fifteen years ago were scarcely to be considered babies now.

He was right about their supporting themselves. During the preceding month the military authorities had issued rations to the destitute Mobilians, white and black alike. To the master race no less than fifty-nine thousand rations had been given away by the Government they had been trying to subvert. Among the negroes only eleven thousand and eighty (or less than one-fifth as many,) had been needed. In June the number of destitute negroes had decreased till they were drawing only one-tenth as many rations daily as were required by the whites. A stranger might have concluded that it was the white race that was going to prove unable to take care of itself, instead of the emancipated slaves, over whose future, unless brightened by some vision of compulsory labor, their late loving masters grew so sad.

The explanation was a simple one. The negroes had gone to work: it was the only way they knew for getting bread, except when the morals of slavery had taught them to steal, and for that there was now small chance. The whites had nobody left to go to work for them, and that was the only way to get bread *they* knew.

Throughout the city the negroes found plenty of em-

ployments. In the country they were already talking
of clubbing together and working plantations. But
I heard of no movement of this kind that promised
success. They had been accustomed to obey a common
master; relieved from his control, each one now wanted
to set up for master on his own account, and "boss"
the rest. There was little doubt that they would make
enough to keep from starving; but there was no prospect of their doing much more. Large cotton crops
were not to be expected from any plantation which negroes controlled.

An evidence or two appeared of the "war of races"
which the mourners over dead Slavery were predict-
ing. Some negroes were heard of, at Montgomery,
who had come into the city with their ears cut off by
their former masters, in punishment for their assertion
of their freedom. Of course, such things were far
from general; but the fact that they ever occurred
gave point to the occasional croakings about negro
insurrections. "Negro insurrections," forsooth! We
need new dictionaries to help us understand one another, when knocking a man down for trying the playful liberty of cutting your ears off becomes "insurrection!"

Mobile houses showed the straits to which the people had been reduced. The pianos all jangled, and the
legs of the parlor chairs were out of tune quite as
badly. Sofas had grown dangerous places for any but
the most slow-motioned and sedate. Missing bits of
veneering from the furniture illustrated the absence of
Yankee prepared glue. The glories of fine window-cur-
tains had departed. Carpets had in many cases gone
for army blankets.

We saw curious rough earthen mugs, that looked as if they had been dug out of Pompeii, where they had been badly glazed by the heat of the lava. These were specimens of home manufacture, to take the place of broken glasses, and had been sold at several dollars apiece, Confederate money. "It did n't make much difference what they asked; it was about as easy to pay ten dollars of that stuff as one. But look out that your own greenbacks do n't soon get in the same fix." A Rebel songster was a rare prize, presented by a Mobile lady to one of our party. Its cover was of wall paper, over which the title was printed; and the paper for the body of the book was scarcely whiter.

Dinners were a sad trial to the old hospitable and luxurious entertainers. They had fine wines left, but champagne must be taken in plain tumblers, and enough to go around the table of one size or shape could hardly be mustered, even with energetic borrowing. Sets of dishes—whatever, in fact, was breaka ble—had undergone like disasters.

"But we 're all poor alike," said a sprightly young friend of Madame Le Vert's. "It makes no difference to us here. Nobody can do any better; so, what is the use of being unhappy about it. I wear this palmetto hat, for example, made in Mobile. It does n't look like the elegant straws of the Northern milliner-shops; but everybody has to wear palmetto, and so I 'm in the fashion. This silk may be very old-fashioned, and I 'm sure the style in which it 's made is; but how were you going to do any better in Mobile? These gloves are not Jouvin's best, but find me any Mobile lady that has them. And as for shoes, we 've all learned not to despise calf-skin, or even something a good deal stronger." And the little foot gave a stamp that certainly never came from a New York gaiter boot.*

A wretched officer, who had been listening, had the heartlessness to add: "And when we came here, a dozen of you could sit in a church pew, where it is now crowded with only four or five." It was true; even crinoline had been added to Mobile wardrobes in less than a month. Most of the dresses still gave ludicrous evidence that they had been made with reference to less expansive underclothing.

---

* Colonel Boynton, writing of his experiences in the interior rural districts of North Carolina, three months later, found, in spite of Wilmington blockade-running, a destitution far beyond that of Mobile.

"Everything has been mended, and generally in the rudest style. Window-glass has given way to thin boards, and these are in use in railway coaches and in the cities. Furniture is marred and broken, and none has been replaced for four years. Dishes are cemented in various styles, and half the pitchers have tin handles. A complete set of crockery is never seen, and in very few families is there enough left to set a table in a manner approaching gentility. A set of forks with whole tines is a curiosity. Clocks and watches have nearly all stopped. Clothing, including hats, bonnets, and ladies' and children's shoes, are nearly all home-made. Hair-brushes and tooth-brushes have all worn out; combs are broken, and are not yet replaced; pins, needles, thread, and a thousand such articles, which seem indispensable to housekeeping, are very scarce. Even in weaving on the looms, corn-cobs have been substituted for spindles. Few have pocket-knives. In fact, everything that has heretofore been an article of sale at the South is wanting now. At the tables of those who were once esteemed luxurious providers, you will find neither tea, coffee, sugar, nor spices of any kind. Even candles, in some cases, have been replaced by a cup of grease, in which a piece of cloth is plunged for a wick. The problem which the South had to solve has been, not how to be comfortable during the war, but how to live at all."

Madame Le Vert herself, with a few other Mobile ladies, made up a pleasant party to accompany us down the river to the forts, under whose guns the Wayanda was lying. The noted little lady seemed to have gone bravely through the war; though at its close she was reduced to quite as great straits as the rest. She steered discreetly clear of dangerous complications; scrupulously said "Confederate" in place of "Rebel," and "Federal" in place of "Yankee," and could hardly consider her literary labors ended till she, too, had contributed her book about the war.

All were bitter about the sudden collapse of the Confederate currency. It had gone down until a dollar was worth only four or five cents, but still it was worth something, "and Heaven knows," ejaculated a lively young person, "there was enough of it, such as it was." But there was no time for such conversions as were possible. There were opportunities for buying real estate with it; Jew brokers were ready to buy up currency and give gold; provisions might at least have been secured with it. But hundreds of widows and orphans still had nearly their whole possessions in Confederate currency; while General Maury[29] assured them they need not be uneasy; that he could hold Mobile against a six-months' siege from the whole army and navy of the United States. Till the last week, and almost to the last day, the confidence of the most was unshaken. Without a word of warning came the surrender, and in an hour thousands were made penniless.

"You ask," said one, "why so many white people are drawing rations. You have the reason. Negroes had nothing, and lost nothing. We had what passed for money; your entrance turns it into waste paper in our purses. Of course, therefore, we are destitute."

[29] Dabney Herndon Maury, Confederate general in command of the District of the Gulf. [Ed.]

All this was plain; but the good Mobilians saw only in part. The negroes had gone to work; the whites too often were listlessly awaiting events, and talking of selling their houses or lands to get bread. The fresh tide of Northern enterprise will soon sweep rudely enough against these broken remnants of the *ancien régime*, and wash them under. The "old families" seem, in many cases, exhausted of force and energy. They had enough originally to gain position; they have not enough left now to retain it; and it waits the grasping hand of the coming parvenues. "New men" will soon be the order of the day, in Mobile and in many another center of Southern aristocracy.

CHAPTER XXIII.

New Orleans and New Orleans Notabilities.

CROSSING from Mobile to New Orleans was going from the past of the South to its present. Till within a few weeks, Mobile had been among the latest strongholds of the rebellion; for some years New Orleans had been held by the national authorities, and had been changing under the operation of Northern influences. Mobile showed us the last of the old South; New Orleans the first of the new.

Before the Wayanda had reached the old battle-ground where what we would now call a sharp skirmish added the 8th of January to our public holidays, and gave the country one of its most famous Presidents, she was met by a tug containing a number of the officials, and some of the prominent lawyers of the city, come down to welcome the Chief Justice. Among them were natives of the South, and gentlemen whose interests were all wrapped up in New Orleans. But a day or two before the city papers had published Mr. Chase's remarks to the Charleston negroes, and much angry comment had been excited by this "desecration of the judicial ermine" and the sanction given to the claims of the negroes for suffrage; yet nothing could have exceeded the cordiality of his reception. His host was a young sugar-planter, born here, and inheriting large estates and many slaves from his father. Fortunately for the young man, much

of his boyhood had been spent abroad, and when, at
the age of seventeen, the sudden death of his father recalled him from St. Petersburg and made him a millionaire, he was measurably free from the ideas which
slavery steadily instilled. When the Emancipation
Proclamation came, his plantations were in the ex-
empted parishes; but he was clear-sighted enough to
see the inevitable end, and sagacious enough to recognize it as already practically accomplished. He gathered his slaves together, told them that henceforth they
might consider themselves free, and proposed a bargain
for their services, if they were willing to remain at their
old places. They stipulated for rations, and an average
of between eight and ten dollars wages per month, which
was promptly paid. They have been working steadily
ever since, and Mr. May now states that, in spite of the
demoralizing effects of the war, to say nothing of the
actual ravages of guerrillas, his principal plantation
has been as profitable under the free-labor system as it
was formerly, when labor cost him nothing.

Like most of the wealthy sugar-planters, Mr. May
keeps up his town house, and, indeed, spends the greater
part of his time in the city, where, for a year or two
past, official duties have required his presence. At the
age of twenty-three, he holds the position of United
States Treasurer, appointed thereto mainly for the reason that he was the most responsible loyal Southerner
then to be found in the city. Even he had served for
a season in the Rebel service—to have stayed out of it,
he says, would have been to have sacrificed his property—but he contrived to get back as soon as New
Orleans fell, and was among the very first to present
himself before General Butler to take the oath of allegiance.

We had been at his house scarcely an hour, and had just gathered about the table, at lunch, when a compact, little, big-chested, crop-headed, fiery-faced officer, in Major-General's uniform, was shown in. He was altogether the most modest, bashful, and embarrassed little fellow we had seen on the whole trip; conversing under restraint, sitting uneasily on his chair, and flushing redder than ever when a lady addressed him. They tell a ludicrous story of his having taken a splendid bouquet to the theater, one evening, to give to a lady whom he knew he should see there. He held it nervously through half the performance; started once or twice from his box to pass around to the one which the lady occupied, but speedily returned, bouquet still in hand, his heart having each time failed him on the way. Finally, summoning one of his staff officers, he directed *him* to carry the bouquet over to Miss ——, with General Sheridan's compliments! Yet, as one looks at the developments on the back of his head, it is easy to understand the tremendous energy and intense love of fighting for the sake of fighting, that have made "Phil. Sheridan" the most famous cavalry officer of the war, if not of the century.

He had but recently assumed command of the Gulf Department, and had been busily occupied with the affairs of Texas. He was by no means satisfied with the situation in the Lone Star State. There had been no real surrender. The officers had availed themselves of the chance for paroles, and the men had gone off, arms in their hands, half expecting a renewal of the war, with the Mexican frontier as a base of operations, and, at any rate, too far from being well whipped to become very quiet or orderly citizens. He did not say in terms that there had been bad faith on the part of

Kirby Smith and the other Confederate officers, but it was evident that he more than suspected it.

Some talk that followed of cotton speculations in Texas, possible and proposed, disclosed pretty plainly a fact which had often been hinted at and as often denied in the newspapers. Either Kirby Smith, or some person assuming to speak for him, had been in indirect communication with our authorities on the subject of closing out the war in the Trans-Mississippi Department, by a big exportation of Confederate cotton on private account. "I've known for a long time that he was for sale," said one, "but I have always doubted whether he was worth the price proposed."

Among the stream of callers that filled up the afternoon was an old gentleman, whom, but for the half-modernized clothes, one might have taken for Dr. Franklin, as he is shown in the marble statue at the Capitol. The countenance had the same strong cast; the thin gray locks hung down, long, over the straight, collarless Quaker coat in the same way; the broad-brimmed hat, the cane, the general aspect of venerable but hearty old age, were all as we have them in the statue. This was Jacob Barker,* a Northern Quaker, whose term of residence in New Orleans counts further back than the lives of most of her citizens, and who had, nevertheless, apparently passed the prime of a prosperous business career before he emigrated to the South. Mr. Barker is now between eighty and ninety years of age. He has many ships carrying his trade to

---

* Since elected Congressman from one of the New Orleans districts, in the hope that his position and age might help to secure the admission of himself and his colleagues. The House, however, proved unimpressible, and he soon gave up an effort after such barren honors, and returned.

foreign and domestic ports. His children approach old age around him, and yet he may be seen almost every day, during business hours, behind the counter, in his old-fashioned little bank on Camp Street, counting money and waiting on customers, like a bank clerk of twenty.

Long ago Mr. Barker sympathized with the generous views of his sect on the sinfulness of slavery. It is even of record that he joined a party once in New York harbor, which steamed out in one of his own tug-boats to a vessel about to sail for Charleston, and rescued a runaway slave she was to carry back to his South Carolina owner. How Southern business has molded Northern consciences may be seen in the fact that, for a generation past, Mr. Barker has been as Southern in his views as the majority of the depositors in his bank; and, indeed, it seems scarcely known in a Rebel community, whose highest confidence he enjoys, that so devoted a Southern politician is not, after all, a Southern man.

We were joined at dinner by three gentlemen who might be taken as conspicuous representatives of the Southern bar, as well as of diverse phases of Southern Unionism. The eldest, a fine old gentleman, whose youthful spirits and ruddy face perpetually contradict the story of his thin gray hairs, is generally held to be the finest civil lawyer here, which is equivalent to pronouncing him the finest civil lawyer in the United States.* As long ago as during the administration of

---

* Throughout the English-settled portion of the United States, the British Common Law is the basis of all our jurisprudence. But the French and Spanish settlements in Louisiana have left it the legacy of the Civil Law, and so made the practice of law in its courts a matter requiring special study, and presenting special perplexities.

General Jackson, his prominence was such that, when it was plausibly argued that a vacancy on the Supreme Bench ought to be so filled as to give that tribunal of last resort at least one Judge learned in the civil law, Mr. Roselius[30] was at once suggested. New Orleans lawyers still tell that he might have had the place if he would; but that the emoluments of the bar are here too great to be exchanged for the honorable beggary of the Supreme Court.

The next was in every particular a contrast to this genial, rosy-faced Nestor of the city bar. He was tall, thin, sallow, cadaverous. His habitual expression seemed saturnine; he had less to say; indulged in fewer compliments; told fewer stories. This was Mr. Thos. J. Durant, the leader of the Radical Free-State party in the State, and an orator whom Northern men pronounce not unworthy of mention in the same connection with Wendell Phillips.

Judge Whitaker,[31] the third of the party (reported to be now an aspirant for the Supreme Bench, to fill the vacancy caused by the death of Judge Catron), though an emigrant to New Orleans from South Carolina, looked rather like one of the free-and-easy Kentucky lawyers in the mountain districts. His collar was carelessly turned down; his tall, loose-jointed figure matched well with his careless toilet, and his hearty ways, and irregular features, lit up with a smile of Western rather than Southern cordiality, all bespoke a different origin.

These three men stand in the foremost rank of Louisiana lawyers, and typify various grades of Louisiana Unionism. Mr. Durant is an intense Radical. In Boston he would be an Abolitionist of the Abolitionists. He speaks at negro meetings, demands negro suffrage,

[30] Christian Roselius, Whig lawyer who opposed secession. [Ed.]

[31] Daniel Kimball Whitaker, lawyer and editor of New Orleans. [Ed.]

unites with negroes in educational movements, champions negroes in the courts. The resident Rebels hate him with an intensity of hatred due only to one whom they regard as an apostate; but all are glad to avail themselves of his legal abilities, and he is daily compelled to reject business he has no time for. Judge Whitaker is far more cautious. He may be as innocent as the dove; but, at any rate, under all his hearty, warm manner there is a good deal of the wisdom of the serpent. He was always a Union man, but he took pains not to make himself personally offensive to the Rebels, and was not disturbed by them during their control of the city. Now that the Union cause has triumphed, he would move very slowly. Negro suffrage may become necessary, but he would wait and see. If there were any possible way of avoiding it, he would avoid it. Mr. Roselius is at once, through age and by temperament, still more cautious. His conservative tendencies led him to oppose secession; the same tendencies lead him to want now a return as nearly as possible to the old condition of affairs—the veritable *status in quo ante bellum.* Slavery, of course, can not be restored, nor would he desire it; but he would have the abolition of slavery work just as few attendant changes as possible. Above all, treat the returning Rebels well; dine them, and wine them; tell them it's high time they would quit making fools of themselves, and that you're glad to see them back.

In the cool of the evening, Mr. May drove us out to see the city. It recalls no other town in the South; reminds one more of Havana than of any of them, and is very much unlike even it. "A town where all their drains are above ground; where a cellar would be a cistern; where the river is as high as the roofs of the houses, and where, when you die, instead of burying you like a Christian, they tuck you away on a shelf, and plaster you in with lath and mortar—that's New Orleans." Such was the description once given by an energetic Yankee, and it conveys as accurate an idea as whole pages might. He should have added that it is a town where half the inhabitants think of Paris as their home, and feel as much interest in the Tuilleries as the White House; that of the other half, the most are cotton factors or commercial men of some sort, with principles not infrequently on sale with their goods; that it is at once the most luxurious, the most unprincipled, the most extravagant, and, to many, the most fascinating city in the Union—the only place that, before the war, could support the opera through an entire winter; the only place where the theaters are open on Sunday evening; where gambling is not concealed, and keeping a mistress is not only in no sense discreditable, but is even made legal. What Boston is to the North, Charleston and Richmond are, in a diminished sense, to the South; what New York is to the North, New Orleans is, in an exaggerated sense, to the South.

The city itself showed no traces of war. Mounted orderlies dashed along the streets; and in front of a few palatial residences guards in uniform paced slowly to and fro. But the superb shrubbery of the Garden District had not suffered as had that of Charleston. The spacious and airy wooden residences in the upper part of the city never looked more attractive; below Canal Street, the quaint, projecting roofs, and curious green-barred doors and windows of the French quarter remained as in the days when Napoleon sold out to the United States, and the inhabitants woke up to find

their allegiance transferred.   Even the levee began to
be crowded again, and business seemed quite as active
as could have been expected in June.

In the evening our host took me down to the office
of the principal newspaper of the city. It has been
started since the national occupation, on the ruins of old
Rebel papers; is, in shape and size, a *fac simile* of leading
New York journals, is crowded with advertisements, and
is paying a net profit of eight to ten thousand dollars a
month.   Yet, with such a start, its proprietors, though
strong Unionists, are afraid to take any decided political stand.   Its main rival, the Picayune, was already
appealing to the returning Rebels, and there was danger, they thought, of their being "cut under."   It was
the old, sad story of making principles as little offensive
as possible, and softening them away, point by point, to
conciliate imperious patrons.   "You call our course
hard names," said one of the proprietors.   "But look
at our condition.   We have the largest circulation and
the business lead.   The interior is just being opened up
to us, and we want to occupy this new field in advance
of any rival.   If we denounce Rebels, or advocate negro
suffrage, we lose what we have here, and throw away,
at the same time, all chance of extending our circulation in the country; for, the moment we say anything
particularly displeasing to the Rebels, the Picayune
stands ready for the chance, and steps into our business.
No, no.   Our only chance is to make a good *news* paper, and politically drift with the tide!"

CHAPTER XXIV.

The Beginning Reaction—Northern Emigrants and New Orleans
Natives.

To BE waked up in the morning by a negro, pushing
your musquito-bar aside to hand you a cup of coffee in
bed; to have him presently return with a glass of iced
Congress water, an orange, and the morning papers, and
to be notified that he'll come back after awhile to tell
you when it is time to get up, are traces of the old style
of living in New Orleans, to which our host scrupulously
adhered. Slavery was doubtless very bad; but it did
one thing we shall never have so well done again—it
trained the best personal attendants to the last possibility of perfection. Under their careful ministrations
the most industrious might be excused for an occasional
languid lapse into seductive indolence. No wonder
some ambitious young writer made the discovery, after
Banks's discomfiture on the Red River, that New Orleans has been the Capua of our Northern armies.

The morning papers began to present an altered
tone. A month ago they sang only the softest strains in
honor of the military management, laughed at the rags
of the Confederacy, and had no squeamishness in speaking of Rebels and the rebellion. Now there were pleasant notices of the returning Confederate braves; rejoicings at the revival of the old appearance of things;
hints about Yankee innovations which would soon be
forced to disappear. The old papers, which had helped

fan the flames of secession, and had only been permitted to continue their publication, after the surrender of the city, under the most comprehensive promises of good behavior, went even further. Mr. Lincoln already began to be referred to as a hard master, whose unconstitutional courses a Southerner like Mr. Johnson could not follow; and the demands of the "Radicals" (whom a few weeks before they had been praising), were denounced in terms quite equal to those of the old invectives against the Abolitionists.

Everywhere one observed the same signs of reaction. The returning Rebel soldiers seemed to have called into active utterance all the hostility to Northerners that for nearly four years had lain latent. Men quoted the North Carolina proclamation, and thanked God that there had suddenly been found some sort of a breakwater against Northern fanaticism. There were whispers that Governor Wells[32] (who had been nominated as Lieutenant-Governor on the ticket with Governor Hahn,[33] under the Banks[34] military reorganization, and who, on Hahn's election as Senator, had succeeded to the Governorship), was about going over to the planting (that is, to the Rebel) party. He had got all he could out of the Free-State party; as his old friends returned, and as the North Carolina proclamation emboldened him, he naturally drifted to the side where his sympathies had always drawn him. But a day or two before, this sallow-faced little official, who, but for the necessities of the Banks reorganization, would never have risen from the obscurity of his remote Red River plantation,* had received a young Northern officer, settled in

[32] J. Madison Wells, Governor of Louisiana, March 1865 to June, 1867. [Ed.]

[33] Georg Michael Decker Hahn, Governor of Louisiana, February 1864 to March 1865. [Ed.]

[34] Nathaniel Prentiss Banks, Union general in command of the department, 1862-1864. [Ed.]

New Orleans, and an applicant for an office which he thought he could fill. The Governor had already begun the free appointment of Rebel officers, but a Northern officer who had been wounded on the loyal side—to the success of which side alone he owed his position—presented a different sort of a case.

"The truth is, sir, that we're very much obliged to you for all you Northern gentlemen have done; but now that you are successful, you had better go home. Louisiana must be governed by Louisianians!"

The bubbling of the political caldron was at its hight. General Banks had removed Mr. Kennedy,[35] the Mayor of the city. In turn, he had himself been superseded, and now it was rumored that the representations of his creature, the Governor, who had betrayed him, having been listened to at Washington, his humiliation was to be made complete by the restoration of Kennedy.

[35] Hugh Kennedy, Mayor of New Orleans, March 1865 to March 1866. [Ed.]

---

* And who subsequently thought it in good taste for *him*, of all men, to refer, in a public speech, to the Chief Justice of the United States, as "the political adventurer who has recently been among us!" A very intelligent correspondent ("V. H.") of the Cincinnati Commercial, writing from the Governor's home, gives the following account of him: "Governor Wells does not seem to have much honor in his own parish. He was sheriff here once, and defaulter to a large amount. His brother, Montford Wells, has since been sued as one of the securities upon the forfeited bond. Montford and Jeff., both brothers of J. Madison (the Governor), married sisters—heiresses. The joint weddings—runaway matches—were a 'spree,' the gay young couples chartering a steamboat, and with a large party of merry guests, setting off from Alexandria, firing a salute, as a note of defiance to the grim, gray old guardian, who had presumed to threaten the course of true love (despite the adage, about to run so smooth down Red River), with vain opposition. Jeff.'s wife has been for some time in the Insane Asylum, and, since the death of Jeff. himself, Montford has been trying to get possession of the estate, in his wife's name, and for the interest of his insane sister-in-law. J. Madison (the Governor), however, had interfered, as the representative of his brother Jeff. Why, I can't understand, for Montford is older than the Governor."

Such was the reward already being reaped for the pro-
scription of Durant, Flanders, and the other genuine
Union men of the State, in the mongrel military reorganization.

Carondelet Street, during these days, presented a curious scene. Sometimes it was impossible to approach
within a couple of squares of the Provost-Marshal's
office, so great was the throng of returning Rebel soldiers, applying for their paroles. It was a jolly, hand-
shaking, noisy, chattering crowd. Pushing about among
them could be seen women, sometimes evidently of
wealth and position, seeking for their brothers or husbands. Nothing could exceed the warmth with which
they all greeted the ragged fellows in gray, and every
few moments one found his own eyes growing dim as
he watched the touching embrace of dear ones from
whom for four years they had been parted.* "Regis-

---

* Bankrupt in all but honor, the paroled soldiers of the Confederacy can only tender to the ladies of New Orleans their undying
gratitude for the cordial welcome which has greeted their advent
in the city, and pray that God will bless the "ministering angels,"
who have lifted from their hearts the dark cloud of gloom and despondency, and turned its "silver lining" outward, brightened
with their smiles. Congregated here only for a brief space, they
will soon be widely scattered, perhaps never to meet again. They
are returning home with blighted hopes and ruined fortunes; all
but honor, and the will which can never be conquered, lost in the
terrible struggle through which they have passed. Many of them
will be voluntary exiles from the fair Southern land which gave
them birth; but wherever their wandering fate may lead, they will
bear with them, among treasured relics of the past, a remembrance
ever more dear and sacred of the noble women of New Orleans,
who have had courage to believe that misfortune may exist without guilt, and, refusing to worship the rising sun, have turned
aside from the prosperous and the powerful, to bestow their prayers,
their tears, and their smiles upon them.—*N. O. Picayune, June* 17.

tered enemies," too, were returning; there was a general
reunion and rejoicing, and amid it all, the men who had
been fleeing before Sheridan, or surrendering under
Lee, soon found it easy to forget how badly they had
been beaten, or how generously their treason had been
treated.

I do not think the Northern men who had come into
New Orleans since its surrender, and who now so largely
controlled its business, were doing much to promote a
healthier tone of public feeling. Most of them were
engrossed in trade. Scarcely any, officers or civilians,
would hesitate to join with the Southerners in talk
against the Abolitionists and the Sumnerites. Nearly
all of them fell readily enough into the current abuse of
niggers and nigger-lovers. And it seemed too prevalent an idea that, in order to secure profitable business,
a man must either sink politics altogether, or fall into
the old habit of pandering to the prejudices of those
with whom he traded. Clearly, the days of Northern
flunkeyism had not entirely passed away.

New Orleans had proved a rich harvest-field to a
crowd of new men and miscellaneous adventurers from
the North. Hundreds had accumulated fortunes since
the occupation of the city. Here is a single case: A
gentleman, unfortunate in previous business ventures,
and without a thousand dollars in the world, came to
New Orleans, to see if something would turn up. The
sugar-planters had all ostentatiously proclaimed that the
Emancipation Proclamation had demoralized their labor
and ruined their business. Some, through spite, others
because they believed it, were absolutely abandoning
the cane as it stood in their fields, on the ground that
the negroes couldn't be trusted to make the sugar.

This gentleman saw his chance. First purchasing the matured cane from the owners for a trifle, to be paid out of the returns of the crop, he went to the negroes, told them he was a Northern man, and would pay them fairly for their work, if they would go ahead and make the sugar. In this way he soon had a dozen or more plantations running again; and in a few months, the end of the sugar season brought him a hundred and thirty thousand dollars net profit!

Subsequently the same man took to purchasing cotton, on a system of what seemed utterly reckless speculation. He would buy a hundred thousand dollars' worth, ship it to New York, and check against his bills of lading for its full value. This money he instantly invested in another lot of cotton of equal amount, which he likewise shipped and checked against; then reinvesting, shipping again, checking again, still making fresh purchases, each with the money thus procured, and so building up his commercial house of card-boards. It thus happened that he sometimes used his hundred thousand dollars a dozen times over, before the returns were half in from his earlier shipments. So enormous became the ventures of this man, who started two years before on nothing, that he had on the ocean, exposed to the perils of ocean navigation, at one time, seven hundred thousand dollars' worth of cotton!

Few of these Northerners had yet made permanent investments in the South. Plantations had not begun to come into the market. Southerners had hardly had time to look about them and decide what to do. But it was already evident that, provided they could make titles which were good for anything, plenty of them would soon be anxious to sell. Northern capital and energy were likely to have still finer openings within a few months, than any that the confusion of a captured city and the chaos of constantly shifting military government had afforded.

Among the earliest callers, the day after our arrival, were General Canby[36] and General Banks. The former is a plain, rather heavy-looking regular, giving you the impression of a martinet, though officers of excellent judgment speak highly of his abilities. He knows nothing about politics, tries to confine himself to the purely military duties of his department, and says he told the Secretary of War he didn't feel fit to undertake the management of the complex questions arising out of the political relations of his department.

General Banks was fully sensible of the treachery which the person he had made Governor was contemplating; still, he seemed to think that if his reorganized government could only have been recognized by Congress, the evils that were then upon the state would have been in some way averted. Now he saw no remedy but in negro suffrage, and for this he was disposed to give hearty co-operation. He had doubts as to whether the General Government would have power to insist upon it; but, in some way or another, not only justice to the loyal blacks, but absolute safety to the loyal whites and to the nation, required it.

A call by the members of the New Orleans bar in a body, to pay their respects to the Chief Justice, gave one an opportunity not often afforded to see the lawyers of this leading city together. They were a fine-looking body of men, mostly of marked Southern accent and manner, very courteous, and, on the whole,

[36] Edward Richard Sprigg Canby, Union general who succeeded General Banks in command at New Orleans. [Ed.]

impressing a stranger as of much more than ordinary
ability. Many of them were by no means as loyal as
they might be; and a few were in sore trouble about
the test oath, which prevented their-practicing in the
United States Court.

In the evening we were taken to a fair held by the
Catholic negroes—mostly of the old Louisiana free-
negro stock. By one of the curious revenges of these
avenging times, the fair was held in the elegant residence of no less a person than ex-Senator and ex-
Minister Pierre Soulé. He who had so often demonstrated negro inferiority and the rightfulness of slavery
was now an exile, seeking a precarious livelihood by
the practice of the law in a foreign language, in the City
of Mexico; while the inferior negroes were selling ice-
cream from his tables and raffling fancy articles in his
spacious parlors, for the benefit of the slave children's
schools!

Nowhere else in the world could that scene have
been witnessed. There were elegantly dressed ladies,
beautiful with a beauty beside which that of the North
is wax-work; with great, swimming, lustrous eyes, half-
veiled behind long, pendent lashes, and arched with
coal-black eyebrows; complexions no darker than
those of the Spanish senoritas one admires in Havana,
but transparent as that of the most beautiful Northern
blonde, with the rich blood coming and going, under
the olive skin, with every varying emotion; luxuriant
flowing tresses, graceful figures, accomplished manners—perfect Georgian or Circassian beauties. Yet
every one of these was "only a nigger." Many of
them had been educated in Paris, and more than one
Parisian wardrobe shimmered that evening under the

radiance of Mr. Pierre Soulé's chandeliers. Some of them were wealthy; all were intelligent, and some conversed in the foreign tongue in which they addressed us, with a vivacity and grace not often surpassed in Washington ball-rooms. But they were only niggers. They might be presented to the Empress Eugenie; they might aspire to the loftiest connections in Europe; but they were not fit to appear in a white man's house in New Orleans, and the Chief Justice was eternally disgraced (according to the talk of the city next day), for having so forgotten dignity, and even decency, as to enter a parlor filled with niggers that were trying to play lady and gentleman!

These people were not always outcasts. Under the great Napoleon they were citizens of the French Empire. It was only when the flag of the free came to cover them that they were disfranchised; only when they were transferred to a republic that they lost their political rights. Hitherto they have held themselves aloof from the slaves, and particularly from the plantation negroes; have plumed themselves upon their French descent, and thus isolated from both races, have transferred to Paris an allegiance that was rejected at Washington.

"But now," as one of them very frankly said during the evening, "we see that our future is indissolubly bound up with that of the negro race in this country; and we have resolved to make common cause, and rise or fall with them. We have no rights which we can reckon safe while the same are denied to the field-hands on the sugar plantations."

Among the negro men present were several who, whether in complexion, clothes or conversation, would never have been suspected in any mixed company at the North of being other than intelligent and polished ornaments of the Anglo-Saxon race. Mingled with these were others of darker hues, ranging down to mulattoes, and even darker still; and among them were several negro officers whose behavior Generals Butler and Banks had highly praised. A group of beautiful ladies, apparently white, was suddenly invaded by a quaint old chocolate-colored dame, with high bandana wound about her head, subscription-book in hand, and the most extraordinary squeaking tones, calling for the taking of shares in her raffle. She was the grandmother of two of the young ladies! Madame Mottier, a mulatto, or quadroon, in whose education I think Boston had some hand, seemed to be the inspiring divinity of the fair, to whom all looked for direction or advice. She is teacher in a colored school.

By and by Mr. Pierre Soulé's piano, under quadroon fingers, began a march, and manly voices—albeit not from Rebel throats—swelled the chorus. And so we left them: negroes raffling fans and picture-frames and sets of jewelry in the Soulé parlors; negroes selling ice-cream in the Soulé dining-room; negroes at his piano; negroes in his library; negroes swarming amid his shrubbery; and yet as handsome, as elegantly dressed, and in many respects almost as brilliant a party as he himself ever gathered beneath his hospitable roof.

Remembering how eagerly they had been buying portraits of Mr. Lincoln, I could not fail to recall, as we drove back, what I had seen in a picture gallery during the day, where there were no obnoxious "niggers" about. A picture of Lincoln hung side by side with one of Wilkes Booth, and above the two was a large, handsomely finished portrait of Robert E. Lee!

CHAPTER XXV.

Among the Negro Schools.

In the good old times, before the advent of Farragut and Butler, the statutes of Louisiana declared teaching slaves to read and write a "crime, having a tendency to excite insubordination among the servile class, and punishable by imprisonment at hard labor for not more than twenty-one years, or by death, at the discretion of the court." When asked, therefore, to visit the negro schools of New Orleans, I was not unduly sanguine in my expectations. Reverend and Lieutenant Wheelock, a keen, practical Yankee preacher, acting as secretary to the "Board of Education for Freedmen," instituted by General Banks, was guide.

The first school-house to which we were conducted was an old store-room, the second story of which had been used as a hall for the Knights of the Golden Circle, and still bore on its walls the symbols of that hollowest and most insolent of Southern humbugs. Rude partitions divided the store-room, and separated the three different grades of the primary school.

In the first we were received by a coarse, ill-dressed, rude-looking man, who evidently sprang from the poor white trash. Ranged along the wall as we entered were a dozen or more boys, reading as boys do read, in the Third Reader—with many a pause and many a tracing of hard words with a great fore-finger that blurs everything it touches. Among the class was a bright, fair-haired boy, who would have been called handsome anywhere. Seated behind the little desks were some large, coarse girls, seemingly eighteen or twenty years of age, conning their spelling-books. The hot air was languidly stirred by the hot breeze from the street windows, which brought in with it the sound of boys at play on the pavement; and one did not wonder at the noise and general inattention that prevailed.

The next room was ruled by a woman as coarse and slatternly as became the neighbor of the man whose school we had just left. A little fellow made some noise to displease her as we entered, and she bowled him against the wall as one would bowl a ball down a ten-pin alley. Children were at work mumbling over charts hung against the wall, and professing, with much noisy show of industry, to be spelling out simple sentences. But their zeal did not prevent surreptitious pinches, when the slatternly school-mistress's back was turned, nor a trade of "five alleys for a bright-colored glass one," on the sly. I think such scenes are not unknown even in model Northern schools.

The teacher in the third room was as great a contrast to the two we had just seen as was her school to theirs. She was smart, bright, looking for all the world like a Lowell factory girl of the better class; and her pupils, though by no means quiet as lambs, were in fine order. Their faces had evidently been washed systematically; long labors had forced upon their comprehension the advantages of clean aprons and pinafores; and they appeared attentive and noisily anxious to learn. This teacher seemed capable of giving an intelligent opinion as to the capacities of her scholars. She had taught at the North, and she saw no difference in the rapidity with which whites and blacks learned to spell and read. There were dull scholars and bright scholars everywhere. Some here were as dull as any she ever saw; others were bright as the brightest. And she called out a little coal-black creature, who had been in school eight days, and was apparently not more than as many years old. The eyes of the little thing sparkled as she began to spell! Eight days ago she had not known her letters. From spelling she went to reading, and was soon found to have mastered every sentence on the charts hung about the walls.

The more advanced scholars were found in the old hall of the K. G. C., up stairs. Here, where once schemes for taking Cuba, or perpetuating slavery in the South, were discussed, forty or fifty boys and girls, lately slaves, stood before the platform where the knights had ranged themselves for initiation, and peacefully recited their lesson in the Fourth Reader! Where once the Knight Commander sat, stalked now a loose-jointed, angular oddity from one of the Middle States—narrow-headed, and with ideas in proportion, which he seemed in nowise fitted to impart. Nigger school-teaching was manifestly not the respectable thing to do in New Orleans; and the Board seemed to have been put to sad straits sometimes for teachers. The reading was bunglingly done, but the teacher didn't read so very much better himself. On spelling the class did better. In geography they had learned by rote the answers to the common questions; and they could point out with considerable accuracy, on the outline maps, New Orleans and Louisiana, and the Mississippi River and the Gulf of Mexico. But one

woolly-headed urchin brought his teacher to grief and
wrath, by selecting Cuba as the proper location for
Iceland; matters were nowise improved by the further
transfer of Asia to the exact latitude and longitude of
San Francisco. Yet, with all the allowances, it was a
fair average school. Boys and girls, ranging in age
from twelve to twenty, read the Fourth Reader passa-
bly; some of them had a fair conception of geography,
and they had even made an entrance on the mysteries
of grammar. Arithmetic seemed to be all plain sailing till they reached long division. Here the process
became too complicated, and they were sure to blunder
in the multiplication of the divisor by the dividend,
or to add where they should subtract, or to bring down
the wrong figures at the wrong time. Was it the fault
of the stupid teacher? or was their previous progress
due to their imitative faculties, and did they fail now
simply because they had reached a point where reason-
ing powers of their own were needed? It is the question which touches the marrow of the whole discussion
about the average negro capacity; but the time has
been too short and the experiments have been too in-
complete as yet to furnish satisfactory data for its
solution.

The next school to which we were conducted was
kept by a middle-aged negro, in gold spectacles, and
with amusingly consequential air. His assistant—
what would not the Opposition journals have given for
such a fact during the late political campaign?—was
an English girl, young and lame, who seemed to have
gone to work here, "among the niggers," very much
as she would have gone to work among the pots and
kettles, simply because a living was to be earned, and
this way to earn it happened to offer. The negro

principal had a short, sharp way of dealing with his pupils; and strap and ferule lay convenient for immediate use beside the books upon his table. He explained that many of his pupils were "contrabans," from the plantations, or negroes that had been "refugeed" from the Red River country; and their experiences in slavery had been such that they knew no motive for obedience but the fear of punishment. "Coax 'em and they'll laugh at you; you've got to knock 'em about, or they won't think you've got any power over 'em." The theory seemed to have made a pretty good school, whether by virtue of the ferule or in spite of it.

The children were having their noon recess when we entered, and the school-room was perfectly quiet. At the sound of the bell they came trooping noisily to the door, and in a few moments the black tide had overflowed all the desks. A Fourth Reader class was called up, which read well—quite as well as the average of such classes anywhere. Now and then one noticed a curious mouthing of the words and a quaint mispronunciation that the forms of the ordinary negro dialect would not account for. In these cases the children were of French parentage, and were learning a language as well as the art of reading. "The children are taught exclusively in English," the Board of Education say sententiously in their report. "Bound by the strong ligament of a common tongue, they will never foster the subtle enmity to national unity that lurks in diversity of speech."

The exercises in arithmetic that followed disclosed the same slower progress in this than in other branches, which had already been observed in the schools previously visited. A few questions of a miscellaneous nature showed that the scholars were by no means destitute of general intelligence; and especially that they had a very keen appreciation of the fact that they had once been slaves, but were so no longer.

We were treated to a special performance before we left—reserved for the closing of the school, except upon grand occasions. An astonishing youth, with wool growing down almost to his eyebrows, beneath which gleamed cunning eyes that alone relieved the face from an expression of utter stupidity, took his place in the aisle in front of the teacher's desk. The hum of the school suddenly hushed, and all eyes were fastened on the droll figure. The woolly head gave a bob forward, while the body seemed to go through contortions caused by some inward pain. As the head ducked down the second time and came up with snapping eyes, the opening of the song was ejected, and the shrill voice was soon drowned in the roar that joined in from the whole open-throated throng.

Such singing may never be heard elsewhere. The nearest approach a Northern reader is ever likely to make to it is when he hears the enthusiastic chorus at some noisy camp-meeting about the time the "power" is supposed to be "coming down, coming down." The song was nothing—a rhyming effort of the gold-spec-tacled teacher himself, I believe, rudely setting forth the joy of the slaves at the great deliverance, and ending in a refrain of thanks and prayer for "Honest Abe." But the negroes, too, have learned to worship the rising rather than the setting sun. "Honest Abe" was very well in his way; but if the schools were to be continued and the teachers paid, there would be more present need of help from his successor. And so the song had been already patched; and the refrain came thundering in for "Andie J." After all, there is a good deal of human nature in negroes!

Some rickety, tumble-down buildings on an out-of-the-way corner had been secured for another school, which we next visited. A motherly old negress here had her brood of little ones gathered about her, learning in concert the alphabet from the chart which she held in her lap. Up the row and down it she led them with the little pointer, which looked as if it might be chosen a double duty to perform. Now one was singled out to name a letter selected at random from some other chart; then the pointer flitted from top to bottom and back to middle of the alphabet, and the shiny-faced urchins eagerly shouted the responses, or winced as the pointer descended threateningly near some naughty hand that was wandering into foreign pockets.

In another room, a bright, lady-like young quadroon, who was similarly occupied, smiled a pleasant greeting as we entered. She had been at the fair at Pierre Soulé's. With ample means and a pleasant home, she volunteered to do this work of duty to her race; and the neat, orderly school-room, with the quiet ways and clean faces of her little charge, not less than their prompt answers, told her success.

In one of the rooms in this building a row of picaninnies, ranging from four to fourteen, stood up to recite in the First Reader. At their head, painfully spelling his way through a sentence as we entered, was an old man of sixty, with white wool and a wrinkled face. He wore a pair of huge brass-rimmed spectacles; but they would not stick on his bullet-shaped head without further contrivance, and so he had tied a bit of packing-cord into the ends of the brass temples, and around his head. I asked the old man what he wanted to learn to read for.

"Reckon if it's good for white folks, good for me too."

"But you're so old, uncle, one would think you would n't care for such things any more."

'Reckon if it's good for chil'en, can't be bad for old folks."

Subsequent talk showed that the old man had a Bible, and wanted to learn to read it, and, further, that he believed, as soon as he could read, he would be entitled to vote. Precisely what good that would do him he did not seem to understand; but he worked away industriously over his well-thumbed First Reader, and scarcely gave a second look to the visitors, at whom the children were staring with all their eyes. It was a trifling thing, doubtless, and the old man may have been very silly to be thus setting himself to children's tasks, in the simplicity of his desire to learn what he knew white folks had found good for them; but to me there seemed nothing more touching or suggestive in all the sights of New Orleans.

We saw no other old men in the schools, and few young ones beyond the age of twenty; but the teachers said the cases were quite numerous in which the more intelligent scholars were instructing their parents at home. In all such instances the parents were sure to enforce regular attendance on the part of their children, and the influence of the school became reflex, first on the scholars, from them to the families, thence back to the school again.

The few schools spoken of above may be taken as a fair specimen of the system in operation in New

Orleans in June, 1865. It was soon destined to give way to the reaction of public feeling, which already began to influence the affairs of the department. But it had now been carried on for fourteen months. Few, even of the most advanced, had, at the beginning, been able to read the simplest sentence. Now there were classes in geography, grammar, and arithmetic, and a very fair proportion of the fourteen thousand seven hundred and forty-one scholars could read quite intelligently. The gate of knowledge had been opened to them; there was little likelihood that hereafter a General commanding would be able to stop the spread of these dangerous arts of reading and writing, by an official notification that the opening of schools for negro children would be very hazardous and unwise.*

So rapid was the progress that, on the 1st of January, 1865, the scholars had advanced so far as to be thus classified:

Writing on slates, 3,883; writing in copy-books, 1,108; studying grammar, 283; studying geography, 1,838; studying practical arithmetic, 1,223; studying mental arithmetic, 4,628; reading, 7,623; spelling, 8,301; learning the alphabet, 2,103.

And from the beginning of the experiment down to the 1st of June, 1865, there had been a regular increase of eleven hundred and fourteen scholars and fourteen teachers per month. Two thousand new scholars had come into the schools in May alone; in April there had been fifteen hundred. The expense of this entire system was about one-half what it cost to support a single

---

* General Emory so admonished Rev. Thomas Conway, months after our occupation of the city. The idea seemed to be, that the Rebel population could not have their feelings agitated by efforts to teach their negroes, without great danger of popular disturbances!

regiment in the field. This expense was to be met by a tax on the property within the lines of military occupation; General Banks's order explaining, for the comfort of dissatisfied tax-payers, that henceforth labor must be educated in the South in order to be valuable, and that if they did n't support the negro schools, they would find it hard to secure negro labor.

Judging, both from personal observation and from the testimony of the teachers and the Board of Education, I should say that the negro pupils are as orderly and as easily governed as any corresponding number of white children, under similar circumstances. There is, I think, a more earnest desire to learn, and a more general opinion that it is a great favor to have the opportunity. There is less destruction of books, less whittling of school furniture, less disposition to set up petty revolts against the teacher's authority. The progress in learning to read is exceptionally rapid. I do not believe that in the best schools at the North they learn the alphabet and First Reader quicker than do the average of these slave children. The negroes are not quicker-witted, but they are more anxious to learn. In writing they make equally rapid progress, and where the teachers are competent they do well in geography. Arithmetic presents the first real obstacles, and arouses painful inquiries as to the actual mental capacity of this long-neglected race.

But, up to this point, the question of negro education is no longer an experiment. In reading and writing I do not hesitate to say that the average progress of the children of plantation hands, as shown in every negro school from Fortress Monroe around to New Orleans, is fully equal to the average progress of white children at the North.

The experiment of high schools is about to be tried among them, under the auspices of a voluntary organization, mainly made up and sustained by themselves. Its constitution was adopted a fortnight or more before our visit, and such men as Thomas J. Durant were uniting with the negroes in an effort to get the enterprise properly started.

On the Sunday after our visit to these schools, we were taken to see a Sunday-school, made up largely of the same scholars, although conducted under the auspices of Mr. Conway, a business-like preacher, in charge of the Freedmen's Bureau in the city. The building into which we were conducted had been, in former times, a medical college. Ranged upon the seats, which arose, amphitheater-like, half-way to the ceiling, sat row after row of closely-crowded, smiling, black-faced, but bright-eyed, Sunday-school scholars, as clean, as smiling, and as prettily dressed as one would see almost anywhere in our Northern rural districts. On the higher benches, where the larger scholars sat, were a few young ladies, tastefully attired in white. At that distance, one had difficulty in seeing that their faces were not of the pure Anglo-Saxon tinge; but, neat and pretty as they looked, they were only niggers, and nigger Sunday-school teachers at that.

A graduate of Amherst met us as we mounted the platform once occupied by the demonstrator of anatomy. He was a sober, sedate figure, in professional black, and, with his dignified ways, might have been taken for a Southern Doctor of Divinity, if you did not look at his face. That was as black as his coat. His son, a handsome, graceful young fellow (always barring the black face and the kinky wool), took his seat at the piano. The sober representative of Amherst rapped on the table, and tapped the little bell, till the children slowly and gradually mastered the almost irrepressible torrent of whispers and laughter. But the bell-taps sounded clearer and clearer; silence at last reigned. A hymn was read; the young negro at the piano softly touched the keys for a moment, and then the whole rich, joyous nature of the children gushed into a volume of melody that rose and swelled till the very air of the old lecture-room was vocal with praise. It was like listening to the grand peals of Plymouth Church itself.

There followed a little address, with, perhaps, a trifle too much of talk about their liberty, and too little of how it should be made profitable; too much about the prejudices against them, and too little about the means for an improvement which should conquer prejudices; too much about the faults of their masters, and too little about their own. But this seems to be the general strain; and perhaps, after all, it may be necessary, in some such way, to gain the confidence of the children before you can instruct them. Occasional questions kept alive the interest, and the lustily shouted answers showed an intelligence that plainly took in the full meaning of the speech.

"What great man freed you all, and was then taken home?"

Surely, if the murdered President could but have been present, beside his old associate, at that scene, he would have thought the shouts that brought back his name the sweetest praise the lips of mortals ever bore him.

"Are you really free now?"

"Yes, yes"

"What would you do if anybody should now try to take your freedom away?"

It was fine to watch the play of surprise and apprehension across the animated faces. "We'd fight," exclaimed a sturdy fellow, twelve or fourteen years old. "We wouldn't let them," said many more. "The soldiers would stop it," murmured the most. That, alas! seemed still the main hope of these submissive, long-enslaved people. They had not reached—not even the oldest of them—the conception of organized effort to protect themselves. "The soldiers would stop it." That was all.

CHAPTER XXVI.

Talks with the Citizens, White and Black

ONE morning we were interrupted at lunch by a message that Mr. Durant had called with the party for whom he had made the engagement yesterday. Remembering that Mr. Durant had promised to bring around some of the "ancient freedmen," as they were called—that, is the free negroes of French descent—I went out a few moments afterward to witness the interview. A group of gentlemen stood about Mr. Chase in the library, and one, a bald-headed, gray-bearded, vivacious, youngish-old man was making an animated little address.

I felt sure that here was a mistake. Imagining that some other party had got into the library by accident—some delegation of Rebel lawyers, perhaps, to remonstrate against the test oath—I turned into the parlors to hunt up Mr. Durant and his French negroes. But they were nowhere to be found; and returning to the library, I saw in the furthest corner Mr. Durant himself, listening to the talk of the bald-headed old spokes-man. Even then it was hard to realize that these quiet, well-bred gentlemen, scarcely one darker than Mr. Durant himself—many of them several shades whiter—were negroes, to be seen walking with whom on the streets of New Orleans was social disgrace. Before their call was concluded, old Mr. Jacob Barker was shown into the parlor. The eminently respectable and conservative old banker looked more like a negro, in point of complexion, than any one out of the twelve or fifteen in Mr. Durant's party.

Every man of them was well educated. All spoke French fluently; the English of all was passable, of some perfect. Some of them were comparatively wealthy, and all were in easy circumstances. They simply asked the Chief Justice to represent to the President, in their behalf, that they paid heavy taxes to support schools for the whites, and could get none for themselves; that they paid heavy taxes to support city and State governments, and were without voice in either; and that they desired to ask whether this accorded with Mr. Johnson's well-known ideas of genuine democracy? They had been citizens of an Empire; when the Republic bought Louisiana they were disfranchised. Now that the Republic was beginning a new life, could it longer refuse them such rights as the Empire had accorded? What answer can legislators give who profess to believe the Declaration of Independence, and who cheerfully confirm a full-blooded Indian in a conspicuous position on the staff of their Lieutenant General?

One pleasant afternoon, when the June sun was a little less fervid than usual, and a moist breeze blew across the lake, we drove up the levee, past elegant country places, embowered in shrubbery and half concealed from the road by luxuriant hedges of Cherokee rose, to the residence of Mr. Roselius, to keep an engagement for dinner. Our genial old host came running out to greet us, hurrying like a boy down the high steps, which, after the prevailing fashion in this moist climate, lead directly from the paved walk to the second-story veranda. A dozen or more gentlemen were in the parlor. Among them I remember two or three noted New Orleans lawyers, one or two sugar-planters who had been absent in Europe during the war, and a Spanish officer, fresh from some one of the perpetually recurring South American revolutions. One noticed here, as at most of the formal dinner parties given during our stay, and at my subsequent visits to the city, the absence of all ladies save those of the host's household. Indeed, except in peculiar cases like this, the prevailing idea of a dinner in New Orleans seems to have for its leading feature copious libations of a great many kinds of the choicest wines— to be licensed by the earliest possible retiracy of the hostess.

Among Mr. Roselius's guests that evening was a modest-looking little gentleman, of retiring manners, and with apparently very little to say; though the keen eyes and well-shaped head sufficiently showed the silence to be no mask for poverty of intellect. It was Mr. Paul Morphy, the foremost chess-player of the world, now a lawyer, but, alas! by no means the foremost young lawyer of this his native city. "If he were only as good in his profession as he is at chess-playing!" said one of the legal gentlemen, with a shrug of his shoulders, as he spoke in an undertone of the abilities of the elder Morphy, and the hopes that had long been cherished of the son. They evidently looked upon the young chess-player as a prosperous banker does upon his only boy, who persists in neglecting his desk in the bank parlor and becoming a vagabond artist.

The gentlemen just returned from Europe expressed

their astonishment at the fortunes that had been accumulated by shrewd adventurers during their absence.
Men whom they had left the masters of Carondelet
Street, they found in a state of genteel beggary. New
names had arisen, unknown to their four-year old
memories of the city. "By the way, Mr. Durant,"
said one, "how does it happen that you haven't profited more by your chances—become Governor, or Senator, say, if you didn't care for any more money?"

> "I should have blushed if Cato's house had stood secure
> And flourished in a civil war,"

was the ready and only response.

Political subjects were scarcely alluded to; but, after
the party had rejoined the ladies, or strolled out among
Mr. Roselius's olive and orange-trees, it was easy to see
that the feeling of the Unionists was by no means
sanguine. Some insisted that the Rebels were certain
to resume control at the first election; others hoped
for better things, but frankly added that there was no
security save in the interference of Congress. "Let
this election go on," said Mr. Durant, "and a Legislature will be chosen which wouldn't hesitate at sending John Slidell and Judah P. Benjamin to the Senate
again! Perhaps policy would prevent the choice of
just those men; but the only change would be in the
substitution of persons with the same principles and
less ability. If you don't get brilliant and artful
Rebels, the lack of genius will be made up by malignity."

Remembering that this Legislature subsequently did
elect Mr. Randall Hunt, I have recalled with special
interest the impressions left by the conversation of that

gentleman, one morning, when he came to breakfast with the Chief Justice, to whom he is remotely related by his marriage into the family of the late Justice McLean, of the Supreme Court.

Mr. Hunt is in the prime of life, though his constitution seems somewhat broken, and his nervousness is extreme. He has been for years one of the leading lawyers of New Orleans. The secessionists seem to regard him as the foremost orator now left them. The Unionists concede that he is a fine speaker, but describe him as given to painfully elaborate rhetoric and ornate delivery. I have been told by Governor Hahn that Mr. Hunt was once asked by General Banks to give up the Rebel cause, and unite in the Free-State movement. It was intimated that, in return for his influence, the Governorship of the State would await his acceptance. Mr. Hunt took a day to consider the matter; then replied that he had supported the Rebel side, was thoroughly committed to it, had near and dear relatives by his advice then out in the armies fighting for it, and could not think of abandoning them! Possibly a whisper of this bit of secret history may have since helped in Mr. Hunt's election as United States Senator by the returned Rebels.

It was easy to see how earnest were his sympathies with the men who had been fighting the Rebel battles. With him, as with most of the better classes in the South, this feeling is wholly unaffected by the utter defeat of all their hopes. To them the Rebel soldiers are still patriots, defeated, but not disgraced, in an ineffectual struggle against mercenary invaders; martyrs without the crown; heroes who have hazarded everything for their native land, and who now deserve only blessings from every true son of the State.

Reconstruction seemed to him an easy task. "We tried to leave the Union. You have defeated us in our effort. What can there be, then, for us to do but to return our Senators and Representatives to the Congress from which we tried to withdraw forever? We acknowledge the defeat, and are ready to send back our Congressmen. That is what you have been fighting for; what more can the General Government have to do with the matter?"

The Amnesty Proclamation had just arrived. Like nearly all other men of Southern sympathies, he thought the exceptions very unwise, and needlessly irritating. "You 've determined to keep us in the Union. Is n't it more statesmanlike, then, to avoid adding to our popular discontent? Is it better to have us a conquered province, or an integral part of the nation—better to have an Ireland on the Gulf, or a Scotland?"

The proposition for negro suffrage seemed to him utterly loathsome. "Surely, sir," said he to the Chief Justice, "you do not know the negro. If you but understood as we understand the condition of these people, their ignorance, their degradation, you would shrink back in horror from your own proposition." Mr. Hunt forgot that these once degraded creatures had been rescued from their native barbarism, and, as he and the other Southern orators have so often told us, had been elevated and civilized by the Christianizing influences of the system of slavery! If their degradation was now so horrifying, these gentlemen must have been formerly mistaken in regarding slavery as such a Christian civilizer. If they were mistaken then, it is among the possibilities that they may be mistaken now

It is a continual source of surprise to observe how these thorough-going Southern gentlemen speak constantly of their knowledge of the negro, as one might speak of the most recondite theorems of the differential calculus. "If you only knew these negroes as we do— but, then, of course, you can't. Why, we were born among them!" To credit such persons, one must regard the negro's nature as something requiring very profound study and long-protracted investigation. I happened to mention to Mr. Hunt the story of "Old Sandie" of Key West. He considered it a very surprising story, "if credible." "But then, if you understood, from a lifetime's experience, the character and debasement of the negro, you would not be misled by such exceptional cases." I mentioned the prosperity of the Sea Islanders, and their beginnings of self-government. "You saw only the one side of the picture. If you had been born among those people, you would have talked in a very different way."

Nothing short of this "being born among negroes" is accepted as qualification for comprehending their nature. And I have observed that the most strenuous in insisting upon it are able editors, eloquent lawyers, and successful business men, who were born in the North, but have lived so long South that they suppose their origin to be unknown.

Mr. Chase's reply to the address of a negro delegation appeared in the papers before we left the city.* It very briefly expressed his own desire for negro suffrage, and his trust that the conduct of the negroes themselves would be such that, sooner or later, it would be found impossible longer to refuse it. The letter closed with a significant sentence, looking apparently in the direction of the proposed policy which Mr.

* See Appendix, note C.

Horace Greeley afterward condensed into the terse
phrase, "Universal amnesty and universal suffrage."
Not more than half the nominal Louisiana Unionists,
who had during the previous winter made up the two
or three factions of the Free-State party, would publicly
approve it. They thought negro suffrage might become a necessity; but they still hoped something less
offensive would offer safety, and preferred to trust in
Congress and wait for something to turn up. Only
those who followed Mr. Durant accepted the naked
issue. They looked to it as the only salvation of the
Union cause; the only means for securing the rights
of the negro, or for protecting the credit of the Government. The Rebels, meanwhile, considered Mr.
Johnson's North Carolina proclamation as settling the
question in their favor, and already began to talk, in
tones subdued only by the presence of the military
authorities, about soon putting an end to the career of
nigger agitators in Louisiana.

It was noticeable that General Banks, who had just
been relieved, seemed to have gained no popularity by
his relaxation of Butler's iron rule. The returning
Rebels appeared in no way grateful for any of the
concessions he was charged with having made to their
prejudices. The Unionists were in no way grateful for
his late conversion to negro suffrage. All described
his administration as vacillating. When Butler said a
thing, they knew precisely what to expect. He might
be severe, but they always knew where to find him.
Banks, they complained, had done too little for the
radical Unionists to command their confidence, and too
little for the reconstructing Rebels to command theirs.
Possibly a General who should have pleased any one

of these parties would have disobeyed his instructions; certainly he would have displeased the rest. But, at the end, the man who marked out his own policy, and inflexibly pursued it, was found commanding a certain sort of respect. All classes, Rebel or Union, expressed it for General Butler. General Banks was less fortunate.

The General was still occupying, with his hospitable family, the elegant residence of an absent Rebel, in the Garden District. General Sheridan was not less comfortably quartered; and one who had heard of Sheridan and his bold riders only from the newspapers, would have been surprised at being led over velvet carpets, through spacious saloons, to find them. "I'd a great deal rather be allowed to take a good cavalry brigade and cross the Rio Grande," said the uneasy soldier. "I'd ride, with such a force as that, from Matamoras to Mexico."

CHAPTER XXVII.

A Free-labor Sugar Plantation.

AT last came the inevitable hour which forever clouds our pleasantest experiences of travel—the hour for parting. It was once or twice postponed, but the advancing summer admonished us to make no more delays. Mr. May insisted that we should not cease to be his guests till he had shown us his sugar plantation, and so a pleasant party was made up to accompany us.

Among them was Mr. B. F. Flanders, a gentleman who, as the candidate of the Radical Free-State men for Governor against the Banks ticket, had been generally called the leader of that party. He is a man of fine presence, with clear, handsome Grecian face. As Special Agent of the Treasury Department, he has had control of millions, yet, I think, no one ever accused him of corruption, though many have pronounced his rulings unjust, and even Secretary McCulloch once went so far as to call him "a very mischievous officer." Like a large proportion of the prominent men in the South, he has been there so long as to be generally considered a native, although he originally came from the North. A quarter of a century ago he was a young school-teacher, attracted Southward by the larger salaries common in that region. Before the outbreak of the war he was Treasurer of the New Orleans and Opelousas Railroad. Some time after the establishment of the Confederacy, New Orleans became too hot to hold him, and, in common with Cuthbert Bullitt, who persisted in hoisting the United States flag on Jeff. Davis's day of thanksgiving, and a number of other more or less prominent politicians, he had to make his escape to the North. Mr. Denison, a young Texas planter before the war (and during Mr. Lincoln's administration, and a part of Mr. Johnson's, Collector of the Port of New Orleans), was another of the party. He, too, had been compelled to abandon everything, and escape North, by a painful and tedious journey through the mountains of East Tennessee. He lost sixty or seventy slaves by the war. "Several of them were preachers, too; none of your common negro preachers, but orthodox fellows, sound in doctrine, and good members of the Baptist Church." "Yes," explained another, "Denison owned six Baptist preachers, two blacksmiths, and a first-rate carpenter among his gang." The expression was almost equal to that in Sherman's famous dispatch from Savannah, about the "mules, negroes, and horses" he had brought out with him in his march to the sea.

Early in the morning the Wayanda landed us at the noted "Dick Taylor plantation," owned, before the war, by the son of President Taylor, and now occupied by negroes, under authority from the United States. The work here did not seem to be progressing so well as on the little farms of the Sea Islanders, and the sugar-planters of the party shook their heads ominously at the prospect. The negroes seemed to have no one to give unity and direction to their efforts. Their old master was gone, and each one now wanted to be master, not only to himself, but, also, to several of the rest. A couple of their head men even fell into a

quarrel about the truthfulness of their respective statements to the Chief Justice, while still in his presence.
The quarters were not clean; the fences had in some
places been taken for fire-wood, and the general aspect
of the place suggested neglect and decay.*

Near this was another plantation, abandoned by its
Rebel owners, and occupied by lessees from the United
States. The absence of responsible proprietors could
be everywhere read in the dilapidated buildings and
the general air of neglect. Still there was a fair crop
of cane and cotton, and the negroes seemed to be working tolerably well for their Northern employers.

A sharp thunder-storm preceded us a few moments
in our visit to Mr. May's plantation, and we found everything in mud. The Rebels had carried off his carriages, and there was nothing for it but to walk up the
bank, and through the sticky alluvial soil, to the beautiful orange grove, in the midst of which we found
the wide, rambling, many-porched, one-story house,
flanked by the negro cabins and the sugar-house. The
guerrillas had repeatedly ravaged the place, and whatever furniture they could not carry off, they took good
care to break. Still enough had been gathered together
to make half a' dozen rooms quite comfortable. In the
first we entered, a sofa stood in the middle of the floor,
with slippers and dressing-gown lying beside it, hastily
abandoned at our approach. A little stand, holding
a lamp and a book about cotton culture, stood at its
head, and above both was hung a voluminous musquito-

---

* These negroes came out at the end of the year with enough
cotton and sugar—after paying for their own support—to divide
only a few dollars to each first-class hand. Even this result was
better than one would have anticipated in June.

bar. It was the overseer's place of retreat when he wanted to read or write. Before we had been in the house many minutes, we began to appreciate the necessity for such fortifications.

Presently the negroes led up horses, and we started for a gallop over the plantation. It was its third year of profitable culture by free labor. The stock of cane had nearly run out during the first and second years of the war, and, from necessity, cotton had been largely planted; although no one knew better than the proprietor that sugar land was unfit for successful cotton culture.

Coming out behind the negro quarters, we struck the beaten road that ran beside the main ditch, down the middle of the plantation, to the swamp at its further side. On either hand ran off the lateral ditches, and before us stretched a thousand acres of cultivated land, without a tree or a fence, as level as a billiard-table, and almost as green. The corn, of which only enough was planted to furnish the "mules and negroes" with food, was beginning to tassel, and, since the rain, one almost fancied the low, crackling sounds proceeding from it to arise from its lusty growth. Most of it waved over the backs of our horses as we rode among it.

Separated by only a shallow ditch from the corn was the cotton, which, for lack of "plant-cane," was being grown on a part of the land. It grew in cleanly-worked beds, that were not unlike a Northern sweet-potato ridge, and was already ten to fifteen inches high. Here and there were a few "blooms"—the first of the season. They had expanded during the night, were now of a delicate, creamy white, would next day be a dull red, and by evening would fall, leaving the germ of the boll, the tiny throne of the coming king.

Crossing other ditches, we came to the waving expanse of sugar, now nearly three feet high, and growing luxuriantly. A few negroes had come out with their plows, since the rain, and were throwing up the rich, fresh earth against the roots. No time was to be lost, for other things grew as rapidly, in the steaming moisture and under the genial heat, as the cane or cotton, and woe to the planter if, by a day or two of delay, he should be "caught in the grass." The negroes drove their mules along rapidly, but, save when speaking to the animals, in perfect silence. There was no conversation among themselves, as they passed or walked side by side on adjacent rows. A few yards away, one would scarcely know the "plow-gang" was in the field. Cross a ditch, and you were in a solitude of boundless wealth, without a trace or sound of the men that made it, and might ride back and forth over the plantation for miles, without finding them again.

Nearly all the negroes had formerly been Mr. May's slaves. "Did you belong to Mr. May before the war?" I said to one stalwart fellow.

"Bress ye, yes. Who'd ye s'pose I b'long to? I b'longed to Mass'r May, of co'se, and to his father afore him."

"Wouldn't you rather belong to him now?"

"B'long to him now! I's free, sah."

"Yes, but don't you think you would rather belong to him still, and not have to take care of yourself?"

"No, sah. I's free."

"But now you have all the trouble of supporting yourself, buying your own clothes, making your bargains, getting your provisions, and the like. Don't

you think you would get along better if you still had
Mr. May to do all this for you?"

"No, sah. We's git along heap better dis way.
We's free."

Wherein he was better off the man did not seem
clearly to understand, but this he knew, "We's free."
He and all the rest spoke warmly of Mr. May, and
whenever he appeared among them, the lifting of ragged hats and brightening of black faces told that here,
at least, the old kindliness said to have existed between
master and slave had been genuine. But not one of
them could be got to say that he would rather be a
slave again. Nearly all the people had remained on
the place. Several times the guerrillas had driven
them away, but they always returned and took up their
quarters in the old cabins. They knew they were perfectly free to go away if they wished; steamboats could
be hailed at almost any hour, and all had money to pay
their passage; elsewhere higher wages were reported.
But they looked upon "May Lawn" as their home, and
Mr. May as the man for whom they ought to work, and
no persuasion could change their minds.

The overseer was well enough satisfied with the new
order of things. You couldn't drive a nigger quite so
hard, but, on the whole, they worked very well. But
the rascals were, if possible, greater thieves than ever.
It would be crazy to let them plant any cotton themselves, as some of them wanted to do; and it would be
better if there were any way to prohibit their culture
of any grain or other product not needed for their own
consumption, in their gardens. If they had a crop of
ten bushels, you might be sure they would sell fifty,
and you would need better locks than any on this
plantation to keep them from getting the other forty

out of your corn-cribs. If they raised no corn, any-body to whom they offered to sell corn would know it was stolen; but if they raised only a single bushel, there was no check on them, and they would keep sell-ing your property whenever they got half a chance. He had even heard of their stealing corn from the troughs where the mules were eating, to sell it.

Mr. May promised a "bowl of mush and milk" for dinner. When it was announced, it was found to con-sist of a round of plantation delicacies, cooked by the late slaves. Beef and mutton were not to be had on the coast, and fish were not to be procured short of Lake Pontchartrain; but turkeys, ducks, and chickens were abundant, and these, with a profusion of vegeta-bles, showed that planters might live well if they would. That in general they did not, before the war, has been the common testimony of travelers, from Fred. Law Olmsted down.

At sunset the Wayanda fired her parting salute for the Chief Justice, and shortly afterward a blank shot from her bow-gun brought too the W. R. Carter,* which had been selected by General Canby for our trip up the Mississippi. There were hurried good-byes, and as the steamer pushed off again, the flaring torch gave us a last glimpse of the faces of our New Orleans friends, and revealed behind them a dusky group of the late slaves, watching the departure of Mass'r May's guests.

This was the first sugar plantation in the United States cultivated by free labor by its old owner; and the free-labor experiment—if, as the planters insist, it is to be regarded as an experiment—has been tried on

* Since lost, by explosion of her boilers, with fearful sacrifice of life.

it for a longer consecutive period than on any other. Its results may, therefore, be profitably studied, as a fair index to the probable value of the system.

No man would be more apt to be a severer judge of the experiment than the one who had lost the slaves whom he now hired. I accordingly asked Mr. May to give me in writing a statement of the workings of his plantation, and of his opinions as to the possibility of cultivating sugar by free labor. This was duly forwarded, and I make some extracts from it here:

"The transcripts from my plantation books, which I send you herewith, do not, in my judgment, give a fair idea of the workings of the free-labor system. I had to contend not only with the complete disorganization of the State, socially as well as politically, but I was subjected, at various periods, to guerrilla raids. These interrupted labor on the estate for days and weeks at a time, and carried off quantities of provisions, live stock, plows, etc., all of which had to be immediately replaced at great cost. The expenses were thus largely increased, while the delays and neglect proportionately diminished the value of the crop. Then, too, it is a sugar plantation, and is not at all adapted to the culture of cotton, being too near the mouth of the river, and being likewise much more liable than ordinary cotton plantations to the ravages of the army-worm. But, during the war the stock of seed-cane ran out, and I had to put the greater part of the land in cotton. In spite of these difficulties and interruptions, and enormous outlay, the estate has never failed to return a handsome revenue. I feel certain that within the next three years I shall reduce the expenses of the free-labor system fully one-third, and, at the same time, increase the returns in an equally large proportion.

"I pay my laborers what I think, even at the North, you would call good wages for that sort of farm work. They get an average, men and women, boys and girls, of twelve dollars a month each, besides their lodging, food, and medical attendance. One-half of these wages I pay them quarterly, the remainder at the end of the year. Each laborer is paid according to his merits. Some of my hands receive as much as twenty-five dollars a month;

others as little as six dollars. This causes great emulation, and consequently more work is performed; all of which results in favor of both employer and employee. I think it wise policy for the planter to give high wages, as he thus secures a better class of laborers, who work not only industriously but cheerfully.

"I am satisfied, in my own mind, that one able-bodied American negro of ordinary intelligence is worth at least two white emigrants. He understands the business, and he has the advantage of being acclimated. I am willing, therefore, to pay the negroes one-third higher wages than any white laborers accessible to us. You may think this extravagant; but during the unsettled state of affairs for the last two years, I have had to try both, and I base my opinion not on my prejudices, but on my experience."

The statements in the last paragraph are widely at variance with the ideas current among the late slaveholders. Scarcely any believe that the negro can be depended on for labor except in a state of slavery; and the most, therefore, throughout the whole season following the surrender, looked upon the sugar and cotton culture as ruined, unless white laborers could be brought in.

The following are the exhibits of the operation of Mr. May's plantation for the years 1863 and 1864, as taken from his books. One thousand acres only of the plantation were cultivated. One hundred and twenty hands were engaged to do it, at an average of $144 per year, with lodgings and food:

1863.

Plantation supply account		$20,315	00
Amount paid to field hands		18,472	25
" " physician		300	00
" " engineer		625	00
" " sugar-maker		600	00
" " carpenter		1,160	00
" " manager		1,800	00
" " sub-overseer		600	00
Total expenses		$43,872	25

Receipts from sale of 360 hogsheads sugar	$51.480 00
" " 740 barrels molasses	17,020 00
" " 204 bales cotton	81,600 00
" " corn	2,743 00

| Total receipts | $152,843 00 |
| | 43,872 25 |

| Net revenue | $108,970 75 |

1864

Plantation supply account	$18,475 00
Amount paid to field hands	17,265 10
" " physician	300 00
" " white workmen	1,785 20
" " manager	1,800 00
" " sub-overseer	600 00
" paid for repairing	1,420 00

| Total expenses | $41,645 80 |

Receipts from sale of 190 hogsheads sugar	$28,500 00
" " 345 barrels molasses	7,590 00
" " 69 bales cotton	40,792 00
" " corn	822 00

| Total receipts | $77,704 00 |
| | 41,645 30 |

| Net revenue | $36,058 70 |
| Add net revenue of 1863 | 108,970 75 |

| Profit for two years | $145,029 45 |

In the two years, during which all his neighbors allowed their plantations to lie idle, because they knew "free niggers never would make sugar or cotton," Mr. May thus realized a net profit of nearly one hundred and fifty thousand dollars. But for the ravages of the army-worm on his cotton in 1864, the profits for the two years would have run well up toward a quarter of a million.

Much of this success was due, of course, to the high prices produced by the war. But if the prices for the

products were high, so were those for every item of
the expenditures. It will be observed that the negroes
were fed and lodged, but not clothed. Mr. May estimated the cost of food and lodging to be at least six
dollars a month. Add this to the monthly wages, and
we have two hundred and sixteen dollars as the actual
annual cost of each field-hand to the planter, under
the free-labor system. Before the war able-bodied
negroes were commanding from fifteen hundred to
three thousand dollars in the New Orleans market.
Counting only ten per cent. interest on the investment,
we find it nearly as cheap to hire the negroes, as it
was in the old days to own them and get their labor
for nothing. But, as yet, slaveholders will reply to all
such calculations, "Free niggers can never be depended
on to grow cotton."

CHAPTER XXVIII.

The "Jeff. Davis Cotton Plantation."

A FEW negro soldiers were standing guard on the river bank, one day, as our steamer touched to land our party at the lower side of the great bend below Vicksburg, for a visit to the adjacent cotton plantations. The officers sent off for ambulances for us. While we were awaiting their arrival, the relief guard came up, marching with a precision and erect, soldierly bearing that spoke well for their drill sergeants, and proved no small source of astonishment to the party of paroled rebels we had on board.

"A nigger 's just like a monkey," growled one; "whatever he sees a white man do he 'll imitate; and he 'll study over it a cussed sight harder 'n he will over his work. But how one o' them black devils with muskets 'd run ef a white man was to start after him with a whip!" And with this he walked up to one of the soldiers, saying, rather harshly: "Boy, le' me see your gun," and offering to take hold of it. The soldier stepped hastily back, and brought his weapon into position for immediate use. "How the war *has* demoralized the cussed brutes!" muttered the discomfited scion of the master race, as he retired.

It was our first experience on the plantation of Mr. Jefferson Davis. Nearly all the nine thousand acres included in the bend of the river here had formerly be-

longed to Joseph Davis, brother to the President of the
late Confederacy. Jefferson was a soldier and a politician, but no planter. He brought reputation and social
position to the family, but no money. His brother balanced the account by giving him, from his own large
estate, a plantation of a thousand acres. Here, down
to the outbreak of the war, Mr. Davis was accustomed
to spend a portion of his time, his brother and the late
General Quitman[37] being his only neighbors. Negro soldiers were now doing duty on the landing whence his
cotton had been shipped, and "runaway niggers"
were tilling his fertile fields on their own account.

The outer levee was damaged by the unusually high
floods which had brought destruction to so many enterprising planters from the North; and for some hundreds of yards our ambulances cut deep into the rich
mud over which the Mississippi had been depositing
fresh alluvial soil. An inner levee had been hastily
hightened, and when we passed this, the sodden, desolate aspect of the country changed. A few cabins, surrounded by small inclosures, seemed to have been used
in the old times for trusty negroes sent to work or
watch at the landing. Beyond these, the road led us
through a broad field of cotton, unbroken by hill or
valley, fence or tree, save here and there a single cotton-wood, whose position by the road-side had saved it.
The whole face of the country, almost as far as the eye
could reach, was plowed into what a Northern farmer
would have taken for low sweet-potato ridges. On the
tops of these ridges, in separate hills, grew the soft and
still tender cotton-stalks, beginning to be well covered
with the white and red flowers; for even cotton wore
the Rebel colors. The petals were soft and flabby, and

[37] John Anthony Quitman, a general in the Mexican War and
later congressman from Mississippi. [Ed.]

the flower was like a miniature hollyhock. For these "earliest blooms" planters keep eager watch, and to have the first in a neighborhood is a distinction, prized as a Northern farmer would prize a premium for the best crop of wheat in a county.

Occasionally a few rows were found carefully tilled and free from weeds; but in very many more, weeds and cotton were struggling for the mastery, with the emancipated negroes reveling in their first taste of liberty, spectators rather than participants in the contest on which their support depended. Doubtless the plantation had looked better under Mr. Davis' control, indifferent planter as he was.

Presently a double row of common negro quarters came in sight, and at their end a white frame house, by no means palatial, but still considerably larger than most of the residences to be found even on the premises of wealthy planters. The road led us up to the back door. "Massa allus meant to turn de road, and bring it roun' in front, under dem trees," explained an old negro. Entering at the back gate, and coming "roun' in front," we found a little lawn, on which a partially abortive attempt had been made to grow shade-trees and shrubbery. The house was a narrow one, having but a single story, with a hall running through the middle, and a couple of medium-sized rooms opening into it on either side. Beyond these, on each hand, was a wing, containing smaller rooms. In front was a veranda, or, as Southerners all call it, a gallery, with pretentious wooden columns; and at either wing was another gallery, with more columns. Above the central piazza was wrought, in sprigs of cedar, a soldier's inscription, drawn from nursery recollections: "The house that Jeff. built;" and over the main door a few more sprigs of evergreen, prettily arranged, spelled out the last word the master of the house would have uttered to any of its recent visitors : "WELCOME." A couple of Yankee school-mistresses were within, and they were the teachers of the boys and girls of Mr. Davis' slaves, and of the runaways from plantations in the interior, to whom the welcome was given. A beautiful little quadroon girl, with clustering ringlets and wondering face, stood in the door-way. She was one of the children of the place, and was the offspring of no Northern "miscegenation."*

All the furniture belonging to the house had long

"* There was a colored woman at Davis' Bend, when our forces took possession of that place—afterward sent to Cincinnati—who can be proved, by the testimony of hundreds, to have been the kept mistress of Jeff. Davis; and she is universally reputed to be the daughter of Joe Davis, the Rebel insurgent leader's brother. We know, also, of at least six persons, the offspring of white Southern women by colored men. One of these children of white women, after narrowly escaping death by drowning at the hands of his maternal uncles, is now a Presiding Elder in the Methodist Church. Another was once sold into slavery by his mother, for a 'flitch of bacon.'

"Moreover, in the course of their official action during the past year, my assistants have become cognizant of four marriages of Southern white men to colored women. One of them was formerly a negro-trader. His quadroon slave and mistress would not live with him without marriage, because, as she said, she had now become free, and it was no longer right to submit to that to which she had been helplessly subjected in slavery. A chaplain, altogether unwilling to assist at mixed marriages, was induced to perform the ceremony in this instance, by the man's saying that he had 'married her in the sight of God five years ago!'"—*Official Report of Colonel John Eaton, General Superintendent Freedmen, Department of the Tennessee and State of Arkansas, for* 1864, *to the Adjutant General U. S. A.*

ago been carried off. Respect for the rights of absent property owners has nowhere been a very marked characteristic of the movements of the Northern armies; and articles from the "house of Jeff. Davis hisself," as one of the soldiers phrased it, were too tempting to be long left unappropriated. Odd pieces of furniture of the most incongruous styles had been gathered up from adjacent plantations, completing as motley an establishment as ever vexed the eye of Yankee housekeeper. A few books lay scattered over the shelves; tactics for Northern soldiers and spelling-books for slaves lying among defenses of the divine right of slavery and constitutional arguments in favor of repudiation and secession.

To the right of the house was a garden full of neglected shrubbery, from which, as we left, we plucked a bouquet of June flowers. Swarms of woolly-headed children lay about the doors and under the little projecting roofs of the quarters; and old men and women filled up the door-ways, to stare at us as we passed. Some of them had "b'longed to Mass'r Jeff.," others to "Mass'r Joe;" others came from the interior. The jail was pointed out, where "Mass'r Joe" used to confine refractory slaves, and at which he used, on Sunday mornings, to hold a court of plenary and summary jurisdiction for the trial of prisoners. A band of iron, four inches wide and half an inch thick, with a heavy chain attached, was one of the relics found in the house. It had been used for the most troublesome slaves. During the day they had to wear it in the fields; at night a padlock secured it to a staple in the wall of the jail.

From the quarters we drove to the dilapidated old

cotton-gin. The floors were partially torn up; boards hung by single nails on the walls; doors were off their hinges or gone. By one of the gin-stands were piled up boxes marked "Enfield cartridges;" and in the lint-room were stacks of muskets. Looking from its window over the cotton-press, we saw in the adjacent cotton-field a regiment of the faithful and affectionate creatures, clad in the "blue on black," at which Rebel newspapers used to laugh, and presenting arms to a former Senatorial colleague of the late proprietor. They had for months protected the freedmen of this entire region from the hostility of their old masters; and but for their presence, the extensive mission schools carried on at another part of the estates inclosed by the bend, must have been abandoned.

Over a thousand scholars, mostly children, have been enrolled at these schools, but the attendance was very irregular. The teachers reported, with an enthusiasm that may, perhaps, have warped their judgments a little, that, wherever the attendance was regular, the progress was as rapid as the average progress of white children in the Northern public schools. This, however, referred only to the primary branches. Too little advancement had been made beyond these to warrant any general opinion as to the average capacity likely to be displayed.

The good missionaries, sent down by Northern Churches, had been zealously laboring at the moral condition of the negroes whom slavery had Christianized. They made encouraging reports, but the facts they mentioned scarcely warranted so cheerful a view of the results of their labors. In the great collections of negroes sent here in 1864, they found marriage practically unknown. The grossest immorality universally prevailed. They had duly married the couples who were living together, which some of them thought a very valuable performance; but it did not appear that the ceremony had yet produced much effect on the habits of the people. They had preached to them and prayed with them, and, as one of them said:

"Their interest in religious instructions is very encouraging. As a people, they are much more easy of access on the subject of religion than white people. When asked if they are pious, they will readily give an answer of yes or no. All professors of religion are free to tell their religious experience. There is no part of religious worship they enjoy so much, and in which they spend so much time, as in singing. In prayer they are generally very earnest, often using expressions that indicate a deep sense of unworthiness. One will often hear such expressions as these: 'Heavenly Master, wilt thou be pleased to hear us?' 'O Jesus, Master, if thou be pleased, do come along dis way by thy Holy Spirit;' 'We know we are not heard for our much speaking.' The gratitude which they have often manifested to me for reading and expounding to them the Scriptures has been a rich reward for my labors."

But the good man was compelled to admit that, when these "professors of religion" came out of the prayer-meetings, they had no hesitation in stealing whatever little delicacies they could find for next morning's breakfast, or in appropriating somebody's mule, and making off before daylight for some other locality. They would very humbly confess their sins on bended knees, and straightway rise to tell some outrageous lie, by which they hoped to get a little money. What reason had anybody to hope that they believed the story they told on their knees any more than the other?

Last year the negroes congregated on these plantations cultivated their crops in their own way and on their own account. The military authorities selected some seventy of the best, and allotted to each a tract of thirty acres. Each was permitted to draw mules and supplies, to be paid for at the end of the year, and each hired as many negroes to assist him as he thought he needed to cultivate the land. The officers say they worked well, and would have made large profits, but for the ravages of the army-worm. As it was, they only gathered one hundred and thirty bales of cotton from their entire plantation, or scarcely one-twelfth of a good crop. White lessees, managing large places on the river, suffered equally from the army-worm, but saved a much larger proportion of cotton. Still, the experiment was a success. The negroes paid back all the advances made them by the Government, and some of them had a balance of between five hundred and a thousand dollars profits.*

These results, it is true, could not have been attained

---

*In the Helena (Ark.) District, negro lessees, cultivating small farms, were in numerous cases comparatively successful. Ten of them, to whom land had been allotted by direction of Mr. Mellen, realized from their crops an aggregate of $31,000. The following were favorable specimens:

"Jerome Hubbard and George West leased sixty acres—planted forty in cotton; their expenses were about $1,200; they sold their crop for $8,000. Napoleon Bowman leased twenty-four acres; he had some capital to begin with, and borrowed some; he employed one hand; his expenses were less than $2,000; sold his crop for $6,000—realizing over $4,000 clear profit. Robert Owens leased seventeen acres; having nothing to start with, he borrowed his capital; he earned by the season's work enough to purchase a good house, with a residue of $300. Samuel Beaden leased thirteen and a half acres; expended about $600 in its cultivation, and sold his crop for $4,000."

They averaged, according to an official report, about $500 profit on every ten acres cultivated.

without Government encouragement and direction; but surely no better way of dispensing charity was ever devised than to make the destitute earn it for themselves, and pay back the advances furnished them. Nor was there anything in the operations of the negro farmers last year, nor in their prospects when we visited them in June, 1865, to warrant a doubt as to their capacity for supporting themselves and managing their own affairs, when once fairly started. Whether they would furnish the country as great an amount of cotton for export, as under the old system, is another and a very different question.

We drove through miles of cotton and corn, rank with the luxuriant growth of a soil marvelous for its fertility. Then came a bad road along a broken levee, through a cypress swamp, where amid the gloom of trailing moss, hanging down almost to the edge of the stagnant, scum-covered water, one could dimly make out the great cypress-knees, and fancy them fit resting-places for the snakes and alligators which are said to constitute the only inhabitants. Finally our ambulances could go no further over the narrow road, and for a little distance we followed on foot the little path beaten by the crowds of negroes constantly flocking to the river. The luxuriant grass waved over and almost concealed it; and here and there it was overgrown with vines, so that every step crushed the juicy dewberries under our feet. The steamboat had passed around the bend, and lay awaiting us as we emerged on its northern side.

CHAPTER XXIX.

Vicksburg to Louisville.

DAVIS'S BEND presented no more striking illustration of the changes of the war than a conversation on our boat, after our return. A brother of General Wade Hampton, the South Carolina Hotspur, was on board. He saw no great objection to negro suffrage, so far as the whites were concerned; and for himself, South Carolinian and secessionist though he was, he was quite willing to accept it. He only dreaded its effect on the blacks themselves. Hitherto they had, in the main, been modest and respectful, and mere freedom was not likely to spoil them. But the deference to them likely to be shown by partisans eager for their votes would have a tendency to uplift and unbalance them. Beyond this, no harm would be done the South by negro suffrage. The old owners would cast the votes of their people almost as absolutely and securely as they cast their own. If Northern men expected in this way to build up a Northern party in the South, they were gravely mistaken. They would only be multiplying the power of the old and natural leaders of Southern politics by every vote given to a former slave. Heretofore such men had served their masters only in the fields; now they would do not less faithful service at the polls. If the North could stand it, the South could. For himself, he should make no special objection to negro suffrage as one of the terms of reorganization, and if it came, he did not think the South would have much cause to regret it.

Vicksburg, city of hills and caves, had already lost most of the traces of the siege, that for a year blocked the progress of our arms in the West, and concentrated the gaze of the continent. Few of the houses showed much serious damage. The hiding-holes dug in the hill-sides, for security against the shells, had been filled up again; stores had been reopened; ox-teams, bringing in cotton, filled the streets; returned Rebel soldiers were looking after their abandoned property, and receiving the heartiest welcomes from their old friends and neighbors.

Carriages were procured, and under the escort of General Morgan L. Smith, the commanding officer, we drove out through the formidable lines of breastworks that run along the successive ridges back of the town, to the spot where Generals Grant and Pemberton met to agree upon the terms of surrender. All the way up the Mississippi, we had been sympathetically quoting General Butler's expressions of delight, after his protracted residence in the flat Southern country, at "seeing hills again." The Vicksburg hills were the first we had seen for a month or more; and we saw quite enough of them. A sudden storm came up; the roads became almost as slippery as ice; the drivers, blinded with the rain, guided their horses badly; and presently one of the carriages was handsomely capsized in the mud, and the other one came within an inch of a similar fate. "Nebber 'n all my born life did so afore, nor nebber will," protested the chap-fallen driver.

From the crest above the unpretending little monument one could trace for miles along the tops of the hills the successive lines of intrenchment, and mark the spots where assault after assault illustrated the various skill of the Generals, and the unvaried gallantry of the soldiers they more than once led to needless slaughter. Cotton already dotted every little spot of arable land within the Rebel lines, and beyond them many a broad field, enriched by Northern blood, was promising a rich harvest to Northern lessees. One, a former Clerk of the Ohio House of Representatives, rode up while we were studying the positions which the respective armies had occupied. He thought there was money down here, and had buried a good deal of it, any way, in these broken ridges.

Everybody was planting cotton; every little valley bloomed with it, and up hill-sides, that further south would have been called waste land, were everywhere to be traced the long undulations of the cotton ridges. As an official report about this time expressed it, "Visions of fortunes were floating before all planters' eyes. The only trouble was scarcity of laborers. A quarter of a million acres, more or less, were waiting to sprout fortunes under every stroke of the hoe. All men seemed mad. Guerrillas were a light matter; the army-worm nothing. Cotton-seed, and land to scatter it on, and blacks to gather in the golden fiber—and lo! Golconda!" Worst of all, nearly every man was over-reaching his means. With capital to carry through a plantation of five hundred acres, he would be attempting a thousand. Negroes were consequently ill-paid; rations were likely to be of the cheapest and scantiest. If the negro, dissatisfied with this specimen of the workings of free labor, broke his contract and ran away, it was a proof that "free niggers would never make cotton without a system of peonage." "We are the only ones that understand the nigger," said a few of the more outspoken Mississippians, emboldened by the growing impression that the President, as a Southern man, was gradually coming over to their side. "Wait till Johnson gets things a-going here, and we'll make a contract law that will make a nigger work."*

Meantime, however, the Northerners were doing most of the cotton-planting. Mississippians were quite sincere in believing it impossible to grow cotton with unrestricted free labor, and many of them, frightened at the prospect of having to pay war taxes, and especially at what the more timorous still thought the danger of negro suffrage, were anxious to sell, for ten dollars an acre, lands that before the war readily commanded forty or fifty.

Memphis showed even more signs of the universal reaction than Vicksburg. The old inhabitants were more generally back, and a longer immunity from the punishments they had at first dreaded made them bolder. The newspapers were almost as unbridled as in the old secession days in their denunciations of Parson Brownlow, the East Tennessee Unionists, the test oath, and the effort to exclude Rebel voters from the polls. But on one point they had been utterly revolutionized. The man whom most of all they used to "decorate with their censure,"† "the drunken tailor from the mountains," "the po' white demagogue,"

---

* They subsequently did. It was like the patent rat-trap. Nobody could make a safer contrivance. Rats could n't possibly get out of it. The only difficulty was that they declined to go in.

† The happy phrase of Mr. Winter Davis in referring, in the United States House of Representatives, to the vote of censure

was now the unfortunate subject of their warmest eulogies.

Business had already shown signs of revival. For the very best part of the cotton-growing region, Memphis, since the completion of her railroad system, had been the natural center and the only serious rival to New Orleans. All this trade was likely to be renewed. Business men were trying to resume, capital was everywhere in demand, and the streets showed more of the life and bustle of a Northern community than those of any Southern city we had seen.

Returned Rebel soldiers swarmed everywhere, in the parlors, at the liquor-shops, about the hotels, in the theaters. A blue uniform attracted attention; the gray flowed all about it in the unbroken stream of the street. If there was any regulation preventing returned Rebels from wearing the buttons and insignia of their rank, it was utterly a dead letter.

At Bolivar, a single standing chimney, as seen from our hurricane-deck, was all that marked the former site of a once bustling town. It was the solitary monument left to tell the tale of the ruin rebellion had brought to that community.

Further up, Fort Pillow showed no signs of either massacre or defense. In fact, one could see nothing but a blank bluff, whence artillery might command a fine range up or down the river.

One evening we landed just as a magnificent sunset was casting an amethyst sparkle over the water, while

passed by the Maryland Legislature for his first public act in co-operation with the Republican party against the slaveholders' policy.

great banks of orange and yellow were reflected from above, and purple and scarlet, partly concealed by a misty blue veil floating over them, spread across half the sky. At a little distance beyond the wood-yard stood a row of the rudest cabins, ranged after the fashion of the negro quarters on a plantation. Entering one, I found a block serving as a chair for a middle-aged negress, who sat on it before the big fire, holding a sick baby, with its little woolly head turned toward a blaze that seemed hot enough to roast it. An old bedstead, nailed together by pieces of rough boards and covered with a tattered quilt, stood in one corner. In the opposite one was a rough table, on which were the fragments of a half-eaten, heavy, sodden "corn-pone." In the fireplace stood a skillet covered by a broken lid, and on an old box were piled some broken dishes. I have enumerated absolutely everything gathered here to make comfortable the happy home of an American freeman.

Returning to the landing, I learned from the negroes standing about that they were refugees from cotton plantations lower down the river, over which the guerrillas " had been a raidin', sah." They had hired here to a speculator, following in the wake of our army, to cut wood for the steamboats. He sold his wood for four dollars a cord, cash; and out of this paid nothing for the wood at all, and only promised to pay them a dollar a cord for chopping it. At this rate they could have made plenty of money, "but de trouble is, sah, he done nebber pay us. He say grillas sunk de steamboat him money come down on, and we'm got to take goods fo' ou' pay. Den he sell us po'k not fit to eat, at tree bits a pound, and de meanest co'n-meal you ever see." Further inquiry showed that they had bought brass rings at five or six dollars apiece, and gaudy cotton handkerchiefs for the head at three dollars; and, in short, had done their best to help the speculator fleece them out of the last penny of their earnings. It was a lonely, desolate-looking spot; the simple creatures were afraid to go away for fear of guerrillas, and here they were completely at his mercy. Scores of such cases were to be found up and down the river. Fortunes were made during the last year of the war out of Mississippi wood-yards, and too often the most successful were the readiest to cheat the poor negroes out of their paltry share of the splendid profits.

At last our long journey approached its close. At Cairo we met floods of Northern newspapers, and, for the first time, became aware that a formidable party was organizing at the North in favor of Southern reconstruction only on the basis of some form of negro suffrage. At Louisville a pleasant dinner party enabled us to meet the last collection of men from the midst of a Rebel community. At that time there was more loyalty in Nashville than in Louisville, and about as much in Charleston as in either. For the first and only time on the trip, save while we were under the Spanish flag, slaves waited on us at dinner. They were the last any of us were ever to see on American soil.

CHAPTER XXX.

General Aspects of the South at the Close of the War.

THE months of May and June were the chaotic period of the returning Rebel States. All men were overwhelmed and prostrated under the sudden stroke of a calamity which the fewest number had anticipated. Many had believed the war hopeless, but nearly all had thought their armies strong enough, and their states-men skillful enough, to extort from the North terms that would soften away, if not conceal, the rugged feat-ures of utter defeat. They expected the necessity of a return to the Union, but they hoped to march back with flying colors, with concessions granted and in-ducements offered that would give them the semblance of a victory. Studious encouragement had been given from the Rebel Capital to such hopes; and outside of Virginia there were scarcely a dozen men in a State who comprehended the straits to which the Confed-eracy was reduced in the winter of 1864–65, or were prepared for the instantaneous collapse of the spring.

The first feelings were those of baffled rage. Men who had fought four years for an idea, smarted with actual anguish under the stroke which showed their utter failure. Then followed a sense of bewilderment and helplessness. Where they were, what rights they had left, what position they occupied before the law, what claim they had to their property, what hope they had for an improvement of their condition in the future—all these were subjects of complete uncertainty.

Here was the opportunity for a statesman to grasp. I speak advisedly, and after a careful review of our whole experiences through the months of May and June, in all the leading centers of Southern influence, when I say that the National Government could at that time have prescribed no conditions for the return of the Rebel States which they would not have promptly accepted. They expected nothing; were prepared for the worst; would have been thankful for anything.

In North and South Carolina, Georgia, and Florida, we found this state of feeling universally prevalent. The people wanted civil government and a settlement. They asked no terms, made no conditions. They were defeated and helpless—they submitted. Would the victors be pleased to tell them what was to be done? Point out any way for a return to an established order of things, and they would walk in it. They made no hypocritical professions of new-born Unionism. They had honestly believed in the right of secession. The hatred of Yankees, which had originally aided the conspirators in starting the movement, had grown and strengthened with the war. Neither the constitutional theory nor the personal hate of their lives could be changed in a day, but both were alike impotent; and having been forced to abandon the war, they longed for the blessings which any peace on any terms might be expected to bring in its train. With unchanged faith in the constitutionality of their secession, they were ready to abandon or ignore it, at the requirement of the victors. Fully believing the debts of their Rebel Government legal and just, they were prepared to repudiate them at a hint from Washington. Filled with the hatred to the negroes, nearly always inspired in any ruling class by the loss of accustomed power over inferiors, they nevertheless yielded to the Freedmen's Bureau, and acquiesced in the necessity for according civil rights to their slaves. They were stung by the disgrace of being guarded by negro soldiers; but they made no complaints, for they felt that they had forfeited their right of complaint. They were shocked at the suggestion of negro suffrage; but if the Government required it, they were ready to submit.

The whole body politic was as wax. It needed but a firm hand to apply the seal. Whatever device were chosen, the community would at once be molded to its impress. But if the plastic moment were suffered to pass ——!

So we found public feeling everywhere along the Atlantic coast. So, by the common testimony of all, it was found throughout the limits of the rebellion, down to the period when the terms of the President's North Carolina proclamation came to be generally understood. On the Gulf we caught the first responsive notes given to that proclamation by the revived Southern temper. By the time we reached New Orleans the change was complete; the reaction had set in. Men now began to talk of their rights, and to argue constitutional points; as if traitors had rights, or treason were entitled to constitutional protection. They had discovered that, having laid down their arms, they were no longer Rebels, and could no longer be punished; as the thief who is forced to abandon his booty is no longer a thief, and may laugh at penitentiaries. As Mr. Randall Hunt dextrously put it, " We withdrew our Representatives from Congress, and tried to go out of the Union. You went to war to keep us in. You have conquered; we submit, and send back our Representatives. What more do you want?" The President had lustily proclaimed treason a crime, but the Southern people took his actions in preference to his words, and were confirmed in their own view that it was but a difference of opinion on a constitutional point, in which, under the circumstances, they were ready to yield.

Not less marked was the reaction on all points connected with the negro. He was saucy and rude; disposed to acts of violence; likely, by his stupid presumptions, to provoke a war of races, which could only end in his extermination. In all this the Freedmen's Bureau encouraged him, and thus became solely a fomenter of mischief. The presence of negro troops tended to demoralize the whole negro population. Negro evidence would make courts of justice a mockery. As to negro suffrage, none but the black-hearted Abolitionists who had brought on this war, and were now doing their best to provoke a second, would dream of seriously asking the South to submit to so revolting a humiliation.

The mistake of the last four or five years had been the one against which Henry A. Wise had warned them in the beginning. They ought to have fought for their rights within the Union. That they must do now.

Throughout the war, the North believed in the existence of a strong Union party at the South. Under the peculiar circumstances of our trip, it would seem natural that, if there was such a party, we should have found traces of it. Individual Unionists there were, of course; noble men, who braved every threat, and stood faithful to the last. But, speaking of a Union party only as comprising numbers of men sufficient to form an appreciable element in political or social movements, I was ready, on our return, to affirm that, save in East Tennessee and small portions of North Carolina, there was no such party in the South. In many of the States the opponents of secession had been in a majority in 1860. But the movement once started, blood once drawn, the honor of the States once involved, secession swept everything before it. The avalanche begins in a little snow-bank. Once set in motion, whatever stands in the way serves only to swell its bulk and augment its power.

Men who had voted against secession at the risk of their lives, again and again told me that they were soon forced to go with the current. The son of one had volunteered, "and, of course, sir, my prayers and hopes went with my boy and the cause in which he was engaged." The property of another was in danger, and to save it he volunteered. At Bull Run his bosom friend fell by a Yankee ball; from that moment he "was a Rebel, heart and soul." " My family, friends, neighbors, old political leaders, all went with the State," said another. " I knew it was madness, but I could not desert them, and I would not be a tory."

Men like Governor Brown and Alex. H. Stephens were thought at the North to be leaders of a Union party. Whatever their private views, neither they nor any other prominent men dared permit themselves to be regarded in that light at home. " They were opponents of the Administration, not of the war," as a Georgian very earnestly explained. " They opposed Mr. Davis, not because he made war at all, but because he did it with less vigor and skill than they demanded."

The belief was prevalent at the North, that, when secession failed, the decimated and beggared people would turn in bitter rage upon the leaders who had brought them to such a pass. But from Fortress Monroe and Key West to Cairo, I never heard one solitary indication of such a feeling.

Many men criticised Mr. Davis' conduct of the war with severity; but wherever an expression was made at all, it was one of sympathy for his fate, and of indignation at the thought of awarding him any other punishment than was allotted to the humblest follower in the cause. "He was but our agent," they said. "He only did our bidding. Our fault with him was that he did n't do it as skillfully as we expected."

General Lee was everywhere reverenced. The common form of allusion to him was, "that great and good man." In Mobile, and throughout the Mississippi Valley, General Jos. E. Johnston was an universal favorite. Beauregard had an ovation when he returned. In New Orleans, the bitterest complaint against the President's Amnesty Proclamation was, that under it they would be compelled to select obscure persons, or new-comers, for Representatives, "instead of our old and tried leaders."

But there were very distinct traces of State jealousy. "Those d——d Hotspurs of Charleston were very keen to get us into this scrape," said a North Carolinian, "and now, after sending us poor troops through the war, they 're sneaking off to Mexico, instead of staying with us to stand it out." Tennesseeans were not general favorites; and it was amusing to hear the contempt showered upon the once petted Kentuckians. "Poor braggadocio devils! After all their strut and swagger, they did n't know which side they were on, and stood, like a pack of half-scared curs, growling at both."

Missouri, on the other hand, was often praised. Several times I heard the statement, that " Missouri troops were among the very best in the Confederate army."

I have already said that we found no Union party in the South, in the months immediately following the close of the war. I should have excepted the negroes. The prevalent stories of their fidelity to their masters were preposterously false. Not one negro in a thousand hoped for the success of the rebellion, or was without some pretty distinct notion of his personal interests in the issue. They often served or saved masters to whom they were personally attached, even in the most critical moments of danger, but this did not in the slightest degree affect their desire for the triumph of the Yankees.

The expectation was general, among the more intelligent, that suffrage would be given them, and many were beginning to assert their claim to lands. How far they were qualified for giving their voice in public affairs, we had no very satisfactory means of judging. We saw mainly those in cities, or near the armies, and in most cases these were the brighter and more intelligent. In Charleston, Savannah, Mobile, and New Orleans, the masses of resident negroes seemed to me quite as orderly, respectable, and intelligent as many of the voters in New York that help to elect mayors like Mr. Fernando Wood.

But we were constantly told that the plantation hands in the interior were a different order of beings. We saw many plantation hands, as on the Sea Islands, and at numerous other points, who were the superiors in good-breeding, and not much the inferiors in education, of many of the "poor whites;"* but these, wo

* I have several times spoken of this class. Lest it should be

were always assured, were only the smart ones, who knew enough to run away. Could we but see the stupid residuum still in the interior, who constituted the vast majority, we would form radically changed notions as to their fitness for any right of a citizen, or, indeed, for taking care of themselves at all. It was not till some months later that I was to see this stupid residuum. Till then, I may fitly leave its description in the language of those who professed to know it best.

But of the great masses of negroes whom we did see in May and June, two general statements may safely be made:

They were as orderly, quiet, and industrious as any other class of the population;* and,

thought that I am exaggerating their condition, let me quote the description of a writer against whom no accusation of prejudice, or lack of familiarity with the subject, can be brought. Mrs. Fanny Kemble Butler says of the poor whites, on page 146 of her Journal of a Residence on a Georgia Plantation, (to wit, that of her husband:)

"They are, I suppose, the most degraded race of human beings claiming an Anglo-Saxon origin, that can be found on the face of the earth—filthy, lazy, ignorant, brutal, proud, penniless savages, without one of the nobler attributes that have been found occasionally allied to the vices of savage nature. They own no slaves, for they are, almost without exception, abjectly poor; they will not work, for that, as they conceive, would reduce them to an equality with the abhorred negroes; they squat, and steal, and starve on the outskirts of the lowest of all civilized societies, and their countenances bear witness to the squalor of their condition and the degradation of their natures."

Fortunately, this class is confined almost exclusively to the Eastern slaveholding States.

* This statement is literally true, but, without another, it might convey a wrong impression. The negroes were everywhere found quiet, respectful, and peaceable; they were the only class at work;

They were far more eager than any others to secure the advantages of education for themselves, and especially for their children.

and in, perhaps, most respects, their outward conduct was that of excellent citizens. But they *would* steal. Petty pilfering seemed as natural to three-fourths of them as eating. Our officers and missionaries thought they saw some reformation in this respect; but there was still abundance of room for more.

CHAPTER XXXI.

Mid-summer at the Capitol.

No PARTY ever made a graver mistake than did the one that had elected the Administration during the summer after the assassination of Mr. Lincoln and the surrender of the Rebel armies. Representatives, senators, leading men of the party in other official stations or in private life, abandoned their new President before he was lost. Dissatisfied with the North Carolina proclamation, they made little effort to convince the President of the justice of their dissatisfaction. Whispering to one another their fears that his Southern prejudices would lead him over to the side of the returning Rebels, they made little effort to retain him. Occasionally some prominent Unionist came down to Washington to see the President, found the ante-room filled with pardon-seeking Rebels, and the city rife with the old Rebel talk, became disgusted and hurried back to the North.

All summer long the capital was filled with the late leaders in Rebel councils, or on Rebel battle-fields. They filled all avenues of approach to the White House. They kept the Southern President surrounded by an atmosphere of Southern geniality, Southern prejudices, Southern aspirations. Mr. Johnson declared that treason must be humbled—they convinced him that they were humble. That traitors must be punished—

they showed him how they had suffered. That only·
loyal men should rule—they were all loyal now.

He had been a "poor white," with all the hatred of
his class to the negroes. They showed him how the
"Radicals" wanted to make the negroes as good as the
white men. As a Tennessee politician, it had been
necessary for him to denounce the "Abolitionists and
fanatics of the North;" to declare, in the stereotyped
phrase of the stump, that he had equal hatred for the
Secessionists of South Carolina and the Abolitionists of
Massachusetts. They asked him if he was going to
let Massachusetts Abolitionists lead him now and control his Administration, while his own native South
lay repentant and bleeding at his feet. He was ambitious, proud of his elevation, but stung by the sneer
that after all he was only an accidental President.
They cunningly showed him how he could secure the
united support of the entire South and of the great
Democratic party of the North, with which all his own
early history was identified, for the next Presidency.

Such were the voices, day by day and week by week,
sounding in the President's ears. He heard little else,
was given time to think little else. And meanwhile
the party that had elected him, simply—let him alone.
The history of our politics shows no graver blunder.

Every day the White House presented the same
scene. Passing through the ante-room to the public
staircase, one always encountered a throng of coarsely-
dressed bronzed Southerners, carrying heavy canes,
tobacco-ruminant, and full of political talk. The un-
furnished desolate-looking room in which visitors
gather, while waiting their turns for interviews with
the President, was always crowded. One day I saw

there two or three Rebel Generals, as many members of the Rebel Congress, and at least a score of less noted leaders. In a corner, occupying the only chair which the room contains, sat a former Secretary of War of the Rebel Confederacy. Not far from him stood Henry W. Hilliard, once United States Congressman from Alabama, and subsequently prominent in the plots which Andrew Johnson so sternly resisted for seducing Tennessee into rebellion.

From nine o'clock until three the President sat in the room adjacent, conversing with one or another as the doorkeeper admitted them. Pardons were discussed, policies of reorganization were canvassed. The pardon-seekers were the counsellors on reorganization—there were none others there with whom to consult. Thus the weary day passed, with a steady stream of Rebel callers. At three o'clock the doorkeeper's hands were full of cards not yet presented to the President, and the ante-room was thronged; then the door was thrown open, and the crowd rushed in as if scrambling for seats in a railroad car. The President stood by his desk; to his left, at another table, stood General Mussey and Colonel Browning, his two private secretaries. On the table in the center of the room lay a pile of pardons, a foot high, watched by a young Major in uniform.

"How the newspapers slandered the President," said a Congressman,* after witnessing such a scene. "Treason is a crime and must be pardoned ! *That* was the rallying cry with which he assumed his office, and the odious newspapers reported him wrong."

A few Union soldiers had been waiting all day to

---

* Judge Kelley, of Philadelphia.

see the President about pardons for desertion, restoration of bounties, and the like. One after another approached, presented his case, received a prompt and generally a kindly answer and retired. A stooped, prematurely old person, wearing several foreign decorations, thin, with nervous face and weary expression, wanted back pay for services as a hospital steward. He gave his name as Geo. Gordon Di Luna Byron, and claimed to be a son of the poet. Hospital-steward Byron was persuaded to seek in the Quartermaster's Department for an investigation and decision of his claims. Sundry gentlemen would be greatly obliged if they could be handed their pardons now. The President was not quite ready; they were made out and lying on the table, but he wasn't just prepared to deliver them yet. "Were not the cases decided?" "Oh, yes; it was all right; they would get their pardons in due time."

"They're not quite enough humiliated yet," whispered an official on-looker.

Others had only called to thank the President for his kindness concerning their pardons. They were about to start home, and it would afford them the greatest pleasure to co-operate in the work of reconstruction, and especially to do all in their power in support of the President's policy.

The District Attorney of Tennesssee wanted to know what course to pursue about confiscations. He had been endeavoring to discharge his duties under the confiscation law, but before he had been able to get through the procedings in any case, the President's pardon had put a stop to it. He was told to call to-morrow.

So the crowd thinned out, one by one. By half-past

five Mr. Johnson was alone with his secretaries—only a few idlers still passing before the open door for a stolen look at the Chief-Magistrate of the Republic.

At the other end of the avenue, in a large, pleasantly-furnished suite of rooms in the basement of the capitol, was a curious contrast. Whoever chose, whatever the degree of his treachery, might go in to stare at the President or ask for a pardon. At the rooms of the Court of Claims, a poor, friendless, cowardly, and cruel Swiss mercenary was on trial for his life for cruelties to National prisoners, known to have been fully reported to the Rebel officials the President was pardoning.

Near one end of the connecting rooms stood a long table, at the head of which, sat the small, nervous figure of Major General Lew. Wallace, and around which were grouped the members of his Military Commission. Among them was General Thomas,[38] the grey-headed Adjutant General of the United States Army; hearty and companionable, General Geary[39] of Pennsylvania; and General Fessenden,[40] of Maine, still limping from his wounds. Opposite General Wallace, at a little cross-table, sat young, long-bearded, pleasant-faced Colonel Chipman, the Judge Advocate of the Commission. Near the latter, shrinking down upon his chair, and mostly seeking to avoid the gaze of the crowd, sat the cringing prisoner on trial for atrocities almost without a parallel in the history of modern warfare. He was badly dressed, in old, shabby-genteel clothes, was slovenly, and seemed to have lost all care for his appearance. He listened in a submissive, helpless sort of way to the testimony. Occasionally something seemed to touch him keenly and he would turn

[38] Lorenzo Thomas, Union general, Adjutant General of the Army. [Ed.]

[39] John White Geary, Union general, later Governor of Pennsylvania. [Ed.]

to his counsel and whisper earnestly; but for the most part, he sat silent, bent-up, cowering, and apparently wretched.

The proofs of his guilt were overwhelming. The man not convinced by them would be the man to doubt whether there was sufficient historical evidence of our ever having had a war with Mexico. But there were others, as guilty as he, guiltier indeed in that they made him the tool to do deeds to which they would not stoop themselves. They should have been seated by his side, to make the trial other than a bitter mockery of justice.

One hot August morning a couple of us, wearied with such scenes, crossed the Long Bridge, (whose opposite ends were guarded, at the outbreak of the war by hostile sentries—Virginia stationing hers at the end where the bridge touched her sovereignty, and General Scott sending his to the other end to watch them), and took the cars for Manassas Junction. The railroad had just been turned over to its old owners by the military authorities, and the cars, provided for the accommodation of the Virginia travelers, still bore the inscription "United States Military R. R."

A motley throng of curiosity-hunters, speculators, sight-seers, returning pardon-seekers, and Southern politicians filled the cars. Among them were a very few Southern women. The leaders of the Old Dominion were not yet able to travel much.

Manassas Junction was being made over again. A few frame shanties had been hastily thrown up. Two of these did duty as "hotels;" nearly all contrived to turn an honest penny by selling villainous liquors for twice the Washington price. Workmen were nailing

<hr />

40 James Deering Fessenden, Union general, son of Senator William Pitt Fessenden of Maine. [Ed.]

on roofs, and hammering at weather-boarding for several more. "We'll open out a store there next week," said an unmistakable Yankee, pointing to a structure still standing in the naked simplicity of bare sills, posts and rafters.

We stopped among the carpenters, while the tavern-keeper was hitching up his horses to take us over to Bull Run, and made some inquiries as to the localities. "That's the road to Manassus Gap," said one, laying down his hammer and nails, with the air of a man glad of an opportunity to quit work and talk. "That's where we came marching up time o' Bull Run." He went on to describe the route his division took. Supposing him to be a Northerner we became utterly confused in trying to square our recollections of the battle with his descriptions. Finally it occurred to us to ask, "Which side were you on?"

"The Virginia side, of co'se! What side 'd ye 'spose I'd be on?"

"He was one of Mosby's guerrillas," whispered a Northern resident standing by.

He reckoned they'd be quiet enough now, 's long 's they'd nothing else to do. They'd been overpowered, but no Yankee could say they were ever whipped. "Didn't we whip you right straight along till you called in the niggers and Dutch to help you? Make it a fair fight and we'd have whipped you all the way through. One of us could whip two o' your men any time in fair fight. It stands to reason. Didn't we whip you all along with only half as many men? Of co'se one o' our men had to be better'n two o' your'n."

By this time our ambulance drove up and we started for the battle-fields. "They talk mighty big," said our Pennsylvania driver, who had heard the latter part of the conversation; "but in spite of all their big talk they do things that down in old Lancaster we'd be mighty 'shamed of. Why, here the other night a fellow comes into our tavern there to buy a bottle of whisky. After he buys it, what does he do, but call in two or three others that had helped him pay for it, and borrow our glasses to take a drink out of his bottle. Why couldn't the stingy cuss 'ave bought it by the drink like a gentleman, if he'd a know'd how a gentleman did?"

The road led us away through a boundless common, waving with golden rod and covered with luxuriant grass. Every fence, for miles, was gone. Here and there solitary chimneys marked the site of an old "Virginia mansion," and sometimes a little of the shrubbery had been spared about the ruins, but there were no other signs of human habitation. Neither were there any signs of the conflicts which have made the neighborhood memorable forever. Few trees were standing to show the scars of shells; the country seemed an absolute solitude; where once the roar of battle had rent the air, we had only the chirping notes of myriads of birds.

Coming out on the brow of a little knoll, near which, in the hollow and across the brook was a double log-cabin, we stood beside the "Bull Run Monument." It is a plain obelisk, built up of the sand-stone found in the neighborhood, roughly-faced down and cemented with coarse mortar. On its sides smooth places had been obtained by daubing on a little square of plaster. On these were painted the words "Erected, June 10, 1865, in honor of the Patriots who fell at Bull Run, July 21, 1861." On either hand stretched the rolling country; below us murmured a little brook; away beyond the log-cabin at the bottom of the hill, a dark forest line shut in the view. A few yards from the monument stood half-a-dozen peach trees, loaded with excellent fruit, with which the driver took care to fill the lunch-basket.

Driving over to the extreme right of the Bull Run ground, we came out into the edge of the woods on the left of the field where the second Bull Run was fought. An old school-house, without doors, windows, desks or seats, had in some way been preserved. A few bullets and fragments of shell could still be found under the trees—there was nothing else to speak of battle, or indeed, of the presence of man for years. Leaving the ambulance here, we walked down through the woods till we struck the railroad-cut, of which Stonewall Jackson made such effective use. Here, too, a few bullets and fragments of shell were to be found; beyond was the long, rank grass covering what had once been cultivated fields. Climbing the hill—with not a few admonitions about the snakes that in the grass do hide—we reached the Second Bull Run Monument, erected by a Northern regiment at the same time with the other, and almost its *fac simile*. The inscription read:

"In memory of the
Patriots
Who fell at Groveton,
August 28th, 29th and 30th, 1862." '

Since the return of the Rebels, after Lee's surrender, another word had been carefully and conspicuously interlined and the inscription read:

"In memory of the
Confederate Patriots," etc.

When the rebellion began arsenals and ammunition were stolen; when it ended we had this more original performance of stealing a monument.

On our return we stopped at the old log-cabin near the center of the first Bull Run battle-field. Its inhabitants, a blear-eyed, hard-drinking poor white and his wife, the latter of whom seemed to be dividing her time between her pipe and the wash-tub, had occupied the house during the whole of both battles and during the subsequent alternate possession of the field by either side. Before the war he had made a living by selling a little whisky; now he had nothing to depend on but his "patch." This, as it subsequently appeared, was gratuitously cultivated for him by a curious old misshapen negro who considered himself in some way bound to the place.

The negro brought us some cider, of indescribable taste. "How in the world did you make this, uncle?"

"Why, sah, I only had few rotten apples, but I's got plenty peaches. So I pounds up de apples and de peaches togedder in a bary, wid a pessle. Den I puts water in to make de juice come, cause its so dry. Den I put away de juice, and gibs it to gemmen, and dey always gibs me somefin den what makes me laugh."

He thought the end of the world was coming, sure, at the time of the first battle. Afterward, when the second came, he wasn't quite so much scared at first, but 'fore it over he thought hisself dead nigger, shore.

Where were all his neighbors? Dey'd all done gone, sence dey got so badly whipped, and nebber cum back. Reckoned some on 'em lost mighty fine farms heah by it.

Didn't he think they were very foolish to fight that way for nothing? He didn't know, twa'n't for him to say. Dey was old enough and ageable enough to know best for demselves.

Thus the freedman. The Virginian of the ruling class was even more cautious. "He hain't nary a politic," explained our driver. "He's been first one thing and then the other, just accordin' to which side happened to be camped around; but he's a poor sneakin' nigger-driver at heart."

We drove from end to end of the two battle-fields, and found these to be its only inhabitants. In fifteen miles of driving through what had once been a cultivated country, we saw but a single fence.

At the railroad station, on our return, we found quite a number of negroes. They had always lived here, and wanted to live here still. They were willing to work, but their old masters weren't willing to hire them. Didn't we think that the Government ought to give them lands?

CHAPTER XXXII.

Richmond, after Six Months of Yankee Rule.

IN my first visit to the Southern States, beginning in the spring of 1865, and ending in mid-summer, there were peculiar circumstances to be taken into account, in drawing conclusions as to any of the questions which the loyal portion of the nation was asking about the South. Our party was constantly surrounded by men desirous of impressing their own views. Southern politicians were endeavoring to convince the Chief-Justice of the returning loyalty of their people. Naturally, they suppressed unfavorable facts and expressions. Intelligent negroes were arguing the fitness of their people for suffrage. Naturally, they did what they could to hold the unfit ones away. Whoever approached the Chief-Justice or his party, was likely to have some special motive for doing so, either of courtesy or of interest Naturally, whatever did not comport with that motive was glossed over, or kept out of sight.

The trip had thus shown us the leaders at their best. I now wanted to see the people, at home and out of company dress. The Secretary of the Treasury, and other members of the Cabinet, had been kind enough to furnish me with letters to the Provisional Governors who had been appointed for all the Southern States; but it was rather the governed than the governors who might be expected to reveal the actual feeling and condition of the community. Acting on what a large mass of his supporters thought a mistaken policy, the President had inaugurated a system of reconstruction. State governments had been set in motion; legislators and congressmen were being elected. It was an opportune time, before Congress met and the ardent Southern sentiment was chilled by the fresh breezes from the North, for a run among the reconstructed, avoiding officials, whether Northern Generals, or Southern Governors, candidates, or Freedmen's Bureau Agents; moving quietly among the people, and seeing in what temper they were carrying on the work to which Mr. Johnson had summoned them.

When I had been last in Richmond—a day or two after the surrender—it was thought to be something of a feat to make the trip in a couple of days. In November, so rapidly had the broken ways been mended and the crooked paths made straight, it was accomplished in a night. The traveler southward left Washington at nine in the evening, and was aroused up next morning at five in Richmond.

The trip naturally inspires an appetite; but among the morning papers I found the following further appetizer from the Richmond Examiner, of Rebel memory:

"A special dispatch to the Baltimore Sun avers that 'it is now pretty clear that the President has at heart the admission of Southern Congressmen, and will make it a measure of his Administration. Those opposing it will be regarded as hostile to the most material points of his policy.' It would appear from this that the President does not agree with the learned librarian of the House,*

* The "learned librarian of the House" had simply published a statement of the laws governing the organization of the House, showing the illegality of any attempt to have the names of the so-called Southern members placed on the roll, prior to the organization. This statement the Associated Press had chosen to pronounce semi-official.

nor with the clerk of the House, who, it is said, will not enter the names of Southern Congressmen until after the organization, and their admission is specially granted by the exclusive members who are to participate. The President, if this be true, will have done a good part in shifting the burden of the difficulty from the shoulders of the Southern members to his own. The clerk and librarian may now have the pleasure of a dispute with his Excellency, if they will, instead of the luxury of looking solemn and severe at some Southern gentlemen they would like to keep out in the cold for a short time."

Paragraphs like this served a special use. They illustrated the temper in which pardoned Rebels, who had sought the Attorney-General's office * as their "last ditch," resumed their duties as loyal citizens. "None so hard to please as a beggar." These men abjured all their rights under the Constitution, and did their best to overthrow it. They were forced back. Yesterday they cringed for pardon at the feet of "the boorish and drunken tailor" they had denounced ; to-day they are harder to satisfy than ninety and nine just men who have no need of repentance.

An ex-colonel of a Virginia regiment was exceedingly anxious to argue his political principles. They were talking, he heard, about keeping the Southern members from participating in the organization of the House, just to enable the Radicals to get all the officers. But he did n't believe they would dare to venture on so grossly tyrannical a course. If it was proposed to conciliate the South, they must no longer be subjected to such iniquitous oppression. The whole war had been of the same sort. The North had no business to begin its attack in the first place—no justification for it under the

* Applications for pardon were first presented to the Attorney-General.

sun. The South was only defending itself from Northern violations of law. Did n't Massachusetts, in her
Legislature, threaten to secede in 1812?* And was n't
there a clause in the Constitution about importing slaves
down to 1808, which was put in for her benefit, and at
her peremptory demand?

" As for your niggers, you 've got 'em on your hands.
They won't work, unless you force them to it, and
they 'll steal rather than starve. You even talk about
giving them suffrage! There are no words to express
the infamy of such a proposition. This is a white man's
government, and must be kept so till the end of time.
It 's true, there are a great many ignorant whites voting
now ; but so much the more need for stopping further
addition to the ignorant vote." There ought to be educational and property qualifications, he thought; but
on no account would he permit negroes to avail themselves of these. Educated or ignorant, rich or poor,
the niggers must be kept down.

In Richmond, and, as it appeared, throughout the
South, there was a general reliance upon the President
to secure the immediate admission of their Senators
and Representatives. Whether all believed or not, all
at any rate claimed, that their Representatives had a
perfect right to participate in the organization of the
House. The President was to see to it that they were
admitted to this right. None of these former sticklers
for a strict construction of the Constitution, hesitated
for a moment at the suggestion that the President was
as powerless in the premises as themselves. " Has n't

---

* " And do n't you know—supposing your statement true—that
she 'd been soundly thrashed if she had attempted it?" interjected
a quiet gentleman who had been attentively listening.

he the army?" they asked. In the better days such a question would have been denounced as treasonable. After their four years of arbitrary rule, it seemed to them the most natural thing in the world.

Richmond was fallen from its high estate, but it was a capital still. The brains, the pluck, and the pride of the rebellion are there, and the Rebel capital still leads the returning Rebel States. The Northern public scarcely appreciated the amount of journalistic talent concentrated there in the interest of the Rebel cause. The newspapers of Richmond, throughout the war, were in many respects the ablest on the continent. Their writing was often turgid, but it was always effective; and it shaped the public sentiment of the whole Confederacy. Mr. Davis himself was not above writing leaders for his organ, and Benjamin is reported to have been a frequent contributor. In the midst of their destitution they managed to keep up double the number of average dailies that we had in Washington, and the editorials of each were generally the productions of educated thinkers, as well as red-hot partisans. Fortunately or unfortunately, a share of the old ability and fervor clings to the revived newspapers of Richmond, and it is curious to see with what avidity the Virginians gulp down the praises of their heroic dead, in which they tend to indulge so freely, since it is no longer so safe to extol the deeds of the pardoned or pardon-seeking survivors.

Yet, with all the fervid zeal of the newspapers, I doubt if the great mass of Virginians cared very much, in November, for any active participation in political movements. At the outset, they were disgusted with their vulgar, drunken Governor. Then their ablest

men were all ineligible to office, because steeped in the
rebellion ; and they had the haughty pride of old families, which revolts against encouraging the aspirations
of unknown or odious upstarts. And, besides, while they
made a great show of establishing civil government, the
galling consciousness remained that, whether they chose
it or not, they *must* walk in a certain path, or be suppressed by the military. As the Enquirer itself said :

"As long as the civil authority is subordinate to the military,
there can not and ought not to be any politics or any principles
among a people so unhappily situated. A paper that is not as free
to censure as to approve, has no virtue in its support, and no importance attaches to its utterances. Approbation is worthless
where censure is forbid. The politics of the Enquirer, therefore,
must be deferred until the return of those good times when a free
press is the bulwark of the State."

Even the hated "Radicals" would be apt to indorse
so lucid a statement of so sound a principle. But they
might possibly make the argument prove more than
would be pleasing to Richmond. If there "ought not
to be any politics among a people so unhappily situated," neither ought there to be the farce of a form
without the substance of State Government.

Though not making exactly this deduction, many
Virginians were still ready for almost any political arrangement that would secure them the quiet and established order of civil government, and leave them to
the task of repairing their shattered private fortunes.
Even yet they had scarcely begun to comprehend the
policy of a plot for bringing the men who had just
been trying to overturn a government into the complete control of it. Many were still ready to accept,
as final, whatever orders the Government might issue,
and to make haste to do their part in obeying them.

"I tell you," said a prominent man, "President John-son can name his Senators and they will be straightway elected. He can say what he wants, and the Virginia Legislature, so-called, will register his edicts in legislative enactments. What we wish is to get settled, to know where we are and what we can depend upon, and then we want to go to work developing our material resources. We're all poor; we want to regain our lost money, and we've got to let politics alone and go to work to do it."

Beneath all this lay, of course, never-abandoned hopes of regaining political supremacy, after the social authority that comes of wealth has been restored. But the first want of Virginians was a settlement; something fixed on which capital could rely. They talked foolishly who said Virginia would not stand this, and the proud Virginians would revolt from that. The proud Virginians would stand anything, for the best of reasons. They could not help themselves. Statesmen might decide upon the course of statesmen for such emergencies; and whether it was pleasant or unpleasant, Virginia would submit, make the best of it, and go to work to improve her condition.

Meantime it was at any rate considered politic to keep the natural leaders of the community in the back ground. A son of ex-President Tyler had published the following significant warning:

"To the Editors of the Republic:

"Without assigning special reasons, I take the liberty, respectfully, but most earnestly, to advise that no person who has held a commission in the civil or military service of the late Confederate Government, *shall permit himself to be a candidate for the Legislature, either Federal or State, at the ensuing elections.*

"It is true, I believe, as a result of the recent struggle, that the entire people of Virginia have accepted the Union and the Government of the United States in good faith. The institution of slavery, too, has been extinguished. As matters now stand, I can not perceive what possible danger to the safety of the Union or the peace of the country could arise by allowing an absolute choice of Representatives to the whole constituent body; *but there are circumstances in the present state of general and national politics which make it imperatively necessary, in my opinion, that those citizens who were prominently identified with the cause of the Confederacy should exercise a rigid political abstinence* AT THIS TIME.

"Very respectfully,
"ROBERT TYLER."

The English of all this was plain: Stand back, now, gentlemen! Your patriotic course has made you a little odious to the Yankees, and we must be careful about offending them till we have got our State representation in Congress again. You're all right personally; we're proud of you, and you shall have plenty of offices by and by, but just "at this time" it is n't expedient to embarrass our cause at Washington, by carrying your conspicuous services in the war on our shoulders! Even school-boys would scarcely be misled thus. They could not forget their

"Timeo Danaos, et dona ferentes."

"I was a Rebel," said a conspicuous Southerner, "I submit because I was whipped, and have a great respect for the men that whipped me; but I shall have less respect for them if they prove such simpletons as to suppose that the Rebels of yesterday can to-day become fit men to be intrusted with the reorganization of a loyal government, by simply swearing an oath of allegiance."

Capital already began to come in from the North.

One gentleman had purchased a large tract of wood-land on the James River, with the plan of selling the wood on it in large quantities. Others were seeking to avail themselves of the magnificent water-power af-forded by the James, just above the city. The business men were anxious for the establishment of cotton fac-tories, and already saw, in imagination, the manufac-ture of the great Southern staple transferred from Northern to Southern hands. There was much talk of mineral lands in the south-western part of the State, and real estate agencies were springing up, to aid in bringing these lands into the market. The papers an-nounced, with many flourishes, that a Mr. Black, whom they styled "a great Scotch capitalist," had leased the famous White House estate, on the lower James, and was about to introduce upon it the Scotch tenantry system.

It was already considered certain that the confiscation law was to be a dead letter, and wealthy Rebels seemed to have no fear of the loss of their estates. But there were harassing confiscation suits, against which there was great outcry. "Are we never to see the end of those frightful lists of libeled property which the marshal and clerk are advertising?" exclaimed one of the papers. "Are costs to be piled, like Pelion upon Ossa, upon the heads of the gentlemen of Richmond and Petersburg, who have already been pardoned? A distinguished gentleman of this city has heard from President Johnson's own lips, language of strong indig-nation at the wholesale confiscation proceedings which have been instituted against certain classes of our peo-ple." Here, as always, President Johnson's will was to be taken as the final expression and force of law.

An indignant correspondent of one of the newspa-

pers* brought heavy charges against the Government
and one of the United States Judges:

"Major Nutt's farm, near Alexandria, and Dr. Bowen's farm,
sold by decree of Judge John C. Underwood, are to be delivered up
to Judge Underwood, Governor Pierpont, and Mr. Downey, the purchasers under the confiscation sale. It now appears that the principal property sold under Judge Underwood's decrees, in and
around Alexandria, was purchased by himself and those connected
with him in the high position he holds, at a fractional part of its
value only.

"Rumor says, and I have never heard it doubted, that Judge
Underwood, during the rebellion, obtained permission to raise a
regiment of negroes in Alexandria, which he succeeded in getting
at a low price, which regiment he turned over to one of the Northern States, at a large advance, thereby realizing a large sum of
money, with which he has been buying up the property confiscated
by himself, under his own decree, in *fee simple.*"

The burnt district, comprising nearly all the business
portion of the city, south and east of the capitol, was
beginning to rise from its ruins. Between a fourth and
a third of it would soon be better than before the con-
flagration, with which the Rebels signalized their abandonment of the city. But business was greatly over-
done by Northern speculators who had rushed down
with heavy supplies of goods immediately after the
surrender. The first pressing necessities satisfied, the
Virginians were too poor to trade largely.

Thanks to Northern loans, in sums ranging as high
(in one or two cases, at least,) as a half-million dollars,
the railroads were rapidly getting into running order,
and old lines of travel were reopening. Already the
Virginia Central Railroad was open to Staunton, and

* Richmond Enquirer, 7th November, 1865.

the Orange and Alexandria through its whole length, over a score or more of our battle-fields. Rival lines of steamers for Baltimore swarmed in the James River. Southward, Wilmington could be reached by rail, and even Charleston, a few gaps being filled by stage lines. South-westward, an unbroken line extended through Chattanooga and Atlanta—historic names—to Mobile.

As was entirely natural, a great deal of sullen bitterness was displayed against the negro. Men did not feel kindly that their old slaves should take time to consider the question of hiring with them, and should presume to haggle about wages. The least manifestation of a disposition to assert obtrusively his independence, brought the late slave into danger. Murders of negroes were occasionally reported; and the late masters made many wrathful promises to kill that were never fulfilled. Half-a-dozen times, in the course of a single day, I observed quarrels going on between negroes and white men. The latter constantly used the most violent and domineering language; the negroes several times seemed disposed to resent it.

Their schools were well attended, and the same good report of their progress was continually made. No man could fail to observe that the poor negroes were making much more earnest efforts to rise than the poor whites.

The restoration of confiscated property was again leaving many of the freedmen houseless. During the convulsions of the war they had left their old homes, and the authorities had established them upon the confiscated estates of absent Rebels. Pardoned, and resuming possession of their property, it was not unnatural that their first step should be to eject the vagrant negroes from their premises. The superintendent of schools under the Freedmen's Bureau estimated the entire number of persons thus rendered houseless in Eastern Virginia, at the beginning of winter, to be not less than seventy thousand.

Small-pox was also making ravages among them. They had not yet learned to take care of themselves; the emancipation had removed them from the care of their masters, and exposure, neglect, and disease were rapidly thinning out the population on which the wasted State had to rely for labor. The prevalent tone of public feeling indicated indifference to this public calamity. Virginians had not yet learned that their interests in laborers did not end when they ceased to own them; and many seemed to gloat over the facts, as a proof of the wisdom of their own opinions, and of the folly of their anti-slavery enemies. "This," exclaimed a newspaper, "is one of the practical results of negro *freedom*—one of the curses that has fallen on this unfortunate race, and one for which *somebody* must be held responsible at the bar of God. Who that *somebody* is, must be determined by a higher authority than human, though many are disposed to believe that the responsibility rests not on the people of the South. But be that as it may, the 'freedmen' are dying by hundreds and thousands. Where are the philanthropists of the North? Where are the Christian Commissions of Boston, and the Freedmen's Aid Societies of Philadelphia? Where are those who wanted an anti-slavery God and an anti-slavery Bible? Yes! where are they, when the negro is freed and is so sadly in need of their kind (?) offices?"

Where it could, the Government was still issuing rations to these poor waifs of the war, but the suffering was beyond any governmental control. Some of the old masters did their best to care for former slaves; but they were themselves impoverished and destitute. November winds already blew sharply—what might be expected before the winter was over?

CHAPTER XXXIII.

Lynchburg—The Interior of Virginia.

THE direct road from Richmond to Lynchburg was not yet in running order again. "One of our fool Generals burnt a big bridge near Lynchburg," explained a citizen, "when there wasn't the slightest use for it, and the bridge has not been rebuilt. Some of our Generals thought if they couldn't have everything their own way, they must ruin everything. They hadn't sense enough to see that it was their own friends they were ruining." The trains from Richmond to Gordonsville, however, and thence to Lynchburg were running with unexpected regularity. But, in at least one respect, Richmond was not to be moved from the good old ways. The train started from the middle of a street; and, in the absence of a depot, the passengers rendezvoused at the shops on the corner till they saw the cars coming along.

Of course, the desolation of Virginia, even in the regions most exposed to the ravages of the war had been overrated. I do not think the white people were starving, or likely to starve, anywhere from Alexandria to Gordonsville, Richmond, Fredericksburg, or Lynchburg; and within these points Virginia had suffered more than in all the rest of the State. A little corn had been grown in the summer, and that little had been husbanded in a style at which a Western farmer would stare in amazement. Every blade had been stripped from the stalks, every top had been cut, and in the center of every little inclosure a stack of blades, thatched with tops, supplemented the lack of hay and other forage for the cattle, while the abundant ears furnished the great staple of diet for the classes most likely to suffer. A few little patches of cotton whitened inclosures near the houses, at rare intervals; but the yield was light, and the cultivation had evidently been bad. Between Richmond and Gordonsville scarcely a dozen wheat-fields were seen. Great surface drains had been furrowed out all over the fields, as if the owners were afraid they had too much wheat in, and wanted a considerable portion of it washed away. Beyond Gordonsville, they became plentier, and the crops had been put in in better style.

But in the main, between Richmond and Gordonsville, as between Fredericksburg and Richmond, abandoned fields alternated with pine forests, destroyed depots, and ruined dwellings. Imaginative writers have described the droves of wild beasts which they represent as having taken possession of these desolated regions; but the sportsman is likely to find nothing more formidable than abundant coveys of quails. Our train brought up from Richmond, and left at different points along the road, numbers of the decayed Virginia gentry, equipped with dogs and fowling pieces, and eager for this result of the war, if not for others of more consequence.

Hanover Junction presented little but standing chimneys and the debris of destroyed buildings. Along the road a pile of smoky brick and mortar seemed a regularly recognized sign of what had once been a depot, and the train was sure to stop. Not a platform or water-tank had been left, and the rude contrivances hastily thrown up to get the road in running order were, in many cases, for miles and miles the only improvements visible. Young pines covered the old wheat-fields and corn-fields. Traces of breast-works wound off through the country in all directions. A coterie of young officers were constantly exclaiming, "Here we whipped the rebs." "There's a place where the rebs got after us mighty sharp. Gray-coated, heavy-bearded, ragged-looking fellows listened in scowling silence, or occasionally beguiled the way by reminding each other how "Here the Yanks caught hell."

At one or two points, where once had been considerable towns, the train was besieged by an outgrowth of the peculiar institution. A score or two of negro women, bearing trays on which were rudely arrayed what they called "snacks," surrounded us, loudly announcing the merits of their various preparations. "Sad" biscuit and fried chicken; "sad" biscuit and fried bacon; "sad" pie-crust, covering wild grapes, constituted the main attractions; and, as a grey-coated passenger sullenly remarked, "played the devil" with the hen-roosts of the surrounding country. Doubtless this petty traffic kept the wolf from many a negro's door through the winter.

The railroads had been supplied with rolling stock bought mainly from the supplies of our United States military railroads, or from Northern shops. One or two cars, however, of the best among all the trains we met, bore the marks of a Richmond firm. The tracks were comparatively solid; but the rails were in the worst possible condition. Looking from the rear platform, one saw every few yards a rail bent outward till he wondered why it did not throw us off; while half of them were crushed at the ends or worn off the face till scarcely half an inch remained for the wheel to touch. The roads hardly pretended to make over twelve miles per hour, and even that was in many places a very unsafe rate of speed. The conductors were, of course, ex-Rebels, so were the engineers and brakemen, and any complaint as to the running of trains was very effectually silenced by a suggestion of the improvement "since six months ago." Gangs of hands are at work on the roads, at distances of very few miles. Negroes and Rebel soldiers worked harmoniously side by side. "I tell you, sir," said a Yankee to a Virginian who did n't approve of this social equality, "a white man has got just the same right a nigger has—to starve if he won't work!"

Perched among its hills, and defended by nature's fortifications, Lynchburg had seen little of the immediate horrors of war. Her sons had gone down to death, but her fields had not been ravaged, her barns had not been burned, her children had not been often startled by the cry of the Yankees at the gates. Men had consequently escaped, to some degree, the impoverishing effects of the rebellion. Business seemed quite brisk; the farmers of the surrounding country were prosperous, and lands were not largely offered for sale.

As our train approached the city, I fell into conversation with a citizen. He rather guessed this little town was in no fix for starving. Niggers might suffer, and doubtless would, if they grew too saucy (pronounced "sassy;") but the people were all right. "Half a million of specie in that little town, sah, when the wah ended. What do you think of that for a little rookery among the mountains, sah?"

I suggested that very few tobacco fields were to be seen along the road. "Plenty of tobacco stored, sah. Did n't raise much last year, because there wa'nt many men at home to manage, but there's plenty more tobacco hid away in this country than people ever dreamed of. Gold will bring it out, sah."

"Greenbacks," it seemed, did not yet have the same magnetic power. Men who had been declaring for four years that the United States Government was over-thrown, could not at once convince themselves that its money was good. Whoever wanted to trade with the Virginians in the rural districts, must prepare himself with gold.

The town was swarming with representatives of Northern capitalists, looking for investments. Balti-moreans were also found frequently among them. The most went further South, over the Virginia and Ten-nessee road; but a few had ideas about the mineral re-sources of these mountains. Many seemed to think it necessary to adopt the coddling policy in their talk with the Virginians. "My policy for settling up these questions," said a Yankee, "would be to banish all the leaders, and tell the rest that they had been soundly whipped, and, now, the best thing they could do would be to go to work and repair their ruined fortunes."

"But how could you punish those equally deserving of punishment at the North, who were just as guilty in bringing on the war?" The questioner was, not a par-doned Rebel, but a speculative Northerner.

"The Lynchburg Post-office is in a church. The Government, it seems, was not willing to pay the rent demanded for the building formerly used for postal purposes, and the rent on churches was not exorbitant. A route agent, whiling away his time while his mail was made up, told how he had taken the oath, and so become an employee of the Government again.

"I was an old route agent, you see, and I wanted to go back to a nice berth. But I had been a magistrate under the Confederacy, and I was required to swear that I had never been. I went to see President Johnson. There was an awful crowd in the lobby, but I cottoned to Captain Slade, and played Yankee a little. Leaving out part of my name, I wrote on a card simply 'Frederick Bruce,' and made Slade promise to lay it before the President without a word. In a moment I was called in; but, as I approached the President, I thought I could see, by the twinkle of his eye, that I wasn't the Frederick Bruce he had expected!* Well, I told him that I took a magistrate's office under the Confederate Government, to avoid having to go into the army. He said the word 'voluntary' occurred at the beginning of the oath, and its force ran through the whole of it, and applied to every clause. 'Now, sir,' said the President, 'it's with your own conscience to say whether you took that office voluntarily or not.' Of course, I didn't, for I was compelled to do it in order to keep out of the army, and so I told the President I would take the oath at once, and he said, 'all right.'"

The narration threw a flood of light on the style of Unionists, with whose aid the Southern States were being "reconstructed." This man was one of the "stay-at-home" Rebels. He made no secret of his entire

---

*His "playing Yankee" consisted in a clumsy attempt to make the President believe that Sir Frederick Bruce, the new British Minister, was waiting in the ante-room to see him.

sympathy with the Rebel cause, but he wanted to keep out of the fight himself, and found it pleasanter to be a Rebel magistrate than a Rebel soldier.

Not very many Virginians seemed disposed to abandon the pleasant mountain homes about Lynchburg, for the doubtful bliss of Mexico or Brazil. The discovery had suddenly been made that there was a good deal more danger of "nigger equality" in either than in the United States, and the newspapers were dolorously warning the dissatisfied, that, if they should go to Brazil, they might happen to be brought before courts where negro judges presided, or be required to submit to laws enacted by the wisdom of negro legislators. It was bad to be forced to tolerate the presence of free negroes in the United States, but, really, it began to look as if they could go nowhere else without finding matters a great deal worse.

In the main, the negroes seemed to be doing well. In the Lynchburg hotels they were paid twenty dollars a month—five dollars more than they received for similar services in Richmond. "Den, besides dat, we picks up 'siderable from gemmen dat gibs us half-dollar for toting deir trunk or blacking deir boots, as I's shore you's gwine to do, sah."* These, however, were only the more intelligent. Through the country the negroes were by no means earning such wages, and, in fact, the most were earning none at all. They gained a preca-

---

* "Intelligent contrabands" all seem to have the money-making faculty well developed. Here is a table of the incomes of some of the freedmen about Newbern, North Carolina, during the third year of the war:

Three hundred and five persons, not employed by the Government, but working at trades of their own, returned a total income o $151,562, the average of all incomes being $496 92.

rious support by picking up occasional jobs, and by a pretty general system of pilfering.

All had the idea that in January the lands of their former masters were to be divided among them; and it

George Hargate, turpentine farmer	$3,000
Ned Huggins, tar and turpentine	3,150
E. H. Hill, missionary and trader	2,000
W. A. Ives, carpenter and grocer	2,400
George Gordon, turpentine	1,500
Adam Hymen, turpentine	1,300
Samuel Collins, dry goods and groceries	1,200
Benjamin Whitfield, grocery and eating-house	1,500
Hasty Chatwick, turpentine	1,000
Limber Lewis, staves, wood, and shingles	1,500
George Physic, grocer	1,500
Sylvester Mackey, undertaker	1,000
Charles Bryan, cartman	1,000
John H. Heath, shoemaker	1,000
William Long, lumberman	1,200
John Bryan, cotton farmer	1,100
Hogan Conedy, cooper and tar maker	1,000
Danzey Heath, grocer and baker	1,500

The average of the incomes of barbers was $675; the blacksmiths, $468; masons, $402; carpenters, $510; grocers, $678; coopers $418, and of turpentine farmers, $446.

While the negroes at Newbern, by patient toil, were putting such facts as these on record, the whole refugee white population was drawing rations.

At Beaufort, of 1,592 blacks in the place, only 300 received help, while, at the same time, 1,200 whites were supplied with rations.

The colony of Roanoke Island, in two years, made improvements whose cost value at the lowest figures was $44,000; more than would have bought the whole island before the war, with all the improvements which the "master class" had put upon it in two hundred years. In two years Sir Walter Raleigh's colony, established here, became utterly extinct.

The negroes in that region have generally preferred turpentine

was, therefore, almost impossible to make contracts with them for labor on the farms through the ensuing year. The inhabitants charged that this idea had been sedulously spread among them by the Yankee soldiers, and that they had been advised never to contract for more than a month's work at a time, until the division of property came. Here is a specimen of the way in which the Lynchburg papers treated the difficulty:

"The refusal of these people to make contracts for labor another year completely deranges all the regular and matured plans of our farmers. They know not what provision to make for feeding their employees; what extent of soil to mark out for seed; what kind of crops to cultivate, or what calculations to make upon their operations. If they sow, they are not certain to what extent they can reap; and if they attempt a variety of crops, (including tobacco,) they have no assurance whatever that their labor will not forsake them at the very moment that it is most indispensable.

"A friend in Amherst suggests that the powers that be should issue an order to the effect that all who do not get homes, or show they have a support within themselves, by the 1st day of January, 1866, will, on the 10th of said month, (nine days' notice being given,) be hired out to the highest bidder. Such an order would, in his opinion, cause all except the most worthless to secure homes before the 20th of December. These suggestions certainly seem to us to have wisdom in them, and to meet the difficulties, to some ex-

---

farming, the work being lighter and the returns earlier, as the product of the first dipping is ready for market before mid-summer. From three thousand to ten thousand trees have thus been leased to single individuals. Many have become rich, hundreds have lived in ease, and considering the difficulties in the way, a remarkable proportion supported themselves. The same opportunities were open to the white refugees, and the result is seen in the report of the number of rations issued in Newbern, the largest camp for contrabands in the State, and the great city of refuge to the whole State. Of 8,000 negroes in camp, only 3,000 drew rations, while in the white camp every man, woman, and child was fed by the Government.

tent, that now so seriously embarrass and retard agricultural pursuits; and we respectfully commend them to the attention of the proper authorities. One thing is certain, that if the negroes are not made to enter into contracts, and to keep them when made, the most ruinous consequences will result to our farming interests, and provisions enough will not be made to feed our people another year. Some fanatics and deluded persons, we know, will laugh at this idea, and tell us that the South has never been so prosperous in the past as she will be in the future under our present system of labor. But taking the most favorable view of the subject, it is still manifest to every one at all familiar with the real condition of things, that freed negro labor never was and never can be made *productive*—that is to say, *accumulative* or *progressive;* and that any reliance upon the *voluntary* work of free negroes, beyond what is absolutely necessary to their sustenance, is both vain and foolish. And we predict now, with regret and pain, what the results will certainly show, that there will henceforth be a steady and permanent decline in all the productions of the South dependent upon negro labor, as there has been in the French and British emancipation islands; and that the negro himself will steadily lose all the civilization which contact with his master has given him, and finally relapse into his native barbarism."

At the same time they were busy inducing these people, who were steadily losing all civilization and about to relapse into their native barbarism, to emigrate to Liberia; by way, it should seem, of hastening the process. One colony had already been sent off, and the papers made much of an address, written by the negro emigrants to their " best friends," to wit, their old masters,* wherein they were made to hint a conviction, in substance the same with that so current in the barrooms, that "Virginia is no place for free niggers."

The people of Lynchburg were all Johnson men.

* That is to say, written for them, and by the old masters themselves.

That is, they believed the President disposed to exact less of them than his party wanted, and they were bound to praise the bridge that promised to carry them safely over. Here, as elsewhere, "sound conservative views" were greatly in demand; these "views" being always found to have a relation, more or less intimate, to the negro. "No man," exclaimed one of the papers, "can fail to see that our future is pregnant with the most momentous issues, and that it will require the union of all right-thinking men to save our country from the blasting curse of a false and most destructive radical sentiment pervading it." To resist this destructive radical sentiment, the union of all the old parties was urged. They felt sure their members would be promptly admitted, and thought it a very great outrage that any opposition should be made to their participation in the organization of the House.

CHAPTER XXXIV.

Knoxville and the Mountaineers—Glimpses of Southern Ideas.

It was only the first week in November, but the morning air was keen and frosty, as I made my hurried preparations for leaving Lynchburg, on the East Tennessee Railroad. The "hotel" served up tough beefsteaks and gluey, blueish hot bread for breakfast. Everything was astir, and the little city wore as cheerful an air as though war had not been near its borders. A crowd of passengers pressed into the gloomy-looking depot. But three cars were provided, of which the last was occupied by negroes and soldiers. Into the second the railway officials carefully sorted the gentlemen, and the one nearest the engine was reserved for the ladies. In all, the glass windows had been broken by the soldiers during the war, and the whole Confederacy was unable to furnish glass large enough to repair them. Smaller sash had been accordingly put in and filled by seven-by-nine panes. There was a scramble for seats, and many had to stand for fifty or sixty miles.

Icicles hung at the pump spouts and around the water-tanks as the train started; and, for miles among the mountains, the first ice of the season could be seen covering the ponds and reflecting back the glowing tints of the autumnal foliage.

From Lynchburg to the Tennessee line (at Bristol,) was a distance of 204 miles, to which our prudent rail-

road managers devoted twenty-two hours, or an average
of a trifle over nine miles an hour! The crowded passengers made loud complaints as they began to ascertain
the rate of progress; but a glance at the road from
the rear platform was enough to silence the growlers.
Crushed rails, occasional gaps where a stone was in-
serted to prevent the car wheels from coming down to the
ties, sharp outward curves (the traces of the twists
Yankee raiders had given the rails,) shaky cross-ties
and fresh earth-ballasting, combined with curves around
mountain precipices, and rough pine trestle-work, where
once were substantial bridges, to give one fresh convictions of the need of Accident Insurance Companies.
The officers had counted the bad rails, and reported that
in an hundred miles an aggregate of not less than sixteen
miles ought to be removed without one day's delay.

A more beautiful route could scarcely be found.
Lovely little valleys peeped out among the hills, pretty
well cultivated, and dotted with houses that showed
comparatively little signs of destitution within. The
mountain sides were covered with forests, and the
abounding cattle found the sweetest blue grass everywhere. Finer grazing lands for cattle or sheep could
scarcely be imagined. Some day Yankee enterprise
will utilize the magnificent water power, convert the
forest into gold mines, and find real gold mines in the
mountain chasms. The mineral wealth of this region
is unimagined. Shrewd geologists were already trav-
ersing it in all directions; and with the next season
we shall have the launch of company after company
with "magnificent mining prospects." The shrewdly
managed will be profitable to the shareholders; the
shrewd managers will find *their* profits always, whether
shareholders do or do not.

Two heavy freight cars followed the last of the passenger cars in our train. They were needed in addition to the regular express car, to carry the accumulations of a single day's express matter at Lynchburg, in the charge of a single company. Southerners were talking largely about the patronage they would extend to General Joe Johnston's Express Company; but just then, they seemed to be doing very well in the way of sustaining its great rival. The express safes in our train contained six hundred thousand dollars in gold. A couple of hundred thousand, the agents said, was quite frequently a single day's consignment. Most of this goes South to buy cotton—a little, also, to buy cotton plantations.

All hands about these trains are Rebels, of course. Our several conductors were full of pleasant reminiscences about their narrow escapes from Yankee raiding parties. "Right yeah I had a hard chase," said one; "I was within a mile of town when I heerd that the Yankees was thar. I run back to the watch-tank and waited. Pretty soon the Yanks heerd I was thar, unloadin' soldiers, and off the fools went, without even destroyin' two cah-loads of ammunition that stood thar. Nobody never tuck no train from me amongst them all," he continued, "except Stone*man*, but he caught me nice. Stone*man* he got a whole train from me a'most before I knowed he was thar. Smart General, that Stone*man*."

Among our passengers were a number of Georgia and Alabama cotton-planters, full of their complaints about the "niggers and the Yanks." A New Yorker, going South to look at some mineral lands, said to give fine indications of gold in paying quantities, sat near

me and began a free and easy talk about the condition
of the negro, resources of the South, etc. He wasn't in
favor of negro suffrage as a condition of re-admission
to Congress, but he thought the Southern States themselves might, before long, come to see that an intelligent
negro would have as good a claim to the ballot as an
ignorant white man. "G—d d—n the infamous, dirty,
liver-hearted scoundrel," exclaimed a low fellow in the
same seat with me, whom I had taken for an army
sutler, but who turned out to be a Georgia planter,
"the dirty Yankee says a nigger is as good as a white
man. The old Abolition sneak," and so on, with epithets far less dainty and moral. The Georgian had
made as great a mistake about me as I had about him.
He took me for a Southerner!

The conversation went on about the Southern prejudices against conspicuous Northerners, like Greeley
and Beecher, and the New Yorker and myself soon
had half the eyes in the cars fixed on us. Presently a
deal of whispering, accompanied with sullen looks,
began. Half an hour afterward, a quiet, meek-looking
individual (who turned out to be a freedom-shrieker,
started in Massachusetts and graduated in Kansas,)
stepped beside me, as we were all on the platform
looking at the country, "Did you know those fellows
got very mad at your Abolitionism? That sallow,
long-haired Macon merchant wanted to have you
lynched, and swore roundly that tar and feathers would
be too good for you." "How did it end?" I asked.
"Oh, a little Georgian said it was all true, and you and
the New Yorker ought to be lynched, but, that since
this d——d war, that thing was played out!" It may
be readily inferred that for the rest of the trip the few

Northerners on board continued to talk Abolitionism enough to have astonished Wendell Phillips himself.

Making a virtue of necessity, the Southerners, after a time, became sociable. My Georgia neighbor told me of his two splendid plantations, not far from Columbus, one of four hundred and eighty acres, and the other of eighteen hundred acres. He had gone North, utterly down-hearted, and willing to sell out for a dollar an acre in gold; but they had treated him well in New York; there was less revengeful, bitter feeling than he had expected; Yankees were coming down to cultivate cotton beside him; and he was going to watch them and profit by it. If they could make money, growing cotton, he knew he could. If they could make the niggers work he would adopt their policy, and he knew he could do as well with niggers, whenever he found out how to get the power to control them, as any Yankee could.

I have conversed with dozens of planters, before and since, whose talk all runs in the same channel. They have no sort of conception of free labor. They do not comprehend any law for controlling laborers, save the law of force. When they speak of a policy of managing free negro laborers, they mean a policy by which they can *compel* them to work. "Why not depend on the power of wages, if they work, or of want, if they don't, to settle the labor question?" I asked one. "They'll work just long enough to get a dollar, and then they'll desert you in the midst of the picking season, till they've spent it all, and have become hungry again." "But Northern laborers are as anxious to save money and get on in the world as capitalists themselves." "Northern laborers are like other men; Southern laborers are nothing but niggers, and you can't make anything else out of them. They're not controlled by the same motives as white men, and unless you have power to compel them, they 'll only work when they can't beg or steal enough to keep from starving."

My Georgia planter, after first mistaking me for a Southerner, next mistook me for a plantation seeker, and earnestly advised me to go into the southwestern portion of his State. "You can make an average of half a bale to the acre on all the lands about there. I grow a bale to the acre on my lands. Went home this year after Lee surrendered, and I got my parole, ripped up half the corn my niggers had planted, and put it in cotton in May, and raised fifty bales, worth two hundred and fifty dollars a bale. Such land as that you can get at five dollars an acre. Then it's far healthier than the rich cotton lands in the west; and you have the best society in the country. Within a few miles of my plantation are half-a-dozen of the very first families in Georgia—the very best society I ever saw!"

But he was anxious to sell, nevertheless. There was no use talking about it, the niggers wouldn't work unless you had the power to compel them to it. Yankees talked mighty big about money bringing them to industrious habits; but, in a month's trial before he left home, he hadn't been able to hire a nigger for next year, or to hear of a neighbor who had hired one. The black vagabonds all expected their masters' lands at Christmas, and the Yankees were putting them up to it. He would take six dollars an acre now for his lands. All through his section (Columbus, Georgia,) lands could still be bought at from three to nine dollars, although prices were now advancing a little. For himself, he always made a bale to the acre; but then his were the best lands in the county. His neighbors never averaged over half a bale.

Altogether his plantation was quite an advantageous one. It was only twenty miles from town, and he could get his letters down quite frequently. They were sent in the care of his Columbus friends, and any person from the neighborhood who happened to be in town brought them out.

He had been in the war four years, and was heartily glad that it was over. Still it was an utter surprise. Neither the army nor the people had ever known to what straits they were reduced; but if the Western army had been equal to the Eastern, it would never have happened. The Army of Virginia was an army of gentlemen. There was no such material in that Western army. All the troops in the world could n't have taken Look-out Mountain from Bob Lee's army. "But you had three things too many for us, the Irish, the niggers, and Jesus Christ. So we're subjugated, and cussed glad for leave to go to work and try to get ahead a little again. But," and he broke out into fearful oaths against, "the scoundrels you hired with money, to butcher our young men, and enslave the bravest people on the face of the earth!"

By and by we came to a place for dinner. "That's the very best railroad eating-house I ever saw anywhere." Fortified by his recommendation, we all went in. Not a thing was there on the table save sour bread and tough steak, smothered in onions. But it excelled in one thing—the bill was a dollar, and the money was to be paid, not merely in advance of the meal, but before you got a sight at the table.

Another Georgian subsequently entered into the conversation. He hoped the Yankees would come down with their money and machinery, and have good luck growing cotton, for their good luck would now be good luck to everybody. "Yankees have always made more money among us than we ever made ourselves. There was ——, a Yankee, who came down to our country without even a change of linen, the poorest poor devil you ever see. He has married two of the best plantations on Pearl River, and is now a million-aire. Another fellow came down from New York, poor, traded a little, made money one way and another, till he got a start, and now he owns four of our best plant-ations.

They agreed in exaggerating the difficulties of the cotton cultivation. It was the very hardest of all crops, they really reckoned. You had to begin your plowing at New Years, and work right along, as close as you could push things, with your whole force. By April you had to plant, and, then, it was one perpetual rush to keep ahead of the grass and weeds, till July. Then you got your arrangements completed for picking; went to work at it as early as you could, and were kept driving till the last of December. Fact was, it took thirteen months to make a good crop of cotton. One hand, they supposed, ought to work twenty acres; ten in cotton, and as many more in corn. Others tried to work twenty-five acres with one hand, but they did n't do it very well. They only plowed three to four inches deep, and were sure that if they stirred up the ground deeper than that, it would be too loose for the cotton to take a firm root!

But free niggers could never be depended upon for such continuous and arduous work. The abolition of slavery was the death-blow to the great cotton interest of the United States. "I honestly believe," exclaimed the young Georgia planter first named, "that in five years the South will be a howling wilderness. The great mass of our lands are fit for nothing else, and you've destroyed the only labor with which we can cultivate them in cotton."

Near Wytheville, accident threw me into conversation with a tall, raw-boned mountaineer, who might have been good looking but for the vulgarity of dyeing his moustache. He had been in the war for awhile, and then had gone to speculating. "I've made a good deal out of the war, and if the cussed thing had n't collapsed quite so soon, I'd been a millionaire—*in Confed!*" He was extravagant in his praises of Floyd,[41] and presently it transpired that he had commanded a regiment on Floyd's right, in one of the early affairs of the war—"Carnifex Ferry," in West Virginia. He seemed delighted to learn that I had myself seen something of that fight—from the other side—and was at once full of inquiries and boasts. "I tell you, we got off mighty smart. The men did n't know we were retreating; had been told they were only going to change their position. You scoundrels got my flag and trunk though. But what in thunder was that infernal racket on your left, after dark, when you were drawing off?" I explained the sad mistake by which a couple of our regiments had fired into each other. "Well, do you know, you scared us worse with that performance of yours than anything else? We felt certain you were going to sweep in on our right." Curiously enough, this precise maneuver had been urged upon General Rosecrans[42] by General (then Colonel) Smith,[43] of the Thirteenth Ohio, and but for the approach of night

[41] John Buchanan Floyd, Confederate general, former Secretary of War under President Buchanan. [Ed.]

[42] William Starke Rosecrans, Union general prominent in the western theater of war. [Ed.]

[43] William Sooy Smith, Union general, engineer and bridge builder. [Ed.]

might have been executed. I gathered from the Rebel Colonel that it would probably have been successful.

"But we came very near using up your Dutch General, when you crossed the river and followed us up to the mountain. Old Bob Lee came down and reinforced us. All our arrangements were made for Floyd to march around to your rear. We were about to start, the guides were all ready, the route selected, and we would have been in your rear before daylight, with Bob Lee in your front; but Lee thought we were too late starting, and made us stop till the next night. By the next night, there was no Rosecrans there."

At one or two points along the line were rows of box-cars, run off on unused side-tracks, and filled with families of refugees. Dirty, frowzy women, with half-clad, tow-headed children, filled the doors, but over their heads we could catch glimpses of filthy interiors that not even negro cabins could equal. Doubtless the poor whites of the South are far better material for voters than intelligent negroes, for we have it on the best of authority—their own—but for dirt, and for utter ignorance of all the decencies of civilized life, no people in America, of any color, can compare with them.* I grieve to add that, in many regions in the South, they

---

* I have said nothing concerning these poor whites, which is not mildness itself compared with the descriptions of other travelers. Here is one of the latest, from the very intelligent Southern correspondent of the Boston Advertiser, Mr. Sidney Andrews. Fortunately the classes he describes are confined, almost exclusively, to the south-eastern States:

"Whether the North Carolina 'dirt-eater,' or the South Carolina 'sand-hiller,' or the Georgia 'cracker,' is lowest in the scale of human existence, would be difficult to say. The ordinary plantation negro seemed to me, when I first saw him in any numbers, at the

are almost the only Unionists. The intelligent people hereabouts are loyal, but in States further South the most loyal are too often the most ignorant.

"How do the negroes get along here?" I asked of an ancient Tennessee matron, looking benevolently down upon us through a pair of brass-mounted spectacles, with an offer of "snacks" for a quarter. "What? O, you mean the niggahs. They's doin well enough, far's I hear." "Are any of them suffering, hereabouts?" "Sufferin? No more'n other folks, I rekon. Everybody gits along well enough heah." "Do the

very bottom of not only probabilities but also possibilities, so far as they affect human relations; but these specimens of the white race must be credited with having reached a yet lower depth of squalid and beastly wretchedness. However poor or ignorant, or unclean, or improvident he may be, I never yet found a negro who had not at least a vague desire for a better condition, an undefined longing for something called freedom, a shrewd instinct of self-preservation. These three ideas—or, let me say, shadows of ideas—do not make the creature a man, but they light him out of the bounds of brutedom. The Georgia 'cracker,' as I have seen him since leaving Milledgeville, seems to me to lack not only all that the negro does, but also even the desire for a better condition, and the vague longing for an enlargement of his liberties and his rights. I walked out into the country, back of Albany and Andersonville, when at those places, and into the country back of Fort Valley this morning; and, on each occasion, I fell in with three or four of these 'cracker' families. Such filthy poverty, such foul ignorance, such idiotic imbecility, such bestial instincts, such groveling desires, such mean longings; you would question my veracity as a man if I were to paint the pictures I have seen! Moreover, no trick of words can make plain the scene in and around one of these habitations; no fertility of language can embody the simple facts for a Northern mind; and the case is one in which even seeing itself is scarcely believing. Time and effort will lead the negro up to intelligent manhood, but I almost doubt if it will be possible to ever lift this 'white trash' into respectability."

negroes behave well?"   "Well's anybody else, I guess.
I don't see much of 'em nor don't want to, the nasty
black things."

The scenery had changed somewhat as we neared
the chief town of East Tennessee. It was not quite so
hilly; and there were more evidences of careful farming. Good wheat and corn-fields lined the road; and
one caught many a peep at picturesque mountain residences, embowered in the abounding orchards. We had
passed out of one great zone of the war into another.
Sheridan, Grant, Lee, were all strange names, that suggested remote operations. We were nearer the theater
on which Bragg, Johnson, Rosecrans, and Sherman had
been the actors. John Morgan's name was a charm
to still the demon of mischief in naughty children.
"This is whar they both belong," said a native, as we
were coming out from the dining-room at Greenville.
It was to President Johnson (whose home was in this
dilapidated little village,) that the reference had been
made. Who the other notability of the place was, no
one understood; till the native explained that he "meant
Andie Johnson and John Morgan, of co'se."

Broken bridges had grown more and more frequent;
and the train crept slowly over long lines of trestle-work
which timid passengers fancied they could see swaying
beneath us. The road led across Strawberry Plains,
where Longstreet was driven back, and wound near
several of the forts.

I was once more doomed to be mistaken. We were
approaching Knoxville. A haggard-looking, rough-
bearded fellow leaned over and whispered in my ear,
"This isn't a good country for you and me. They're
all tories here, every d——d scoundrel of them. I've

been chased off from my home because I had been in the Confederate army. For three weeks I've dodged about in the woods, and now I'm a going to get out of this Yankee country. But you had better keep mighty quiet; they'll suspect you quicker'n me." I advised my confidential friend to get further South as fast as possible, and the last I saw of him he was making a rush, in Knoxville, for the Dalton and Atlanta cars.

Burnt houses and solitary chimneys over one whole quarter of the city, showed that the heart of East Tennessee loyalty had not been without its sufferings. The best part, however, of the little city seemed to be saved. Straggling up and down hill, stretching off to the precipitous banks of the clear, sparkling river that skirts it, with few pretensions to elegance in its stony streets or old-fashioned architecture, but with a great deal of homely substantial comfort, Knoxville is a very fit capital for the mountain region of East Tennessee. It seemed prosperous, and likely, under the new order of things, to continue to prosper. Its people had not been accustomed to depend for support upon their slaves; they suffered the less, therefore, from the sudden disappearance of slaves. Land-owners in the vicinity held their property at enormous prices; the people had plenty; and, in a rude way, they lived very comfortably. For a time there had been a strong conflict between Unionists and their former oppressors. Men who had been driven from their homes or half-starved in the mountains, or hunted for with dogs, were not likely to be very gentle in their treatment of the men who persecuted them; and one readily believed what all observers said, that in no place through the South had the bitterness of feeling, engendered by the war, been so intense, or the violence so bloody in its consequences. Returned Rebels had not unfrequently been notified that they must leave the country, under penalty of being treated precisely as they had treated Union men when they had the power. Sometimes they were shot before such notification; sometimes after it; when, in a foolhardy spirit, they remained to brave it out.

But the prevailing tendency to violence was now turned in a new direction. The niggers were presuming to talk about getting the right to vote. The inborn poor-white hatred of the negroes was all aflame at this, and every man felt it his duty to help set back the upstart niggers. Every few nights, I was told, a negro was shot in some of the back streets, "nigger life's cheap now; nobody likes' em enough to have any affair of the sort investigated; and when a white man feels aggrieved at anything a nigger's done, he just shoots him and puts an end to it."

Doubtless there was in this a spice of exaggeration; but it was manifest that East Tennessee radicalism, however earnest on the question of punishing Rebels, did not go to the extent of defending the negroes. There was, I should judge, absolutely no public sentiment in favor of negro suffrage, and scarcely any in favor of negro education. The prejudices against them were, with the most, intense; and if any way of driving them out of the country can be found, it will be very apt to be put in force. The freedmen have more hope from Virginia Rebels than from East Tennessee Loyalists, if the public sentiment of Knoxville may be accepted as a test. In this, as in all their other political feelings, the Mountaineers are fervidly in earnest.

A prophet is generally without honor in his own country, and it is not surprising that there should be other places in the United States where they have more confidence in President Johnson than at Knoxville. The people of Greenville are very proud of having given a President to the country; but in Knoxville they are inclined to reserve their praises. "What in h—ll is he palavering with the Democrats for?" asked one. Others could hardly be brought to express an opinion about him; and I found very few except the office-holders who were warmly and without reservation his friends. "He's pardoning cursed scoundrels all the time, such as we've been shooting out here, on sight." "Why don't he hang Jeff Davis, as he said in the Senate he would?" "Well, he's got to play his hand out pretty soon, and we'll see whether he's going to desert us." Such are some of the voices I heard in November among the East Tennesseans. They didn't give Mr. Johnson up; in fact, they still wanted very much to believe in him; but they had more faith in Parson Brownlow.[44] More hanging and fewer pardons would, as they thought, better suit the existing wants of the South.

The chief newspaper of the place is "Brownlow's Knoxville Whig and Rebel Ventilator." Its name is a pretty good index, at once to its contents, and to the temper of the people among whom it is a favorite. The Rev. Governor and Editor tersely summed up his views of the political situation:

"The Southern leaders still have the devil in them, and presuming upon the leniency of the President, they are losing sight of their real positions. Louisiana is proposing to elect ex-Governor Allen, now a refugee traitor in Mexico, to gubernatorial honors, on the ground that he is endeared to the people because of his services rendered

[44] William Gannaway ("Parson") Brownlow, Governor of Tennessee, 1865-1869. [Ed.]

in the cause of the rebellion. In North Carolina, Georgia, and Alabama, unpardoned Rebels are running for Congress, boasting that they are still unpardoned and do not intend to change. We are sorry to see this state of things, but it is just what we predicted from the start. The war was closed out two years too soon. * * The mild and benignant policy of the President has been abused; is not at all appreciated by Rebel leaders, but is insultingly demanded as their *right!* These Southern Rebels have their fate in their own keeping, and they are nursing their wrath to keep it warm. We feel confident that the President will not yield any more ground to them, if indeed he does not withdraw from them what he has conceded."

On many accounts East Tennessee offers peculiar advantages to the poorer classes of Northern emigrants, who wish to avail themselves of the cheap prices of lands in the South. There are few large planters; small farms are easily purchased; the community is made up of men not ashamed to labor for themselves, and not disposed to sneer at the emigrant who fences his own fields and does his own plowing. Lands about Knoxville commanded high prices—fifty dollars per acre and upwards—but through the greater part of the country they could be bought, in November, at prices ranging from two to ten dollars. The soil is a rich, dark limestone, producing good crops of corn, oats, wheat, hay and potatoes. Much of the country is admirably adapted for grazing; and horses, mules, sheep, cattle, and hogs are reared in great abundance. The climate is delightful. Water-power is abundant; iron and coal are found in almost every county; copper, zinc, lead, and the famous Tennessee marble also abound. Give East Tennessee her long-sought railroad connection with Cincinnati and the North, and the emigration thither from all the over-crowded localities of the Middle States can not fail to be very large.

CHAPTER XXXV.

Atlanta—Georgia Phases of Rebel and Union Talk.

FROM Knoxville I went direct to Atlanta, Georgia, the key of the great campaigns in the West, the memorable surrender of which re-elected President Lincoln, and proved the beginning of the end.

The city was adapting itself, with remarkable rapidity, to the new order of things. "Sherman, his mark," was still written too plainly to be soon effaced, in gaping windows and roofless houses, heaps of ruins on the principal corners and traces of unsparing destruction everywhere. The burnt district of Richmond was hardly more thoroughly destroyed than the central part of Atlanta; yet, with all the advantages of proximity to the North, abundant capital, and an influx of business and money from above the Potomac, Richmond was not half so far rebuilt as Atlanta. What is more remarkable, the men who were bringing a city out of this desert of shattered brick—raising warehouses from ruins, and hastily establishing stores in houses half finished and unroofed—were not Yankees, but pure Southerners. These people were taking lessons from Chicago, and deserved to have, as they then seemed likely to have, the foremost of the interior cities of the Gulf States.

Not less than four thousand mechanics were at work; and at least as many more would have been employed,

it it had been possible to secure building material
enough to supply the enormous demand. A hundred
and fifty or two hundred stores were already opened;
and others found themselves unable to rent rooms for
their goods. The streets were blockaded with drays
and wagons. The four railroads were taxed to their
utmost capacity, without beginning to supply all the
demands upon them. The trade of the city was a third
greater than it had ever been, in its most prosperous
days before the war.

But the faces one saw on the streets or behind the
counters were not the faces of men with whom you
would choose to do business. "I have spent five days
here," exclaimed a simple-hearted scientific man, as he
greeted me; "I have spent years among the Black Feet,
and have been pretty much over the world, but I never
saw such demoralized faces. The war has destroyed
their moral character. There isn't one man in a score
here I would trust with my carpet-bag." The geolo-
gist was too severe, but the traces of the bad passions
and disregard of moral obligations which the war has
taught, are written almost as plainly on the faces as
are Sherman's marks on the houses of Atlanta. More
tangible evidence of the war's demoralization was to be
found in the alarming insecurity of property and even
of life. Passing about the dark, crooked streets of
Atlanta after night, unaccompanied and unarmed, was
worse than attempting a similar exploration of the
Five Points, in New York, ten years ago. Murders
were of frequent occurrence; and so common a thing
as garroting attracted very little attention.

The soil of the country, for many miles in all directions, is poor, but prices of land in the immediate vicinity were run up to fabulous rates. The people

were infected with the mania of city building; and
landholders gravely explained to you how well their
plantations, miles distant, would cut up into corner lots.
Cotton is, of course, the only staple. It ought to be
raised in abundance, for the soil will produce nothing
else, but he would be a skillful cultivator who should
get an average of a third of a bale each from many
acres. Ten or twelve bushels of corn to the acre would
be a great crop. Indeed, throughout wide stretches in
the interior of the cotton-growing States, so worthless
was the soil for any other purpose, that the planters
used to buy their corn and pork for the mules and negroes, and thus reserve all their arable land for the
undivided growth of cotton.

A few Union men are to be found in the region to
which Atlanta is the natural center. All complained
that it was worse for them, under the progressing reconstruction, than for the original Rebels. "We are in
no sense upheld or encouraged by the Government;
public sentiment is against us because we opposed the
war; or, as they said, because we were tories; but,
when the Government triumphed, we were secure because we were on the winning side. But you pardon
Howell Cobb and every other leading secessionist;
they at once become the natural leaders in an over-
whelmingly secessionist community; and we, through
mistaken kindness of our own Government, are worse
ostracized to-day, in the new order of things, than we
ever were during the war."

The feeling among the Rebel portion of the community against the course of the Convention was strong.
"They have repudiated the debt they incurred themselves. If that Confederate debt isn't honestly due,

no debt in the world ever was. If we ve got to repudiate that, we may as well help the Democrats repudiate the debt on the other side too. What's fair for one
is fair for the other."*

In spite of their new-found love for President Johnson, they could not help grumbling a good deal at "this
Presidential interference with the rights of a State."
They seemed utterly unable to comprehend that, after
they had once submitted, they could possibly labor
under any disabilities on account of their effort to over-
throw the Government. "Treason is a crime, and the
greatest of crimes," vociferated the President. His
Southern friends seemed to regard this as only a little
joke. To interfere, for a moment, with the free action
of their Conventions and Legislatures, half made up
as yet of unpardoned Rebels, was monstrous. "What's
the use o' callin' it a free country, ef you can't do as
you please in your own Legislater?" asked one indignant Georgian. "It's a pretty note ef we've got to
take men as went agin the State through the wah to
make laws for it now. For my part, I hain't got no
use for sich."

The political phraseology of these Southern gentlemen is at once peculiar and concise. Every desirable
thing, politically, is described as high-toned and conservative. Everything dangerous to the settled order of
things, everything looking to an establishment of the
results of the war, or tending to an indorsement of the
political grounds on which the North suppressed the

* Mr. Simmons said in the Georgia Convention: "Let us repudiate only under the lash and the application of military power,
and then, as soon as we are an independent sovereignty, restored to
our equal rights and privileges in the Union, let us immediately
call another Convention and resume the debt."

rebellion, is to be abhorred and avoided under the name of radical. President Johnson was greatly praised, " because he is conservative on the nigger."

"Johnson knows niggers,. I tell you," said an Atlanta worthy. " He's not going to let any such cursed radicalism as inspired Lincoln trouble him. If Johnson had been President, we wouldn't have been embarrassed by any infernal Emancipation Proclamation." So all good conservatives were exhorted in all the papers to convince the South of their desire to reconstruct the Union by admitting at once the Southern Representatives and Senators; and, above all, it was to be understood that sound conservative men of all parties must unite in the repeal of the odious radical oath. It absolutely prevented Rebel office-holders from at once becoming national law-makers.

Mr. Jas. F. Johnson aspired to represent the Senatorial District in the General Assembly. He furnished an excellent type of what passes among Georgians for a respectable and proper sort of Unionism. He stated his position, in an advertisement in the public papers, thus:

"As a member of the Georgia Convention, entertaining the views I then did, I opposed the immediate secession of the State from the Union, and used every effort in my power to prevent it, until I became satisfied that a controlling majority of the Convention entertained different views. I then yielded my opposition, believing it to be the best interest of the State to be united in supporting the action taken by a majority of the Convention. And since that time, until the surrender of the Confederate armies, I did all in my power, both in person and means, to sustain the resolution of the Convention, and establish, if possible, the independence of the Southern States.

Another style of Unionism might be inferred from

the phrase heard a dozen times every day: "I've taken the oath," or, "I've got my pardon; and I'm just as big a Rebel now as ever I was." "I've got just the same rights now that any of the d——d Yankees have," added one, "and I mean to demand my rights. I'm pardoned; there's nothing against me, and I mean to demand fair treatment." He had Confederate cotton, which he insisted should not be taken from him, since, although he had subscribed it to the Rebel Government, he had never made the actual delivery.

Between Atlanta and Knoxville one passes over the track of the destroyer. Down to Dalton the damage from the war has not been very great; but for the rest of the route, solitary chimneys and the debris of burnt buildings everywhere tell the old, old story. If the country did not reveal it so plainly, it might still be read in the faces of our passengers. Every one of them was a record of some phase of the contest, of its squalor and misery, of its demoralization, of its barbarism, or of its ennoblement. Bright, fair faces that ought to have adorned happy rural homes, grown coarse and brassy, flaunted beside young officers. They were the transformation of the camps—the results of its license and lax-morality. Trembling old refugees watched the conductor as he counted their hard-earned gatherings, to see if the little pile of fractional currency would be all exhausted in paying their fare home. Aimless young men in gray, ragged and filthy, seemed, with the downfall of the rebellion they had fought for, to have lost their object in life, and stared stupidly at the clothes and comfortable air of officers and strangers from the North. By the roadside, here and there, might be seen—as I saw on a public corner, in the midst of all the bustle and whirl of Atlanta—a poor, half starved, half naked white woman, gathering her little children about her, and cowering in the gray dawn over the dull embers by which, in dull wretchedness, she had watched through the weary night.

And, as one looks over the scene, and takes in the full sense of all this sad destruction, a Major from Longstreet's staff sits down to talk. "If you of the North want now to conciliate and settle the South, you must do one of three things : re-establish slavery ; give the old masters in some way power to compel the negroes to work ; or colonize them out of the country, and help us to bring in white laborers ! " A handsome man he is ; tall, bearded like the pard, brown with campaigning, battered, clad in worn-out Confederate gray, but with good army blue pantaloons, taken, doubtless, from the body of some dead or captured soldier of the Republic. Such waste and destruction all about us ; and still these insatiable men—these handsome tigers—want more conciliation !

Some Southern merchants, from different points in Alabama and Georgia, were returning from New York, after making their purchases. They could not say too much about the kindness with which they had been met, and their disappointment at not finding the Yankees all eager to drink their blood for desert after dinner. But in a moment after such expressions they would break out into the most fearful and blasphemous invectives against some conspicuous Northerner, who had the misfortune to differ from them as to the best mode of re-establishing peace throughout the Rebel regions. These people have discovered that they must tolerate the opinions of others, but their intolerant spirits have not yet been sufficiently disciplined to it ;

and so it happens that sometimes, now, their utter im-
potence only serves to increase their malice. Must the
poor negroes prove the vent for this rage that dare not
reach to higher objects?

Manifestly the negroes themselves have no faith in
them.   At one of the railroad eating-houses I happened to ask a fine looking old "uncle" what wages he
received.

"Twenty dollahs a month, sah; but I'se gwine to
quit. 'T ain't enuff, is it?"

"O yes, uncle, if they give you twenty dollars a
month and your boarding, you are getting fully as
much as you would get at the best places in the North
for this kind of work. In Richmond they are only
getting fifteen dollars."

"You tink, den, sah, dat we ought n't fur to quit—
dat when dey pay us twenty dollahs dey ain't a cheatin'
us?"

"By no means. Work straight ahead, and do the
best you can, as long as you can get such wages."

"Well, den, sah, I'll do as you say. I was afeared
of dese men cheatin' me, because I knowed dey would
if dey could. But I'll do jus as you say, sah. If you
say wuck on, I'll do it." And three or four of the servants who had gathered about, nodded and grinned
their approval of the old man's conclusions.

"That's just the trouble," exclaimed a young Alabamian, to whom, a few hours later, I was narrating
the incident. "These fellows have all got to believe in
the Yankees, and to think that we, who have always
been their best friends, want to cheat them. It's going to ruin the South. Five years hence, I firmly believe, the cotton-growing regions will be an utter waste,
unless you Yankees, who don't know anything about

cotton growing, come in, learn it, and get the niggers
to work for you. They won't half work for us."

"Won't a fair day's wages, in the long run, be sure to
bring a fair day's work?"

"No. I tell you, the nigger *never* works except when
he is compelled to. It• is n't in his nature, and you
can 't put it in. He 'll work a day for you for good
wages, and then will go off and spend it; and you 'll
not get another lick out of him till he's hungry, and
has got nothing to eat."

"Possibly, at first. But remember, these people are
intoxicated with their first draught of freedom. Wait
a little while, and as they get settled, and see something
of the rewards of steady industry, they 'll be as eager
to accumulate and save, as any other class of laborers."

"Not a bit of it. I tell you, niggers are niggers.
You 're talking about a different class of laborers altogether. That 's always the way. You know, and every
Northern man knows, that we have been the best friends
the nigger ever had. Yet this is the way they treat us.
They 'll work for you a little while, and then they 'll
serve you in the same style."

An old negro on the platform, at the very moment,
was droning out a curious commentary on the Alabamian's complaints: "One-half of dese niggers," said he
to the brakeman, "one-half of dese niggers ought to be
killed, any how. Dey don't do nuffin but hang roun'
and steal from dem dat work." His old brass watch, it
seems, had been stolen, and he was scowling through
his brass-mounted goggles in the direction in which he
supposed the thief had gone.

I told the Alabamian of the persistent labors of the
Sea Island negroes. He utterly refused to believe that
I had not been deceived. Finally, the crucial test was

mentioned—the balances to their credit in the National Bank.*   "Well, I do n't understand it.   There were never any such niggers around in our country."   And with that he suddenly ended the talk.

* Some weeks before this, on the 17th of September, 1865, the balances to the credit of the Sea Island negroes, in their National Bank, amounted to $195,587 08.

CHAPTER XXXVI.

Montgomery—The Lowest Phase of Negro Character—Politics and Business.

FROM Atlanta I took the railway for Montgomery, Alabama. We had been traveling, thus far, in third-class passenger cars. Now we came down to box freight cars, around the sides of which a board bench was placed for the accommodation of such passengers as cared to sit down.

"'Ere's your Cincinnati and Nashville papers, Gazette, Commercial, Press, and Times! All about the execution of Champ Ferguson!"

"Yes, and I wish it was all about the execution of the scoundrels that tried him."

The scene was a box-car on the West Point (Georgia) Railroad; the speaker an Alabama planter, on his way home from Atlanta.

I have been seeking to exhibit, as fairly as I could, the actual talk and temper, not of the office-holders or office-seekers, who are, of course, all things to all men, but of the people one meets on the cars, in the hotels, at the wayside, and on the plantations. The expression above quoted, about Champ Ferguson, is but a specimen of what was often heard among men proverbially outspoken, and, then, more than ever disposed, in the bitterness of their defeat, to let out all the gall that was

in them.   The Tennessee guerrilla had far more friends
and sympathizers throughout this region than had the
men who convicted him.   The unjust detention of Mr.
Jefferson Davis was everywhere deplored.   "By —,"
exclaimed an Alabamian to me to-day, with a horrible
oath, "are you going to hang Jeff. Davis?   That's what
I want to know.   You might as well hang all the honorable men in the South, for he was only their trusty
agent."   Even Wirz was covered with the broad mantle
of Southern charity.   It was universally thought that
his trial had been grossly unfair; that Government
gave him no opportunity to get witnesses, and that he
was entirely innocent.*   The report of his execution
had just arrived, and while some refused to believe it,
others took great delight in repeating the words of the
dispatch, as sweetened to suit the prevailing taste, by
some Southern news agent: "He died bravely, protesting his innocence."

I do not mean that these people are nursing a new
rebellion.   For many years they will be the hardest
people in the civilized world to persuade into insurrection.   But they nurse the embers of the old one, and

---

* About this time the New Orleans True Delta, (quite recently
the organ of General Banks,) spoke of "the gloating of the cold-
blooded, viperous, vindictive editor of the Chicago Republican,
over the hanging of Henry Wirz," and "his atrocious wickedness
and unparalleled fiendish malignity, in endeavoring to connect
Jefferson Davis' and General Lee's names with the alleged crimes
of Wirz."   At the same time the Epoque of the same city protested
against the execution of Wirz, and against brutal military commissions, complained that a Confederate Major-General and Captain Petit were both held for similar sacrifice; hoped that President Johnson would stay such merciless and exciting proceedings,
and asked, supposing them guilty of all alleged against them. and
such guilt was to be punished, why Butler still lives?

cherish its ashes. They are all Union men, in the sense that they submit, (since they can't help themselves,) and want to make all they can out of their submission. But to talk of any genuine Union sentiment, any affection for the Union, any intention to go one step further out of the old paths that led to the rebellion, than they are forced out is preposterous. They admit that they are whipped; but the honest ones make no pretense of loving the power that whipped them.

It has been currently supposed at the North, that the desolation wrought by the war, would lead to an intense hatred of the leaders who brought it on. But this hatred has taken another turn. Instead of hating their own leaders they hate ours. They do not realize that such men as Mason, Yancey, Davis, and Toombs led them, for selfish purposes, into this sea of blood; they followed these leaders willingly, believe in them still, and insist that the North brought on the war by illegal encroachments, which they were bound in honor to resist. Such were the expressions I heard everywhere around me, and, however little might be said for their loyalty, their honesty and candor could not be doubted. The men to suspect of dishonesty are not these who frankly, admit that they are defeated and bound to submit, but still insist that they were right in the start of the quarrel. The men who make haste to adjure all the principles they fought for, and to acknowledge their dead brothers and sons to have been traitors, *they* are the ones whose new-born "loyalty" is sown upon the sand. When the nutriment of the offices is withdrawn, look out for a withering.

One or two plantations between Atlanta and West Point showed gangs of negroes at work clearing off the lands, and preparing for a cotton crop; but by far the greater number seemed still abandoned. Since leaving East Tennessee, I had not seen one white man at work. The negroes, who were breaking up the cotton lands, did it with little "bull-tongues," such as Northern farmers use to cultivate their corn. A good, moldboard plow seemed unheard of.

At West Point, a village of cheap frame houses, where we stopped for dinner, large piles of cotton bales filled the public square. Even the primitive cultivation we had seen, seemed to produce fair crops. Half a bale to the acre was above the average yield. There were few large plantations; and the population seemed mainly composed of small farmers, cultivating from one to four or five hundred acres.

At Opelika we reached the ultimate in the matter of railroad traveling. The Macon train pushed out with a couple of box cars, containing no seats, into which were loaded passengers, baggage, freight, and fuel. The locomotive bore only the battered remnants of what had been a smoke-stack; the machinery was rusty; the head-light was gone, and even the bell was broken. On the Montgomery train we congratulated ourselves on better fortune. We had ordinary box freight cars, into which we climbed, ladies and gentlemen alike, through the sliding doors at the side; but in each car half-a-dozen pine board benches had been arranged, across which the ladies scrambled to a corner, free at once from dust, light, and ventilation, and over which every one trampled in getting into or out of the car.

With less fear of dust, and more love for fresh air than my fellow travelers, I established myself in the door. While we waited for the engine, a plantation negro, who seemed to belong to the lowest possible grade, approached us. He was not idiotic, but he seemed hopelessly and inconceivably stupid. No such existence as his would be possible on a large plantation. It is only where the attrition of social intercourse is almost wholly removed that a human being can possibly grow to manhood with so little advancement beyond the condition of the brutes around him.

He was clad in the coarsest negro cloth, ragged, dirty, ill-fitting. Head and feet were bare. I asked him if he knew he was free.

"Ya-a-a-s, sah."

"Well, are you ready to live with some good man, and go to work to earn your living?"

"I reckon."

"How much do you think you ought to have per month?"

"Dunno." And the stupid stare was broken by a puzzled expression, as if this seemed a very hard and a very serious question.

"Do you know how to raise cotton?"

"Ya-a-a-s, sah, I kin make cotton well's any man."

"How much can you make to the acre, on your place?"

"Dunno."

"How much did you make altogether this year?"

"'Bout bay an' half, dis yeah; but we's done hab 'bout eight bays over from las' yeah."

"What do you think of Andie Johnson?" interjected an amused auditor of the conversation.

"Who him?"

"He's President of the United States. Do you know what that is?"

"Who him?"

"Who?"

"Why, Pres' den'?"

Evidently he was not strong on politics; so we reverted to something he might be expected to be more familiar with.

"Did you ever see a bigger town than this?'

"N-n-no."

"This is the biggest town in the world, isn't it?"

"No; I's heern dat C'lumbus is heap sight bigger."

"Columbus is the biggest town you ever heard of, is it?"

He scratched his head for some time at the unwonted exercise it was getting, but finally concluded as how he'd heern tell dat Mobile was bigger still.

"How much do you suppose you'd sell for?" This was asked, because it was said in some places that the ignorant negroes didn't know they were free, and even had no knowledge of the meaning of the word.

"I's free. Ain't wuf nuffin."

"How much were you worth before the war?"

"Wen old massah died, him praisement said I wuf fifteen hunder dollah."

"When did your master die?"

"Dunno."

"Was it a year ago?"

"Spec it was a yeah."

"What did he die of?"

"He'm drunk and fell off him hoss.'

The public sentiment of the listening crowd seemed to decide that inquiries had been pressed far enough in that direction. I next fell back on something they were all interested in.

"Would you work for five dollars a month?"

He seemed a little puzzled, but thought he wouldn't, "harly."

"Would you work for ten?"

"Spec I would, sah."

"Would you stick at it, if a man hired you?'

"Ya-a-a-s. Ef I once 'mence, and git money, I's wuck on. Jis git me money an' I wucks."

I wrote this conversation down carefully at the time. The negro may fairly be taken as a sample of the most ignorant plantation hands, in the interior of the poorest cotton-growing districts, and the conversation may therefore have a certain value, as showing the lowest degree of intelligence among the class on whom it is proposed to confer the right of suffrage.

All the trains on which I had traveled for some days, had contained numbers of Northerners going down to look at the cotton lands. Many went prepared to buy; all went either to buy or lease, if they found the prospects as encouraging as they hoped. To all these, the central belt of Alabama seemed a promising field. Its lands are the richest east of Louisiana and west of the South Carolina and Georgia Sea Islands; and the country is entirely healthy, which is more than can be said of either of the other regions. A bale to the acre could be made on the first-class lands, and the Alabama bale means a hundred pounds more than that of Louisiana or the west. Nearly all the lands could, with careful culture, be made to average half a bale. Then, within easy railroad connection, is Mobile on the south, while on the north, a twelve hours' ride carries the debilitated planter to the bracing breezes of the mountains.

In September and October these lands were selling at five dollars an acre. In November I imagine that the average was very nearly ten, and it was constantly rising. The papers were full of advertisements of plantations for rent or sale. The great rush was from men of small means at the North, who wanted from four hundred to a thousand acres; but a few were looking for heavier investments. Here are a couple of specimens of the kind of lands offering:

"For Sale or Rent.—A plantation on the Alabama River, containing fourteen hundred acres, one thousand of which are cleared, under good fence and in fine order for a crop. It has a three-story brick gin-house, a large brick stable and corn-crib, a new, well-finished dwelling with four rooms on the floor, all covered with tin roofs and built in the most substantial manner; nine double tenement framed negro houses, with piazzas in front; a large kitchen and smoke-house, a good blacksmith-shop, two never-failing wells of excellent water, some seven or eight miles of Osage-orange hedge. No plantation on the Alabama River lies better or is prob. ably more healthy. The quality of land about the average of Alabama River. I think I risk nothing in saying it is the best improved plantation in the State of Alabama."

"For Sale or Rent.—My plantation, one mile above Montgomery, immediately on the river, containing about 2,000 acres, 1,300 in cultivation. There is a steam grist-mill, which propels two gins, on the place, and every other improvement which constitutes a complete plantation. I will rent for a share in the crop. This is well known as one of the very best cotton farms in the State."

When these plantations were rented, the owners asked three to five dollars rent, payable 1st of January, 1867; or, if he furnished all the mules, corn, bacon, and everything else except the labor, he would require one-half the crop.

The old planters seemed utterly despondent about raising cotton by free negro labor. A few thought of watching the Yankees and imitating their policy; but the most of those who did not propose flying to Brazil, were dreaming of imported white labor. The following was one of their fine schemes:

"WHITE LABOR AGENCY.—Rates of Hire of White Laborers:

Men, per year............... ....$150 00
Women, per year... 100 00
Children, of 12 or 14 years of age, per year.................... 50 00
House Servants, per month... 15 00

Payable at the end of the year.

They contract for one year, to do the same work as the negro; live in the same cabins, and on the same rations; clothe themselves and pay their own doctor's bills. Time lost by sickness deducted from wages.

One in every six of Germans agree to speak English. Cost of transportation, $15 per head, to accompany orders, but to be deducted from wages.

An order will be forwarded to New York on Saturday, the 11th instant."

A "Planters' Convention" was to be held in a couple of weeks, to agree upon a policy for making the negroes work. But they had no faith in it, unless they could have power to seize upon every idle negro they found, put a hoe in his hand, and vigorously apply the lash. The local papers were calling out lustily to "checkmate the Freedmen's League." This association, it seemed, had "taken upon itself to fix the wages of freedmen at ten dollars per month," a rate higher than had been heretofore ruling. "Teach the darkies," urged one of the papers, "that this leaguing is a game that two can play at. If they assume to dictate, we will oust them; and supply their places with better laborers, whom we can import from the North;" and it greatly encouraged itself herein, by its interpretation of a recent speech by the President: "President Johnson, in his speech to the negroes, plainly intimated that the Lincolnian idea of everything for the negro, and everything by the negro, had no receptacle in his brain."

A pioneer company of planters, disgusted with "free niggers," the United States Government, the defeat, and everything connected with the country, were about to sail for Brazil, taking with them farming utensils and provisions for six months. "The present destination of the colony," it was laconically explained by the managers, "is the city of Para, on the Amazon; its ultimate location on a tributary of that river, between five and ten degrees south latitude. Length of voyage two thousand miles; sailing time about three weeks."

Others were proposing to send agents North from every county, to secure white emigrants. Public sentiment was against the sale of lands to the Yankees; "Get white laborers," they urged, "and in a year you 'll make enough to be able to hold on to your lands."

Montgomery was the first capital of the Confederacy. It has none of the characteristics of a capital, no collections of able men, mainly occupied, officially or unofficially, in public affairs; no tone of government and of the world; it is simply a beautiful and well preserved little inland Southern city; well built; sandy, of course, like all Southern towns; regularly laid out, and, for a wonder, well drained. The Southern taste for huge columns and tawdry architectural display, is conspicuous; but many of the private residences are elegant. The residence of the President of the Confederacy, (at the time when Montgomery was the capital,) is a large, substantially built and commodious house; less pretentious in style than the most; and in every way more desirable than the one subsequently presented to the Confederate Government, with such a flourish of trumpets, by the city of Richmond, for Mr. Davis' occupancy.

Business seemed quite brisk; and very heavy stocks of goods—far too heavy, one would think, for the impoverished country—had been sent down on credit by New York merchants.

Cotton filled the ware-houses, and drays loaded with it, crowded the streets, and the river bank, where it was shipped for Mobile. Some of it was Government cotton; more had belonged to the Rebel Government, and had been stolen by private individuals. Such were the results of the policy of meddling with this cotton at all by Government agents. Infinite scandal and no profits accrued. Thieves of Rebel cotton had been paying seventy-five dollars a bale to have the cotton carried by steamer to Mobile! There the gauntlet was to be run again; but if successfully passed, the net profits on each bale were still over a hundred dollars.

The newspapers found it difficult to realize that free speech and a free press were at last established. The Montgomery Mail thought these correspondents from the North ought to be kept in their own section—they did nothing but misrepresent and slander. Similar suggestions occcurred every day. The temper which used to display itself in lynching gentlemen whose writings were not satisfactory, now found this safer outlet.

But they all indorsed President Johnson; the despot of Tennessee, the tory who had deserted his section and attempted to grind down his people; the drunken tailor and demagogue, had suddenly become the pattern of all statesmanlike virtues. A new associate editor, making his bow in the Montgomery Ledger, found it necessary to say: "I believe him a true friend of the ill-fated South, and lifting himself above the mad waves of Black Republican fanaticisms, that are dashing and breaking themselves around his elevated position, I think that he is endeavoring to rise to the patriotic duty of leading his country, out from its distracted condition, into the calm sunshine of national repose and prosperity."

It was a curious exemplification of popular tastes, that the newspapers surrendered their editorial columns to elaborate disquisitions on the circus. The citizens talked of it as people in the similar pretensions at the North would of the opera; and for days before its advent it seemed as if everybody was preparing for its coming. But why not? Did not the leading journal announce in double leaded type, in its leading column, that "The circus has always been a favorite amusement with the South, and the Southern taste upon the subject has ever been so fastidious and demanded so much, that it is a well known fact, that as the term goes, a circus that would go down well on the European continent and elsewhere, would be criticised and ignored in the South?" And did it not gratefully announce that "we have the pleasure to hail, as an evidence of returning peace and prosperity, the advent of a real circus, one of the old time establishments; with all its concomitants to allure, please, and give satisfaction?"

It even grew eloquent on the history of the performers, thus:

"It is no small feature upon their escutcheon to know that the old Southern favorite, gentleman and actor, Mr. S. P. Stickney, with his charming daughter and talented son, are on the list of performers, and eliciting vast applause whenever they appear. Some years ago a little boy came here with a circus company, about whom nothing was particularly noticeable, save vivacity and sprightliness of manner, and a rather large amount of good looks; in fact, he was what the ladies call a sweet little boy. That little boy is now the eminent clown and original jester, Jimmy Reynolds, sharing the honors with Dr. Thayer; and if we mistake not, Doctor, you must look to your laurels, or Jimmy will snatch the chaplet from your brow. Jimmy is well aware of the prejudices of the Southern people with regard to expression, and will take good care they are not invaded."

This opinion, it was to be understood, was one of weight and moment; for the editor haughtily added:

"We claim to be sufficiently well acquainted with the principal artists in the equestrian business to know those of merit, who have visited the South, and whose names are a guarantee against any aggression upon refinement and delicacy."

And, finally, the timid were reassured on an important point:

"An admirable arrangement has been perfected by which Freedmen will be comfortably accommodated in a section of the pavilion, fitted up expressly for them, and entirely distinct from the rest of the *audience*, with a separate entrance. By all the indications, we have no fear but that this great company will achieve a success here commensurate with its merits."

The Mayor of Atlanta, the editors, and sundry other important personages, published a card in the papers of that city about the circus, "commending the establishment to public favor and generous patronage in its tour throughout the State and the South."

Mr. Gorsüch and other gentlemen who had been connected with the Rebel "Bureau of Niter and Mining," were busy with a great speculation by which they all felt sure of retrieving their fortunes. They had organized a monster oil company—on paper—and had already leased over a quarter million acres of lands, in Central and Northern Alabama, and adjacent parts of the neighboring States. Some Northern geologists, who had been exploring this region, were inclined to laugh at them, but they were full of dreams about spouting wells and flowing fortunes.

Some of them seemed, however, to imagine that the gold regions west of the Coosa River, were likely to prove more profitable. Hitherto they had paid but little; but there was much talk about what scientific work would do for them.

Some very worthy people of Montgomery were much disposed to plume themselves on their Southern blood. A Baptist peacher, who kept a book-store, (and had once been known as editor of a series of school books,) was a specimen. "I've got my pardon," he began, warmed into confidence by a trifling purchase, "and am all right for the future. I've done well, too, by the war, and my profits were mainly invested North. But I'm tired of this crowd of Yankees that is pouring down here. The more I see of them, the more I am convinced that they are a totally different class of people, and can never assimilate with us Southerners. What a miserable picayune way of doing things by retail they have, to be sure!" The worthy gentleman was asked where he was born. "Well," he admitted with a wry face, "I was born in New Jersey, but then I've been in the South from childhood, and am completely identified with her!" Precisely similar was the reluctant confession of a planter here, who had been exalting the virtues of pure Southern blood, and complaining of Yankee meanness. He was born in northern New York!

There was no indication whatever of the slightest disposition to foment another war. "I've had enough of fighting to last me my life-time," said a young man who was hoping to resume work on his plantation. "We're all glad it's over," said a business man. "Still we think we were right in the outset. We believe in the right of secession as much as we ever did; but what difference does that make? What's the use of your right to do a thing, if you know you'll get soundly whipped if you attempt it?"

CHAPTER XXXVII.

Selma—Government Armories—Talks among the Negroes.

From Mongomery I went down the River to Selma, Alabama.

Colonel McGee,[45] of Illinois, commanding the post there, had cut down a small oak which interfered with his hanging out the large garrison flag in front of his headquarters. The inhabitants complained bitterly about the sacrifice of the oak. "I tell you, gentlemen," responded the Colonel, "not only trees but many brave men have been cut down that that flag may float!" Silenced, but not convinced, they took their revenge in mutterings; and the fair ladies of the place walked out into the sandy street to avoid passing under the Yankee colors. The public journals and the politicians thought it a great outrage that their representatives should not be immediately admitted to Congress, on the presentation of their certificates!

Selma is the center of the rich cotton-growing belt of Alabama, and the lands there are probably unequaled by any to the eastward, and by only the Mississippi and Red River lands on the west. But this temper of the inhabitants caused Northern investers some anxiety. The better classes were, undoubtedly, anxious that Nothern capital and skill should be thrown into cotton cultivation; and were ready to welcome every respectable Northerner who came among them. But the baser sort also abounded. With no pecuniary

45 Probably David Wood Magee, Colonel of the 47th Illinois Regiment. [Ed.]

or political interests to risk, and still full of the feeling that made the Selma ladies walk out of their way to avoid Colonel McGee's flag, there was reason to apprehend petty outbreaks of malignity against Yankee incomers, which had to be taken into account in any calculations about the openings there for Northern enterprise.

All agree that the negroes would do more for the Yankees than for anybody else. The disposition of respectable Rebels was equally encouraging. They had been fairly whipped in fight; they frankly acknowledged it, and desired, above all things, to go to work and repair their shattered fortunes. Capital and enterprise they wanted among them, and would gladly receive from any quarter. But officers shook their heads if asked whether, when military protection was removed, Northerners would be secure from annoyance from the more vicious classes.

Lands were not so freely advertised for sale as about Montgomery, but there was the same disposition either to sell or rent. A treasury agent mentioned to a few friends his purpose to go into the land agency business. In a day or two he had twelve plantations put into his hands, to be sold at fixed prices, ranging from seven to fourteen dollars per acre. Before the war these lands were valued at from fifty to a hundred dollars. A few miles out from Selma was a large plantation, three thousand two hundred acres in extent, one thousand eight hundred acres cleared land, of the kind they call cane-brake, or prairie, the very best for cotton in Alabama. On this plantation were the entire stock and equipment for its cultivation—sixty or seventy mules, two hundred head of cattle, corn enough for next year's feeding, large droves of hogs, etc. The planter was anxiously seeking for a buyer for land, stock, and everything, at sixty thousand dollars. Estimating the grain and live stock at current rates, this would leave the land at a valuation of ten dollars an acre. The run from the North was mainly for smaller plantations than this, and the prices on them had advanced considerably. Two months earlier the average price of all lands there was a third less.

The productiveness of all these lands seemed to be systematically overstated. Throughout the rich cotton-growing regions of Alabama, planters always assured me that their prime lands would, with careful cultivation, yield an average of a bale to the acre. But strict inquiries as to results actually realized, failed to show an average of more than two-thirds of a bale. Then it cost from three to ten dollars per bale to get the crop down to New Orleans.

Northern men were pressing in rapidly. Many officers were in Selma in November, arranging for pretty heavy operations; and soldiers who had gone home, talked about returning to lease small plantations. General McArthur, of Illinois, had leased five in Central Alabama. Generals Charles and William R. Woods, of Ohio, were getting some; so were Colonel Gere, of Iowa, and a number of others. Their plan was to rent at three to five dollars an acre, one-third down and the remainder payable 1st January, 1867. Then they hire, at liberal salaries, competent overseers for each plantation. In this mode of operating, everything, of course, depends on skillful management. I should judge it a splendid opening for careless men to lose money.

West of this region, on the Tombigbee, New Orleans capitalists began to come in. A purchase of five thousand acres, in one tract, had just been made by a New

Orleans sugar-planter, in company with a former Tribune correspondent. Another company, composed of New Orleans gentlemen, proposed to run five or six plantations; and others were beginning likewise to extend their operations in this direction.

But these were the speculations of moneyed men. The South had its speculations to offer for small farmers as well as for capitalists. With reasonable prudence and skill, they might hope to realize at least double as much as could be expected from an investment of the same amount of capital in farming at the North. Scores of plantations, averaging from one to four hundred acres of arable lands, could be bought or leased, at prices not generally exceeding fifteen dollars per acre for purchase, or four dollars for lease. Purchases were made in cash; leases were paid either quarterly or one-third down, and the rest at the end of the year's work.

A Northern farmer, himself working in the fields with his hands, could probably make the crop on a hundred acres with six hired negroes, depending upon subsequently hiring a few more to help pick it out. His account, then, would stand somehow thus:

```
100 acres yield, say 60 bales of 500 pounds each, at 25c...... $7,500
Deduct hire of six negroes, at $15 per month........... $1,080
         food for same, say half as much..................   540
         food for six mules, say.......................   400
         incidentals, say.......................................   300
                                                          ——  2,320
                                                              ————
                                                              $5,180
```

The farmer could afford, out of this, to pay four dollars per acre for his lease, and still have a handsome year's earnings left.

Selma bore rough marks of the Yankee General Wilson,[46] who passed through it on his raid, just before the capture of Mr. Davis. A third or more of the city was in ruins, and the large machine shops and founderies of the Confederacy were thoroughly destroyed. On a public corner, where a large cotton warehouse had stood, was a broken safe, lying among the debris. Some resident had taken the pains to label it, so that the Yankee garrison might understand what it meant, "Always safe, except in case of Wilson, U. S. A." On another side was a different inscription: "Business Cards! Wilson & Co., U. S. A., General Burglars and House and Safe Openers. Orders respectfully solicited." The third side bore the following: "Insured safe from dangers of fire and dampness, Wilson and his Thieves (*sic*) only excepted."

Wilson's work had been thoroughly done. The gun foundery and machine shops which he had destroyed, were only to be compared to great Government establishments like those at West Point or Fort Pitt. A confused mass of bricks and mortar covered the ground, and from the debris rose fourteen tall chimneys, the blackened monument of what had been. About a hundred great guns were lying about in various stages of manufacture. Wilson had carefully knocked off the trunnions. Among them were the heaviest siege-guns, iron field ten-pounders, guns with wrought iron muzzles screwed on, Brooks' guns, and other varieties. One still lay on the lathe, where the workmen had been turning it when Wilson and his raiders came.

On the other side of the town were the ruins of an extensive manufactory of small arms. Hundreds of musket barrels lay among the bricks and mortar, be-

[46] James Harrison Wilson, Union general who took Selma. [Ed.]

sides shot-gun barrels innumerable, and great sheaves of bayonets, fused together by the heat. But for the utter collapse of the rebellion, at about the same time, this destruction of these shops would have been justly considered the weightiest among the crowding calamities of the rebellion.

An accomplished Northern mineralogist,* who went over the ruins with me, pronounced the iron ore, which had been used in making the great guns, nearly equal to the Marquette ore from Lake Superior. He thought it would average sixty-five to seventy-five per cent. of pure iron, and possibly even higher. It had all been brought from the mines near Talledega, where, also, a number of founderies for the Confederate Government had been established. The war had found these people ignorant of their mineral resources, without machinery, workmen, or materials. At its close they had developed a mineral wealth which ages could not exhaust, and had built up here, as I have said, a manufactory of guns, great and small, with which only three or four in the United States could be compared.

The burnt houses in the business part of the city were being rapidly rebuilt. Negro carpenters and masons seemed to have exclusive control of the work. An old negro, who worked as hod-carrier, explained that he was paid a dollar a day. " By de time I pays ten dollars a month rent fo' my house, an' fifteen cents a poun' for beef or fresh po'k, or thirty cents fo' bacon, an' den buys my clo'es, I does n't hab much leff. I's done tried it, an' I knows brack man cant stan' dat." He had been " refugeed " from Tuscumbia; now he

---

*Professor of Mineralogy and Geology in the University of Pennsylvania.

could not get back. He had been doing his best to save money enough, (forty dollars,*) but he could n't seem to get ahead at all with it.

His people were all going to work well, he thought, on cotton plantations where they were sure of good pay. Of course, they would work better for the Yankees, 'cause dey freed 'em. There was no talk of insurrection among them—had never heerd of sich a thing. What should they rise for? There were no secret societies among them.

On the other hand, the people had many complaints of insubordination, so great that they were in actual fear for the lives of their families! Some of the newspapers thought "the scenes of bloodshed and massacre of St. Domingo would be re-enacted in their midst, before the close of the year." "We speak advisedly," continued one frightened editor, "we have authentic information of the speeches and conversation of the blacks, sufficient to convince us of their purpose. *They make no secret of their movement.* Tell us not that we are alarmists. After due investigation and reflection upon this matter, we have determined to talk plainly, without fear or favor, and if our voice of warning is not heeded, we, at least, will have the consoling reflection that we have performed our duty."

All this silly talk was, doubtless, utterly without foundation. Negroes neglected to touch their hats to overseers or former masters whom they disliked; and straightway it was announced that they were growing

---

* Negroes are required to travel in very bad cars, often in freight cars, or on open platforms ; but they are charged full first-class fares. Now and then a negro objects, but is always silenced by a short argument. "You're free, aint you? Good as white folks, aint ye! Then pay the same fare, and keep your mouth shut."

too saucy for human endurance. They held meetings and sung songs about their freedom, whereupon it was conjectured that they were plotting for a rising against the whites. They refused to be beaten; and, behold, the grossest insubordination was existing among the negroes.*

Near the ruins of the Selma armory was a village of huts, filled with the lowest order of plantation negroes. One or two were riding about on abandoned Government horses; more were idly watching them. They were "'joying their freedom." A little round furnace

---

* Carl Shurz gave an instance in point:

One of our military commanders was recently visited by a doctor living in one of the south-eastern counties of Georgia. The doctor looked very much disturbed.

"General," says he, "the negroes in my county are in a terrible state of insubordination, and we may look for an outbreak every moment. I come to implore your aid."

The General, already accustomed to such alarming reports, takes the matter with great coolness. "Doctor, I have heard of such things before. Is not your imagination a little excited? What reason should the negroes have to resort to violence?"

"General, you do not appreciate the dangers of the situation we are placed in. Our lives are not safe. It is impossible to put up with the demonstrations of insubordination on the part of the negroes. If they do not cease, I shall have to remove my family into the city. If we are not protected, we can not stay in the country. I would rather give up my crop to the negroes than the lives of my wife and children."

"Now, Doctor, please go into particulars, and tell me what has happened."

"Well, General, formerly the slaves were obliged to retire to their cabins before nine o'clock in the evening. After that hour nobody was permitted outside. Now, when their work is done, they roam about just as they please, and when I tell them to go to their quarters, they do not mind me. Negroes from neighboring plantations will sometimes come to visit them, and they have a sort of

stood some distance from the huts. At its mouth sat
an old negro, far gone with fever and greatly emaciated.
His story was a simple one. He had been sent here,
by his master, from Northern Alabama, to work for the
Government. Yankees had come along, and his paper
to go home (his transportation) done wuf nothing no
more. He begged a little, picked up a little, slept in
the furnace, and so got along. He might last through
the winter, but it was very doubtful. He was, apparently, sixty or seventy years old, and there was not a
soul, black or white, to care for him.

meeting, and then they are cutting up sometimes until ten or eleven.
You see, General, this is alarming, and you must acknowledge that
we are not safe."

"Well, Doctor, what are they doing when they have that sort of
a meeting? Tell me all you know."

"Why, General, they are talking together, sometimes in whispers and sometimes loudly. They are having their conspiracies,
I suppose. And then they are going on to sing and dance, and
make a noise."

"Ah, now, Doctor," says the imperturbable General, "you see this
is their year of jubilee. They must celebrate their freedom in
some way. What harm is there in singing or dancing?   Our
Northern laborers sing and dance when they please, and nobody
thinks anything of it; we rather enjoy it with them."

"Yes, that is all well enough, General; but these are negroes, who
ought to be subordinate, and when I tell them to go to their quarters, and they do n't do it, we can't put up with it."

"By the way, Doctor, have you made a contract with the negroes
on your plantation?"

"Yes."

"Do they work well?"

"Pretty well, so far. My crops are in pretty good condition."

"Do they steal much?"

"They steal some, but not very much."

"Well, then, Doctor, what have you to complain about?"

Most of the negroes congregated here had either been sent to work in the Rebel shops, or had come since the end of the war to " 'joy their freedom."

"You were just as free at home as here," I said to one who had patched up an abandoned tent, under which he lived.

" But I 's want to be free man, cum when I please, and nobody say nuffin to me, nor order me roun'."

" De Lo'd tole we to come heah," another said. " De Lo'd him 'll take car' ob us now."

" O, General," says the Doctor, dolefully, "you do not appreciate the dangers of our situation."

"Now, Doctor, to cut the matter short, has a single act of violence been perpetrated in your neighborhood by a negro against a white man?"

" Yes, sir; and I will tell you of one that has happened right in my family. I have a negro girl, eighteen years old, whom I raised. For ten years she has been waiting upon my old mother-in-law, who lives with me. A few days ago the old lady was dissatisfied about something, and told the girl that she felt like giving her a whipping? Now, what do you think? the negro girl actually informed my old mother-in-law that she would not submit to a whipping, but would resist. My old father-in-law then got mad, and threatened her; and she told him the same thing. Now, this is an intolerable state of things."

CHAPTER XXXVIII.

Mississippi Tavern Talks on National Politics—Scenes in the Interior.

From Selma to Mobile the best route is by the way of Meridian, Mississippi. Meridian boasts numerous hotels. Lusty porters, clad in Nature's black and Rebellion's gray, lustily chant their respective praises. "If a gemmen wants a gemmen's accommodation he goes to de Henrie House." "'Ere ye are for de Snagsby House; only place in town for a gemmen." "All de gemmen in town go to de Jones House." I went, at a venture, to the Snagsby. I am therefore well prepared to recommend any of the others to subsequent travelers. They cannot fare any worse, and they have a chance that inheres in all things sublunary, of possible improvement.

What I saw of Meridian was this: A frame one-story shanty, labeled, "Liquors for sale;" two straight railway tracks in the midst of a wide expanse of mud; a crowd of yelling negro porters; half-a-dozen houses that may have been used for storing cotton and whisky; the hotels aforesaid; some disconsolate looking negro huts; and a few shabby residences that differed only from the huts in the extent to which the disconsolate appearance was made possible with them by the larger scale of their construction. There may have been other things in Meridian last November, but, if so, they were buried in the mud.

But I forget the Snagsby House. There being neither carriage, nor omnibus, nor dray, one was forced to wade through the mud, amid the encouragements of the porter who "toted de trunk," and the anathemas of the half-dozen whose offers to "tote" it had been disregarded. Emerging thus from the mud, one looked upon the Snagsby as really inviting. Such is the power of circumstances.

There were four rooms. One of them was the ladies' reception room and parlor. It had only four beds. The others had each two or three bedsteads, and about eight beds spread on the bare floor. In each was a smoky wood fire. In the passage way was the office, where you paid your three dollars for supper, lodging, and breakfast, in advance. And to the rear, in a separate building, was the negro kitchen, in which, to do the house justice, were served the best meals I have found in the country towns of these States. It may be interesting to know what a Mississippi hotel, in the interior, is like; the above is a faithful statement.

Adversity breaks down reserve. We were all in the Snagsby House together. And so we became social. There was no candle in the room. It has been observed that this increases sociability.

"You're from Washington, I see from the register. Is there much change there in the last five years?"

I mentioned a few of the more prominent improvements the Yankees had wrought.

What do they think there of Joe Johnston's great Express Company? Surely the Government won't interfere with it?"

"Possibly not. Indeed, I fancy neither the Government nor the public think very much about it. But I

have heard express men suggest that General Johnston
was not accustomed to close financial calculations, and
not likely, therefore, to make the best manager for a
struggling enterprise."

"They were fools, then, who hadn't sense enough to
understand General Johnston. He's the ablest man in
the country, and everybody but a blockhead knows it."

I looked around in some little surprise. The tone
indicated that the speaker did not mean to be personally rude, though the language certainly grazed the
border of politeness. In the dim firelight I made out a
soldierly-looking personage with an empty coat sleeve.
When he went to the window, a moment later, some
one whispered, "That's General Loring, a classmate of
Joe Johnston's, and one of his Division Generals."

The conversation that followed soon disclosed Major
A. D. Banks, an officer of Joe Johnston's staff, (at one
time Postmaster of the House at Washington, and at
another, for a short period, editor of the Cincinnati
Enquirer,) as another member of a group that was
filled out by a Government cotton agent and half-a-
dozen Rebel planters.

The first important question with all these Southern
gentlemen was, "Will the Southern members get in?"
"Possibly, during the winter," I replied, "on the reception by the Government of adequate guarantees for
the future, but certainly not at the organization."

"Why not at the organization?"

"Because, Mr. McPherson, the Clerk of the House,
construes the law governing his action in making up
the roll so as to preclude him from inserting their
names."

"But the tremendous pressure we can bring to
bear," suggested an old Washington stager, "can give

him new ideas as to the possible construction of the law."

"Pressure is not likely to affect an honest man in a conscientious interpretation of an explicit law."

"Well, a bigger office might?" "I tell you," continued the same speaker, "the whole question turns on what Mr. Johnson wants to do. I have reason to believe that he means to side with us. If he does, he can buy up Congress. There's no use in you Yankees talking. Johnson can force through Congress anything he wants."

"But why do you think him on your side? How long has it been since, in the Senate, he was denouncing you all as traitors?"

"We think him on our side because of what he has done, and what we know him to be. Last spring, you can form no conception of the utter, abject humiliation of the Southern people. We were all prostrate, helpless, and abased to the dust, but out of this abject condition Mr. Johnson has partly lifted us. He has made us feel that we have some standing ground, some chance still to battle for our rights; and for this, there has now sprung up throughout the whole South a warm feeling of regard and gratitude. Johnson knows this. He knows that if he continues in this way, he will be able in 1868 to count on the South as a unit for his re-election. There would be no thought of contest—he would be nominated by acclamation. Now, he is a man of strong will and boundless ambition. Of course he wants to be re-elected. He doesn't want to quit the stage as an accidental President. And he knows perfectly well that, with the South as a unit at his back, his enormous patronage will enable him to carry New York and Pennsylvania, and defy the whole Black Re-

publican pack. Those States will be enough to elect
him. A blind man could see the game, and Andy
Johnson has got plenty of nerve to play it."

Such are almost the very words in which were thus
frankly revealed the hopes of the Southern politicians.
Later in the evening and next morning, as my Yankee
proclivities began to attract more attention, my Rebel
acquaintances grew more cautious and reticent. "How
do you all feel toward Sherman, who ravaged your
country so mercilessly?" I asked one of them. "The
truth is, sir, the Southern people have been so soundly
thrashed that just now they've got d—d few opinions
of any kind. All we want now is to get back to civil
government and the making of our own laws!"

What struck me most, however, in the conversation
of all these gentlemen was the utter scorn with which
they treated any professions of principle. "A first
foreign mission would give McPherson new ideas of his
duty as clerk." "Don't tell me Southern members
won't get in if Johnson decides that he wants them in.
Things have changed mightily if he can't buy up enough
Congressmen to carry his ends." "It's as sure as fate,
that the Democratic party will carry the next Presidential election. You say it died, in the late New
York struggle, for want of principles? Nonsense. It
can soon get together all the principles it wants to win
on. Remember its old stagers have been hungry eight
years, while the Black Republicans have been feeding
at the public crib?"

Their old prejudices against Northern public men
seemed unchanged by the war. Sumner they spoke of
with loathing. Chandler was a beast and a blackguard
in a breath. Seward had the ability but not the courage

to be a first-class devil.* Chase was the greatest of Yankee public men, and had subjugated the South by keeping up the Yankee finances, but, d—n him, he would some day get his reward, for taking a side he knew to be wrong, in order to gratify his ambition. Yet in the midst of all this talk, that called up so vividly the Southern politician of five years ago, there was one notable change. You could talk abolition as safely in that Mississippi country-tavern as in Faneuil Hall. Since entering the cotton States I had not seen, on the whole trip, an indication of the slightest desire to interfere with free speech. Off the lines of travel, in remote quarters where neither railroads nor good wagon-roads penetrate, I heard that the case was different; but in all the out-of-the-way places I reached, I felt just as safe as in Washington and just as free to express my opinions.

But I saw cause for thankfulness, more than once, that I was not a Government cotton agent. On the road between Selma and Meridian, near Demopolis, it was necessary to embark, for a short trip, on a steamboat on the Tombigbee River. In the cabin, I entered, a violent altercation was raging. A short, portly old planter, florid-faced and white-bearded—the impersonation of the fine old Southern gentleman, who could finish half-a-dozen bottles of claret at a sitting, and had been doing it, any time, for the last dozen years— was berating a black-bearded, trim-built and very resolute Yankee. The oaths were fearfully blasphemous, but the substance of the old man's complaint was that he had delivered up to the agent a quantity of cotton

* Four months later they were speaking of him as "our great Conservative Minister of State."

which he had originally subscribed to the Rebel cotton loan, and that, as he had subsequently learned, he was entitled, by such voluntary surrender, to one-fourth of the value of the cotton; which sum he accused the agent of unjustly withholding. "But I'll follow you, sah," he vociferated, shaking his fist in the very face of the agent. "I'll follow you to General Wood's, aye, and to Andy Johnson! I'll follow you, sah, to hell and Illinois, but you shan't swindle *me*, sah."

"You'll follow me to Mobile, sir, if you want to; that's where I live, and you'll never have any trouble in finding me."

The agent stood, trim, compact, cool as an icicle, evidently ready for anything, and watching the fiery planter, as a pugilist might watch for the instant to strike. The stout old man, tremulous and hoarse with passion, blustered up and shook his fist in angry gesticulation, but the agent never moved a muscle. One grew proud of him, and even the Southern crowd, forming a ring about, evidently respected his bearing. Two or three friends bustled up to the old planter, twined their arms about his neck, and finally coaxed him out of the throng. The agent then turned on his heel and walked away. "Is he a gentleman, or is he a Yankee?" I heard one of the passengers inquire. "He is a scoundrel, of course," said another, "for he's a Government cotton agent, and I wish the old man had shot him, as his fellow was shot, the other day, at Montgomery." I subsequently learned that, only a few weeks ago, a son of the white-bearded old planter had shot a Northern soldier in some brawl at the polls. Life is cheap here, and the Northern papers report that the demand for pistols from the South is brisk!

The little quarrel with the cotton agent being over, the planters on board fell to discussing the labor question, as we slowly steamed down the Tombigbee. "You're all going crazy," said a top-booted personage, who turned out to be a Rebel mail contractor that had recently transferred his allegiance to Governor Dennison. "You're crazier even than I thought you. First you lost your slaves, and now you propose to give away your plantations! Give them away, I say," he continued dogmatically. "Lands that are worth sixty and eighty dollars an acre, you're selling for ten and twelve. Why, you can rent them for half of that."

"But what's the use of lands when you can't work them?"

"We've got to change our whole system of labor," said another planter. "Let the Yankees take the niggers, since they're so fond of them. Why, I was talking, down to Selma, the other day, with Jim Branson, up from Haynesville. We figured up, I don't know how many millions of coolies there are in China, that you can bring over for a song. It will take three of 'em to do the work of two niggers; but they'll live on next to nothing and clothe themselves, and you've only got to pay 'em four dollars a month. That's our game now. And if it comes to voting, I reckon we can manage that pretty well!"

But they all agreed that, unless the Yankees raised it, there would be no cotton crop grown in these States next year.

Dinner was announced, on the boat, and we all went in, belligerent cotton agent and cotton-planter among the friendliest. There were on the table water, soggy corn-bread, raw onions, sweet-potatoes, and beans, and that was absolutely all The bill was a dollar. "At them licks a man must be made o' money, to stand it long." Thus said a plethoric planter.

Between Selma and Demopolis we passed through the garden lands of Alabama. A little cotton could still be seen, standing in the fields. Fine houses appeared occasionally along the road. The fences were standing, cornstalks showed the extent of last year's cultivation, and not many traces of war were perceptible in the face of the country.

After we returned to the cars, beyond the Tombigbee, the appearance of the country was somewhat changed. The cane-brake and prairie were exchanged for pine barrens, and we had passed the most desirable cotton lands.

A Georgian, emigrating to Texas, with his whole family, had seats in our car. One of the children grew noisy. "General," said the father, reprovingly, "General, if you do n't behave yourself I wont call you General Beauregard any longer. I'll call you some Yankee name."

Cigars were freely smoked, it being taken for granted that the ladies had no objections. Pistols and Bowie-knives were shown, and one had a comparison of views as to the proper mode of using these weapons to the best advantage.

It was in a county not very far from here, that sundry wise resolutions were adopted, as,

"WHEREAS, We have for four years most bravely and gallantly contended for our rights with the United States; and,

"WHEREAS, We have been overpowered by numbers,

"*Resolved*, That we will, for the present, submit to the Constitution of the United States, and all laws in accordance with the same."

Somewhat similar seemed the view of all of our passengers who had anything to say. "Mighty ha'd on
po' Confeds. We're the unde' dogs in the fight. We're
subjugated. I would n't fight no mo' for the stars and
bars than for an old dish-rag." "Nor for the stars and
stripes nuther," exclaimed his companion, and the sentiment elicited general approval.

CHAPTER XXXIX.

Mobile Temper and Trade—Inducements of Alabama to Emigrants.

BETWEEN Meridian and Mobile, the railroad passes only very small tracts of land that appear at all inviting to Northern eyes. Much of the country is grown up in pine. Possibly lumbermen might find it a good location, but planters are likely to keep away from it.

All in all, however, Alabama offers better inducements to the Northern emigrant than almost any of the other Southern States. The feeling against Northerners is not so bitter as through most of the South. The climate of the northern half of the State is delightful, and throughout the State it is more healthy than at any point in the same latitude to the westward. Northern, and a portion of Central Alabama, are well adapted to the growth of Northern crops, wheat, corn, oats, hay, or flax. Cotton can be grown anywhere in the State; although the only first-class cotton lands lie in the central belt. The mountain regions are admirably adapted for stock-raising. Apples may be well grown in the same localities. In the southern sections, all the semi-tropical fruits flourish in the greatest luxuriance. Worn-out and abandoned lands, within easy distance of Mobile, may be bought for trifling prices,* on which oranges, figs, bananas,

---

* Sometimes as low as two or three dollars per acre.

peaches, apricots, plums, pears, strawberries, black-berries, raspberries, and melons can be grown in per-fection, and with comparatively little labor. Fruit-growing has hitherto been much neglected in Alabama, but no branch of industry gives permanent offer of better rewards. Off the coast the fisheries are almost as productive as those of Newfoundland, and they abound in rare and valuable fishes not now known to any considerable extent in commerce.

It would be much better for Northern men, who seek to avail themselves of these advantages, to go in small colonies. They should not be too large, lest they grow unwieldy. Half-a-dozen families, purchasing farms of one or two hundred acres apiece, adjacent to each other, may thus make up a little neighborhood of their own, which can sustain its own school, and which will be sure to form the nucleus for further accretions from the North. A farm of a hundred acres can thus be bought, in many localities, for five or six hundred dol-lars, half or more of it on long credits. No emigrant should be without half as much more, to put at once into improvements for his family.

The Mobile and Ohio Railroad, down which I went from Meridian to Mobile, seemed to be in better condi-tion at that time than any of the other Southern rail-roads, and the cars ran heavily loaded. Even then they were making the trip between the mouth of the Ohio River and Mobile, in forty-eight hours. The mails here, as elsewhere on the entire trip from Wash-ington, were carried with a degree of carelessness that showed how little the gratuity of keeping up a mail service for them was yet appreciated by the Southern-ers themselves. Often no one was at the station to receive the mail. Sometimes it was handed to any chance negro boy, with instructions to deliver it to the postmaster. Occasionally it was thrown out on the ground. The route-agents, on the other hand, were not free from fault. Often, especially at night, they went to sleep, carried mails past a dozen stations before they waked again. But they were not always to be blamed. One route-agent told me he had to make the entire trip from Columbus to Mobile, two days and two nights, without sleep! Enough agents had not yet been appointed; and the few on duty were making an effort to do the work of the full force.

The greatest embarrassment, however, was for lack of postmasters. " 'Twill be a long time 'fo' you get any postmaste' heah, 'less you 'bolish that lyin' oath," said a strapping fellow who received the mail at one place. "He was not appointed postmaste', but he tuck pape's and lette's to 'commodate 'em. You mout git wimmen for postmaste's or niggahs; but you can't git no white men; cause they all went with their State. An' mo'— ef you fetch any d—d tories heah, that went agin their State, and so kin take the oath, I tell ye, 'twill soon be too hot to hold 'em. We haint got no use for sich."

In the Spring of 1865, when I had last seen Mobile, it was a city of ruins; warehouses ruined by "the great explosion," merchants ruined by the war, politicians ruined by the abject defeat, women bankrupt in heart and hope. Emerging from the chaotic interior, in November, one rubbed his eyes, as he was whirled through the bustling streets, to be assured that he was not deceived by an unsubstantial vision. Warehouses were rising, torpedoes had been removed from the harbor, and a fleet of sail and steam vessels lined the

repaired wharves. The main thoroughfares resounded
with the rush of business. The hotels were overflowing.
The "new blood of the South" was, of a truth, leaping
in right riotous pulsations through the veins of the last
captured city of the coast.

Everywhere, in the throng of cotton buyers, around
the reeking bars, at the public tables, in the crowded
places of amusement—two classes, crowded and com-
mingled—Northern speculators and Rebel soldiers.
These last come on you in every guise. Single rooms
at the hotel were out of the question, and I received a
jolly fellow, who looked as if he might be magnificent
in a charge—on the breakfast table—as my room mate.
He turned out to have been chief of staff to a conspicuous Southern General. I fell into a conversation with
my neighbor at dinner, which soon drifted from requests
for the mustard into a discussion of the claims of Southern "members" to seats in Congress. By and by
he casually admitted that he had been in the Rebel
service, which might interfere with his taking the
test oath !

Nothing could exceed the general cordiality. Formerly a Southerner was moody, and resentful of approaches from Yankee-speaking strangers, unless they
came properly introduced. Now he was as warm and
unrestrained without the introduction as he used to be
after it. That was about the most marked change one
noticed on the social surface. But there was no abatement in the old ambitious pretensions. The North, we
were told, must have the Southern trade; and with that
trade it was to be corrupted. The North would be
politically a power divided against itself; the South
would be a unit, and it would rule again as it always
had ruled. "Which side will we take?" answered an

adept in political shuffling, whose presence graced many a caucus in Washington in the old times, "Why, the side that bids the highest for us, of course. And you need'nt be at any loss to know which side that is. You've been whipping us right soundly. We acknowledge the whipping, but we don't kiss the hand that gave it—not by a d—d sight! We'll unite with the opposition up North, and between us we'll make a majority. *Then* we'll show you who's going to govern this country."

The theory of reorganization, which prevailed during the war, based itself upon the belief in the existence of a Union party at the South. But there was no such party. There were "reconstructionists" who believed, from the day of the defeat at Gettysburg, that Southern independence was hopeless, and therefore wished to end the struggle on the best terms they could get; but these men loved not the Union more, but Jeff. Davis less. Now, when we sought for Union men to reorganize civil government there were none to be found. It was on precisely this point that the North failed, prior to the meeting of Congress, to comprehend the situation. Immediate reorganization meant restoration of civil power to the defeated Rebels. No other reorganization was possible. Many may say now that no other was desirable; that a community must always of necessity be controlled by its leading men. But in November the North thought differently. It was eager for reorganization, but determined that it should be effected only by Union men. Such reorganization would have meant merely that, instead of an honest government representing the great majority of defeated Rebels, a handful of aggrieved and vindictive refugees should be held up by aid from without, to sway power in the forms of republicanism over a people who, but for the bayonet, would submerge them in a week.

No such farce had been attempted in this region. In Alabama and throughout the greater portion of the Gulf States, the men who were taking the offices were the men who had just been relieved of duty under their Rebel commissions. The men who were to legislate safely for the Freedmen were the men from whom the national victory extorted freedom to the slave. The men who were to legislate security to the national debt were the men for whose subjugation that debt was created. Whether these are or are not desirable things, I do not here and now argue. But *the fact* is of importance to men of all parties.

People innocently asked, What is the temper of these reorganizing rebels? A remark quoted a moment ago, was the universal answer. They wanted to make the best for themselves of a bad bargain. They wanted to get the best terms they could. They still believed themselves the aggrieved party; held that the Abolitionists began the war; thought themselves fully justified in seceding; believed in the necessity of compulsory labor, and would come just as near as we would let them toward retaining it. There was the whole status in a nutshell.

Mobile talked, however, rather of plantations and cotton than of politics. Dozens of Northern men were on the streets, buying cotton on speculation. Every steamboat swelled the number of Yankees on the lookout for plantations, and of planters anxious to sell or lease. These planters were entirely honest in the idea which lies at the bottom of their convulsive grasp on slavery. They did not believe the negro would work without compulsion. Accordingly, they considered themselves absolutely destitute of reliable labor, and were anxious to be rid of their lands. The Yankees had faith in Sambo and propose to back their faith with abundant capital. If they succeed, their cotton fields are better than Nevada mines. If they fail—but a Yankee never fails in the long run.

CHAPTER XL.

Phases of Public Sentiment in New Orleans before Congress met.

"MEMPHIS is a more disloyal town than New Orleans," said some one, during the winter, to General Butler. The cock-eye twinkled as the General answered: "I'm afraid, then, they never had the gospel preached to them in its purity, in Memphis!"

That General Butler's gospel was preached with all plainness of speech and freedom of utterance, in New Orleans, was a fact to which the whole city testified; but still, if Memphis was worse, it was bad indeed.

"What about the Union party here?" I asked of a conspicuous gentleman, the day after my arrival. "There is no Union party, sir. We are all washed under, and the most of us only live peaceable lives by the sufferance of our Rebel neighbors."

I was constrained to confess the remark nearly if not quite just. Remove the military power, and the next day such men as Ex-Marshal Graham, Benjamin F. Flanders, and Thomas J. Durant would live in New Orleans by bare sufferance. One of the newspapers soberly reproached Mr. Flanders with ingratitude to "the people of New Orleans," who only drove him out of the city in 1861, when they might just as easily have hung him for his unconcealed hostility to the State! After this signal proof of personal kindness to him, the newspaper continued: "Mr. Flanders had the ingratitude to persist in stirring up strife in our midst, by presuming, contrary to the laws of the State and the feeling of our citizens, to make speeches to assemblages of negroes!"

A charge to the grand jury by a city judge, published in the papers, menaced Flanders, Durant, and others of the ablest men of New Orleans, with imprisonment, for illegally addressing negro meetings! Was it any wonder that the few Unionists grew cautious, or that they complained of having been washed under by the returning Rebel tide?

I do not use the word Rebel as a term of reproach—these people themselves would hardly regard it in that light—but simply as the best distinctive term by which they can be accurately described to Northern readers. It must not be understood that they still resisted the United States authority—on the contrary, they were profuse in their acknowledgments of being subdued; nor that they plotted new rebellion, for they would shrink from it as burnt children from the fire. But the great mass of the adult white male population of New Orleans (nine-tenths, indeed, of the white male population of Louisiana) were in sympathy, or, by active efforts, supporters of the rebellion. No reorganization was possible on a white basis which should not leave these men in full control of the civil government by an overwhelming majority. He was blind, therefore, who failed to see that any government then set in motion by the votes of these Rebel Louisianans, must be composed of Rebel officers, chosen because they were known to be in full sympathy with their Rebel electors.

Of course, these Rebels and Rebel sympathizers, and registered enemies, *et id omne genus*, all now professed to be Union men. They were Unionists according to their interpretation of Unionism. They meant by it that they accepted the fact of defeat, and the necessity for giving up just so much of their old policy as that defeat compelled them to give up—not a whit more.

Thus they abandoned the doctrine of secession. Most of them honestly said that they still believed it a constitutional right; but that having appealed to the verdict of arms, instead of the verdict of the Supreme Court, they were bound to acquiesce in the decision which the trial by battle had given. So they abandoned slavery. Three-fifths of them still insisted that slavery was an institution beneficial to both races, if not indeed indispensable to Southern prosperity; but they appealed to war to sustain it, and they yielded to the logic of accomplished facts in admitting that war had destroyed it.

So much they gave up, because they realized that they must. More they would have yielded in like manner, if equally convinced that more must be yielded. But all the concomitants and outgrowths of slavery and State sovereignty, doctrines which lie at the foundation of secession, and beliefs which reject the possibility of free negro labor, or the prudence of conferring legal rights upon free negroes, remained in full strength. They were imbedded in constitutions, they were walled about by the accretions of a century's laws, they were part and parcel of the accepted faith of the people. They would be given up as was slavery—not otherwise. Every step must be by compulsion.

What need, then, could there be to point out the further danger, inseparable from this state of affairs, that, being compelled to such reluctant abandonment of their life-long policy, it would be equally hard to bring them to tax themselves to pay for such compulsion? In other words, that being whipped, and thus driven to give up the points in issue, they would be still less ready to pay our bills for the whipping. Politicians, whose status depended on the admission of the Louisiana members to Congress, professed great readiness to pay the National debt; but I did not hear one private citizen make a similar expression. They did their best in the rural districts to discredit the National currency; till the military interfered, they did the same in some of the city banks; and throughout the early part of the winter, outside the moneyed centers, the notes of the National banks were held at a discount of twenty to fifty per cent.

The politics of all Louisianians, (except a body of Union-men-from-the-first, less than five thousand in number,) as full and freely expressed up to the time when Congress refused to receive their members, might be thus summed up:

They freely acknowledged that they had been badly defeated.

They acknowledged, in consequence, the fact (not the rightfulness) of the destruction of slavery.

In the same way, and with the same limitation, they admitted the impossibility of secession.

These they regarded as all the concessions which they ought to make, in order to be restored to their old relations and powers in the Union, On the other hand,

They honestly disbelieved in the capacity of the late slaves to support or to protect themselves. Therefore, their tendencies were to the establishment of some sort of enforced labor system; and to the refusal of any right to the negroes to testify in courts,* or of relief

---

* The New Orleans Daily South, of 19th November, 1865, said:

" Ethiopia has invaded the Mississippi Legislature. Some of the

from other civil disabilities, which made the gift of freedom to them a mockery.

And, honestly believing themselves right in the out-set of the quarrel in which they had been worsted, they were ready to array weighty influences in favor of an ultimate repudiation of the National debt.

The question, therefore, for the Washington states-men to decide was a simple one. Should these posi-tions of the Rebels be taken as satisfactory, and should they be thereupon restored to civil power? Or should further guarantees be exacted, and reorganization de-layed until they were furnished?

In the one case, the work of the Provisional Govern-ments might be accepted. In the other, it was neces-sary either to give suffrage to the negro, or to delay reorganization till time had elapsed for passions to cool,

members of that body, favoring Judge Sharkey's transcendental views on the subject of negro testimony, have been talking about 'justice to the negro.' The white man seems to be forgotten in the recent gabble about the eternal negro.

"Negroes care nothing for 'rights.' They know intuitively that their place is in the field; their proper instruments of self-preser-vation, the shovel and the hoe; their *Ultima Thule* of happiness, plenty to eat, a fiddle, and a breakdown.

"Sambo feels in his heart that he has no right to sit at white man's table; no right to testify against his betters. Unseduced by wicked demagogues, he would never dream of these impossible things.

"Let us trust that *our* Legislature will make short work of Ethi-opia. Every real white man is sick of the negro, and the 'rights' of the negro. Teach the negro that if he goes to work, keeps his place, and behaves himself, he will be protected by *our* white laws; if not, this Southern road will be 'a hard one to travel,' for the whites must and shall rule to the end of time, even if the fate of Ethiopia be annihilation."

and opinions, based on old facts, to conform to the new ones.

Much of the above applies to the condition of the Gulf States at large, in the beginning of the winter, quite as well as to Louisiana alone. The case here was, in fact, complicated by the hybrid nature of the attempted reorganization. Elsewhere we had Provisional Governments instituted under appointments from President Johnson ; here we had an organization instigated by General Banks, sanctioned by President Lincoln, and already sold out to the enemies of both. While, to complete the chaos, the policy of the returned Rebels, already advocated in most of the newspapers, and freely talked in all political circles, was, to have the Legislature call a new Convention, whose first act should be to declare all the State offices vacant, in order that citizens absent (in the Rebel armies or as registered enemies) when the present ones were chosen, might have a fair share in the voting!

We'll get Congress to sanction such a Convention," said a lawyer. "For that matter we can buy up Congress. It doesn't want to humiliate us, or, if it does, we have money enough to control it."

"When we get in," continued the lawyer, diverging into general politics, "we'll put an end to this impudent talk of you Yankees about regenerating the South by Northern immigration. We'll require you to spend ten years in the State before you can vote." "Of course we don't love the Union," he went on. "We're not hypocrites enough to make any such professions. I have no love for the flag. It never protected me ; it *has* robbed me and mine!" That man could be believed. He honestly said what he plainly thought. But how should we regard the office-seeking class, who,

after four years' war against the flag, had suddenly
been beaten into new-born but most ardent love for it?

One of the public journals, protesting against the
charge of treason, cited President Buchanan's book, as
to the causes of the war, and exultantly exclaimed:

"Such will be the verdict of history. The triumphant party may
apply to the people of the South all the opprobrious epithets known
to the vocabulary of hate, but they can not efface historical records,
or rebut documentary testimony. The guilt of being the origina-
tors of the late civil war lies at the door of the Abolitionists.

" The people of the South know very well where the guilt and
odium of causing the war rests. While they accept and abide by
the result as a finality, they do not now, nor will they ever, stand
before the world as culprits and felons. They may sorrow over
the war and its results, but they have no cause for shame or re-
morse.

CHAPTER XLI.

Cotton Speculations—Temper of the Mississippians

WESTERN men, seeking Southern speculations, mainly centered in New Orleans during the winter. Competition had already put up prices enormously. An army officer had recently *leased* a cotton plantation, above Miliken's Bend, for seven dollars an acre! A few months earlier he might have bought such plantations at a similar figure; but in November he was able to sell out his lease at an advance of three dollars an acre! Within another month rents advanced to twelve and fourteen dollars an acre, for good plantations, fronting on the Mississippi. From Memphis down, wherever the river plantations were above overflow, they commanded prices that, compared with those of three months before, seemed extravagantly high, although they did not yet reach the average of prosperous times. Two-thirds of these plantations were fairly roofed in with mortgages, so that enforced sales were soon likely to become abundant. Scores of planters were already announcing their anxiety to borrow money on almost any conceivable terms, to carry on operations for the next year. Many sought to borrow on the security of the consignment of their crops. Others offered still higher inducements. Small planters from the interior of Mississippi, proposed to a heavy capitalist, in considerable numbers, to borrow severally ten to fifteen thousand dollars, to mortgage their plantations as security for the loan, and give the consignment of one-half the crop as interest for the year's use of the money. Manifestly all such men were making a desperate venture, in the hope that a combination of good crops and high prices might enable them to hold on to their lands, and escape bankruptcy.

Everybody was overrun with "estimates," presented by sanguine planters, as proof of their ability to repay the money they were borrowing. Here is a specimen of this speculative figuring, made out by a Lake Providence lessee, for his fifteen hundred acres of heavy, rich cotton land:

Lease at $10 per acre	$15,000
Cost of 100 mules, at $200, (best mules are required for these heavy lands)	20,000
Wages of 150 negroes, at $15 per month	27,000
Cost of supporting them, say $7 per month	12,600
Cotton seed and incidentals	10,000
Total expenditures	$84,600

RECEIPTS.

1,500 bales, at 25c. per pound	$150,000
Deduct expenditures	84,600
Net receipts	$65,400

With all deductions from such estimates, and all omissions, it was still manifest that, giving the two essentials of a bale to the acre and twenty-five cents per pound for it, and there could be little doubt about the lucrative results to be reasonably expected from free-labor cotton growing.

It was noticeable that planters from the Mississippi Valley, from the Red River country, and from Texas, were all much more hopeful of free negro labor than

Georgians and Alabamians had been. Few apprehensions were expressed as to the labor question, and the only want concerning which much was said was the want of capital.

General Beauregard had become the President of the railroad connecting New Orleans with the capital of the State of Mississippi. He may be an admirable man for the post, but his road was a very bad one.

Between New Orleans and Jackson, one saw little to admire in the pine flats that lined the railroad for nearly its whole length. "The rossum heels live in thar," a newsboy on the train informed me. Lands are cheap, and dear at the cheap rates. There are but few places where a Northern man in his senses would be disposed to make investments with a view to cultivating cotton. For anything else the land is generally regarded as worthless.

Scarcely a postmaster was yet to be found along the route. The mails were handed out by the route-agents to any one who happened to be standing about the station, and they were delivered or not, as was convenient. Nobody could be got to take the offices, because nobody was able to take the oath. It had been proposed, by some wise person, to remedy the difficulty by appointing women. That would be "jumping from the frying-pan into the fire," indeed. Where the men were Rebels, after the Mississippi pattern of earnestness, some new word must be discovered to define the extent of the hatred the women bore to the Yankee Government. Such mild titles as "Rebel," failed to meet the case.

Of old, travelers in the South were perpetually regaled by the siren song of the affection between the negro and his master. "Free them all to-morrow, and it would make no difference. They know instinctively that their masters are their best friends. You could no more make them fight against us than you could make them fly." On all hands one heard of this bond of attachment between the races; was pointed to the devotion of favorite servants; assured that no law was necessary to hold them; reproached with the fanatical prejudices of the North against color.

With the downfall of the rebellion there came a change. He would be blind and deaf, who, after a day's stay anywhere in the interior of Mississippi, failed to discern aright the drift of public opinion toward the negro. The boasted confidence in the slave, and the generous friendship for the helpless freedman were all gone. There were, of course, many individual exceptions, but the prevailing sentiment with which the negro was regarded, was one of blind, baffled, revengeful hatred. "Now, that you've got them ruined, take the cursed scoundrels out of the country." "D—n their black souls, they're the things that caused the best blood of our sons to flow." "The infernal sassy niggers had better look out, or they'll all get their throats cut yet." "We can drive the niggers out and import coolies that will work better, at less expense, and relieve us from this cursed nigger impudence." "Let a nigger dare to come into *my* office, without taking off his hat, and he'll get a club over it." Such were the voices I heard on every hand—in the hotels, on the cars, in steamboat cabins, among returned soldiers, grave planters, outspoken members of the "Legislature," from every party, and from men of all ages and conditions. More or less, the same feeling had been apparent in Tennessee, Georgia, Alabama, and Louisi-

ana; but it was in Mississippi that I found its fullest
and freest expression. However these men may have
regarded the negro slave, they hated the negro freeman. However kind they may have been to negro
property, they were virulently vindictive against a
property that escaped from their control.

With coarser illustrations of the universal feeling the
public prints have been crowded—stories of ear cuttings
and shootings, and the like. Doubtless many of these
stories were exaggerated; for even in Mississippi murder is not practiced with as much safety as the other fine
arts; but no man could mingle in the community and
not be convinced that the feeling was there, and that
only prudence restrained its exercise. A railroad conductor was possessed with some delusion about my
ability to help to his appointment as post-office agent, and
he accordingly exhausted all his arts to entertain. The
burden of his talk was " the blasted, imperdent nigger."
"Just think, sah, down here, the other day, at ———,
a nigger sergeant ordered his men to shoot me. I
never heard of it till I'd got twenty miles away, or I'd a
raised a little speck of Jerusalem in that nigger camp.
What did he want me shot for, sah? Why this was the
way of it. I was writin' on a platform car, where a
d—d nigger guard was a trampin' back and forrard,
and says I, 'Can't you keep still thar, you nigger;
don't you see you're a shakin' the car?' The black
scoundrel never said a word, but kept on trampin' his
beat. I spoke to him again, kinder sharp, but he didn't
mind me no more nor if he'd never heerd me. Finally
I couldn't stand it no longer, and broke out: 'G—d
d—n your black heart, you dirty Yankee nigger, I'd
just like to cut your throat from ear to ear for your infernal impudence.' At that he walked off to the ser-

geant and kept a whisperin' till I got ready to start.
But I heerd afterward that the cowardly nigger sergeant told him to stand his ground and shoot me if I
interfered with him. Just think of the nigger impudence we've got to bear, sah!"

In a crowded bar-room, among a group of cronies
who evidently looked on him as the oracle, swaggered
a "hotel-keeper," whose guests were taken in and
fleeced, at a point on the railroad between Jackson and
New Orleans. He was boasting of his success with the
" cussed free niggers." " We've got a Provo' in our
town that settles their hash mighty quick. He's a
downright high-toned man, that Provo', if he is a Yankee. I sent a nigger to him, the other day, who was
sassy when he came into my office, and said he wouldn't
work for me unless he pleased. He tucked him up, guv
him twenty lashes, and rubbed him down right smart
with salt, for having no visible means of support. That
evening I saw Tom, and asked him whether he'd rather
come home. ' Bress ye, yes, massa,' says Tom. ' But
Tom,' I told him, I'll take that old paddle of mine with
the holes in it, and paddle you soundly, if I think you
deserve it.' ' Bress you, massa, Tom likes dat all de
time better dan dis.' That's a downright high-toned
officer, I tell ye, that Provo' of our'n!"

"A nigger's just as good as a white man now," argumentatively observed a bottle-nosed member of the
Legislature, " but I give my Sam t'other day to understand that he wasn't a d—d bit better. He came into
my room without taking off his hat. ' Take off your
hat, you dirty black scoundrel, or I'll cut your throat,'
I yelled at him. D—n him, he had the impudence to
stand up and say he was free, and he wouldn't do it

unless he pleased. I jumped at him with my knife, but he run. Bimeby he came sneakin' back, and said he was sorry. 'Sam,' says I, 'you've got just the same rights as a white man now, but not a bit better. And if you come into my room without takin' off your hat I'll shoot you!'"

This Bowie-knife and pistol style of talk pervaded all the conversations of these people about their late affectionate bondsmen. Nothing less gunpowdery, it seemed, would serve to express their feelings. I fancy, however, that, as with all such talkers, there was a great amount of throat-cutting in words to a very small percentage of actual performance.* Nor must it be forgotten that the provocations were not wholly on one side. The negroes would be more than human, if suddenly enfranchised, clothed in the army blue, and taught to use the muskets in their hands, they should

---

* The following was, however, a well-authenticated case:

"A physician and planter, near Greenville, Mississippi, called a freedman in his employ to account for some work which he alleged he had neglected to do as directed. The freedman said he had received no such directions. The doctor told him if he dared to dispute his word he would kill him on the spot. The negro replied that he never had such directions. Thereupon the doctor, without any other provocation being alleged, drew his revolver, and the negro ran. After some little pursuit, and after discharging several shots, he killed the negro dead in the field. The murdered man's wife interposed to save his life, when the doctor fired several shots at her, and was only prevented from a double murder by the efforts of his own mother, who, with difficulty, saved the poor woman's life.

"Colonel Thomas, Superintendent of Freedmen, caused the arrest of the murderer. He was taken to Vicksburg and placed in military custody."

not strain the bounds of prudent freedom. They were not always respectful in their bearing toward men who talked of cutting their throats; and sometimes they had an indiscreet way of pressing claims, which it had been wiser for them to waive. "Get out of this car, you black puppy," shouted a young blood, who evidently bemoaned the loss of the right to larrup his own nigger, as a handsome negro sergeant, fully equipped, modestly established himself in the corner of a first class car. The negro stood his ground but made no reply. Presently some one else ordered him to the negro car, quietly explaining that no negroes were allowed in the ladies' car. "Ise paid my passage, same as de rest of ye. Ise goin' on Government business, and Ise got as good right to what I pays for as anybody else." The logic might have been hard to answer; but the conductor, who by this time had been summoned, didn't trouble himself with logic. "I expect you're on the Major General's business, cuffee, but if you don't get out of here mighty quick, bag and baggage, I'll have you pitched off the train." As there was but one against a train full of white men, he succumbed, though with an exceedingly bad grace. I have heard of other cases, where several soldiers were together, in which they stood their ground.

Embittered feelings, of course, follow all such controversies. The negro feels himself aggrieved by the petty spites of the men who can no longer hold him enslaved; the master feels himself outraged that one over whom his power had been so absolute should "go to putting on airs this way" in his very face. Against the negro troops, who alone kept these smouldering elements from breaking forth, the hatred of the commu-

nity was especially intense.*   Some timorous souls had
great fears of a negro outbreak at Christmas, and even
our officers believed that, in some cases, the negroes were
distributing arms, to be used to enforce their claims to
their masters' lands.   There was not a particle of
foundation for the fears.   They got arms, indeed, but
what of it?   Was not every man armed?   Could you
brush closely against any ragged neighbor without being bruised by his concealed revolver?   People had not
got over regarding negroes as something other than
men; and when it appeared that they were imitating the
example of the whites, and preparing to protect themselves, forsooth we had straightway cock and bull stories
of impending negro insurrections and a war of races!

* The official organ of the city of New Orleans thus editorially
explains this feeling:

"Our citizens, who had been accustomed to meet and treat the
negroes only as respectful servants, were mortified, pained, and
shocked to encounter them in towns and villages, and on the public roads, by scores and hundreds and thousands, wearing Federal
uniforms, and bearing bright muskets and gleaming bayonets.
They often recognized among them those who had once been their
own servants.   They were jostled from the sidewalks by dusky
guards marching four abreast.   They were halted, in rude and
sullen tones by negro sentinels, in strong contrast with the kind
and fraternal hail of the old sentinels in threadbare gray or dilapidated homespun.   The ladies of villages so guarded, ceased to appear on the streets, and it was with much reluctance that the citizens of the surrounding country went to the towns on imperative
errands.   All felt the quartering of negro guards among them to
be a deliberate, wanton, cruel act of insult and oppression.   Their
hearts sickened under what they deemed an outrageous exercise
of tyranny.   They would have received white troops, not indeed
with rejoicing, but with kindness, satisfaction, and respect; but
when they saw their own slaves freed, armed, and put on guard
over them, they treated all hope of Federal magnanimity or justice
as an idle dream."

The heel of the destroyer had been on Jackson too; and solitary chimneys and shattered ruins attested the thoroughness with which the work was done. The same recuperative power was not displayed, with which the stranger was so impressed at Atlanta or Selma. The Mississippians seemed more listless. In traveling several hundred miles in the State, I did not see a white man at work in the fields, or very many at work anywhere or anyway. Cotton, however, continued to come out—a satisfactory proof that the " niggers " had still been able to do something. Piles of it were stored near the railroad; and through the interior one noticed an occasional wagon drawn by a couple of oxen, with, perhaps, a mule in front, bringing a few bales to the nearest station.

The " Legislature," in session in Jackson, seemed to me a body of more than average ability. Leading Mississippians, however, even of the ultra type, denounced it as impracticable. There could be no question of its rebellious antecedents. Scarcely a dozen, probably not half so many of its members, could be named who did not in some way actively countenance or support the war. But they were all Union men now; that is, as one of them tersely stated it, " we are whipped, can't get out, and want now to get back on the very best terms we can possibly make, and with the least possible loss from our failure ! "

The tone of the Mississippi papers, like the tone of the Mississippi talk, was bitter. A Jackson journal soundly berated anybody who should presume to insist that the President required the admission of negro testimony in the courts. Mississippi, at any rate, should not be crawling to the President's feet to ask what she should do. She should walk erect, assert her rights, and demand their recognition! And a Vicksburg paper spoke its views thus:

"If any radical was ever black enough to suppose the people of Mississippi would endow negro schools, for their ilk to teach the rising eboshin hatred of his former master, but his best friend, then such chaps had better take to marching on with John Brown's soul; they will hardly reach the objèct of their desires short of the locality where John is kicking and waiting. The State has not opened them, nor has she the slightest idea of doing anything of the kind."

CHAPTER XLII.

Memphis—Out from the Reconstructed.

OF the trip between Jackson, Mississippi, and Grand Junction, Tennessee, I only remember a dismal night of thumpings over broken rails, and lurches and contortions of the cars, as if we were really trying in our motion to imitate the course of the rails the Yankee raiders had twisted. At one point all were waked up, hurried out into the mud of a forlorn little village, and informed that, some way or another, they must get over the burnt bridge to the train half a mile on the other side. Clambering over cotton bales into the cars of the new train, we found everybody who preceded us shivering with cold. The freight cars attached to the train were loaded with cotton, it seemed; and orders had been given to extinguish all fires in the passenger cars, lest the sparks might set fire to it!

Finally, an hour or two before daybreak, the conductor discharged his passengers in the mud at Grand Junction, much as a cartman would shoot out his load of rubbish. In the darkness no depot was to be seen; and, at any rate, every passenger was compelled to watch his baggage, as there was nobody to attend to it. Fortunately some one had matches. A fire was soon started on the ground, and the railroad company's pile of lumber was made to furnish fuel. Seated around that fire on their trunks, in the cold night air, and half-blinded by the smoke, were ladies who, before the war, had been among the wealthiest and haughtiest in the South. Some of them were going to Texas to hide their poverty. It was nearly three hours before the train for Memphis took us up.

Memphis, in June, was full of returning Rebel soldiers. Now it was full of Rebel business men, and the city, like New Orleans, had passed completely over to the control of the great majority of its citizens, who throughout the war hoped and labored for the success of the rebellion. It was rather to their credit that they made no concealment of their sympathies. They were outspoken in denunciation of Governor Brownlow, and the entire State Government, which Mr. Johnson himself had set in motion. The "Radicals of the North" were as odious as in the old days of the war; and the tone of the newspapers was as fierce as when they were wandering from point to point in front of the steadily advancing National armies.

Next to New Orleans, Memphis seemed to be doing the heaviest business of any Southern city. The streets were filled with drays, and the levee was crowded with freight.

General Frank Blair, who engaged in cotton planting on the opposite side of the river, was in town. Many other adventurous cotton planters from the North made Memphis their head-quarters. None seemed to suffer the slightest inconvenience from any unfriendly disposition on the part of the people. On the contrary all Northern men, bringing capital to stock and conduct these great plantations which had hitherto made the prosperity of Memphis, seemed to be sure of a fervid welcome.

Between Corinth and Stevenson lies as beautiful a country as the South can anywhere show. Huntsville, Decatur, Tuscumbia, and Florence are the principal towns. Around them stretches a lovely valley, which constitutes the chief charm of Northern Alabama. Far enough South for the profitable cultivation of cotton, it is still adapted to all the Northern grains. The people have generally more education and refinement than in other parts of the State; their public improvements are better, and their country is every way more attractive. It is not surprising that lands here are commanding prices nearly as high as in Central New York or Ohio. The people are rarely compelled to sell; and there is a strong prejudice against either Yankees or Tories, (that is, Southerners who went against their State.) Western men seem to be more welcome.

After a weary day's riding through the wild mountainous country along the Upper Tennessee, our train shot in beneath the great overhanging cliff, and approached Chattanooga at nightfall. Fires had been raging through the pine forests.

A soldier at my side pointed out the famous localities, Mission Ridge, Lookout Mountain and the rest. He grew fervid as he told the story over again—how the troops charged up precipitous ascents, where not even Hooker had expected them to go; how they shouted, and cheered, and struggled upward; how, from below, long lines of blue, faintly gleaming as the light struck their muskets, could be traced up the mountain side; and at last the hight was gained, and the rush was made, and the flag was seen floating over all. As he spoke, the scene grew vividly upon one; and, looking from the darkened window, lo! the battle-lines, all aflame, stretched up the mountain side, and the fire fantastically wrought out again the story.

Was it so? The battle had been fought and won— from this flame-covered Lookout Mountain to the Gulf. Was the victory to be now thrown away, that later times might witness the contest over again?

CHAPTER XLIII

Congress Takes Charge of Reconstruction

THE Capital had been full of exciting rumors for a fortnight, on the subject of the admission or the rejection of the Southern Representatives and Senators; and, finally, the action of the House Union Caucus had been announced; but, still the Southern aspirants hoped against hope.

At last came the decisive day. Floor and galleries, lobbies, reception-rooms, passage-ways, and all manner of approaches were crowded. The Diplomatic Gallery—so called, because diplomats are never in it— beamed with many new and many familiar faces. The Reporters' Gallery—so called, because the members of the press are always crowded out of it on important occasions—was crammed by persons who, for the nonce, represented the Daily Old Dominion and the Idaho Flagstaff of Freedom's Banner. Elsewhere the "beauty and fashion," (as also the dirt and ill manners, for are we not democratic?) of the Capital looked down upon the busy floor, where members, pages, office-holders, office-seekers, and a miscellaneous crowd, swarmed over the new carpet and among the desks. Thus from ten to twelve.

Then the quick-motioned, sanguine little Clerk, with sharp rap, ends the hand-shaking, gossip, and laughter among the jovial members.   A moment's hasty hustling into seats; the throng of privileged spectators settles back into a dark ledge that walls in the outer row and blockades the aisles; the confused chatter subsides into a whispered murmur, and that, in turn, dies away.

"The hour having arrived for the assembling of the Thirty-ninth Congress, the Clerk of the last House of Representatives will proceed, in accordance with law, to call the roll of Representatives elect.   From the State of Maine: John Lynch, Sidney Perham, James G. Blair," etc.

Members quietly respond, the busy subordinates at the desk note responses, and everybody studies the appearance of the House.   There are enough old faces to give it a familiar look, and yet there are strange changes.   The Administration side has, in more senses than one, been filled too full.   It has spilled over the main aisle till half the Democratic seats are occupied with its surplus, and the forlorn hope, that still flies the banner of the dead party, is crowded into the extreme left. James Brooks, however, smooth, plausible, and good-natured, sturdily keeps his seat by the main isle.*   Directly in front of him, two or three desks nearer to the vacant Speaker's chair, (which neither is destined to fill,) sits a medium-sized, handsome man-of-the-world-looking gentleman, with English whiskers and moustache—Henry J. Raymond.   "Grim old Thad.," with wig browner and better curled than ever, occupies his old seat in the center of the Administration side; and directly behind him, greeting his friends with his left hand, which the Rebels left uncrippled, is General Schenck.[47]   Toward the extreme right is Governor

---

* Since ejected, on the score of alleged frauds in his election.

[47] Robert Cumming Schenck, Union general, later U.S. minister to England. [Ed.]

Boutwell,[48] in his old seat; and beside him is a small but closely-knit and muscular figure, with the same closely-cropped moustache and imperial as of old, the jaunty, barrel-organ-voiced General Banks, ex-Speaker, ex-Governor, etc. Next to him is a bearded, black son of Anak, with a great hole in his forehead, which looks as if a fragment of shell might once have been there—General Bidwell,[49] one of the new members from California. Garfield[50] is in his old place near the Clerk's desk, and just across the main aisle from him, on what used to be the Democratic side, when there was a Democratic party, is that most nervous and irritable-seeming of all figures, the best-natured and crossest-looking man in the House, John A. Bingham.* He has been absent from Congress for a term, has filled arduous posts and won high praises, and comes back, they say, to take high place on the committees.

Away across, in the midst of the Democratic desks, rises a head that might be called auburn, if the whiskers were not brick-dust red. It is a brother-in-law of the semi-Rebel Governor Seymour, of New York—one of the ablest Republicans of the House in old times, defeated two years ago, but sent back now, more radical than ever—Roscoe Conkling. If he had been a little better tempered the House, in the Thirty-seventh Congress, would have placed him within the first five in the lists of its most honored and trusted members. Near him, one naturally looks to the desk of the candidate opposed to President Johnson at the late election. Alas! a West Virginia Unionist fills the seat of George H. Pendleton. Back of him is the desk of the

---

* Representative of the Government, in the trial of the assassination conspirators.

[48] George Sewell Boutwell, former Governor of Massachusetts, later Secretary of Treasury under Grant. [Ed.]

[49] John Bidwell, Congressman from California for one term. [Ed.]

little joker of the Ohio delegation. But the little joker played his tricks too often, and has been dismissed to a second-rate claim agency business, while another West Virginian occupies his seat in the House.

In the front row of desks on the Union side is a clumsy figure of gigantic mould. The head matches the body; and in old times (when such men as A. Lincoln were his colleagues,) Long John Wentworth proved that there was a good deal in it. His immediate predecessor in the representation of Chicago, now sixth Auditor, is in the lobby.

So one's eye ranges over familiar faces or picks out noted new ones, in this House which is to administer on the effects of the great Rebellion, while the Clerk vociferates the roll.

"Samuel McKee" has just been called, and the young Kentuckian has answered; "Wm. E Niblack," continues the Clerk. He has skipped, on the printed roll, from Kentucky to Indiana, omitting Tennessee. From the very heart of the Massachusetts' group rises the "black snake of the mountains," the long, black-haired, black-faced, Indian-looking Horace Maynard. Every man knows and honors the voice, but it can not be heard now. He shakes his certificate of election from Parson Brownlow and begins to speak. The sharp rap of the Clerk's gavel is followed by the curt sentence, "The Clerk declines to be interrupted during the roll call. William E. Niblack; Michael C. Kerr;" and so the call goes steadily on. At last the member from Nevada had answered; the territorial delegates had answered; Mr. Maynard rose again. But "The Clerk can not be interrupted while ascertaining whether a quorum is present." Then, reading from the count of the assist-

50 James Abram Garfield, Congressman from Ohio and later President. [Ed.]

ants, " One hundred and seventy-five members, being a quorum, have answered to their names." " Mr. Clerk," once more from Horace Maynard. " The Clerk can not recognize as entitled to the floor any gentleman whose name is not on the roll." And a buzz of approbation ran over the floor as the difficult point was thus passed.

Then, as if poor Mr. Maynard's evil genius were directing things, who should get the floor but that readiest and most unremitting of talkers on a bad side, Mr. James Brooks. Mr. Morrill[51] had moved to proceed to the election of Speaker, but had made the mistake which at once suggested how defective he was likely to prove in the leadership of the House, to which rumor already assigned him—had forgotten to call the previous question.

Brooks never misses such an opening. He proposed to amend the motion. He thought the roll ought first to be completed. He couldn't understand why a State good enough to furnish the country a President wasn't good enough to furnish the House members. If Mr. Maynard, of Tennessee, was to be kicked out by the party in power, he hoped they would proceed to perform the same operation on their Tennessee President. And then he told how, in the years of the war, he had heard the eloquent voice of this persecuted and rejected Tennesseean ringing on the banks of the Hudson, on the side of an imperiled country. But he forgot to add (as his hearers did not forget to remember,) how earnestly he had himself then taken—the other side! And, as if determined to stab poor Maynard as dangerously as possible, he even dragged up the Rebel Virginians, (" Sandie " Stuart at their head,) placed

[51] Justin Smith Morrill, Congressman from Vermont. [Ed.]

them by the loyal East Tennessecan's side and claimed for them equal rights!

Long John Wenworth made his *début* by slowly rearing aloft his ponderous hulk, and calling, like a stentor, for order. The Clerk, handsomely and fairly, decided the speaker in order. Long John sank down, and Brooks improved his chance: "When the newly arrived gentleman from Illinois becomes a little more familiar with matters in the House, he will be a little slower in undertaking to find me out of order." Presently he essayed a tilt against Thad. Stevens, but came out from that, as most men do, badly beaten, with House and galleries roaring at his discomfiture. Finally, Brooks was ready to close and sought to yield the floor to a Democrat; the Unionists were quick enough, this time, and objected. Points of order were raised, and old heads tried to entangle the Clerk; but he was clear as a bell, and his rulings were prompt, sharp, and decisive. The moment a Unionist fairly got the floor, the previous question was moved, and the contest was over. "If Maynard had spoken," says Judge Warmoth,[52] the delegate from the "Territory of Louisiana," "I should have claimed the right to speak too."

The stoop-shouldered, studious looking, thin-voiced Mr. Morrill, rises. "I nominate for Speaker, Schuyler Colfax, of Indiana." Across the way a ponderous Democrat: "I nominate James Brooks, of New York;" and some person of bad taste titters, the laugh is infectious, and breaks out all over the floor, and runs around the galleries; while Brooks tries to look solemn for a moment, then makes the best of it, and laughs with the rest.

Four members of diverse parties take their seats beside the Clerk to count, and in a moment the call begins.

[52] Henry Clay Warmoth, later Governor of Louisiana, 1868-1872. [Ed.]

"Sydenham E. Ancona." "James Brooks" comes back for the first response, and the ill-mannered galleries laugh again. Then follows a running fire of "Schuyler Colfax," "Schuyler Colfax," "Colfax," "Colfax," with here and there a scattering shot for "James Brooks." A moment's figuring; the tellers rise; Mr. Morrill steps out in front of the Clerk's desk. "The tellers agree in their count. One hundred and thirty-nine votes have been cast for Schuyler Colfax, and thirty-five for James Brooks." Laughter again, while the Clerk repeats the figures of the result. Then, "Hon. Schuyler Colfax, one of the Representatives elect from the State of Indiana, having received a majority of all the votes cast, is duly elected Speaker of the House of Representatives of the Thirty-ninth Congress. Mr. Morrill, of Vermont, and Mr. Brooks, of New York, will act as a committee to conduct the Speaker elect to the chair; and Mr. Washburn, of Illinois, who has been for the longest time a member of the House, will administer the oath of office." And with this the bright-faced little Pennsylvanian steps down.

The Speaker turns as he reaches the steps to the chair, shakes hands again with the committee, and leaving them, ascends to his place, unfolds his roll of manuscript and reads his graceful little speech.

While he reads, one may move around and see who make up the crowd standing about the outer row of desks and filling the space back to the cloak-rooms. Near the door the portly form and handsome face of Secretary McCulloch are noticeable. The other Cabinet officers seem not to be present. An amazing shock of black, curly hair, of formidable length, surmounting a boyish face, in which the queer incongruities are completed by a pair of spectacles, can not be overlooked. Its owner moves about with some constraint; naturally enough, for the Rebels shot away his leg at Port Hudson, where he was one of the commanding Generals, (Wisconsin sent him,) and the wooden one is not quite perfect. Another spectacled hero, with fiery whiskers, and an asserting nose with the blooded race-horse thinness of nostril, is conspicuous—General Carl Schurz, for the time chief Washington correspondent of the New York Tribune; and, as all men know, the most eloquent foreigner taking part in our American politics. Half a score of Senators have come over; the ubiquitous and good-looking Henry Wilson, prominent among them.

But the Speaker elect closes; a ripple of applause runs over the audience; the bluff, hearty, downright Washburne is taking his place, book in hand, in the little space in front of the Speaker:

" You, Schuyler Colfax, a member of the House of Representatives of the United States, do solemnly swear that you have never voluntarily borne arms against the United States since you have been a citizen thereof; that you have voluntarily given no aid, countenance, counsel, or encouragement to persons engaged in armed hostility thereto; that you have neither sought, nor accepted, nor attempted to exercise the functions of any office whatever, under any authority or pretended authority in hostility to the United States; that you have not yielded a voluntary support to any pretended Government, authority, power, or constitution within the United States, hostile or inimical thereto. And you do further swear that, to the best of your knowledge and ability, you will support and defend the Constitution of the United States against all enemies, foreign and domestic; that you will bear true faith and allegiance to the same; that you take this obligation freely, without any mental reservation or purpose of evasion; and that you will well and faithfully discharge the duties of the office on which you are about to enter: So help you God."

It is the oath which the laws require and which the higher obligations of public safety demand, and it is the oath, facing which most of the Southern States have sent none who could take it without perjury. Even the venerable Jacob Barker would make a pretty figure taking that oath—especially if he should happen to see General Butler watching him while he swore!

Next comes the swearing of the members. State by State, they gather in rows around the Clerk's desk; and the new Speaker descending from his chair, and standing in the center of each group of uplifted hands, reads over again the oath.

This scene of unavoidable confusion over, an unkinder thing than even the oath is thrust before the Democrats. Wilson, of Iowa, looking as honest as ever, downright proposes to elect McPherson and the remaining House officers by resolution. The Democrats squirm and protest; but Wilson guards every point; insists on the previous question, and carries the matter through with a whirl. The Democrats stand up, on the call, and their corporal's guard contrasts so ludicrously with the great crowd that rises from all parts of the hall when the Union side is called, that the galleries can't refrain from another burst of laughter. "We want at least the poor privilege of complimenting our candidates for these offices by nominating and voting for them" pleads one; but Wilson is inexorable, and the Democrats are not permitted even to make a nomination.

There remained one thing to do. The door had been shut in the Rebel faces; it was still to be bolted. Thad. Stevens getting the floor, sent a little paper to the desk, with this:

Resolved, By the Senate and House of Representatives in Congress assembled, That a Joint Committee of fifteen members shall be appointed, nine of whom shall be members of the House and six of the Senate, who shall inquire into the condition of the States which formed the so-called Confederate States of America, and report whether any of them are entitled to be represented in either House of Congress, with leave to report at any time, by bill or otherwise; and until such report shall have been made and finally acted upon by Congress, no member shall be received in either House from any of these said so-called Confederate States; and all papers relating to the representatives of the said States shall be referred to said Committee without debate.

This is the last straw, and the burdened opposition determine to fillibuster. They object, under the rules, to its reception. Stevens grimly moves to suspend the rules. They demand the yeas and nays, and get them; one hundred and twenty-nine to their beggarly thirty-five. They move to lay on the table, and demand the yeas and nays again, with like uncomfortable fate. Ashley wants to make a slight amendment, but members all around shout, "No! no!" The Democrats abandon the hopeless contest for their friends; and the resolution passes.

The galleries have thinned out, and the members have become inattentive. One or two trifling matters are offered; an effort is made to adjourn; the House refuses; some notice of a bill is given; the effort to adjourn is renewed; the House listlessly votes again; the Speaker rises: "The House stands adjourned till to-morrow at twelve o'clock.

The organization is perfect, and the bars are put up before disloyal representatives of lately rebellious States—the day's work is well done. All thanks to the true men whose honest purpose insured its doing. And so auspiciously opens the Thirty-ninth Congress.

CHAPTER XLIV.

Southern Feeling after the Meeting of Congress.

DECEMBER broke the earliest hope of the revived Southern temper. The preponderating Rebel element, which reorganized the State Governments under Mr. Johnson's proclamations, first expected to take Congress by a *coup de main*, organize the House through a coalition with the Northern Democracy, and, having thus attained the mastery of the situation, repeal the war legislation and arrange matters to suit themselves. Defeated in this by the incorruptible firmness of Mr. McPherson, the Clerk, they next hoped by Executive pressure, combined with Southern clamor, to force a speedy admission of all Representatives from the rebellious States who could take the prescribed oath. These once in, the rest was easy. They were to combine with the Northern Democracy and such weak Republicans as Executive influence could control, repeal the test oath, thus admit all the other Southern applicants, and turn over the Government to a party which, at the North, had opposed the war for the Union, and at the South had sustained the war against it.

By the 1st of January all knew that the plot had failed. A few days later, I left the Capital again for the South.

Traveling wholly by land from Washington to New

Orleans, taking the trip leisurely, with frequent stoppages and constant intercourse with the people, I had abundant opportunities for discovering at once the marked change in the tone of public sentiment. In November I had found it buoyant and defiant. In January it was revengeful, but cowed.

Prominent public men were much more cautious in their expressions. They talked less of their demands; were more disposed to make elaborate arguments on their rights. There were few boasts as to what the South would do, or how heartily that true Southern man, the President, would sustain them; there was more tendency to complain that they had been whipped for trying to go out, and that now the door was shut in their faces when they tried to come in.

A very few, whom I should judge to have been Union men through the war, or to have been so thoroughly disgusted with the rebellion as to accept its defeat with cheerfulness, professed their entire satisfaction with the action of Congress. "It is none of our business to be making a fuss or demanding anything," said one of these. "We've been guilty of a great crime; we have reason to be thankful that we are treated as leniently as we are, and it becomes us to keep quiet, and hope for the best."

Such were the expressions of two classes. Together, they were but a small minority.

Everywhere, on the cars, in the hotels, on the streets, at public meetings, in social intercourse with the people at their homes, the great majority held very different language.

A little east of Lynchburg, an officer in the national uniform happened to pass through the cars. "There's one of the infernal villains," exclaimed an old man in homespun behind me. "Well," said his companion, "perhaps it is n't right to talk so, but how can we help hating them? They 've burned our houses and made us paupers, and now they kick us out of the Capitol. May be my sons may feel differently, by the time they 're as old as I am, if they have to live with them, but I always expect to hate the sight of a Yankee till my dying day." These were plain old Virginians from the mountains, apparently farmers.

At Grand Junction, Tennessee, I whiled away half a day in the bar-room of a dilapidated little frame house called a hotel. A wood contractor from one of the interior towns of Northern Mississippi was the leading talker. For hisself, he 'd rather be a pauper all his days than do business with the dirty, mean, low-down Yankees. Certainly four out of every five in the room at any period during that half day, in some form or another re-echoed the sentiment.

On the cars of the Mississippi Central Railroad, a party of girls, attended by one or two rustic beaux, going down to New Orleans to see the sights and have their winter "society," monopolized the conversation, and did it in no whispered tones. The burden of all their discourse, the staple subject that never failed them—when questions as to how long Sam stayed the other night when he came to see Sally, were fully exhausted—the *pièce de resistance* to which they always reverted, was the meanness, the ignorance, the hatefulness, the cowardice of the detested Yankees. One had to leave school because the dirty Yankees were too near. Another's "par" had lost all his house servants because the sneaking Yankees had enticed them away. Another knew that the Yankees were all cowards, and would never have overpowered us if they had n't called in the Dutch, Irish, niggers, and all the rest of their superiors in creation, to help them. "Did n't my brother Tom—you know, Lizzie, he 's as brave and gallant a man as ever lived—did n't he tell me hisself, with his own lips, that he chased five of 'em, in full uniforms, with swords in their hands, and plenty of revolvers, full gallop, out of Holly Springs? His own self, mind you, by hisself." The presence of an officer in uniform in the car, part of the day, only served to increase the volubility and virulence with which these Mississippi ladies delivered their utterances.

By and by one of the beaux, having run out of subjects for talk with the ladies, took a seat beside me, and produced the unfailing Mississippi substitute for an introduction—a whisky bottle. "Try some, stranger; do n't be afeard. Jist sample it. You 'll find it the rale stuff." "Did n't that Yankee officer look sheepish just now, when the gals was givin' it to him so hot?" he asked, after our acquaintance had progressed smoothly for some time. This was a little too much for Northern flesh and blood, and I informed him that I was a Yankee myself.

"Stranger, you 're jokin'." I insisted that it was a solemn fact.

"Whar 'd you come from?"

"From Washington City."

"Well, who 'd a thought it? But, stranger"——and a prolonged stare followed.

"I say, stranger, take another drink," and the uncorked bottle of villainous whisky was thrust to my lips. "I rather guess, stranger, you must be pretty well used to hearin' that sort o' thing, if you 've been down heah long. The truth is, you do n't look like one o' them sort, and I do n't b'lieve y' are one o' the mean kind anyway; but we do all hate the Yankees like pizen—thar's no use tryin' to hide it."

I traveled one day through Northern Alabama and Western Tennessee with a Texan, who had been North, begging merchants to give him credit again, and help him on his legs.

"I tell you, you don't none o' you know anything about the meanness of the Yankees. I've been among them—I understand 'em. Why, do you know, a little thing a Texas store-keeper 'd throw in 'thout thinking to tell you of 't, one o' them New York fellers 'll make you out a bill for, and ten to one he 'll reckon in the interest till paid."

In such a strain he entertained his listeners for hours. By his account, Northern hotels were sponging houses, as compared with similar establishments in the South. Northern railroads were wholesale swindles, the churches were like the circus, and a "high-toned gentleman" was unknown. From this the talk naturally digressed to life in Texas. We had vivid accounts of little personal differences with the Bowie-knife; precise instructions as to the best way to stand to make your antagonist miss you in a duel, while you got a good shot at him; and challenges to anybody to name as charming a town to live in, under this Yankee-cursed Government, as Galveston, Texas. Nobody named one.

At last we came to an eating-house. "We 'd better hurry," some one suggested. "Oh, there 'll be plenty of room," said the Texan. There 's a lot of cowardly Yankees in the front car. You don't ketch them payin' a dollar for dinner. They stole enough at the breakfast-table to last till to-morrow mornin'."

All this was, of course, the merest froth, thrown not

without scum to the surface of the social agitation. A civil engineer, holding a responsible position on a leading Southern railroad, whom I encountered the next day, expressed very clearly the prevailing views of the better classes.

"What do they mean at Washington? They said the war was to maintain the Union. They succeeded in it and would n't let us go out. What then? Why, they next refuse to let us in."

This man was a gentleman; he was intelligent, familiar with political questions, apparently not bitter. Yet, when I tried to explain to him the view at the North, that every one who had in any way attempted to overturn the Union was a traitor to it, not to be again invested with civil rights till atonement for the treason had been made, or, at least, till security was given against its repetition, he seemed to regard it as something monstrous, unheard of, not to be endured.

"It all resolves itself back into this: we honestly thought we had a right to go out. You thought differently; went to war about it, and established by numbers what you could not by argument. We submit. We accept the situation. Then, having refused to let us out, you slam the door in our faces and won't let us in. During the war you maintained that we were not out, and never could get out. The war over, you now maintain that we are out, and must stay out till you subject us to fresh humiliations."

"I tell you," he continued, with evident sincerity and deep feeling, "no free people in the history of the world were ever treated with such indignity. There was some feeling, not of love for the Union, but of readiness to be at least obedient, even though we could not become affectionate children. They are destroying all this at Washington. Our people feel that you are cruelly and wantonly trifling with us—yes, insulting us; that, having conquered, you have not the magnanimity of brave conquerors, but are bent upon heaping humiliation on your unfortunate victims."

"Do you mean that the people feel like making armed resistance to the action of Congress?"

"Feel like it? Yes. Likely to do it? No. You have us at your mercy. We are powerless, impotent. You can work your will upon us; but men do not forget things seared into their hearts. The time will come when the Yankees will learn to regret their present course."

Of a hundred conversations with intelligent gentlemen from different parts of the interior (not politicians), this one gave the clearest statement of the common feeling. I believe it to have been almost universal in Mississippi, and to have been entertained by a majority of the citizens in West Tennessee, and in the interior of Georgia and Alabama.

The mistake made by Northern statesmen, through the whole winter of 1860, was in not believing the South to be in earnest. They thought the conventions were political bluster; the secession itself a piece of bravado. Perhaps there is danger of a similar mistake again. To us, all this talk of defeated traitors about the humiliation of not being immediately reinvested with political rights in the Government they tried to destroy, seems very absurd bluster. Perhaps their politicians see it in the same light; but their people do not. Very many in some of the States, certainly a majority, actually smart under the exclusion of their representatives as a studied, brutal insult to a beaten and helpless enemy.

A change in the feeling toward the negroes was also manifest from the first day's entrance within the cotton region. In November nothing could exceed the hatred which seemed everywhere felt to the freedmen. Now, this feeling was curiously and almost ludicrously mingled with an effort to conciliate them. Cotton was no longer king, but the cotton-maker was. Men approached the negro with an effort at kind manners; described to him the comforts of their plantations, and insinuatingly inquired if he would n't like to enter into contract for a year. The sable owner of muscle, his woolly head greatly perplexed with this unwonted kindness, held aloof, and seemed, as he respectfully listened to the glowing inducements, to be wondering whether the fly would make anything by his visit to the nicely-arranged parlors of the Mississippi spiders.

The anxious planters argued and pleaded, and the puzzled negroes—kept up their thinking, I suppose. At any rate, very few contracts were yet made in many parts of the interior, especially in Mississippi, though by this time it was near the close of January, and the season for beginning the year's cotton work was rapidly passing away. They were willing to contract on the Mississippi River, and, to some extent, along railroads; but they were very shy about venturing into the interior at all, and, when they did, insisted on remaining in sight of the towns. "I could have got plenty of hands at Vicksburg," complained a planter returning from an unsuccessful trip for labor, "if I had only been able to pick my plantation up and move it twelve miles across the country to Holly Springs." Another came nearer success: "I could have got plenty right at home, if my quarters had been at the other side of my plantation, where it joins the corporation-line of the village; but the black rascals would n't trust themselves the width of my plantation away from town for fear I would eat 'em up."

An old Mississippian was returning from New Orleans in a great rage: "Do you believe, sah, I even demeaned myself so much as to go to a d——d nigger, who called himself a labor agent, and offered him five dollars a head for all the hands he could get me. He promised 'em at once, and I was all right till I told him they was to be sent to ———, Mississippi. To think of it, sah! The black scoundrel told me flat he would n't send me a man. 'Why not,' says I; 'I'll give you your money when they start.' 'I would n't send you a man ef you gave me a hundred dollars a head,' said the dirty, impudent black dog. And why? All because the sassy scoundrel said he did n't like our Mississippi laws."

I subsequently learned that these statements were literally correct, and that many Mississippi planters who had gone to New Orleans for laborers, found they could engage plenty, but lost their hold on every man as soon as they let him know that it was in Mississippi he was wanted. Through the interior, planters were complaining of the disappearance of the negroes. They could n't imagine where the worthless things had suddenly sunk to, until it occurred to some of them to observe that this disappearance began shortly after their reconstructed Legislature had embodied its wisdom in laws on the negro question.

CHAPTER XLV.

Political and Business Complications in the South-west.

NEW ORLEANS in January was a very different city from New Orleans in November. Trade had swelled to its old volume; the city was crowded beyond its capacity; balls, theaters, the opera, crowded upon one another, and all were insufficient to satisfy the wants of this amusement-loving community.

But these changes were nothing, compared with that in the tone of political affairs. Governor Wells had accomplished another revolution on his axis. Lifted into power by the Banks *régime*, he had congenially betrayed it, in order to make interest with the returning Rebels; had appointed them to office by scores; had turned out the Unionists that elected him wherever he could find Rebels to take their places; had made over himself and his power without reserve. They used him, and threw him aside; the betrayer was in turn betrayed, and had nobody to pity him.

The Legislature had passed a bill authorizing a new election for city officers in New Orleans, avowedly to get rid of the Union appointees, and elect "men who were the choice of the great majority of the people "— that is, undisguised Rebels. The Governor, seeing that the movement boded him no good, had broken with the Rebels and vetoed the bill; and they had

promptly passed it over his head.* The leader in this
movement was Mr. Kenner,[53] an old Rebel politician,
and member of the Confederate Senate at Richmond,
recently pardoned by Mr. Johnson. Such was the return he was making for the forgiveness for his treason
which he had begged and received.

Nevertheless, the general feeling was much less defiant than in November. Then they had been sailing,
with favoring winds and under full headway, straight
into their old power in Congress and control of the
country's legislation. The check had been sudden, and
they were not fully recovered from the shock. Business interests, too, had come into play. Trade always
softens away angularities of prejudice, and too often
of principle also. Northerners having money to invest
in the South, men were very willing to forego manifestations of Rebel spite toward them for the sake of
furthering their chances of a good bargain.

I was frequently a guest at the "Varieties Club,"
an organization composed almost exclusively of former
Rebels, and sharing with the "Boston" the favor of
what was considered the *crème de la crème* of New Orleans. The "Varieties" differs from every other club
in this country, in the fact that it is the owner of the
favorite theater of the city, in which the best boxes
and orchestra chairs are always reserved for the use
of the members and their friends, free of charge.

* Under authority of this bill they at once proceeded to elect
the old Rebel Mayor of the city, whom Butler had been compelled
to imprison for his outrageously rebellious conduct. The Union
offices were also filled, almost without an exception, by returned
Rebels. The significance of such an election could not be misun-
derstood, save by the willfully blind. In effect it gave the Rebels
absolute control of the political machinery of the State.

[53] Duncan Farrar Kenner, Representative of Louisiana in the
Confederate Congress. [Ed.]

One evening I happened to enter just as some scene was being enacted in which the hero is suddenly pounced upon and disarmed by a couple of ruffians. As he stood helpless between them, he interpolated a sentence to suit the latitude, exclaiming, "Let me go, let me go; *I'll take the oath!*" The whole audience burst out into uproarious laughter and cheering, which for some little time delayed the action of the play. It was manifest that they had a very clear apprehension of the average value of oaths of loyalty.

The first night I was there, a Union Major General was also one of the guests. Sitting at the same table with him, drinking his whisky—if there are any places in the country more remarkable for hard drinking than the Varieties Club of New Orleans, I have never seen them—and hob-nobbing in the most companionable way, was an officer of the Rebel army who had surrendered to him in Texas. A number of other Rebel officers, some of high grades, members of the Rebel Legislature, registered alien enemies, and a crowd of resident Rebels, were passing through the room. Nothing could exceed their genial courtesy, or the "hospitality" (so called in the South) with which they pressed their whisky.

The next day, I heard that, in the organization of a new club, expressly intended to be established on a loyal basis, the word "Union" had been stricken out of the title by an overwhelming vote. "Do you know," said a resident Northerner, "I was very much in favor of that myself? I am determined that I will have nothing to do, down here, with any social organization into which politics are permitted to enter!" In his mind the use of the word "Union" as part of the title of a club was the introduction of an offensive political distinction! A few days later, in the reading-room of this new club, I noticed, conspicuously hung on the walls, side by side, five portraits of General Sheridan (the commander of the department), and of General Robert E. Lee.

Mr. Flanders was very bitter in his denunciations of what he called Northern toadyism. "With the Northern men and the Northern capital we have here, we could absolutely control this city. But we can't make use of our power, because of these miserable toadies. They imagine it is necessary to truckle to Southern men in order to get trade and acquire influence. Poor fools! can't they see that the moment Southern men get power, they'll kick them all aside? Even now they despise them."

"Give us a couple of hundred Northern men, with money and brains, who were not flunkies, and their honest, straightforward talk would do wonders," he continued. "But the traders are nearly all flunkies. Those who have gone on plantations are more manly, but they are in positions where they have less influence." It was the old, old story.

He insisted that the abatement of Rebel violence, then visible everywhere, was only a torpor, not a radical change. They were discouraged now about their chances. Let them get in again, and they would be up and hissing at once.

Others made the same complaints about the tendency to conciliate Southern prejudices. Begun in the praiseworthy desire to exhibit the most generous consideration to the vanquished, it had degenerated, they said, into the very flunkyism of which Mr. Flanders complained. "Here is General Herron," exclaimed one. "A better or manlier fellow we didn't have in our

army. He has settled down as a commission merchant
here; has plenty of capital, and ought to do well. But,
do you know that he can't get as many favors, soldier
though he is, at the Quarter-masters' and Commissaries'
head-quarters here, in the way of legitimate business,
as can any resident Rebel? Why? Because it's the
thing to display distinguished consideration to these
fellows, in order to convince them that we're willing
to forget the past, if they'll only be good enough to
do the same. Of course, then, it's all smooth sailing
in business intercourse; but, in the bottom of their
hearts, how they must despise us!"

At the residence of a friend, I met, one evening, Mr.
J. Ad. Rozier, a lawyer of considerable prominence,
whose record during the war might, I was informed,
be described as that of a conservative Rebel. He was
greatly delighted with the recent election of Alexander H. Stephens to the Senate by the Legislature of
Georgia, because he "believed in brains." There was
no abler or fairer man, he thought, in the whole South
than Mr. Stephens. He would be, as he had been
before, an honor to the South in the Senate of the
Union.

I couldn't help suggesting that, according to the
appearances then, there wasn't much chance for his
doing a great deal very soon either to honor or dishonor the South in the Senate.

"Oh, he must get in soon. It won't be possible to
refuse admission to such men. The position of the
Republicans is so utterly untenable that they must
soon find it out."

The Republican party, he insisted, was not at all an
Administration party. "It is only coquetting with

Mr. Johnson. Pretty soon it will turn against him openly."

I suggested that, as it had control of both houses, in any event it made very little difference whether Mr. Johnson agreed with it or not, so far as the present question, the immediate admission of the Southern Representatives, was concerned.

"Ah, but the present Congress does n't reflect the real views of the Northern people. It was elected under a war pressure, and it is proving itself utterly unfit to deal with the issues which the peace has brought forward. You may be right about the admission of Southern members now; but the next Congress will soon fix things."

Nothing, he thought, could exceed the indignity with which Congress had treated honorable Southern gentlemen elected to it in good faith by Southern constituencies, in refusing them the empty privilege of seats on the floor. That was an extraordinary way to meet the returning loyalty of the South. Perhaps it was honest in thinking them not entitled to membership; but the refusal of seats to men bearing certificates of election was a gross and studied discourtesy which could not be forgotten or forgiven.

Among men of Mr. Rozier's class I found a general disposition to restrict rather than extend the suffrage. Negro suffrage, they argued, would only be another step in a path which had already led to most of our existing troubles. Too many voted now, instead of too few. What business had any man to cast a vote for the imposition of taxes who had no taxes to pay? What right had any man to a share in shaping the legislation of the country who had no settled interest in the country? Or what sort of government could be expected from the votes of men too ignorant to know anything about government? In short, no man ought to vote unless he had landed property and was educated. The gentlemen of the country should be the ruling class of the country.

But this was only the talk of the clubs and the dinner-tables. The mob who made up the Rebel vote and the Rebel army, and who now furnish the substratum for the universal Rebel feeling, heard nothing of such sentiments. The discussion of them—like their principles themselves—belonged exclusively to the "natural governing classes," and in a special degree to the late slaveholders.

Still, no evils of republican institutions were likely now to drive them out of the country. They had heard enough from their Mexican explorers. Bad as the nigger equality was here, they had discovered it to be much worse there and in Brazil. But their whole hearts were with the Imperialist party in Mexico. Part of this came from the French sympathies of a large portion of the population; another part was due to a general preference for monarchical institutions. The Monroe doctrine had come to be considered a Yankee notion. The impression common at the North, that war with France would help heal the wounds of our own strife, was manifestly untrue, as to Louisiana. It would there be regarded as another Yankee crusade. It would probably meet no open resistance; but it would unquestionably find no support, unless of the coldest.

The great rush of Northerners seeking plantations was already over. Along the Mississippi, and in other favorable localities for cotton-planting, prices had gone

up so largely that men who had only been tempted
South by the hope of ruinously low bargains, took
Northern exchange for their money and went home
again. Others, who had made investments in the interior of Alabama and Mississippi, were greatly discouraged by the temper of the people and by the scarcity·
of laborers. Lands were being leased on the Mississippi, from Natchez to Lake Providence, at rents ranging from eight to as high as twenty-two dollars an
acre. The lessees, after paying these enormous prices,
had still in most cases to stock the places with everything, erect fences, contend with a two to four years'
growth of Caco and Bermuda grass, and pay fifteen
dollars a month, with rations and medical attendance,
for laborers. And then, after incurring the expenses,
they had to take the risk of overflow, and face the
prospect of a steadily declining cotton market. With a
good year and good fortune, they were certain, after all
these outlays, of a large profit remaining; but the con-
tingences were so numerous and the risks so great, that
an investment in Mississippi bottom cotton plantations
seemed to many business men very much like an investment (heretofore very well known on the Mississippi), on the chances of turning up sevens or holding
aces.

The city was full of negroes. They felt their new
power, of which it was impossible that they should be
ignorant while the demands for their services were so
pressing; and they were very slow about making contracts except on terms entirely satisfactory to themselves. They had no doubt of their safety in the
cities; but they feared to trust themselves in the old
Rebel communities in the country.

For even the limited number of plantations which

were being worked, the supply of labor was wholly inadequate; nor would all the idle negroes in the cities have made it up. There seemed no reason to doubt that during the war there had been an actual and very great disappearance of negroes. A few had gone North; some, the rumor had it, were being carried to Cuba; but disease and privation accounted for the most. Their new-found freedom had soon liberated them, in very many cases, from all services on earth.

CHAPTER XLVI.

The Sugar and Rice Culture in Louisiana—Profits and Obstacles.

A NEW ORLEANS friend of mine had recently purchased a fine sugar plantation, twenty-seven miles up
the river from the city. He was going up to see how
the season's work was beginning, and I accepted his
invitation to spend a day or too looking into the details
of sugar culture.

Steaming up the lower Mississippi is about the
dreariest form of traveling. Within is the same round
of novel-reading, card-playing, eating ill-cooked meals,
and swilling bad liquors at the bar, under penalty of
offending every chance acquaintance who insists upon
extending the hospitalities of the occasion. Without,
you catch glimpses, occasionally, of the roofs of old Creole houses peering above the levees. These, and the
stretches of reclaimed swamps on either hand, running
back to the cypress brakes which invariably shut in
the view, constitute the scenery.

But we left New Orleans at nearly sunset, and the
night was brilliant with starlight. Word had been
sent up the day before of our intended visit. As we
approached the plantation, a great fire was seen on the
levee, built to guide the pilot in making the landing.
Grouped about it were two or three negroes and a
couple of white men; the light from the burning logs
casting its fantastic shadows over them. The boat's

bow struck the bank, we leaped off and a couple of negroes caught our traveling-bags. The boat rebounded by its own elasticity, the off-wheel gave a backward revolution, the captain shouted, "Good night," to us from the hurricane-deck, and the vessel was already under headway, again up the stream, as we turned to receive the greetings of the old Creole overseer and the new proprietor's agent.

From the landing, a wagon-road led across the levee and behind it up the river for a few yards, till we entered an old-fashioned garden, laid out in the stiff Dutch flower-bed style, and stood in front of the "mansion." It was a fine old country house, built in the French style, with only dining-room, pantry, ice-closets and the like, back of the row of round brick-stuccoed columns below. Stair-cases ascended at the diagonal corners from the pavement to the second story gallery, which encircled the building, and from which glass doors opened into the parlors and bedchambers. The floors, posts, and in fact nearly all parts of the wood-work were constructed of the best red cypress, and looked as if they might yet last for half-a-dozen generations. The lower story had a tesselated marble pavement; and outside the lower gallery a pavement of brick extended for a yard or two out from the house on all sides. Even with these precautions, the lower story was damp, and to live in it (or to live in the lower story of any house on the coast*) would, in the estimation of the inhabitants, be almost certain death.

"Once it vas very fine house," said the French over-

* The narrow belt of bottom land, reclaimed from the swamps on either side of the Mississippi for sugar plantations, is called "the Coast." Above New Orleans, to the northern limit of sugar

seer, with a shrug of his shoulders; "but des soldats;
dey vas so bad as you see nevare. Dey pasture deir
horses on our flowers and stable dem on dis marble
pavement. I am desolèe," he continued, "to have
not ze power to entertain you as I should like, but
dey took all our liqueurs, and drank our champagnes—
sacre—as if dey tought is vas lager beer. Dey broke
all our dishes; and Monsieur Paine, he buried ze silver
to save it, and found it again nevare."

Still, the old place disclosed unexpected treasures of
claret, which it gladdened the heart of the Creole to
see us taste; and the house servants succeeded in making the spacious but half-furnished bed-chambers comparatively comfortable.

Next morning, while the new proprietor was looking
into the arrangements made in accordance with his
orders, for stocking the place and beginning operations,
I busied myself with explorations. From the front
gallery, into which the glass-door of my bed-room
opened, I looked out upon a broad, brick pavement,
running through the garden to the public road which,
here, as for hundreds of miles up the Mississippi,
everywhere skirts the levee. In the middle of it was
a brick column, three or four feet high, serving as a
pedestal for a leaden sun-dial, which had formerly been
set with accurate care in mortar on its top. During
the military occupation, the soldiers had amused themselves by firing from the gallery at this dial, and one
too good shot had struck it fairly in the center leaving
its deep indentation, and breaking the whole dial loose
from its bed in the mortar.

culture, is the Upper Coast. Between New Orleans and the mouth
of the Mississippi is the Lower Coast.

The garden had evidently taken much of the time and no small share of the profits of the former proprietor. Even yet, notwithstanding the destruction by the troops and the neglect during the war, many of the rarest shrubs and flowers were in luxuriant growth. It was still January. I had left Washington in the midst of a heavy snow storm, and the telegraph brought accounts of continued cold weather; but in this deserted garden we plucked bouquets of rare flowers, growing in the open air, which scarcely a green-house in Washington could have equalled. Fig and banana trees were of course abundant. Oranges had been served at breakfast which had been plucked from the trees last fall; and, in the edge of the garden, we now found others on which the oranges were still hanging in spite of the winter's frosts. Most of these were wild; but several trees, bearing fruit that after all its exposure was still pleasant to the taste, had escaped the gathering of the soldiers and the after-gleaning of the negroes. China trees, filled with mocking birds, formed a short avenue in front of the house; and in a corner of the garden was one of the rarities, which the Creole overseer delighted to exhibit, a cork tree, already quite large, which in a few years might furnish all the corks they wanted for bottling their own wines from the wood. The green-house was in utter ruin. The soldiers had amused themselves by shattering its glass-roof; and the shelves, on which the potted plants had been placed, were rotted away and broken down.

"Jim," the sugar-maker, called me from the flowers to see the sugar-house. He was a middle-aged, shrewd looking negro, who had been sold here by one of the

Virginia patriarchs at a very early day. He could remember learning a trade in Virginia; "but I's been
heah so long I dunno much 'bout de ole place. I'd
like to go back to see it, for pears like it was mity fine
place to live; but I would n't stay dare now. Dis is
my home."

To the right of the house stood the "quarters," a
double row of dilapidated frame cabins, each containing two rooms, with a porch in front, covered by the
projecting roof. Each room was supposed to furnish
accommodations for five adults. If they were all in
one family, very well; if not, two or three families must
go together. For these five persons there was, in the
single room, space for a couple of bedsteads, a little
table, two or three chests, and as many chairs. Each
had a fire-place, a door and a hole in the wall opposite,
closed by a wooden shutter, which they called a window. "These quarters ought to be whitewashed," said
the proprietor. "Wait till the niggers all get back and
they'll do it themselves, and we'll save that expense,"
replied the agent.

Beyond the quarters, in a large field well-set in Bermuda grass, stood the sugar-house. Everything about
it seemed damp and soggy. We approached it over
ground yielding to our tread from the moisture, and
ascended to the door by a wooden stair case, covered
with a slimy growth of fungus, and half-rotted away.

Within stood a fine engine, which "Jim" exhibited
with pride. "Eberything dar, sah. Dem brasses you
see gone, I done locked up to keep de niggers from
stealing 'em. De pipes and de valves, all locked up
safe, sah. I ken set her a runnin in a day, sah, and
you don't need to send to Orleans once for nuffin."
Near the engine were the boiling pans, and in a long

"L" of the building was the wide trough into which the fluid was run off for cooling and crystallization. Everything here seemed scrupulously neat, although the fact that the negroes had worked the place by themselves, last year would not generally have been taken as a guaranty for cleanliness.

"Jim" was greatly disgusted with his last year's effort to make the niggers work. "I sposed, now we's all free, dey'd jump into de work keen, to make all de money dey could. But it was juss no work at all. I got so 'scouraged sometimes I's ready to gib it all up, and tell 'em to starve if dey wanted to. Why, sah, after I'd ring de bell in the mornin' 'twould be hour, or hour 'n half 'fore a man 'd get into de fiel'. Den dey'd work along maybe an hour, maybe half hour more; and den dey'd say Jim, aint it time to quit? I say, 'No, you lazy dog, taint ten o'clock,' Den dey'd say, 'Jim, I's mighty tired,' and next thing I'd know, dey'd be pokin' off to de quarters. When I scold and swear at 'em, dey say, 'we's free now, and we's not work unless we pleases.' Sah, I got so sick of deir wuflessness dat I sometimes almost wished it was old slavery times again."

"How did they live, Jim? If they wouldn't work, I don't see what they had to live on."

"Well, the trufe is, sah, dey stole eberyting dey could lay deir han's on."

It ought to be added that the negroes all complained that "Jim" was a hard task-master, and that he was "harder on them than white folks." His old master, Mr. Payne, on the other hand, pronounced him invaluable; said he was one of the most intelligent and skillful slaves he ever saw, and declared his determina-

tion, if he ever went to planting again, to hunt "Jim"
up and hire him.

There were not more than half-a-dozen negro families
on the plantation at the time of our visit. The agent
of the new proprietor had been attempting, through
the past week, to hire them, but they had refused to
enter into any contract which he thought admissible.
They all wanted special privileges of one sort or another. Many wanted considerable tracts of land set
off to them on the plantation, which they could cultivate on their own account. Some thought they ought
to have two or three acres to plant in cotton. Nearly
all wanted to grow corn. "Let 'em have an acre of
either," said the agent (and the Creole overseer fully
agreed with him), "and they would pick more than you
would get from any half-dozen acres you've got. Give
them the slightest opening for growing the same crops
you grow, and you've opened the flood-gates of unlimited stealing. You have no sort of check on them."

One fellow wanted permission to keep on the plantation two horses, a mule, and a cow, besides hogs,
chickens, and goats innumerable. "How could he
feed them?" innocently asked the proprietor. "Feed
them? Out of your corn-crib, of course. You couldn't
put a lock on it he wouldn't pick the first dark night.
He would steal the corn you fed your mules with at
dinner, out of the very trough from which the mules
were eating it. Haven't I caught them at such tricks,
again and again?"

The agent had accordingly set his face as a flint
against all these special claims preferred by the negroes. He would give them the wages then customary
along the Coast (ten dollars a month, with clothing,
lodging, food and medical attendance), would give them

Saturday afternoons and Sundays for themselves, would give plenty of land for gardens, and mules and plows to cultivate it; and that was all he would give. The negroes might enter into contract on these terms or leave. They did n't want to do either. They would n't contract, but they made themselves comfortable in the houses and evidently considered themselves at home, contract or no contract. Thereupon the agent brought matters to a crisis by telling them that he gave them till Saturday morning to contract, if by that time they had made no engagement they must shift for themselves. Saturday morning came; and not more than half-a-dozen besides the two drivers had signed the contract.

"They thought, by standing out, they could force me to terms about their mules and cotton. But I soon undeceived them. I rigged up the carts, packed their traps into them, and sent them bag and baggage off the place. They went down to a sort of free-nigger settlement a few miles below. Now they're sneaking back every day and asking leave to enter into contract."*

The Creole thought they worked so badly last year that it did n't make much difference whether they returned or not.

"But dey'll do better, sah, wid you. Dey wants a white man to gib orders. Dey would n't min' me las' yeah, 'cause I's nigger like demselves. I tink dey do better dis yeah." Such was "Jim's" view of the case.

"Jim" spoke English—such as it was. This he owed to his Virginia birth. All the rest of the ne-

---

* About half of them, I believe, returned before the spring work had been fairly begun. The rest sought new homes, and in general fared no better than those who returned.

groes spoke French exclusively. They had been quite as successful in forming an unintelligible *patois* from that, as other plantation negroes have been with their English. Some of our party spoke French fluently, but they could make nothing out of the talk of the negroes. The Creole overseer gave his laughing explanation. "It's nigger French, zey speak, sare; of course you can not it understand." And with that he broke into a volley of gibberish, the words coming like chain-shot, in couples, to which the negroes at once responded. "Jim," in addressing them, made use of the same mongrel French; he had learned it from his long residence among them. Now and then one could catch a pure French word; and the general sound was similar to the French; but it had been so distorted, the overseer told us, as to constitute a distinct dialect, which must be learned by all who undertake the control of the Coast negroes.

Exaggerate four-fold the peremptory style in which military officers generally think it necessary to deliver their commands, and project the words with a rapidity which nobody but a Frenchman could conceive, and you have the manner in which our Creole constantly spoke to the negroes. The words came from his lips with a rasping, spasmodic sort of energy, that really seemed to infuse a little life in the slow-motioned creatures; though I observed that most of the energy inspired by his tones seemed to be expended in the quaint *patois* of the replies. Directions to hitch up an enormous, broad-tired, inconceivably clumsy sugar cart, required an amount of shouting that would have sufficed for a western barn-raising; and I feel sure that fully an hour was spent by two able-bodied negroes in the process of harnessing the mules to the shafts, tandem-

fashion. A similar storm of "nigger French," brought
us, in the process of time, a number of horses sufficient
for the party; and, under the guidance of an old head-
negro, pleasantly named "Voisin," we set out for a ride
over the plantation.

Voisin was the plow-driver. Over every foot of the
twelve hundred acres he had maneuvered his gang of
plows, as a military officer would maneuver his bat-
tallion, and he was ready to pour into the ear of the
proprietor all the traditions of the plantation; that this
land was too wet for cane and ought to be left in grass;
that all on this side of the leading ditch had been used
for corn from time immemorial; that the finest cane
always grew on this side of that levee by the cross-
ditch; that that back-land was too stiff for anything,
and he'd better not attempt to plow it if he did n't
want to kill off his mules; that cotton ought not to be
grown at all; but, if it must be, this land nearest the
front levee was the best for it; and so on interminably.

When we rode out of the inclosures around the
quarters, sugar-house, and stables, we were in the one
field which comprised the entire plantation. From the
levee by the river bank it stretched in an unbroken
flatness, gradually descending, back to the cypress
swamp that bounded the arable land in the rear, and
shut in the view. The field was cut by two deep leading ditches, one running down the middle to the swamp,
and the other leading from side to side of the place,
intersecting the first about midway between the river
and the swamp. Into each of these smaller ones
emptied, at distances of thirty to sixty yards, and
the entire field was thus intersected by a net work of
open ditches; the water from all of which flowed back

to the swamp until it met the obstruction of the back levee.

To understand the object of this, and the nature of the difficulties which the Louisiana sugar-planter has encountered, it must be remembered that all this land bordering on the river was originally a swamp. Successive overflows naturally deposited the most of their sediment near the river banks. Thus the land became highest at the river, and the drainage, instead of inclining in the natural direction, went backward to the swamp. Thenceforward there was a double trouble confronting the adventurous planter who sought to utilize this amazingly fertile soil. The river in his front was dangerous; but the swamp behind him was worse. His levees might protect him from the Mississippi itself; but crevasses, hundreds of miles above, might overflow the back country, or the back streams themselves might do it; and presently, while he was watching the flood at his door, the water from the swamp behind him was creeping up over his land and ruining his prospects for the year.

There was no resource save to fight the water on all sides. Each plantation was therefore protected by front and back levees, and resembled in shape a huge dish; which, but for the energy of its owners, would become a lake. A fresh difficulty was then encountered. The land, being below the surface of the water on both sides of it, was kept constantly soaked by infiltration. Ditches might drain this water back to the swamp, but here the levee met them. A pumping machine thus became necessary; and during the wet season the water was to be fought with levees, before and behind, and that which filtered in was to be pumped out into the swamp.

We found the back levee cut open, and water from the ditches was flowing out through the gap. Voisin explained that as soon as the water in the swamp began to rise, the levee must be closed again, and the pump put in operation.

To Northern eyes, the "swamp" began far enough inside of the swamp levee. Voisin assured us that in old times there was no better land on the plantation; but, riding along the beaten road by the main ditch, over which all the wood used for the engine and at the house was drawn, and along which the cattle were daily driven, our horses sank over their knees in the alluvial mud. On either hand the water stood in small pools over the entire surface of the "back cuts." A New Englander would have declared it fit for nothing but cranberries. Some of the planters insisted that such land was *then* in the very best condition for plowing— "it turned over so much easier when it had water standing on it!"

The supply of cypress in the swamp was inexhaustable. Nothing prevented it from being far more profitable than the sugar grown under such difficulties, except the expense of hauling it out, to the river. Sugar-planters generally make little or no account of their swamp land. They reckon their "leveed" land, fronting on the river, and give little attention to the depth back into the swamp the surveyors may have given them. Probably not half of them have ever seen their back lines.

This plantation, only twenty-seven miles from New Orleans, considered among the best on the west side of the river, with its sugar-house and the expensive machinery attached in a condition to be used, with residence comparatively uninjured, quarters for all the hands, good levees, and some cane, sold at auction on terms which represented a cash investment of about fifty-five thousand dollars! I know cotton plantations, further up, which *rented*, acre for acre, for over two-thirds of this sum! The title was perfect, and there was nothing to prevent the plantation from making as high an average yield as it ever did, as soon as the cane should be reset, unless the free labor system should fail. Other places along the river have since sold at higher figures; but I believe that any one who is willing to devote two or three months to watching for an opportunity, may make equally favorable purchases any time within the next two years.

Extravagant living left nearly every planter enormously in debt when the war came. Since then their affairs have gone from bad to worse. Many are now making desperate efforts to retrieve themselves, and some will succeed. The sheriff will close out the rest, and bargains await the watchful capitalists. "By gare," said the Creole, "le proprietuer of zis place, before Monsieur Payne, lived as you vould nevare beleive. He had over seexty slaves for house servants. Seex carriages stood tere in ze carriage house, for ze use of ze family, beside buggies, saddles horses, et tout cela! He had four demoiselles; every one moost have tree slaves to vait on her! And ze dinnares, and ze trips to New Orleans! Den, sare, let me explain to you; ze jardin himself cost ovare seexty tousand dollare."

This family, of course, had gone to the insolvent's court. The next proprietor was caught by the war; and now Mr. A. C. Graham was trying to revive the neglected culture. He had bought a quantity of plant-cane from the Dick Taylor place, lying immediately below; had secured mules, by sharp bargaining, at a hundred and sixty-two dollars a head; and, if he could only be sure of laborers, had a fair prospect for a hundred and fifty hogsheads of sugar and twice as many barrels of molasses in the fall. Some cotton had to be planted, although there was small hope, in this heavy sugar soil, of its doing much more than paying expenses; and corn and hay enough would be grown to make the plantation self-sustaining for next year's operations.

We rode over to the Dick Taylor place to look at the plant-cane. This was cane which had been cut from last year's crop, and instead of being ground for sugar, had been buried in "mattresses" for planting in the spring.* We could see only a confused mass of dry blades, not unlike the blades of Indian corn. Voisin dug into the mattress and brought out fine large canes, fresh and moist. They had been buried thus, overlapping each other, with the ends of each layer in the ground, and had been preserved through the winter without injury from the frost.

Plows were already starting to prepare the land. As soon as possible, these canes would be laid in the furrows, two or three side by side, across the whole field, and buried with the fresh earth. When the young canes are sprouted up from the joints, they would be seen stretching across the plantation like rows of Indian corn. Then would begin the battle with the grass and

---

* The sugar-cane is propagated from the stalks; the stalks from one acre being enough to plant four. They will then remain productive for three years; after which they must be replanted. In the warmer climate and dryer soil of Cuba, they last for ten years. Hence the advantage Cuban planters have in the sugar-culture. In Louisiana it is only an exotic, and but for the protection of a high tariff, would perish.

weeds, to last without a day's intermission until June or July. In mid-summer the cane would be "laid by," and a three month's interval would follow, corresponding to the winter's leisure of the Northern farmer. During this time cypress would be cut and hauled for the engines, the fences would be repaired, and every preparation for sugar-boiling made in advance. Meantime the luxuriant cane, arching from row to row, would by its own shadow keep down all weeds and leave the furrows clean to act as ditches in carrying off the flooding summer rains.

Early in October an army of cutters would attack the field, armed with a broad-hooked knife, with which they would sever each stalk, close to the ground, strip it of its blades, and cut off its top at the uppermost joint. Some day Yankees will invent machinery to do all this; but now, the unequal length of the stalks and the necessity for cutting each one at the upper joint to exclude the injurious juices of the top, are supposed to require this slow labor-consuming process. Great "broad-tread" carts, with a stout mule hitched in the shafts and a pair of lighter ones in front, are used to haul the cane to the mill. There the fires never go out, and the mill never stops, day or night, for the ensuing three months. The negroes are arranged in sections to relieve each other; and every man on the plantation is expected to do eighteen hours of work daily. Abundant rations of whisky, presents of tobacco, free draughts of the sweet syrup, and extra pay, carry them through. The expressed juice is boiled in vacuum-pans till nearly all the water is driven off; then, when it is run out to cool, the sugar crystallizes, (with the aid of lime and bone-black to purify it,) and the residuum is drawn off in the shape of crude molasses.

The machinery for all this is expensive. Sugar-mills, with all the appurtenances, cost from twenty up to one hundred and fifty thousand dollars; and the more costly ones are by far the more economical. This statement at once discloses the great difficulty of adapting the free-labor system to the culture of sugar. A freeman naturally looks forward to the time when he can own the soil he cultivates. But for a negro, or for a Northern farmer without capital, to attempt the sugar culture on a small scale, would, as matters now stand, be utter folly. Perhaps, in time, we shall have large sugar-mills erected here as flour-mills are at the North; every man's growth of cane to be manufactured for a fixed toll, or sold to the miller at current rates; but till then, the growth of cane for sugar must be left to men of capital.

Two hundred miles further north, the owners of these amazingly fertile swamps may yet find more formidable rivals than the Cubans. Every cotton-planter requires large quantities of molasses for the use of his negroes. Yankees will not grow cotton long till they begin growing the sorghum to manufacture their own molasses. And Yankees will not continue many years manufacturing the base of sugar, without forcing the secret of sorghum, and finding how to crystallize its syrup into sugar. Already the negroes, who have once tasted the sorghum molasses, insist on being furnished with it in preference to that made from cane. Demand will not long exist here, among the new elements of this changing population, without creating a supply.

Meantime the sugar-culture along the coast must, at any rate, revive slowly. Even if the capital were all ready to be invested, so complete has been the neglect of the plantations, that a full crop can not be made short of three to four years. The crop of 1861 was four hundred and forty-seven thousand nine hundred and fifty-eight hogsheads, from twenty-four parishes of Louisiana. In 1865 it had dwindled to six thousand seven hundred fifty-five hogsheads. In 1861 there were one thousand two hundred and ninety-one sugar-plantations under cultivation in these parishes. There are now one hundred and seventy-five. These figures tell their own story.

On the Payne plantation, the negroes about the quarters were pounding out rice in a little wooden mortar. Large stacks of rice stood near the stables. A little mill was pointed out as having been formerly used to hull rice sufficient for the use of the hands; and back toward the swamp, we were told, were excellent rice lands; on which, in old times, fine crops had always been made.

While the place was being slowly reset in cane, it would doubtless be profitable to grow rice; but the negroes were unwilling to undertake it. Here, as in the rice lands of South Carolina and Georgia, there was every prospect that free labor would prove absolutely fatal to the culture. Men *would* not work in rice swamps except under compulsion. There is a species of rice, which grows like wheat, on uplands; but it only yields about one-fourth of a crop. On good rice lands the yield per acre varies from thirty-five to fifty bushels. Exceptional crops have run up as high as ninety bushels. With good cultivation on good soil, one might reasonably hope for an average of forty bushels, or eighteen hundred pounds per acre—worth (with rice ranging from nine and a half to twelve cents per pound) about one hundred and eighty dollars. This is much more lucrative than cotton at twenty-five cents a pound; nearly as much so as cotton at fifty cents.

It is a golden opening—but the free laborers decline to step into it. Five years ago the rice crop of the United States was about a quarter of a million casks. Last year it was seven thousand!

CHAPTER XLVII.

A Cotton Plantation—Work, Workmen, Wages, Expenses and Returns.

A FEW days afterward I embarked again upon a Mississippi packet, at New Orleans, to make a visit to some noted cotton plantations near Natchez.

A good steamboat should make the trip in about thirty hours; but the packets lengthen the time one-half by their frequent stoppages. Every few miles we ran into shore, the gang-plank was thrown out, and half-a-dozen barrels of pork, or double as many of flour, or a few bales of hay were rolled off. So wedded are most of the old residents to their old ways of doing business, that they see all these supplies steadily carried past their doors by the "up-river boats," but wait until they reach New Orleans, pass through the hands of their old commission merchant, and thus return with double freights and double commissions, to be landed at the very places they passed the week before. Ask one why he does not buy above, and have the goods shipped direct to his plantation, and he will reply that Mr. So-and-so, in New Orleans, has sold all his cotton or sugar, and purchased all his supplies for the last ten or twenty years, and he doesn't want to be bothered making a change.

Among the passengers was a short, florid-faced, red-whiskered gentleman, with an empty coat-sleeve, who seemed a general favorite. "Poor fellow," said one, as he passed near, "the war pretty much broke him, I guess."

"Broke *him!* well, now, you just go below and look at the seventy-five mules he's got on board, bought in New Orleans for his plantations, at two hundred dollars a head, cash, and see whether you think he's broke."

"I'm mighty glad he's got his property back," said another. "He owns three of the finest plantations in Louisiana; and one good crop will put him all right again, and let him go into politics if he wants to."

All shared in the expressions of good will, and it was evident that the red-faced, one-armed little gentleman was a popular favorite. It was General Yorke, late of the Rebel army, scarred with three wounds, and back among those for whom he had unsuccessfully fought. At Monocacy he led the final charge which swept back Lew Wallace's forces and opened the way for Ewell and Breckinridge to the Capital. At Spottsylvania a bullet struck him in the head; in another Virginia battle he was wounded in the shoulder; from several he came out with clothes riddled with bullets and all his horses shot under him; at last, in the Wilderness, his arm was carried away.

It was common at the North to regard such men as the leading criminals of the rebellion, but I would rather trust General Yorke in Congress, unpardoned Rebel as he is, than a single one of the pardoned Congressmen elect from Mississippi or Louisiana.

"You do n't know what you're talking about," he exclaimed, impetuously, to some one who was haranguing against the tyranny and cruelty of the government; "I tell you, sir, you have got and I have got the most

merciful government in the world. What's the use of
our trying to disguise the facts? We attempted to destroy the government and failed; any other would have
hung me for my share in the matter; and would have
had a perfect right to do it. I consider myself a standing proof of the mercy of my government. It confiscated my property, while I was gone, fighting against it.
I don't complain; it did perfectly right. Since then
I've got my property back; a thing I had no right to
expect; and I'm very grateful for it. I only want a
chance to prove my gratitude. If we get into a war
about this Mexican business, I'll try to show the government how I appreciate its generosity to me."

Very few of his hearers seemed to like the General's
views—much as they all admired him personally. To
them it seemed a very great outrage that while he was
losing his arm under Lee, in the Wilderness, government lessees should have been cultivating his splendid
cotton plantations, within the national lines, at Natchez.
What business had government to be interfering with
the rights of property?

Some one said the war was n't over yet. "Isn't it?"
said the General. "Well, may be *you* havn't had enough
of it. But I tell you, the men that did the fighting
have. What's more, they are satisfied to quit and to
take things as they can get them. More still, I don't
know of anybody that is n't satisfied to quit, except the
stay-at-home sneaks that have never yet made a beginning. You're very full of fight now, all of a sudden,
when it is n't needed. Why did n't you show some of it
when we wanted you in the trenches at Richmond?"

Yet the General was as firm a believer in the right
of secession as ever: "I have my own views as to the
constitutionality and rightfulness of our course; I

thought our cause just, and I did all I could to make it successful. But we were beaten, badly beaten. Some of those fellows that have been hanging around Natchez, or making money out of army contracts, may not be subjugated, but I am. And now, having submitted, I do it in good faith. What difference does it make now about our beliefs and our arguments in favor of secession? All that has been settled against us in the court to which we appealed; we have submitted to the verdict; and, as honorable men, we have no right to revive the controversy."

The General assured me that his negroes were working well; and that he had not experienced the slighest difficulty in getting all the labor he wanted. "My people all knew well enough that I had been a kind master to them before the war; and you could n't have hired any considerable number of them to leave me. Why, when I came back here to White-Hall,* from the army, it was a perfect jubilee. They picked me up and carried me into the house on their shoulders, and God-blessed me, and tanked de Lo'd for me, till I thought they were never going to get through."

All this, as I had subsequent occasion to learn from numerous sources, was but a moderate statement of the facts. His old slaves had unlimited faith in him; his plantations had all the labor they needed; and the work on them was as well advanced as on any along the river.

At last our boat reached Natchez, having consumed

---

*The name of one of his plantations, only three miles from Natchez, fronting on the Mississippi. It contains seventeen hundred acres of open land, besides a pecan grove and an enormous tract of cypress.

over forty-eight hours in traveling the two-hundred and seventy-five miles from New Orleans. High bluffs rose above us, and perched upon them could be seen the roofs and steeples of an important little inland town. Between the river and bluff was crowded the most miserable, straggling, shabby-looking village imaginable. This was what is left of Natchez-under-the-hill. Once fine rows of brick warehouses lined the banks; but the steady encroachments of the river undermined their foundations, and one after another disappeared. Thirty or forty feet from the water's edge a large deserted building still stood, with one corner of the wall washed away by the "last high water," and the rest of it tottering, to fall with the next. Negroes filled the nasty little shops, where tobacco, whisky, sardines, calicoes, and head-handkerchiefs were displayed. The street was full of dirty idlers, and the whole appearance of the place was unprepossessing in the extreme. Up the river a saw-mill and lumber-yard shut in the view.

Altogether, it was about the most unlikely place imaginable in which to look for any display of art or appreciation of natural beauties. But, the day after my arrival, a citizen, to whom I had brought letters of introduction, taught me how to find a rare gem in this shabbiest of settings. Driving past the saw-mill, we approached the residence of the sawyer, nestled close, as it seemed, under the bluff, which, a few yards further up, jutted out against the river. Passing from the lumber-yard and the whisky shops, we entered, as my enthusiastic companion said, "the garden of Eden." Hedges of the most beautiful flowering shrubs led up to the airy, many-galleried house. Graveled walks led off on either hand to pleasant summer-houses, covered with vines, and bordered with the rarest exotics. Great mounds, covered with shrubs and flowers, stood sentry on either side the gate. The air was heavy with perfumes, and vocal with the music of the full-throated little songsters that flitted about among the branches. Citizens of Natchez boast that the sawyer's garden is the finest in the South. They might enlarge their boast, by a little modification, and safely pronounce it the most surprising one on the continent.

Natchez-on-the-hill, (to which passengers from the boats ascend by a long carriage-way, cut out of the perpendicular face of the bluff,) would be called, at the North, a flourishing county-town; dusty, and by no means specially attractive. But it is the aristocratic center of the lower Mississippi Valley cotton-planting interests. Before the war, it was regarded as a most desirable residence, and wealthy Southerners sought plantations within a range of thirty or forty miles up or down the river, in order to be able to fix their own residences at Natchez. Few resided on their plantations; many owned several—in some cases as high as eight or nine—the smallest rarely, if ever, falling below a thousand acres in extent. These lands were all of the richest alluvial soil; and, before the war, were worth, after being cleared, from sixty to a hundred dollars per acre. Recent sales had been made at about forty dollars, but the leases were all disproportionately high. I heard of cases in which thirty thousand dollars had been paid in cash, and in advance, for one year's lease of fourteen hundred acres. This, however, was probably the highest lease paid along the river. Fifteen thousand dollars seemed a common rent for a thousand acres of good land, with the use of agricultural implements, gin, and saw and grist-mills. It was always, however, an important consideration that the former slaves should all be on the plantation. Here, as elsewhere, labor was the great desideratum. That secured, speculators were ready to pay almost any price for the use of the land.

Around Natchez is a beautiful rolling country, abounding in park-like scenery. Showy, and, in some cases, elegant residences crown the little knolls; and the country, for several miles back into Mississippi, wears an air of wealth and comfort. On the opposite side of the river are "the swamps." But the swamps are the gold mines; it is only those who draw their support from the rich, low lands of the neighboring parishes of Louisiana who can afford the display that crowns the hills about Natchez.

Buildings in Natchez, which the Government had seized, were being restored to their former owners. Business had revived. Northern men had established themselves as commission merchants and dealers in plantation supplies, and were infusing new energy into the town. They said they had all the business they could do, made no complaints of hostility from the people, and said they believed it would be better for all parties if the troops were removed. So far as they were themselves concerned, at any rate, they professed that they would not have the slightest apprehension.

Many of the small planters in the interior (hill country) of Mississippi, who used Natchez as their base of supplies, were anxious for assistance from capital, from whatever source it might come. Some had supplies enough to carry them through till their cotton should be half made. Then they wanted to borrow money enough to last till they could begin to receive returns from their crops, and were willing to pay such extravagant rates as two and even two and a half per cent. per month for it.

" Cotton square " was crowded with ox-teams from these hill plantations. Each brought in two or three bales of cotton, and returned with pork, meal, and molasses to support the negroes. The planters themselves, rough, hairy, wild-looking men, wearing home-spun, bargained in the shops, where they sold their cotton, for Calhoun plows, harness, drills, and denims for the " niggers," and an occasional article for themselves. The whole scene was primitive, and rude in the extreme; yet these tobacco-chewing, muddy-footed men from the hills were among the best customers the Natchez merchants had. They were nearly all small planters, working from six to thirty, or even forty hands, raising from fifty to three hundred bales of cotton, and handling more money in a year than half-a-dozen Northern farmers, each of whom would have his daily newspaper, a piano in the house, daughters at the nearest " Female Seminary," and sons at college.

A steam ferry-boat sets passengers, once an hour, across the Mississippi, from Natchez-under-the-hill. A pleasant drive for a few miles down the levee, (passing but two plantations on the way—one to a mile of river front is a small allowance here,) brought me to the plantations I had come to visit. They lay beside each other, and belonged to the same man; but each had its separate set of quarters and gang of negroes, and the work on each had always been kept distinct. The levee formed the boundary of their arable land. Outside this were two or three hundred acres, thickly set in Bermuda grass,* and fringed with a dense growth of young willows. This was covered with water when the Mississippi rose to its highest point, but at all other seasons it furnished pasturage for the mules and other stock of the plantations. A negro on each, enjoying the title and dignity of "stock-minder," was charged with the duty of "carrying out," daily, all the stock not in use, and herding it on this open common.

A lane led down between an old gin-house on one hand, and an old stable on the other, to the broad-porched, many-windowed, one-story "mansion." China and pecan trees surrounded it. On one hand was a garden, several acres in extent, to which the labors of two negroes were steadily devoted ; and on the other were the quarters—a double-row of frame, one-story houses, fronting each other, each with two rooms, and a pro-jecting roof, with posts, shutting in an earthern porch floor. Down the middle of the street were two or three brick cisterns; at the foot of it stood the church. Back of each cabin was a little garden, jealously fenced off from all the rest with the roughest of cypress pickets, and carefully fastened with an enormous padlock. "Niggers never trust one another about their gardens or hen-houses," explained the overseer.

Back of the house and quarters stretched a broad expanse of level land, gently sloping down to the cy-press swamp, which, a mile and a half in the rear, shut

* An admirable pasture grass, flourishing only in warm climates and free from shade. It was first introduced into Louisiana as a protection for the levees, its thick mat of roots preventing the high water from washing away the base of the levee; but it spread rapidly over the adjacent cotton lands, and thus became one of the greatest pests to the planters, who find it almost impossible to exterminate it.

in the view. Not a stump, tree, or fence broke the smooth monotony of the surface; but half-a-dozen wide, open ditches led straight to the swamp; and were crossed at no less than seven places by back levees, each a little higher than the one beyond it. The lands were entirely above overflow from the Mississippi in their front; but the back-water from the swamp, when swelled by the overflows from crevasses above, almost every year crept up on the land nearest the swamp—coming sometimes before the planting had begun; sometimes not till the first of June. Then began the "fight with the water," as the planters quaintly called it. An effort was made to "catch it at the back levee." Failing in this, the negro forces retreated to the next levee, a hundred and fifty yards further up; closed the leading ditches, and went to work trying to raise this levee to a hight sufficient to check the sluggish, scarcely moving, muddy sheet of water that, inch by inch, and day by day, crept nearer to it. The year before they had failed here, and at every levee till they came to the one nearest the river. On the two plantations, out of twelve or fourteen hundred acres of cotton land, they saved less than three hundred. The rest was planted in the ooze, as the waters receded, late in June; the negroes following close behind, men and women knee-deep in the alluvial mud, drilling in the cotton-seed, and covering it by rubbing along the row the flat sides of their hoes. "Ten or twelve barrels of whisky.got it done," the overseer explained. But the crop, like all late ones in this region, was attacked by the worms; the grass got ahead of the plows, and less than a quarter of a bale to the acre was realized on lands that had been made to produce a bale and a half.

Along the inner levee, at which the water had been

finally "caught," led a fine, beaten wagon-road down
to the quarters on the other plantation. These differed
in no way from those already described, except that
they were less regularly arranged. Instead of a "mansion," there was at the front only a double cabin, which
in old times. served as the overseer's house. Now both
plantations were managed by the same overseer; and at
this lower place were eighty-five field negroes, besides
children and old people, without a white man nearer to
them than at the house on the upper place, a mile off.
"They get along nearly as well as if they were watched,"
said the overseer. "We have about as much trouble at
the upper place as here."

By the inner levee were, at points about three-quar-
ters of a mile apart, the ruins of the two steams-gins
that had once been the pride of the plantations. The
boilers were still in their places; and fragments of the
engines and machinery strewed the ground for many
yards in each direction. One was lost by the carelessness of an unaccustomed negro engineer; the other
had been destroyed by the guerrillas. From this point,
for a distance of thirty miles down the river, nearly all
the steam-gins were burnt. The guerrillas were determined, they said, that the Yankees, or men that
would stay at home and be friendly with the Yankees,
should n't make money out of them. A few had been
rebuilt; but, in most cases, the planters were relying
upon clumsy horse-power arrangements for ginning
out the next crop.

We rode out to see the negroes at work. They were
back half-way between the river and the swamp. Two
gangs made up the working force on each plantation;
and each was under its own negro-driver, who rode

about on his horse and occasionally gave sharp, abrupt directions.

The plow-gang, containing fifteen plows, each drawn by a pair of scrawny mules, with corn-husk collars, gunny-bag back-bands, and bed-cord plow-lines, was moving across the land, after a fashion which would have broken the heart of a Northern farmer, at the rate of about eighteen acres a day. They had been at work since the middle of January, and would continue plowing, without interruption, till the first of April, by which time they hoped to reach the swamp. The land was plowed in beds; each occupying about five feet. Each plowman started down, what had been the "middle," between last year's cotton rows; returning, he threw another furrow up to meet the one he had turned going down. Two more furrows were then thrown on each side, and the bed was completed, ready for planting. On one of the plantations, however, they were only "four-furrowing" the land; i. e., throwing up two furrows on each side, but leaving the middles still unbroken. "If we done gits behine, we's plant on dem beds, and knock de middles out afterwards;" so the plow-driver answered my question about his object for leaving part of the work undone. Two or three women were plowing, and were said to be among the best hands in the gang.

A quarter of a mile ahead of the plows a picturesque sight presented itself. Fifty women and children, with only a few weakly men among them, were scattered along the old cotton rows, chopping up weeds, gathering together the trash that covered the land, firing little heaps of it, singing an occasional snatch of some camp-meeting hymn, and keeping up an incessant chatter. "Gib me some 'backey please;" was the first salutation as the overseer rode among them. These were the "trash-gang." After the cotton is planted, they become the hoe-gang, following the plows, thinning out the cotton, and cutting down the grass and weeds which the plows can not reach. Most of them were dressed in a stout blue cottonade; the skirts drawn up till they scarcely reached below the knee, and reefed in a loose bunch about the waist; heavy brogans of incredible sizes on their feet, and gay-checkered handkerchiefs wound about their heads. As evening approached the work moved more slowly, and the sharp remonstrances of the energetic driver grew more frequent and personal. The moment the sun disapppeared every hoe was shouldered. Some took up from the levee, where they had been lying through the heat of the day, army blouses or stout men's overcoats and drew them on;* others gathered fragments of bark or dry lightwood to kindle their evening fires and balanced them nicely on their heads. In a moment the whole noisy row was filing across the field toward the quarters, joining the plow-gang, pleading for rides on the mules, and looking as much like a caravan crossing the desert as a party of weary farm-laborers.

The drivers were all comparatively intelligent men, and they occupied positions of considerable responsibility. Each plow-driver had charge of about thirty-five mules, was required to see that these were properly fed, to prescribe for them when sick, and to decide when they were too tired too work and must be replaced by fresh ones. It was his duty to have his plowmen out

---

*Nearly all the women on plantations have a great fancy for thus arraying themselves in their husband's coats. Not a few also adopt the pantaloons, half concealing them with the scant cotton skirt.

by sunrise, keep them steadily at work, to change them from part to part of the land to find that in the best condition for plowing at that particular time; to have broken plows repaired at the plantation black-smith shop; and, in general, to get as much plowing done and in as good style as possible. The "hoe-drivers" had larger numbers under their command and more troublesome material to deal with. "Dem women done been a squabblin' 'mong deirselves dis afternoon, so I's harly git any wuck at all out ob 'em." "Dem sucklers ain't jus wuf nuffin at all. 'Bout eight o'clock dey goes off to de quarters, to deir babies, an' I don' nebber see nuffin mo' ob 'em till 'bout eleben. Den de same way in afternoon, till I's sick ob de hull lot." "De 'moody (Bermuda) mighty tough 'long heah, an' I couldn't make dem women put in deir hoes to suit me." "Fanny an' Milly done got sick to-day; an' Sallie's heerd dat her husban's mustered out ob de army, an' she gone up to Natchez to fine him."

On each plantation, as soon as the people reached the quarters, the hoe-drivers began giving out their tickets. Each hand received a white ticket for a full day's work, or a red one for half a day. These they preserved till the end of the month, when they were paid only for the number presented. Under this arrangement the overseer said he had very few sick people on the plantations. Sometimes in fact they went to the fields when really too sick to work, lest they should lose their wages for the day. In unpleasant weather too, when the ground was a little muddy, or when a fine mist was falling, they were far less anxious to quit work than formerly.

The tickets distributed, the women were soon busy

in the quarters getting supper. Meantime the plow-gang had gathered about the entrance to the overseer's part of the house. He'd done promised dem a drink o' whisky, if dey'd finish dat cut, an' dey'd done it. The whisky was soon forth-coming, well-watered. The most drank it down at a gulp, from the glass into which the overseer poured it; others, as their turns came, passed up tin cups to receive their allowance, and went off boasting about "de splennid toddy we's hab to-night." Then came a little trade at the store. Some wanted a pound or two of sugar; others a paper of needles or a bar of soap, or "two bits worth o' candy." Some had money; other offered in payment their tickets, just received; which were taken at their face value. In an hour the trade was all over and the quarters were as silent as a church-yard.

Next morning at four o'clock I was waked by the shrill "Driber's Horn." In a couple of hours it was blown again; and looking from the window, just as the first rays of the sun came across the level field, I saw the women filing out, and the plowmen slowly strolling down to the stables, each with his harness in his hand.* At twelve the horn blew again, and they came in; at half-past one again, and from then until sunset they were in the field.

The overseer said he "couldn't get as many hours of work out of 'em" as in old times; nor was he quite sure that they worked as well during the shorter time they were at it. Still he had never heard of gangs of white laborers of equal size, in which better or more

---

*They even steal one another's corn-husk collars; and so every plowman carries home his harness at night and locks it up in his cabin.

cheerful work was done. On the whole, he was perfectly satisfied with the free-labor system; and, if the water only kept away, was sure of making a hundred thousand dollars net profit this year for the proprietors.

On the two plantations there were one hundred and seventy-six laborers on the pay-roll. The first-class men were paid fifteen dollars per month, first-class women ten dollars, and drivers forty dollars. The wages for the entire number averaged between ten and eleven dollars per month. They were furnished a weekly ration, for each laborer, consisting of

> 4 pounds mess pork.
> 1 peck corn-meal, or
> 8 pounds flour.
> 1 pint molasses.
> 2 ounces salt.

Each family, in addition, had its garden and poultry; and they were always paid for Saturday afternoons, but were given the time for their own work.

The expenses on these plantations for the year could be quite accurately calculated. The items would stand nearly or quite as follows:

60 mules @ (average) $180..		$10,800
175 hands @ $10. pr. month,* wages............................		21,000
SUPPLIES.		
Pork, 182 bbls. @ $29..	$5,278	
Meal,† 442 bbls. @ $5..	2,210	
Molasses, 1,137 gallons @ 70c..............................	796	8,284
Corn for mules, 5,400 bushels @ $1.......................		5,400
Hay for mules, 100 tons @ $30..............................		3,000
Incidentals..		3,000
		$51,484

* The lost time would more than bring it down to this average.

† They mostly took meal, of choice, and to simplify the calculation it alone is counted.

Economical management and the personal supervision of an interested party might undoubtedly reduce these expenses at least ten per cent., but under the loose expenditures of overseers the calculation was none too large. The amount would still be swelled by at least twenty thousand dollars for rent, and two thousand as wages of the overseer, so that the expenses of conducting the plantations for a year might be pretty accurately set down in round numbers at seventy thousand dollars.

With a good season and without overflow, the yield ought to be twelve hundred bales of cotton, worth, say, a hundred dollars per bale. Taking all the risks, therefore, and using this heavy capital, the proprietors were likely, under the most favorable circumstances, to have, at the end of the year, fifty thousand dollars and sixty mules, as their net profit. On other plantations, where they paid less exorbitant rents, they anticipated, of course, larger returns.

CHAPTER XLVIII.

Among the Cotton Plantations—Rations and Ways of Work.

A DAY or two after my visit to the plantations just described, I started on a little horseback trip down the river. I was furnished with letters to a planter, nineteen or twenty miles down, and I supposed that the distance might be easily made in three hours. I left Natchez at two; but the delays at the ferry made it three before I reached the Louisiana side of the river. The February frosts had been keen, but the afternoon was oppressively warm. For miles along the bank of the river the horizon was blue and misty with the columns of smoke from the trash-gangs on the plantations. Here and there an ox-team was passed by the roadside, hauling willow-poles from the river banks to repair the fences. The negroes were at work on every plantation—the plows near the road, the trash-gang further back toward the swamp that everywhere shut in the view. Houses appeared at but rare intervals, not averaging one per mile. But few seemed to be more than the mere lodgings for the overseers. There were no poor whites in this country, from which the aristocratic planters had driven them. Behind or beside each house stretched the unvarying double row of quarters, with the little mud-floored porches in front, and the swarms of little picaninnies tumbling about in the sunshine. Every one had accommodations for at least a hundred negroes. Coveys of quails and broods of pigeons started up with a whir by the roadside; and, occasionally, from the fields came faintly the shout of some plowman to his team. Other sounds they were none—the country seemed almost as silent as the unbroken wilderness. Not a traveler was seen on the whole road.

I had miscalculated the strength of my horse, and nightfall found me six or seven miles from my destination. For some time the road had been leading along the top of a high levee, a little distance from the river. The plantations were very low and partially covered with water. Finally the levee led off directly into the cypress swamp at a point where the land had been thought too low to be worth clearing out. Briars grew over its sides and occasionally stretched across the path; the road was very rough, and to leave it, on either hand, was to ride down the side of the levee into the swamp. Finally the exhausted horse could carry me no further, and I was compelled to dismount and plod slowly along on foot. Now and then the whir of a covey of quails sounded startling in the darkness—on either hand could be heard the rush of ducks and geese in the water. There were deer in the swamps, I had been told, and likewise bears. The latter suggestion was scarcely a pleasant one.

By and by the darkness became less profound on the river side of the levee; and straining my eyes to make out the dimly defined objects, I saw what seemed a two thousand acre plantation, with a large set of negro quarters *outside* the levee. Outside or inside, I was determined to stop there. Starting down the side of the levee I soon found that the ground was swampy. Returning, and following along the beaten road, I presently came directly up to the river—stopped short, in fact, within half-a-dozen feet of its brink. Turning up the bank I started again for the quarters, now more clearly seen. It was no slight disappointment to discover that they were unoccupied! The plantation had been thrown outside the levee, on account of a change in the current of the river, had been abandoned for years, and was under water every spring!

Groping my way tediously back to the road, I started again down the river. Half an hour's walk brought me to a light, glimmering through the open windows of some negro quarters. The blacks showed the way to the house—further back from the levee—and here explicit directions were given for the plantation I was seeking. I had only to go down the river a couple of miles further, then turn off through a gate, follow the road across a little lake and along its bank for a quarter of a mile. All went well till I crossed the lake. Then, near where I supposed the house ought to be, bright lights were shining, and a beaten path, through an open gate led to them, and so I walked half across the plantation to find that the trash-gang had been firing some dead cypress trees, and that, instead of the house, I was near the swamp!

It was after ten o'clock when at last, groping my way among the negro quarters, I reached the double cabin, fronting the street, where the overseer lived. No other person was at home, but the welcome was a hearty one. Fried bacon and corn-bread were speedily served up for supper, and the fatigues of the journey forgotten as the jovial overseer told his experiences in running off slaves to Texas, when the Yankees came, and his disgust, that after all his trouble, the whole work proved useless.

This plantation contained eight hundred acres of land cleared for cotton, besides a thousand or twelve hundred of timber-land, covered with hackberry, cypress, and cotton-wood; a portion of which ran down to the river bank and afforded an excellent site for a wood-yard. Plenty of negroes could be hired to chop wood for a dollar per cord. Half a dollar more would pay for its delivery on the river bank, where steamboats bought all they could get for five dollars per cord—thus affording the proprietor of the wood-yard a net profit of three dollars and a half on every cord.

Less than fifty hands had yet been hired on the plantation; not as many by at least thirty, the overseer said, as were absolutely needed to cultivate the eight hundred acres; but with this inadequate force the work on the plantation was further advanced than on any I had seen. The most cordial good-feeling seemed to exist between the negroes and the overseer. "Him allus good man in de ole slavery times. He allus did jussice to us niggers," said one of them. For twenty years this man had done nothing but oversee negroes. He boasted of having made, one unusually good year, seventeen bales to the hand. Here he expected to make about twelve or thirteen—not less, if the high water did not interfere, than a bale to every acre of the whole eight hundred. The proprietors paid ten thousand dollars for the lease. Twenty thousand dollars would probably pay the running expenses, (including the hire of additional hands, if they could be got,) and the net profit therefore ought to be nearly or quite fifty thousand dollars in a favorable year.

The laborers here went to the fields at daybreak. About eight o'clock all stopped for breakfast, which they had carried with them in their little tin buckets.

Half an hour later they were at work again. At twelve they went to the quarters for dinner; at half-past one they resumed work, and at sunset they could be seen filing back in long noisy rows across the plantation, shouting, singing, and arranging for the evening dance.

They were divided into three gangs: the "hoes, log-rollers, and plows." The plantation had been neglected for the last four years; briars grew everywhere, and the ground was covered with logs. The whole scene, when the laborers were at work, was one of the utmost animation. The overseer kept the three gangs near each other, the hoes ahead, pushing hard behind them the log-rollers, and shouting constantly to the log-rollers to keep out of their way the plowmen. The air was filled with a dense smoke from the burning briars and logs. Moving about among the fires, raking together the trash, chopping the briars, now seizing a brand from a burning heap, and dextrously firing half-a-dozen new ones, then hurrying forward to catch up with the gang, singing, laughing, teasing the log-rollers to "cotch us if you kin," were the short-skirted, black-faced damsels, twenty or twenty-five in number, who composed the trash-gang.

Before the little heaps were half burnt the log-rollers were among them. A stout, black fellow, whisky bottle in hand, gave directions. At least half the gang were women, each armed, like the men, with a formidable handspike. They were very proud of their distinction, and wanted it understood that dey was n't none ob you' triflin' hoe han's; dey was log-rollers, dey was. Selecting the log hardest to be moved, as the center for a heap, the driver shouted, "Now, heah, hurry up dat log dere, and put it on dis side heah!" A dozen hand-spikes were thrust under the log, and every woman's voice shouted, in shrill chorus, "Come up wid de log! come up wid the log!" Sometimes the spikes were thrust under, and the log was lifted bodily, the foreman shouting, "Man agin man dere! gal agin gal! all togedder wid you, if you 'spec any water out o' dis bottle!"

Sometimes, before these heaps were fired, the plows were upon them, every plowman urging his mules almost into a trot, and the driver occasionally shouting, "Git out o' de way, there, you lazy log-rollers, or we plow right ober ye." The land was a loose loam, turning up like an ash-heap; and both negroes and mules seemed to thrive on the hard work.

The overseer rarely left the field. With one leg lazily thrown across the pummel of his saddle, he lounged in his seat, occasionally addressing a mild suggestion to one of the men, or saying to the driver that the other gangs were pressing him pretty close. Then, riding over to the next, he would quietly hint that the trash-gang was getting ahead of them, or that the plows would catch them soon, if they were n't careful. All treated him with the utmost respect. I am satisfied that no Northern laborers, of the same degree of intelligence, ever worked more faithfully, more cheerfully, or with better results.

On the first of April, the overseer told me, he intended to stop plowing and plant the land then prepared. Then he should resume plowing, and keep on plowing and planting till the whole eight hundred acres were taken up. If he could finish it by the middle of May he should feel sure of a good crop. Planting ended, he should go over the land, throwing the earth *away* from the young and tender cotton-plant, with a moldboard plow. The hoes would follow the plows, carefully dressing up the rows, and thinning out the cotton to one stalk for about every eighteen inches. Then fresh scrapings, and plowings, and hoeings, continued, without intermission, till perhaps the middle of July. Then would follow a month of leisure, to be spent making cotton baskets, repairing fences, and preparing the gins. By the middle of August, the lower bolls would be opening, and the pickers would take the field. A couple of days later the gin would be started. From that time until Christmas there would be one constant hurry to pick and gin the crop as it bolled out. Fifty bales a week were the capacity of the gin, and the overseer expected to keep it driven to the utmost. Every Saturday, the cotton baled through the week would be hauled to the river bank and shipped to New Orleans. By the last of August, returns would be coming in from the crop, and from that time the financial battle for the proprietors was over.

A day or two later I rode several miles further down the river, to a plantation of two thousand five hundred acres, one thousand two hundred of cleared land, which had recently been purchased for fifty-six thousand dollars by a Northern man. The house was a comfortable two-story frame, with abundant porches and large windows, looking directly out through the carefully trimmed shrubbery, upon the Mississippi, which flowed scarcely twenty yards from the door-step. At the North, it would have been considered a very proper residence for a substantial farmer owning a couple of hundred acres. On the river-bank stood a curious log structure, built from the fragments of two or three old flat-boats. Here, with genuine Yankee thrift, the new proprietor had established a store to catch the negro trade. Its business was done entirely for cash, and its sales averaged over fifty dollars a day—all made at an average profit of one hundred per. cent. Calicoes, cottonades, denims, shoes, hats, brass jewelry, head handkerchiefs, candy, tobacco, sardines, cheese, and whisky were the great staples. The latter was always watered down at least one-fourth, and the "fine" was kept up by a liberal introduction of red pepper-pods.

The work here did not seem to be progressing so well as at the plantation last visited. The negroes were dissatisfied—why they seemed scarcely able to explain. The new proprietor had not yet acquired their confidence; he had perhaps been unfortunate in not properly yielding on one or two points to their prejudices, and his overseer, with whom he had quarreled, was doing his best to foment the discontent. This overseer, it seemed, had been assigned a room in the house with the family. To the great disgust of a daughter of the proprietor, he brought a negro women with him. She couldn't "stand such goings on under her roof;" and, in the absence of her father, she promptly notified the overseer "to turn out that nigger or leave." The overseer preferred the latter alternative, moved out to the quarters with the woman, and speedily had the negroes in such a dissatisfied state that the proprietor discharged him, drove off a number of the negroes, and went to Georgia for more. Near Eufala he found a number who had formerly belonged to the plantation. The most of them were getting nothing but rations and lodging for their labor; six or eight dollars per month were the highest wages any received, and all were eager to go back to Louisiana, provided they were sure they wouldn't be taken to

Cuba and sold. He had partially convinced them on this point, and he hoped soon to have fifty or sixty fresh laborers, who would enable him to snap his fingers at the discharged overseer and the dissatisfied laborers.

The owner of this plantation, on his discharge from the army two years before, had come down to this country not worth a hundred dollars. He opened a wood-yard, got some fortunate wood contracts with the government accumulated a little money, and the next year leased some plantations. His money was soon exhausted; but, by the aid of dextrous manipulations of his credit and unlimited bragging about the value of his crop, he worried through. His profits were about forty thousand dollars, out of which he owed ten thousand dollars lease, and, perhaps, as much more in small sums for supplies. His creditors, growing impatient, sued him. This suited him exactly; the law's delays were all in his favor; and meantime he took the money and bought this plantation; mortgaged it at once and so borrowed enough to carry him through the year. Thus he was in two years the owner of a property which, before the war, had been valued at two hundred thousand dollars; and with one good crop would be entirely out of debt.

Next day I went to another plantation, not more than a mile or two distant, to witness the Saturday issue of rations. It was a small plantation, of six or eight hundred acres cleared land; but the owner had, as yet, only twenty-five negroes, and did not expect to raise more than three or four hundred bales. He had no overseer, went among the hands himself, supervised their operations, and in his absence trusted mainly to the two or three negroes to whom the rest had been accustomed to look up as leaders.

The little, one-story double cabin stood fronting the double row of quarters. The street was thoroughly cleaned, the quarters all looked neat, (for negro quarters,) and the negroes themselves seemed in the finest spirits. A group of them stood gathered about the door of one of the cabins, which was used as a store-room, with a motley collection of tin buckets, bread-bowls, troughs, old candle-boxes, little bags, and the like, in which to receive "de 'lowance," One of the negroes chopped up the rounds of mess pork, and weighed out four pounds to each, carefully shaving off, with a knife, till the scales were exactly balanced. The meal was measured by the proprietor himself, who had a pleasant word or a joke for every applicant as she approached. Then a negro took a tin cup, and baring his brawny arm to the elbow, dipped down into the molasses barrel, bringing up cup, hand, and wrist clammy with the black, vicous fluid, which was soon daubed over clothes, barrels, and faces promiscuously.

Room was presently made for a wrinkled, white-wooled old auntie, blear-eyed, trembling, and thin-voiced. "Please, massa, can't you gib me little piece ob meat?" and she laughed a low, oily gobble of a laugh, as though she thought her presuming to ask for it rather funny. "Why, auntie, I thought you were so old you did n't eat any now?" "Bress ye, sah, I eats lots, an' wen de cotton come, sah, I picks some for ye. Aint strong 'nuff to pick much, sah, but I picks little for ye, close to de house."

"Massa" handed her a piece of meat, and filled her outstretched apron with flour; and the old woman stepped back into the crowd, her face fairly aglow. A moment afterward, one of the girls said, as she took her flour, "I wants meal dis time; had flour las'." "You g'long!" exclaimed the old woman with unwonted animation, "if you can't take what white folks gibs you, go widout."

"Heah, Lucy, you do n't want none." Thus said the sable meat-chopper to one of the women, young, and, according to negro ideas, pretty. "Jus' trus' me wid your'n, den. You'll be shore I would n' steal it, ef I do n' wan' none." "Lo'd! might jus' 's well frow it 'way 't once. Take you' meat and g'long wid you!" But the beauty stood her ground, pork in one hand, and pail of meal balanced on her head, distributing her dangerous glances around, in a manner manifestly disconcerting to more than one of her admirers.

Nothing could exceed the general good humor. "They're always so," said the owner. "If I had fifty more such hands I'd make a fortune this year; but they really seem to have disappeared from the country." Still he hoped to pick up a few more as the season advanced.

CHAPTER XLIX.

Plantation Negroes—Incidents and Characteristics

THE months of February and March, with a portion of April, I spent mainly on Louisiana and Mississippi plantations, seeking to gain some insight into the workings of the free-labor system on these large estates, and especially to study the various developments of the plantation negro character. It has been popularly supposed that the negroes in the cotton-growing regions of the South-west were, from their isolation in the swamps and their rarer contact with the whites, the most ignorant, degraded, and unfit for freedom of their race. They had escaped the careful observation given to the character of the emancipated slaves along the coast; and, as it seemed, offered therefore a comparatively fresh and inviting field for study.

Whether these plantation negroes would do less or more work now than in a state of slavery, I found to be an unsettled point. Every old slaveholder, I might almost say everybody in the old slaveholding communities, vehemently argued that "niggers wouldn't do more'n half as much, now that the lash was no longer behind them." On the other hand, Northern experimenters told different stories. Some were disgusted with the slowness and stupidity of the negroes; others said all they needed was prompt pay. Give them that, and they would work better than the average of uneducated white laborers.

On three plantations, where I had the opportunity of watching their performance critically at various periods during a couple of months, I was convinced that when they were employed in gangs, under the supervision of an overseer who had the judgment to handle them to advantage, they did as well as any laborers. They seemed, by nature, gregarious. Put one at some task by himself, and there was every probability that he would go to sleep or go fishing. Even in gangs, not half of them could be depended on for steady work, except under the eye of the overseer or driver; but, with his direction, they labored cheerfully and steadily. Doubtless they worked more hours per day while in slavery; but, they were perfectly willing now to work as many hours as any employer ought to ask.

On many plantations they rose half an hour before daybreak, when the horn first sounded. A few minutes before sunrise, the horn sounded again, and they all started for the fields. By sunrise the whole force, nearly one hundred and seventy hands, were at work. At noon they stopped for an hour and a half—then worked till sunset. On others, the first bell rang at four o'clock; at daybreak the second rang, and every hand started for the fields—the wages of the tardy ones being docked. They carried their corn-bread, boiled pork, and greens in little tin buckets, and about eight o'clock all stopped for breakfast. In half an hour the drivers called them to work again, which continued till twelve. Then came an hour and a half's rest, then work again till sundown.

I never saw hands more cheerful or contented than some managed on this last plan were. They had a new plantation, cut out of the swamp, to cultivate. It had eight hundred acres of arable land, nearly the whole of it incumbered with fallen logs. The cypress trees had been "deadened" in 1859 and 1860; during the years of the war, they had fallen, until the place was perfectly covered with them; and the task of rolling the logs and preparing for the plow, was almost as great as that of the original clearing. They had begun this work about the middle of January, with only forty-two hands, little and big. The working force was gradually increased, till in April they had sixty-five. By the first of April they had six hundred and seventy-five acres bedded up and ready for planting. The old estimate was, that each first-class hand should cultivate ten acres. Here were hands, not first class, but men, women, and children, who had under unusually unfavorable circumstances, cleared off and prepared for planting, an average of nearly thirteen acres to the hand. And the overseer, an old Southern one, said he had no doubt at all about being able to cultivate all the cotton he could get planted.

I observed, however, that when he thought they were not getting on fast enough, he always found it necessary to offer some reward in addition to their regular wages, to revive their drooping energies. One day he would promise the plowmen all a drink of whisky, provided they finished a certain "cut" by evening. Then a plug or two of tobacco would be given to the hand who did the best work through the entire day. If they got all the land cleared off in time for planting, they were to quit for a day, go off to the lake across the swamp in a body and have a big fish-fry. Still, the main motive, under the stimulus of which pretty steady work was secured, was always that "at fust ob next month, Mass'r —— (the proprietor) will be 'long wid greenbacks enuff to shingle a house for us."

The house servants seem singularly worthless. The praises of this class of Southern slaves have always been loudly sung by their owners, but the good cooks and rare housekeepers have certainly disappeared. On one plantation which I visited, there resided at the "big house" only the overseer and, for perhaps half of each week, the young proprietor. To keep house for these two men, required the united energies of four able-bodied negresses. One cooked; another assisted her; the third waited on the table and swept the rooms; and the fourth milked the cows—two or three in number—and made the butter! With all this muster of servants, the two much waited-on white men lived no better than the average of Northern day-laborers.

After the new planter had once secured their confidence, nothing seemed more characteristic of the negroes than their constant desire to screw a little higher wages out of him; or, in one way or another, to make him turn over to them his superabundant greenbacks. All regarded him either as an adventurous swindler, without any money at all, or as a Crœsus, made of money. So long as they doubted his ability to pay them, they were suspicious and watchful; captious as to the quality of the flour and meal furnished them; severely critical on the pork, and perfect almanacs as to the approach of pay-day. The crisis passed, supplies abundant, money promptly paid when due, the planter then found himself under constant siege, perpetually approached under covered ways, which infallibly led to the citadel—his pocket.

"Mass'r, I 'se got my own 'pinion ob you," 1 heard one gray-wooled fellow say to his employer, with scrape of foot, tug at cap, and every insinuating means of expressing profoundest respect and regard; "I does n't tink your'm de hardest mass'r in de world; an' all I wants is to hab you 'sidah my case. I 's all 'lone; I 's allus been good niggah. Rain or shine, me an' my hoss am at your service. We hauls de feed for de mules to de lowah place ebery day; and on Saturdays we hauls for Sundays too, kase I 's 'ligious, an' would n't work on Sundays no how. Now, mass'r, I wants you to please 'sidah my case. Does n't you tink dat for dat extra work on Saturday you ought to 'low me anoder day's wages?" and he tugged off his cap again, and gave an extra scrape to the No. 14 shoe which encased his foot.

The facts in his " case " were, that he was employed to drive a wagon from the granary on one place, each day, to the stables on the one below it, both being controlled by one man, who, living at the upper place, preferred to keep all his supplies under his own eye. The old man never handled the grain; it was put in and taken out by others, and his sole duty was to drive this wagon from one place to the other once a day. This work done, he was generally sent to the swamp for a load of wood. But on Saturdays, in consideration of his having two days' supply of grain to haul, he was given no other task. Now the shrewd old fellow proposed to get extra pay for what he thus called extra work.

A sickly young man, on one plantation which I visited in April, had been hired to watch the stables at night; mules not being safe even from the negroes on the place, much less from those roaming about over the country. He could not make a "half hand" in the fields, but, in the hope that good wages would make him faithful, he was engaged at precisely the same rate with the first-class hands, although his work was the easiest, and, during the greater part of the year, the pleasantest on the place. He seemed perfectly satisfied for two or three months; then, suddenly, he discovered that he was working Saturday and Sunday nights extra, and for them must have extra pay. "Did n't you contract to watch those nights as well as the rest?" "Yes." "Did n't you contract to do this work regularly for fifteen dollars a month?" "Yes." "Well, what right have you to charge extra for these two nights, after that bargain?" "Well, it's been mighty cold, sah, nights; but I wanted to watch to 'blige you; but I's sure you pay me extra for workin' when de oder hands do n't work!"

At one place a man who was unable to do field work, had been hired to feed the mules. He made his bargain, and was supposed to be entirely satisfied. At first the mules were fed only at noon and in the evening. After a while, orders were given to feed also in the morning. Straightway Morton presented his claim for extra pay for this extra duty. Soon afterward he had another claim for extra work—throwing in corn to the mules on Sunday! And yet the whole work of this man consisted in putting corn and hay for thirty mules in the troughs, both being delivered to him at the door; and for this he was being paid the same wages as the plowmen!

"We's worked mighty hard for you;" thus said a stout, pleasant-faced negress on an upper-coast plantation to the proprietor, on the occasion of his long-expected visit. "We's cut down de briars, all de briars on de

whole plantation for you, and dey was mighty high
an' tough ; an' we 's all in rags, for de briars done tore
up all our coats,* an' we want you to gib us new
ones."

"But, girls, I 've just paid you off. Now, you ought
to take that money and buy your own clothes ; that 's
the way free laborers do up North, and the world
over." "But we done tore our coats cuttin' down you'
briars, and we 's all rags. Why, if anybody 'd come
along heah you 'd be 'shamed ob us, 'deed you would,
we looks so bad. An' we all wants you to gib us new
coats. Den we fix up Sundays, an' you be mighty
proud o' yo' niggers." This last appeal was irresistible,
and the girls got their " coats," at a cost to the planter
of about two hundred and fifty dollars.†

---

* The Yankee change of the good old English "gown" into "dress,"
has been outdone by the plantation negroes in Louisiana. Instead
of asking for " dresses," they ask for " coats." " What a splendid
coat dat 'ar calico 'd make ! "

† In Charlestown harbor, the spring previous, Admiral Dahlgren
showed our party the plantation book of a heavy coast planter.
He was a devout man, paying tithes and giving God thanks for the
good things of this life. At the end of a successful year's operations he humbly returned thanks to a bountiful Providence, (as it
was duly written down by himself,) for having been blessed to the
extent of a net profit of thirty thousand dollars. Thereupon, in
token of his gratitude, he ordered a distribution of money to every
slave he had—*six and a fourth cents cash to each and every one !*
He had forbidden the slaves wandering about to other plantations; but they wanted to sell their garden vegetables, and so he
established a domestic market. Everything was to be sold at the
house, at the fixed rates which he established. Eggs were to be
bought at one cent per dozen. Chickens were six and one-fourth
cents per dozen, except in the case of a favorite old man, who was
to be paid double price for all he had to sell.

The feeling among the negroes about education varied considerably with the locality.

On the Fish Pond plantation a few soldiers, just discharged, had recently been added to the working force.
The old hands, most of whom had belonged to the
owner of the plantation, and had rarely traveled a
dozen miles from its lines, were disposed to look with
critical eyes upon the new-comers. The latter, in turn,
were very eager to dazzle the "home niggers" with a
display of their acquirements.

"Don't you know figgers?" inquired one of them,
rather pityingly, of the young head-driver; selecting as the time for making his inquiry, an occasion
when a number of girls from another plantation were
making them a visit. The driver had not been at all
satisfied with the questioner's performance in the field.
"No, I does n't pretend to nuffin' more 'n I *does* know,
like some people dat 's lately come to dis plantation.
But I tell you, Dan, if I 'd a had you heah fo' yeah ago,
and you did n't wuck no better 'n you 'm doin' now, I 'd
made figgers on you' back! You miserable, good-for-
nothin' nigger, you done broke more harrers dan you 'm
wuf already, an' you ha' n't wuck two days yet!"

"Wat 's de use ob niggers pretendin' to lurnin?" he
continued, warming with his subject. "Dey 's men on
dis yeah plantation, old 's I am, studyin' ober spellin'-
book, an' makin' b'lieve 's if dey could larn. Wat 's
de use? Wat 'll dey be but niggers wen dey gits
through? Niggers good for nothin' but to wuck in de
fiel' an' make cotton. Can 't make white folks ob you'-
selves, if you *is* free."

"Dere 's dat new boy, Reuben," chimed in one of the
others. "Massa Powell sent me to weigh out his 'lowance. He brag so much 'bout readin' an' edication dat

I try him. I put on tree poun' po'k, an' I say, 'Reub, kin you read?' He say, 'Lord bress ye, did n't ye know I 's edicated nigger?' I say, 'Well, den, read dat figger, an' tell me how much po'k you'm got dar.' He scratch him head, an' look at de figger all roun', an' den he say, 'Jus seben poun' zacly.' Den I say to de po' fool, 'Take you' seben poun' an' go 'long!' Much good *his* larnin' did him! He los' a poun' ob po'k by it, for I was a gwine to gib him fo' poun'!"

I was surprised to find a good deal of this talk among many of the plantation negroes. Wherever old Southern overseers retained the control, and the place was remote from the towns, there was at least an indifference to education, strikingly in contrast with the feverish anxiety for initiation into the mysteries of print, everywhere strikingly manifest among the negroes in cities and along the great lines of travel.

Elsewhere, however, I saw plantations where the negroes asked the proprietors to reserve out of their wages enough to hire a teacher for their children. All were willing to consent to this; those without families as well as the rest. They preferred a white teacher, if possible, but were willing to take one of their own color, if no white one could be obtained.

Even here, the proportion of young men and women who could spell out simple sentences was not more than one or two in a hundred. Men of middle age, often of considerable intelligence, professed their utter inability to learn the alphabet. "'Pears like taint no use for we uns to be tryin' to larn; but ou' chil'n, dey kin do better."

On an extensive Mississippi River plantation, thirty or forty miles below Natchez, which I visited two or

three times in the months of February and March, I
was shown a negro who, in the old times, had been
considered the most vicious and dangerous slave in the
entire neighborhood. His owner, so the neighborhood
gossip ran, had once sent him over to Black River to
be killed; and, at another time, had himself been on
the point of shooting him, but had been persuaded by
his neighbors to try milder measures. Twice, last year,
the overseer had tried to shoot him, but each time the
cap on his revolver had snapped, and before he could
try again the negro had escaped behind the quarters.

"When I came here," said the present overseer, himself a Southern man, who had been an overseer all his
life, "I was warned against him, and told that I had
better drive him off the place; but I liked his looks and
thought I could make a good nigger out of him."

The "boy" walked across the space in front of the
house, as he was speaking, and respectfully lifted his
hat to the overseer. He was a model of muscular
strength, and had a fine intelligent face; though there
were lines about it that spoke of high temper and a
very strong will of his own.

He had now been under the new overseer's management two months. There was no better hand on the
plantation. He had naturally taken the place of foreman of the log-rolling gang; the negroes cheerfully
followed him as a leader, and he was doing splendid
work. There had not been the slighest trouble with
him ; had never been need for the use of a single harsh
word to him. "I believe he'll steal when he gets a
chance," said the overseer; "but 'I'd like to see the
nigger on this or any other plantation that wo n't do
that." In fact, so handsomely had the vicious slave
behaved under the altered conditions of freedom and

kindly confidence, that his wages had been voluntarily increased one-third, and he had once or twice been sent out as a trusty man to try and hire more hands for the plantation.

"There's a proof," said the Northern proprietor who had recently come into possession, "of the evil influences of the old system. A man of any spirit was sure to be driven into revolt by slavery, and then you had a very dangerous nigger. Freedom makes a first-class hand of him."

The case seemed clear and convincing; and, for myself, I was fully satisfied. During the next fortnight I remember often referring to it, in conversations with the old slaveholders, and always, as I thought, with clinching effect. But they all shook their heads, and said they knew that nigger too well to be hoaxed that way.

The next time I visited the plantation there was a manifest commotion among the hands, although they were working steadily and well. "It's all along o' that d—d reformed nigger of ours," growled the overseer. "I'll never give in to the new-fangled notions again. A nigger's a nigger, and you only make a fool of yourself when you try to make anything else out of him!"

It seemed that, the previous Saturday, when the overseer came to give out rations, he discovered that the lock of his "smoke-house" had been tampered with, and that nearly half a barrel of mess pork, (costing, at that time, thirty-four dollars per barrel, delivered,) had been stolen. A little investigation revealed the loss of several gallons of whisky, and of sundry articles, from the store-room. He said little about it, but quietly made some inquiries; saying nothing, however, to or

about the "reformed nigger." But on Monday morning the boy failed to go out to work with the rest.
Being asked the reason, he replied that "the niggers
had been lying on him, saying he had stolen pork and
whisky, and he was n't gwine to stay among no such
set; he was gwine to leab de plantation." The overseer
told him that would be a breach of his contract; but
he said he did n't care, and privately told some of the
hands that "he was n't afraid of the overseer nor of no
other d—d white man arrestin' him!"

An hour or two later, the overseer, on riding out to
the plow-gang, found the fellow sitting there among
them with a loaded gun in his hand. One of the drivers
told him Philos had threatened to kill "two niggers on
dis plantation 'fore he leave."

"I never carried arms in the field afore in my life,"
said the overseer, "but I rode straight back to the
house then, and buckled on a 'Navy-six' under my coat.
I 'spect, if that nigger had stayed there, holding up his
gun, and lookin' so sassy, I 'd a shot him when I got
back; but he suspected something, and put out. At
night, however, the scoundrel came back, and fired off
his gun back of the cabin where one of the drivers
lives. He 's got two guns and a pistol, and the niggers
is all afraid of him as death. One of the men he has
threatened to kill is his own brother-in-law. He 's
hangin' 'round the place somewhar yet, tryin', I suppose, to sneak off his clothes, and get his wife and some
of the other niggers to go with him."

I found, on careful inquiry, that the story was true
in all its details. My model reformed negro had back-
slidden, and proved a sad reprobate. He had been
stealing whisky for weeks, by means of a false key, and
had been selling it at nights and on Sundays, to the

negroes at a wood yard, a few miles further down the river. He was enraged at being found out, and particularly at the negroes whom he suspected of having informed on him.

It is very rarely, indeed, that one negro will expose another. "They think it's taking the part of the white man against their own people," explained a Mississippi overseer. "If, by any chance, some house servant does tell you of the thefts of a hand, it will only be after exacting innumerable promises that you will never, never, on any account, tell how you found it out."

In the case of the backslider, a warrant was at once procured for his arrest on the charge of theft. "The officer told me there was another law, recently passed, under which I could arrest and imprison him for carrying weapons on the plantation without my consent. He appointed me special constable to make the arrest, and promised me that if the boy would agree to go to work, after I'd had him shut up in jail three or four days, he'd waive proceedings; let me take him out and try him, and then arrest him again if he made any trouble. Fact is, this officer's very much like the old provost marshal, last year. You just tell him exactly what you want done, and he'll be very apt to do just about that thing."

The remark may serve to illustrate how laws are administered, amid the difficulties of the present chaotic state of affairs, in most cases, when the subject race is involved.

Hearing of the warrant, the boy ran away. In about three weeks he returned, very defiant, and boasting that no white man could arrest him. He had been to the Bureau, and knew the law; he was armed, and **meant to go** where he pleased. But he was promptly taken, without resistance, before a justice of the peace. Three negro witnesses conclusively established his guilt, and he was committed to jail to await a trial by court, with every prospect of being sent to the penitentiary for a year or two. Among the witnesses against him was one of the men he had threatened to shoot. When Philos was being locked up he called to this man and said:

"Arthur, you know I's allus hated you, and talked 'bout you; but you was right, when you tole me not to git into no sich troubles as dis."

"Philos," ejaculated Arthur, precipitating his words out in shotted volleys, "I allus tole you so. You said, when you come back, dat you'd been to de Bureau—know'd de law—dat no white man could arrest you. I tole you den you didn't know nuffin 'bout law—dat no law 'lowed you to carry on mean."

"Well, I t'ought I did know sumfin 'bout law, den, but I shore, now, I don't."

"Dat's so, Philos; but I tell ye, you'm got in a mighty safe place now, whar you'm got *nuffin in de wo'ld to do but to study law!* Reckon, Philos, by de time you git out you'll be mighty larned nigger 'bout de law! Good-bye, Philos."

"The worst thing about these niggers," explained the justice, "is that they seem to have no conception of their responsibility. That boy, Philos, can't see why a word from his employer isn't enough now to release him, as it would have done while he was a slave. He doesn't comprehend the fact that he has committed an offense against the State, as well as against his master."

"Tol'able well, myself, but I'm not well contented,"

replied one of the best plowmen in the gang, on another plantation, which I visited in March, to the inquiry of the young Northern proprietor, as to how he was getting along.

"Why, what's the matter, Stephen?"

"Sah, I tell you de trufe, I don't git enuff to eat. Matter enuff, dat is, for a man as works hard all day long."

"But, Stephen, you get the same rations with the rest, and the same that your employers gave you all last year."

"Shore, sah, but I nebber had enuff, den, nuther, dough I nebber say nuffin to nobody 'bout it, kase I's not one de talkin' kine."

"Bress you, sah," grinned the plow-driver, who had been listening to the conversation, "he nebber had 'nuff in his life. He'm allus hungry. He's de powerfullest eater I eber did see."

"Dat's fac'. I don't brag on myself, but I kin eat a heap. I's good hand. I plows wid de bestest, and no man nebber pass me. When I hire for man, I do best I kin for him, and take de best care I kin ob his mule; but it mighty hard not to hab enuff to eat."

The difficulty of making an allowance in the weekly issues of rations, for his inordinate appetite, without making the other hands dissatisfied, was explained to him.

"I's got common sense. I kin see dat. But I don't want to work for a man and den have to buy what I eat. To be shore, I got de money, and de chilen do eat a heap; but you don't make no 'lowance for dem, and I don't want to spend de money what I earn by hard work buyin' bread for dem."

A promise of a drink of whisky pacified him. As

we rode off the overseer burst out into a hearty laugh. "Why, do you know now," and his manner indicated that he thought it a capital joke; "do you know—that fellow's just the biggest thief on these plantations! Lor' bless you, how he *can* steal! He not got enough to eat! Well, hog meat must be mighty scarce in all the nigger cabins around him when *he* hasn't got enough! Why, I had to discharge him last year for stealing. It got so bad that the very niggers couldn't stand it. Even Uncle William's piety was disturbed by him. One Sunday morning Uncle William's pig was gone, and he couldn't find hide nor hair of it. He knowed where to hunt, and he pitched into Stephen's cabin. I got down there just then; and Uncle William was a talkin' at him, I tell you. There was some hair there, which Uncle William declared come off his pig; and he wanted to know what that hair was doin' in Stephen's cabin, if Stephen hadn't seen the pig! Nigger meetin' was broke up, that day, with the row. So things kept goin' on till I had to discharge Stephen. He cried like a baby, and begged to be took back, but I wouldn't. Then he went off. Three days later, back comes Stephen with a first-rate mule. He cried and begged so that I let him go to work again, and hired his mule. Three days afterward, who do you think should come along, but a nigger guard a huntin' for Stephen. But that nigger was too sharp for them. They got the mule; but Stephen took for the tall cotton, and nobody saw him for two days. Come to find out, he had gone back into the country, when I turned him off, and had found an old nigger woman on some little patch in the woods plowin' with a mule. He told her that was too hard work for her, and that if she would go to the cabin and get some dinner for him he'd plow for her. Soon as her back was turned, he mounts mule, cuts and runs. Do you think, when I scolded him for it, the nigger said he would n't have stole the mule, but he was afraid I would n't let him come back, and he thought if he brought me a nice mule I might be more favorable to him! That's the kind o' niggers you believe, when they tell you they do n't get enough to eat!" And again the overseer enjoyed his hearty laugh.

A succession of rains kept me shut up on a Louisana cotton plantation for several days, early in April. When Sunday came I accompanied the overseer down to the negro church. It stood at the end of the street, on either side of which were ranged the quarters. It had originally been a double cabin, intended for a couple of slave families, like the rest of the quarters; but the middle partition had been knocked out; and space enough was thus secured to accommodate a much larger congregation than that which we found gathered. But with frugal mind, the worthy overseer had determined not to waste all this valuable room. A couple of beds had accordingly been set up at one end of the cabin, and a negro family with a sleepy-looking baby and one or two grown daughters had this for their home. As you entered you had your choice— you could visit the family or go to church, as you preferred.* At the other end stood the pulpit—a rough platform, fronted by a contrivance which looked like the first bungling effort of a carpenter's apprentice at the manufacture of a rough, pine mantle-piece. Four or five benches in front served for pews; and on either

* Another church, which I found on a cotton plantation in Mississippi, was located above the stable—the staircase leading up to it on the outside, from the barn-yard.

side of the pulpit other benches were ranged, on which gathered the fathers and mothers of this negro Israel. Square holes in the walls, filled with swinging wooden shutters, answered the purpose of windows. Above were the joists, brown with the smoke of many a year, festooned with cobwebs, hung with here and there a string of red-peppers, or a poke of garden herbs "for the ager," and covered with a collection of carefully preserved fishing rods. Against the weather-boarding, which served also instead of ceiling or plastering, were fastened pictures of Grant and Joe Johnson; and near the pulpit was a rough, enlarged copy of Brady's well-known photograph of Mr. Lincoln, with "Tad" standing at his knee, looking over an album. The imaginative copyist however had added a meaningless face, with hair smoothly gummed to the temples, which was supposed to represent Mrs. Lincoln. Directly behind the preacher's head was nailed a New Orleans merchant's advertising almanac-card.

Services were just beginning as we entered. One or two of the headmen bustled about to get chairs for us; the rest continued their singing with less stareing and turning of heads than many a white congregation exhibits over late comers. The women all wore comparatively clean calico dresses; and the heads of all were wrapped in the inevitable checkered and gay-colored handkerchief. Even the preacher's head was bound up in a handkerchief, none too clean, and over this his brass-rimmed spectacles were made secure by means of a white cotton string.

The old fellow, (who was none other than the plantation gardener,) was not one of those who fail to magnify their office. He seemed pleased at the chance to level his broadsides at two white men, and he certainly showed us no mercy. "White men might tink dey could git 'long, because dey was rich; but dey'd find demselves mistaken when damnation and hell-fire was after dem. No, my breddering an' sistering, black an' white, we must all be 'umble. 'Umbleness'll tote us a great many places, whar money won't do us no good. De Lo'd, who knows all our gwines in an' coming out, he'll 'ceive us all at de las', if we behave ou'selves heah. Now, my breddering an' sistering, white an' black, I stand heah for de Lo'd, to say to ebery one ob you heah, be 'umble an' behave you'selves on de yearth, an' you shall hab a crown ob light. Ebery one ob you mus' tote his cross on de yearth, eben as our bressed Master toted his'n."

This was about the average style of the sermon. Part of it was delivered in a quiet, conversational tone; at other times the preacher's voice rose into a prolonged and not unmusical cadence. He was really a good man, and wherever any meaning lurked in his numberless repetitions of cant phrases, picked up from the whites to whom he had listened, it was always a good one. The small audience sat silent and perfectly undemonstrative. The preacher once or twice remarked that there were so few present that he did n't feel much like exhorting; it was hardly worth while to go to much trouble for so few; and finally, with a repetition of this opinion, he told them "dey might sing some if dey wanted to," and took his seat. "D——n the old fellow," whispered the overseer, "he do n't do no retail business, it seems. He wants to save souls by hullsale, or else not at all!"

A young man, wearing the caped, light-blue army overcoat, rose and started a quaint chant. The congregation struck in and sung the line over. The young man chanted another line, and the congregation sang it after him; another was chanted, then sung; then another, and so on. It was exactly the old Scotch fashion of "lining out," except that instead of reading the line which the congregation was to sing, the leader delivered it in the oddest, most uncouth and sense-murdering chant ever conceived. Presently several of the older members joined the young man in the chant; then united with the chorus in thundering over the chanted line again. Meantime, a number of the women began to show signs of an effort to get up hysteric excitement. They drew up their persons to their full hight, swayed back and forth, and right and left, then gave a curious "ducking" motion to the head, bent down, seemed to writhe in their efforts to rise; then drew up and began again. Presently one came marching over toward our side, with eyes nearly shut, an absurdly-affected expression of the ugly black features, grasped my hand with effusion, and squeezed it as if it were a nut she wanted to crack. Then came a squeaking " O-o-oh!" supposed to express unspeakable delight; and she passed to the black man and brother by my side, catching both his hands in the same vice, and going through the same performance. Thus she moved from one to another around the church, while the singing grew fast and furious, and the sisters twisted their bodies about hysterically as they sang, and shouted "glory!" between the lines.

The prayers were made up in about equal proportions of " Oh-a-o-ahs," " O merciful Father," " Ooh-ooh-oohs," profuse snuffling, and wiping of eyes and nostrils, and ludicrously perverted repetitions of the common forms of addressing the Deity, which they had heard among the whites. Many of them seemed almost entirely destitute of any distinct, intelligible meaning. The women furnished a running accompaniment, entirely novel to me. One, a stout negress, with lungs like a blacksmith's bellows, set up a dismal howl through her nose. The rest joined in, in different keys, and the combination furnished a sort of chant, without one word in it, or one effort to articulate a word, which kept pace with, and sometimes drowned out, the prayer.*

Singing and prayer alternated several times. The demeanor of all was earnest; and, so far as the emotions went, there could be no doubt of their sincerity. Finally the preacher rose, announced that on "next Sunday dere would be baptisin', an' all dat was ready for de water mus' be present. On de Sunday followin' dere would be de funeral. Some forty or more had died since de las' one, and he mus' hab deir names now afore de funeral come off. Ef de water wasn't too high, he would hab it outside de levee, at de buryin' groun'; but ef de water was ober dat, dey would try an' git 'mission of Mr. ——, (naming the overseer,) to hab it in front ob de house, for der'd be a great crowd."†

---

* This they call "mourning for their sins, as the angels mourn." The sounds were certainly the reverse of angelic. There are no words in the "mourning;" it is simply a nasal, aggressive, persistent boo-hoo, in chorus, by half the women present. Not a tear is to be seen, and the girls often rise from their knees, and in half an hour are begging the overseer for a drink of whisky.

† When a dead person is interred, they call it simply the "buryin'." After thirty or forty deaths, they have a big meeting and a funeral for the whole of them; thus distributing funeral honors, as the overseer said the preacher did his salvation, "by hullsale." At this time the water was nearly over their burying ground, which was outside the levee.

And with that, he reverently pronounced the benediction; and a few struck up a lively hymn tune, while the rest dispersed to the quarters.

It was very absurd; but, after all, who shall pronounce it valueless? Perhaps they do rise from their knees to steal—even white church members have been known to do the same. Perhaps most of them are too ignorant to comprehend religious matters—but it is on white, not black, shoulders that the sin for their ignorance rests. This very preacher had more than once been dragged from the pulpit and given forty lashes for presuming to repeat passages of the Bible, and talk about them to the slaves.

CHAPTER L.

Further Illustrations of Plantation Negro Character.

I WITNESSED the monthly payments on several large plantations. On one the negroes had never been paid before; their masters having retained control of them till the end of the war. They had been hired about the middle of January, and had worked till the beginning of March, without asking for money. The lessee rode into the quarters and up to the overseer's house, one day at noon, and it was soon whispered among the negroes that they were to be paid that night. Numbers of them, however, had complicated store accounts, and it took the lessee longer to interpret his overseer's imperfect book-keeping than had been expected. The night passed without a word being said to the negroes about payment; they never mentioned it, and next morning were promptly in the fields before sunrise.

The following evening, however, they kept watching about the overseer's house; one and another making some little errand that would excuse him for loitering a few moments by the steps or on the long gallery, and presently all understood that "we's to be paid green-backs, shore enuff."

Finally a table was placed in the door of one of the rooms. The pay-roll, store-book, and some piles of greenbacks and fractional currency were spread out upon it, a couple of candles, fastened to the table by smearing it with melted tallow and dipping the ends in it before it congealed, furnished all the light. A hundred eager eyes watched the proceedings from the doors of the quarters. At last the bell was tapped by one of the drivers. In a moment or two the gallery was covered by the "whole stock of the plantation," (as the overseer expressed it,) men, women and children.

They stood at respectful distance in a circle around the table, and with wide-eyed curiosity awaited developments. The lessee read from the pay-roll the contract, and asked them if they understood it; all said they did. Then he explained that, as they had only worked a couple of weeks in January, he had n't thought it worth while to go to the trouble of a payment for so short a time. Accordingly they were now to be paid for this part of January and for the whole of February. But they were only to be paid half what they had earned. The rest was to be reserved till the end of the year as a security for their faithful fulfillment of their contract. "That's the security on one side. Perhaps, as most of you have n't known me very long, you'd like to know what security you have, on your side that, at the end of the year I'll keep my part of the contract and pay you this money?" They said nothing, but looked as if they *would* like to know. "Well you're going to raise a big crop of cotton, are n't you?" "Yes, *sah*," with emphasis. "Well, the bigger the crop the bigger your security. Every bale of that cotton is yours, till you are paid for your work out of it, and the Freedman's Bureau will see that it pays you."

Then he read over the long pay-roll, told each one how many days he or she had worked, and how much had been earned; how much of this was due now, and how many dollars or cents were to be paid at the end of the year. "Dat's so," occasionally interrupted one in a reflective manner. "I did miss five days, I'd done forgot all 'bout it till you tole me."

Next he read over the charges in the plantation store against a number of them. Then began the payments. Looking out from the lighted doorway into the darkness, one could see the fringe of black faces lining the gallery, their eyes shining as the light from the candles struck upon them. Beyond was blackness and a confused murmur of many whispers; within, the circle advanced one and another to the table to receive the currency rapidly counted out. The lessee carefully explained to each how much there was, and that a similar sum was still due; counted the money, note by note, folded it up, and handed it over. The negro looked with a puzzled air, took the money as if it were fragile glass, and must be handled very carefully or it would be broken, and went off very much with the air one always imagines, the man must have worn who drew the elephant in a raffle.

"Missah ——," exclaimed one, "I done wuck mighty hard fo' you, chop briars and roll logs, and you haint paid me nuffin at all."

"Haven't I? Didn't you get two new dresses, three rings, and a breastpin out of the store?"

"Well, but you don' gib me no money." And it took not a little laborious explanation on the part of the lessee, before the finery-loving young negress could be made to understand that she could n't take up her wages in the store and still draw them in money—could n't both eat her cake and have it.

"Missah ——, how much does you pay me a month?"

"Ten dollars."

"Well, you done gib me, you say, only dollah and six bits."

"Yes, but you've been working only a few days. Don't you know, you've had the chills nearly all the time?"

"Well, but you say you pay me ten dollah a month, and you doesn't do it. Aint you payin' for de month? An' if you is, why don't I git my ten dollah?"

Cases of this sort, however, were rare. Here was a more common one:

"Missah —— doesn't you pay me fifteen dollah a monf?"

"Yes."

"But you aint done gib me a bit o' money."

"No; but how much did you get out of the store, Ben?"

"He didn't git nuffin in de wo'ld 'cept stuff fo' one shirt an' a pair o' boots," interposed his old mother.

"No, auntie, you're mistaken; he got several things for you. Don't you remember having a box of sardines for dinner, a week or two ago?"

The old woman 'peared like she did 'member dat.

"And haven't you had cheese, three or four times?"

Nebber in de wo'ld but onct, she was shore, or most-ways, more 'n twict.

"Now, auntie," said the lessee, improving the occasion after the fashion of the divines, "you have a right to spend your earnings any way you please; you're free. It's none of my business what you do with your money. But if you would let me give you a little advice, I'd tell you all not to waste your money on fish, and candy, and rings, and breastpins, and fine hats. If you will have them, we'll sell them to you, but you had better not buy so freely. Look how Ben. has wasted his money!" And he proceeded to read the following account:

BEN. BROWN,	DR.
To one pair Boots	$7 00
" Mackerel	50
" Sardines	50
" One Ring	1 00
" Shirting	2 00
" Candy	50
" Mackerel	1 00
" Cheese	50
" Two Rings	2 00
" Breastpin and Ear-rings	6 00
" Whisky	1 00
" "	50
" Tobacco	50
" One Ring	1 00
" Two Rings	2 00
" Mackerel	50
" Whisky	50
" Candy	50
" Sardines	50
" Candles	50
" One Ring	1 00
" Hat	2 50
" Tobacco	50
" One Skillet	1 50
" Candy	50
Total	$34 50

As every item of this precious account was read, Ben. nodded his head. Presently the people began to laugh, and the reading ended in a roar. Ben., it seemed, had a good many sweethearts, and the whole plantation knew, better than his old mother did, where the wondrous succession of brass rings had gone. To the girls who wore them, the joke seemed particularly funny, and Ben. got no sympathy in his discomfiture.

About two hundred dollars served to complete the

entire payment for sixty-five hands. Half of them had already been paid all, and more than all, that was due them, from the store. In such cases, the lessee, while giving the overseer strict instructions to credit them no more, unless in cases of absolute need, was very careful to conceal from them the entire amount of their indebtedness. "There's danger of their running off," he argued, "if they knew how deep they had got into us."

One old woman asked for her full wages, saying she wanted to go to another plantation to be nearer her husband. "Don't you know that you contracted with me for a year?" "Don't know nuffin about it. I wants to go 'way." "Haven't you been well treated here?" "Yes." "Well, I'm keeping my part of the contract, and you've got to keep yours. If you don't, I'll send you to jail, that's all."

On another plantation the mode of dealing with the negroes approached nearer the cash basis. Nearly all were well supplied with clothes and other necessaries, when hired, and there was, therefore, no necessity for giving them credit in the plantation store. Tickets were issued for each day's work. If anything was wanted before the end of the month, the tickets were received for goods at their face value; but no goods were sold without payment either in money or tickets.

The payment began in the evening as soon as the day's work was over. The proprietor took his place in the overseer's room. The people gathered on the gallery and clustered about the door. As the names were called, each one entered the room, producing from some cavernous pocket-book or old stocking-foot a handful of tickets. The overseer rapidly counted them, the negro closely watching. Often it was insisted that there ought to be more. In every such case they were at once counted over again, slowly and distinctly. It rarely happened that this did not end the dispute. Sometimes, however, fresh search in some unexplored pocket, or a return to the quarters and examination of the all-concealing bed-clothes, would produce another ticket or two.

The number announced, the proprietor called off the amount earned, and counted out one-half of it, while the overseer wrote an informal due-bill for the other half, and the next name was called, while the slow-motioned negro was gathering up his change and due-bill.

Outside could be heard the grumbling of those who thought they ought to receive more, the chucklings of the better satisfied, the speculations of the unpaid as to how much they would get; and over all, the plans of the women as to what they would buy wid de money, fus' time we's go to Natchez. Sometimes one would be absent when the name was called. The rest shouted it in chorus, and presently the missing negro would come running up, tickets in hand, crying, " Heah me! " "Heah me! "

They seemed to have poor success in keeping the money. At the very payment I have been describing, an old blind carpenter, (who, strangely enough, really earned ten dollars a month, in spite of his blindness, making hoe-handles, plow-handles, and the like,) lost his pocket-book. Next morning it was carefully placed under his door, but the money was all gone, with the exception of an old Confederate five-dollar bill, which had been considerately left behind. The next day the elder of a family of three girls took out her pocket-book, containing the money of all three, from its hiding place in the bed, to buy some candy. She replaced it at once, and went out of the cabin. On her return, a few minutes later, the pocket-book was gone, and the poor girls were twelve dollars poorer.

In general, the girls spent their money almost as soon as they got it. Most of the men were more economical. Some of them had a hundred or more dollars saved up.

The pay roll disclosed some quaint freaks of nomenclature. "They've had the greatest time picking names," said the overseer. "No man thought he was perfectly free unless he had changed his name and taken a family name." "Precious few of 'em," he slily added, "ever took that of their old masters."

One boy was called "'Squire Johnson Brown." It seemed that his mother, "since dis time come," (as they always say when they mean since their emancipation,) had chosen to call herself Brown; and, like a dutiful son, he thought it would be no more than respectable that his last name should be the same as his mother's. But there was a 'Squire Johnson over on Black River, for whom he had a great regard; and, as he had a name to take, he insisted on taking Squire Johnson's. This, however, was quite a minor performance compared with that of another boy, whose name was duly written down, "States Attorney Smith!"

Neither here nor at any point through the regions of the great plantations did I discover any such knowledge of their Northern benefactors as would naturally be evinced in names. There were no Abraham Lincolns among them; no Charles Summers; no Wendell Phillips; or Owen Lovejoys. There were plenty of Chases, but I could not find that any of them knew they bore the same name with the Chief-Justice, or had selected it with the slightest reference to him.

An old man, white-headed, with shrunken eyes and broken voice, came in. "If't please you, sah, I hears as you's ou' new mastah. I's old nigger on plantation, sah, an' I's come to ask you if you'd be so good as to please be so kin' to ole nigger as has allus worked faithful all his days, as to git me a little piece o' groun' to plant co'n and punkins, to help keep me an' ole 'oman?"

"O, yes, uncle, we'll give you a garden."

"But, sah, I's got garden already, what ole mastah gib me, long time ago, and I's allus had. But, mastah, you mus' considah I's got to buy my close now, an' my shoes, an' my hat, an' my ole 'oman's close; an' I wants to make a little meat; an' if you'd be so good as to please let me hab patch of groun' for co'n an' punkins besides."

"How old are you, uncle?"

"Sebenty-five yeah, sah."

"Have you no children who could support you?"

"You's got 'em hired for you, sah. Dere's John, an' Ruthy, an' Milly, an' Jake. But dey's got deir own fam-'lies; an' when man gits ole dey do n't care so much. Sometimes dey gib me piece o' meat, and sometimes dey say dey haint got none for me; den it comes pretty hard on me an' ole 'oman. You gibs me half 'lowance, sah; ef't was n't for dat, I spec we could n't lib 't all."

The South is full of such cases. In most instances, to their credit be it said, the old masters give the worn-out negroes a little land to cultivate and houses to live in; but very often they have no ability to go further. Sometimes the children support their aged parents; sometimes, as here, they plead that they have their own families to maintain, and seem to feel sure that, rather than see them starve, the whites will take care of them.

Northern lessees feel all their notions of conducting business on business principles outraged at the idea of having to support all the old negroes, in addition to hiring the young ones; but, in the main, their feelings get the better of their business habits. The instances are very rare in which old and helpless negroes, deserted by their children and by their former masters, are driven off or left to starve by the new-comers. In this case, the old man was allotted about an acre and a half of land, was furnished a house, and supplied with half rations; all of which was pure charity, as there was no possible way in which he could make any return to the hard-pressed lessee, who had already paid an exorbitant rent (twenty-five dollars per acre) to the old master for the land.

The wife of one of the head-drivers on a Louisiana plantation, had been for some months confined to the house, and most of the time to her bed, by a very curious gangrenous disease, which had attacked one foot. It became necessary, in the opinion of the physicians, as well as of the old woman herself, and of her husband, to amputate the entire foot. "It really *is* necessary in this case," explained the physician privately; "But nine times out of ten, when these niggers will come to you and beg you to cut off a leg or an arm, there is no real need for any operation at all. They have a great notion for having amputations performed; and really, sir, I'm afraid that sometimes our young physicians have been tempted by the fine chance for an instructive operation, to gratify them when they should not."

In many parts of the South, the number of these young physicians is somewhat startling. Young men who felt the desirability of having a profession, although without either necessity or desire for practicing it, have resorted to medicine, as at the North, under similar circumstances, they would have adopted the law. Medicine has been the aristocratic profession.

At the time appointed for the amputation, in the case of the driver's wife, a young gentleman came to see the operation performed. He was the son of a South Carolina rice-planter. For two years he had not heard from his father, and he was very anxious to know whether I had observed the condition of the old homestead on Edisto, when among the Sea Islands, the previous spring. Formerly, he had been a rice-planter himself; but now he had to take up the practice of his profession; and he had thus of late been led to give his attention to some plan for organizing proper medical care for the poor negroes, who now had no kind masters, bound by self-interest, if not by affection, to secure them the best possible attendance. In short— to strip away his delicate circumlocution—he wanted to get a contract on the plantations by which each able-bodied negro would pay him fifty cents a month, (making a net profit of say fifty dollars a month from each plantation,) in return for which he would prescribe for them when they needed anything. He thought that if ten or fifteen plantations would give him such a contract, he would be able to live by it. I thought so too.

Like most South Carolinians he had no difficulty in expressing his political views. As to secession, he supposed it was settled by the argument of force. On that, and on slavery, the only thing the Southern people ought to do was simply to accept the situation. But to whip them back into the Union, and then keep out their representatives till the Northern States had prescribed a rule of suffrage for the South, which they wouldn't adopt themselves, was a subversion of republican principles. "I'd stay forever without representation, first, and let them govern us as territories. But I tell you what our people will do; I say it with shame; but even South Carolinians, of whom I am particularly ashamed, will do it. They will all submit to whatever is required. They'll do whatever Congress says they must; and so our only hope is in the noble and unexpected stand Johnson is taking for us.

"After all," he continued, after a moment's thought, "it's very curious that we should be depending on such a man. I'm glad of his stand, because he's on our side; but what a miserable demagogue he is and always was!"

We waited and waited for the physician in charge of the case, but he broke his engagement completely. When two or three days afterward, he was seen and asked about it, he explained that this young South Carolinian had told him he had been called in as a consulting physician in the case. "I thought it very strange; and I'm very cautious about these consulting physicians with whom I have no acquaintance. I lost a life through one of them once. I always called that death, killing by courtesy; and my conscience won't stand any more of it; so sir, I stayed away."

It seemed that he had once been summoned to amputate the leg of a negro, injured by some accident at the cotton-gin. He found another physician in charge, who was expected to assist him. I asked the fellow to control the circulation while I prepared for the operation, which was to be performed not far from the ankle. D—n the blockhead, sir; what do you suppose

he did? Why, sir, he applied the tourniquet to the
femoral artery almost at the top of the thigh! But
what could I do? I did venture to ask him if he felt
quite sure that would stop the bleeding below the
knee, and he bristled up as if I had insulted him. To
have said any more would have been to have had a
duel on hands with the son of one of our first families,
and to have been ruined in the community whether I
fought him or not. So I had to go ahead and perform the operation. The very first motion of the
knife deluged me with blood! The poor negro bled to
death, of course; and I called it killing by courtesy. I've
done with that sort of thing. I'll perform that operation out there, for it is sadly needed; but you must
keep that 'consulting physician' away. I have nothing
to do with consulting physicians about whom I know
nothing!"

I subsequently witnessed the operation. Three or
four negro women were in the room. The stolidity
with which they watched the carving and bleeding of
their sister's person seemed amazing. Only once did
they manifest the slightest emotion—when the saw
began to grate on the bone. Yet they were kind
enough to the poor sufferer; though I could not resist
the impression that her life or death was a matter of
comparative indifference to them. "Niggers never care
for one another much," said the overseer. Could he be
right? They often manifest abundance of emotion—is
it *so* abundant as to be without depth?

The husband, however, professed great joy. "I's
tuck care o' 'Manda dis long. She done cost me more 'n
tree hundred dollars, but I's spend tree hundred more,
if dey's needed. Nebber you cry 'Manda. I'll watch
you long 's you live, and after you's dead. I's watch

you long's a bone's leff." He gave an account of the origin of the disease:

"One night, she done been hollerin' all de night long. In de morning she git me look at her foot. Juss as I look, she gib a big scream, and out of de little sore on him bottom dere popped de last rattle from de end ob a rattlesnake tail. Den I know what de matter. Did n't I, Mr. Smith?" appealing to the overseer. "Did n't I go straight to you an' tell you some o' dem bad niggers been a conjurin' wid de debbil on my wife? Den I ax you for some whisky dat no man nebber mix no water wid. You gib me some. Den I tuck dat rattle-snake button out o' my wife's foot down to de ribber, an' I conjure on him. Fust I say words ober him. Den I sprinkle whisky, dat dere's nebber been no water in, ober him. Den I sprinkle some whisky in de ribber. Den I frow him in after de whisky. Den I sprinkle more whisky atop of him. An' den I tuck good drink o' whisky, dat dere's nebber been no water in, myself."

But the other negroes conjuring with "de debbil" were too much for poor Charles, whisky and all; and his wife's foot had grown steadily worse. When I first saw her, she was propped up in a chair, screaming every minute or two as if she were in mortal agony, and em-ploying the alternate moments in gnawing at a huge stick of peppermint candy which her husband had brought her. After the operation was performed, she seemed highly pleased, and there was every reason to hope that she would recover.

"She not my wife berry long," explained the driver, with an appearance of actual pride in the announce-ment. "She done been my sweetheart, long afore she been my wife. I had two or tree chil'en by her while she my sweetheart. When my old wife die, de moder of dese gals you see here, I tought dere was no use foolin' 'bout so much, so I sends to de corral where 'Manda was, an' I done hab her ebber since."

In all this he was but a type of the whole class of plantation negroes in Louisiana. I have seen hundreds of such cases. I do not think it too strong an expression (judging from the evidences on every hand, and from the concurrent testimony of all parties, Northerners, Southerners, whites and blacks) to say that, among the old plantation slaves of Louisiana and Mississippi, virtue was absolutely unknown. Neither men nor women had any comprehension of it; nor could I learn that the highest standing in their churches made the slightest difference. Yet who shall deny the Christianizing influences of slavery? Have not doctors of divinity attested it; and do we not know them, that their testimony is true?

In the last days of March I was riding with a Northern lessee of a fine plantation on the Mississippi, over his back land. Sixteen double plows and a gang of fifty hoes were rapidly diminishing the distance between the land "bedded up, ready for cotton-planting," and the swamp at which their labors were to terminate. The field resounded with the ringing snatches of song from the merry women in the hoe-gang, and with the cries of the plowmen: "Git up, Mule!" "You, Bully, I say, whar you gwine to!" "Mule, didn't I tell ye, las' week, I'd thrash you if you sarve me dat trick agin!" "Now, Mule, don' you fool wid me any more!" "Git up, Morgan, you heifer you!"

The fiery-red clouds which marked the sun's place, had sunk till they were casting their shadows through the swaying moss on the cypress in the swamp, and the overseer was just riding over from the hoe-gang to tell the plowmen to turn out for the night. A stout, broad-faced women, big enough and strong enough to knock down almost any man on the plantation, came stalking up to the proprietor, as he lounged in the saddle, with his right leg thrown over his horse's neck, watching the last labors of the day:

"If you please, sah, I's a good han' as everybody know, an' I'll go farder, an' do cleaner dan any woman on dis place; an' I ax ob you juss one favor; an' I want you, sah, fur to please fur to grant it; an' I'll be mightily obleged to you."

"What is it, Aunt Susan? I know you're a good hand—none better."

"Dat's so, sah. You set me to work by myself an' you'll be 'sprised. I's do more wuck one day dan you spec from any tree women you got on de plantation. I allus good nigger, an' I wucks faithful fur you allus. An' de favor what I ax of you, an' I wan' you to please fur to grant it, is dat you let my daughter Maria, heah, come home to me from your upper place, an' stay heah wid me, her mudder."

"Why, auntie, she's Jasper's wife. You don't want to take her away from Jasper. He's one of our drivers, and one of the smartest men on the upper place."

"Well, I dunno 'bout dat. I tought him smart too; but Jasper done beat my Maria hisself, an' dat wat I don' think he do right. But to-day de women up dere, fur I tell you de trufe, dey all hate my Maria. You don' know dem niggers as I knows 'em. 'Fore God, dere aint nuffin in dis wo'ld, as God is my helper, so mean as a mean nigger. I know dem Scotland niggers. Dey's a mighty mean set; and dey's all togedder 'gainst my Maria. To-day at noon, you had Jasper away, and dem women know'd it. So dey tole lie an' sed Maria done tore up Flora's dresses; an' dey gits around her, an' double-teams on her an' beats her mos' to death; an' I wants you, sah, if you please, sah, to let Maria come down from dat mean upper place, an' stay heah wid me."

"What! and leave Jasper?"

"Dunno nuffin 'bout Jasper. Reckon if he care much for her, he can come and see her'n; if he do n' nobody 'll care. He can come or stay 'way, jus' as he please."

The girl, Maria, stoutly confirmed her mother's story. "Dey all done double-team on her, an' beat her mos' to deff. Ef Jasper 'd been dere, dey would n't 've done it, but dey know'd Jasper was gone." She was altogether the prettiest girl on either of the plantations, with regular and really quite expressive features, small hands and feet, and a well-formed person. Withal, she was as black as jet.

"De trufe is, sah, she won' tell you, but I will. Jasper done been runnin' after oder women up dere too much, an' dat 's de reason dey hates Maria. Jasper's mammy, she 's agin Maria, an' de pore chile haint a fren on de whole mean place, an' I wish you would *please* let her come down an' stay wid me. Dey try to poison her las' yeah, an' now dey try beat her to deff. But *please* let her come to her mammy, an' I 's take care ob her!" And she shook her mighty fist in earnest of the way she meant to do it.

It was finally arranged that she should bring Maria back to the upper place, (from which she had run away after the quarrel at noon,) that Jasper should be called in, and the affair arranged in any way they could agree upon.

So, by seven o'clock in the evening, up they came, sure enough. Meantime it had been ascertained that the girl had really slipped into the house of Flora Aitch, of whom she was particularly jealous, and had torn all her fine dresses. Flora was in high dudgeon, swore she would strip dat Maria naked 'fore God an' man but she'd have pay or revenge. Jasper, too, had been consulted. He said Maria was lazy, and he had been compelled to whip her several times; but he would have got along well enough if it had not been for that sneaking, meddling mother-in-law. Altogether, it was very much such a complication as will break out some-times even in the social relations of the "master-race."

The proprietor was by this time pretty well broken in. He had become used to a great many droll per-formances, and divorcing a married couple seemed about as easy to do as anything else.

"Well, are you all satisfied to quit? Jasper, what do you say?"

"I says dey do jus' as dey please. Dey did n't 'suit me fust, an' I hab no'ting to do wid it last. M'ria's mammy done treat me like dog all de time. If she want to take M'ria 'way, she can do it. I 's nuffin to say."

"Maria, you said, out in the field, you loved Jasper dearly. Do you want to leave him?"

"So I does lub Jasper. But I do n' wan' dem women to double-team on me, an' beat me when he 'way."

"But do you want to leave him, and go to live with your mother again?"

"No use axin' her," interrupted Jasper angrily. "Ax dat 'oman dere, her mudder. She got all de say, an' done hab it ebber sence I had her daughter."

"Yes, you mean t'ing; an' you beat my chile, an' run off from her arter oder women."

"Dat not true. I nebber done nuffin ob de sort, neb-ber; but you done keep tellin' pack lies on me all de time."

By this time both were talking at once, at the highest pitch of their voices, and gesticulating with correspond-ing violence. The poor girl stood between them, her hands meekly clasped together, awaiting the result of the quarrel. The overseer looked on with a contemptuous smile, "he'd seen such rows among niggers all his life;" and three or four women—with the curiosity said to be occasionally evinced by some of their sex—had slipped in the room to watch the contest.

The proprietor quietly waited for one or other of the parties to get out of breath. Each had a decided dis-position to "get into the wool," of the other, but the pres-ence of white folks prevented. At last Aunt Susan's tones could be made out amid the din:

"You went off wid Flora Aitch, you good-for-nothin' nigger! I was dar, dough you didn't know it! I seed you! Den w'en you cum back to your wife, w'y didn't you make much ob her, an' try to make up? But, no! you goes to wuck an' beats her!"

"Ob co'se I beats her, kase she need it; I allus will! Who'd hab a wife ef he didn't beat her w'en she didn't behave herself? But I allus treats M'ria well, an' you knows it, an' so does my mammy."

"I do n' care nuffin 'bout your beatin' her w'en she deserve it, but w'en you go off after oder women, you no business to come back an' beat her."

And on that rock they split. Jasper maintained the indefeasible right of a husband to flog his wife, and the mother, while admitting the general principle, insisted that there ought to be exceptions.

"Well, I'll settle this very soon," said the proprietor

at last. "Aunt Susan, take Maria down with you. I hold you responsible for making her work as much as Jasper did."

"T'ank you berry much, sah!" And out they went, divorced by this summary process, and apparently all the better friends for it.

But in the quarters there was soon fresh uproar. They had gone to Jasper's cabin to get Maria's clothes, and had here encountered Jasper's "mammy." The two old women began storming at once, and the full vocabulary of negro billingsgate rang through the entire quarters. A crowd collected about the door, and in a moment Flora Aitch appeared, rampant in her demands for pay for her torn dresses, "afore dat sneak-in' gal carries her rags 'way from heah!" "Or I'll strip you," she yelled at the open door, "'fore God! I's strip you naked's soon's you set your dirty foot out-side. I's pound you! I's cut you up! I's eat you blood-raw! I's mad, I is, an' I's do anyt'ing, if you don' pay me for dem tore dresses!"

The calmer negresses approved the justice of Flora's complaint. "She ought to be made to pay for dem." "It ought to be tuck out ob her wages." "If 't was my dresses she done tore, she would n' git off so easy." Nobody seemed to think anything of Flora's alleged criminality with Jasper. Maria's provocation to the offense was as nothing. It was a mere matter-of-course; "but dem tore dresses was a burnin' shame."

At last Maria's effects were all bundled up, and she her mother appeared at the door. Flora was by this time quite composed, especially as she saw the overseer near, and ready to prevent blows. "Dere she come, a totin' her rags. Leb her go. She done brought nuffin but rags when she come heah, an' she got nuffin but rags to take away, 'cept what Jasper fool enough to gib her. But she pay me yet for dem tore dresses, or I eat her blood." It was hinted by some of the peaceably disposed that the women might slip down the road, between the two plantations, and waylay Maria. Accordingly the overseer, followed rather sulkily by Jasper, accompanied them down to the "line ditch."

"Well, dat's breakin' up mighty easy," said one of the women. "Lo'd help me, *I'd* make more fuss 'fore *my* husband should leave me. I'd hold on to him tight, I would. I'd tear him coat all off ob him, any way, 'fore he git off."

"Dat would n't help you none. I's smarter'n dat," said another. "I'd my man afore white man up to Natchez; an' I done got paper to hole him. Jus' lef him leab me if he dar'; I take dat paper to de provo', an' he go to jail, or he come back an' lib wid his wife, me." She had procured a marriage certificate. The most laughed at her; said that would n't keep a man, if he wanted to go, and that the best thing was to get somebody else.

"Tell Jasper come and see me," said Maria to the overseer, as they parted. "If he do n't, I'll go back an' see him."

"Dat won't do her no good," growled Jasper, when he heard it. "I's glad to git rid ob her, an' she never need come back to me. I won't hab her no more."

"Pshaw, they'll be better friends than ever in a month. Jasper will get another wife now, and have Maria for his sweetheart." Thus said the practical overseer.

And so ended the new proprietor's first divorce case. It may serve to give an insight into some of "our domestic relations."

CHAPTER LI.

Payments, Strikes, and other Illustrations of Plantation Negro
Character.

On one of the "best-stocked" plantations that I visited in Louisiana, I witnessed, in March, a "strike" of
the entire force. It was a curious illustration, at once
of the suspicions and the docility of the blacks.

The negroes had been hired by a Southern agent,
who had formerly acted as factor for the plantation.
These gentlemen are never likely to fail in magnifying
their offices; and in this particular case it happened
that the agent left very distinctly upon the minds of the
negroes the impression that he was hiring them on his
own account. When, therefore, a month or two later,
the proprietor went out and assumed charge, they became suspicious that there was something wrong. If
they had hired themselves to the old factor, they did n't
see why this new man was ordering them around, unless, indeed, he had bought them of the factor, which
looked to them too much like the old order of things.
Not one word of this, however, reached the ears of the
proprietor. Before him all was respectful obedience
and industry.

It happened that some little difficulty occurred in
procuring the large amount of fractional currency
needed to pay them off; and pay-day came and passed
before it was obtained. The negroes had never men-

tioned payment to the proprietor. He asked the overseer, who replied that probably they would never know
it was the beginning of a new month, unless he told
them, and that therefore it was best to say nothing
about the payment till the money came up from New
Orleans.

One afternoon, a day or two later, the proprietor
spent in the field with the laborers. Riding up among
the plow-gang, he dismounted, talked with the plowmen about the best way of working, took hold of one
of the plows himself, and plowed for some little distance. Everybody seemed cheerful. Going over to the
trash-gang, he found there the same state of feeling;
and after mingling with them till nearly sun-down, he
returned to the house without the remotest suspicion
of any latent discontent; or, indeed, as he said afterward, without having himself once thought of the deferred payment.

Next morning the overseer came dashing up to the
house, before breakfast, with the alarming news that
"the hands were on a strike; declared that they did n't
hire with the man who was now on the plantation, that
he had n't paid them, and they would n't work for him."
Not one, he said, would leave the quarters; and they
were complaining and plotting among themselves at a
great rate. The proprietor took the matter coolly, and
acted on a shrewd estimate of human nature. Fortunately for him, the house was, in this case, some distance from the quarters. Directing the overseer to
hurry off to the Freedman's Bureau and bring down
the agent, he quietly resumed his easy chair and newspaper. The mules had all been taken from the plowmen as soon as they refused to work, and brought up

to the house. They could not go to work, therefore, without asking permission.

The negroes expected to see the proprietor down at the quarters the moment he heard of their action. He had peremptorily refused to give them an acre of land apiece, to plant in cotton; and their plan was to refuse now to work till he promised them this land, and satisfied them about the payments. But hour after hour passed, and no proprietor was seen. Growing uneasy, they sent out scouts, who speedily returned with the news that he was reading his paper on the front gallery, just as if nothing had happened. Manifestly, he was not alarmed, which greatly disappointed them; and was waiting for something or somebody, which might be cause of alarm to *them*. In short, instead of being masters of the situation, they were suddenly eager to get out of a scrape, the outlet from which began to look very uncertain. By-and-by, they sent the plow-driver up to the house to ask if they could have the mules again. The proprietor told him "not just at present;" and added that after a while he should go down to the quarters. Meantime no person must on any account go to work.

About twelve o'clock the overseer returned with the agent of the Freedman's Bureau, a one-armed soldier from the Army of the Potomac. They rode down to the quarters where the whole force was gathered, uneasily waiting for developments. He asked what was the matter.

"We's not been paid di's monf."

"Did you ask for your pay?"

' N-n-no, sah."

"Did you make any inquiry whatever about it, to find out why you were n't paid?"

"N-n-no, sah."

"Did n't you have plenty of chance to ask? Was n't Mr. —— out among you all yesterday afternoon? Why didn't you ask him whether it was n't time for your payment?"

"Well, sah, we dono Missah ——; we hired ou'selves to Missah ——, (naming the New Orleans factor,) and we's afeard we git no money. We nebber heern o' dis man."

The agent read over their contract; and explained to them how, being busy, the proprietor had simply sent an agent to attend to the business for him. All professed themselves satisfied at once, save one lank, shriveled, oldish-young fellow, who said, in a very insolent way, that "He'd done been cheated las' yeah, and he wanted his money now, straight down. He was as good as any other man; but tree o' four time now dis yeah new man, wat pretended to be boss had passed him in de fiel' without ever lookin' at him, much less speakin' to him fren'ly-like; and he was'n' agoin' to stand no sich ways." The agent sharply rebuked him for such language; and finally told him that he had already broken his contract, by refusing to work without sufficient cause, and that if he gave a particle more trouble, he would arrest him for breach of contract, and throw him into jail. The rest seemed ashamed of his manner. As it subsequently appeared, he had been the leader in the whole matter. The plowmen had gone to the stable in the morning, as usual, for their mules. This fellow met them there, persuaded them that they were going to be cheated out of their money, and induced them to return to the quarters. Several of them wanted to go to work; and took good care to inform the proprietor that, "Dey did n't want to quit, but dere was no use in deir wuckin' by demselves, cause de rest 'd say dey was a turnin' gin deir own color an' a sidin' wid de wite folks."

By one o'clock, half an hour earlier than the required time, every man, woman, and child of the working force was in the field. Since then there has not been the slightest trouble on the plantation.

In all such cases the Freedman's Bureau seemed invaluable. The negroes had confidence in its officers; and, in general, obeyed them implicitly. I knew that but for this very agent not less than a dozen heavy planters would have been compelled to suspend operations. All availed themselves of his services. Rebel generals, and men whose families carefully stepped aside into the street lest they should pass under the United States flag, were equally ready to call on the agent on the occasion of the slightest misunderstanding with their negroes. His authority was never disputed.

Some negroes on a plantation which I visited in February, were determined to wheedle or extort permission from the new lessee to plant cotton on their own account. There were about forty men on the plantation, each one of whom insisted upon at least an acre of land for this purpose, besides his half acre for a garden, and an acre more for corn and pumpkins. One Saturday afternoon, when they were up in Natchez, they met the lessee on the streets, and at once began preferring their claims.

"Boys," said he, "I have never thought of the matter at all. I don't know how much land I could spare you; and I don't know whether there would be objections to your growing cotton for yourselves or not.

I'll look into the matter; and the first time I'm down there will give you my conclusion about it."

"No, sah; one time's juss as good as anoder You can tell us now juss as well's any time."

"Can't you wait till I look into the matter?"

"No : you can tell us juss as well now's two weeks later. Ob co'se you'm got de lan' dar, an' you can gib it well's not."

"You won't wait for an answer then?"

"No, sah; we wants it right off."

They thought they were sure of it, and determined to strike while the iron was hot.

"You must have an answer right off?"

"Yes, sah."

"Very well. Here it is then. NO!" And without another word he walked off and left them. His overseer had been watching the affair. "If you'd a yielded an inch to 'em then," he said, "you'd a been pestered and run over by 'em all season. 'S long 's they think they can browbeat you into- givin' 'em things, they'll do it; an' if you'd a let 'em plant cotton, every acre they'd a had in would a brought three or four bales. They'd a picked all over your fiel' at night to get their cotton out."

One Sunday, a week or two later, the lessee was passing about among the quarters. The men gathered around him, and one of them introduced the cotton-planting question again.

"Berry, wasn't it you that spoke to me about this, up in Natchez, the other day?"

"Yes, sah, you said you'd tink about it."

"So I did; but you refused to let me. Didn't you tell me you must have an answer right off?"

"Y-yas, sah; but may be, if you'd tink 'bout it, it'd be better for us."

"Did n't you say though that you must have an answer right off?"

"Y-yas, but"——

"*Stop!* Did n't you get your answer right off?"

"Yas, but"——

"*Stop!* You got it. Well, I always keep my word. If you had waited, I might have given a different answer; but you would n't wait so you got your answer; and it is all the answer your going to get."

Meantime the crowd was chuckling at the discomfiture of Berry. It did n't seem to concern them so much that they were losing their case, as it amused them to see how Berry had entrapped himself. Every time he attempted to renew the discussion, the lessee stopped him with the reminder that he had demanded an answer in Natchez, and had got it; and each time the laughter of the crowd at their own champion grew more uproarious.

While this was going on in the street between the quarters, I stepped into one of the cabins. Stretched out on a bench lay the corpse of an old man; for many years the head driver on this very plantation. His head was partially covered; the body was rudely wrapped in cotton cloth; and over his stomach was placed a delf saucer, full of coarse salt.

"Dat's to keep him from swellin' 'fore we bury him," explained the bereaved wife; who, with a house-full of people looking on, was engaged in dressing herself for the funeral. Her sick baby was in the hands of another negress—its feverish and parched little head absolutely inside the chimney, in which a great fire was blazing. The woman said they had made so much noise last night, after the old man died, that the child had got no sleep. "Reckon you'd make noise too, ef you los' you' husban'. Husban's ain't picked up ebery day. Dey's plenty ob men you can hab, but taint ebery day you can git a good husban'."

In the afternoon they buried him. The rough board coffin was lifted into a cart, to which one of the plantation mules was attached. A great crowd, composed of negroes from three or four plantations followed, singing a hymn in mournful, minor chords that, rendered in their wonderfully musical voices, seemed at a little distance almost equal to the finest performance of the "Dead March," in Saul. The grave was in the plantation burying-ground, in the common outside the levee. It was only about four feet deep; yet it seemed half-full of water. A lusty young fellow rolled up his pantaloons, jumped down into the grave and vigorously baled out for ten minutes. Even then the coffin sank out of sight, and the little clods which each one hastened to throw in upon it only fell, with a splash, into the muddy water. "Dis is de length an' breadth of what we's all a comin' to," began the old preacher; and for a few moments he continued in the most sensible strain I had heard from any one at any of their religious exercises. Then came more singing, while the grave was filled up; and then they all started back, chatting and laughing as they went.

The passion for whisky is universal. I never saw man, woman, or child, reckless young scapegrace, or sanctimonious old preacher among them, who would refuse it; and the most had no hesitancy in begging it whenever they could. Many of them spent half their earnings buying whisky. That sold on the plantation was always watered down at least one-fourth. Perhaps it was owing to this fact, though it seemed rather an evidence of unexpected powers of self-restraint, that so few were to be seen intoxicated.

During the two or three months in which I was among them, seeing scores and sometimes hundreds in a day, I saw but one man absolutely drunk. He had bought a quart of whisky, one Saturday night, at a low liquor shop in Natchez. Next morning early he attacked it, and in about an hour the whisky and he were used up together. Hearing an unusual noise in the quarters, I walked down that way and found the plow-driver and the overseer both trying to quiet Horace. He was unable to stand alone, but he contrived to do a vast deal of shouting. The driver said, "Horace, don't make so much noise; don't you see the overseer?" He looked around, as if surprised at learning it.

"Boss, is dat you?"

"Yes."

"Boss, I's drunk; boss, I's 'shamed o' myself; but I's drunk! I 'sarve good w'ipping. Boss; boss, s-s-slap me in de face, boss."

The overseer did not seem much disposed to administer the "slapping;" but Horace kept repeating, with a drunken man's persistency, "slap me in de face, boss; please, boss." Finally the overseer did give him a ringing cuff on the ear. Horace jerked off his cap, and ducked down his head with great respect, saying, "T'ank you, boss." Then, grinning his maudlin smile on the overseer, he threw open his arms as if to embrace him, and exclaimed, "*Now, kiss me, boss!*"

Next morning Horace was at work with the rest; and, though he has bought many quarts of whisky, he has never been drunk since.

On one occasion I saw a novel example of the difficulties that sometimes occur in the best regulated plantations. On this one, there were no better plowmen
than Alfred and Moses. Each, however, had a young
and pretty (i. e. jet black and regularly-featured) wife.
The women were disposed to attract all the admiration
they could, and the boys grew very jealous. Several
times they gave their wives sound beatings; but this
did 'nt seem to reach the root of the complaint. In their
turn the wives grew jealous, doubtless not without ample cause, and not being able to beat their husbands,
the did the next best thing, and attacked their husbands' "sweethearts." In such encounters they came
out second best more than once.

Finally they resolved that "Dey was mighty mean
niggers on dis plantation, an' we 's gwine to leave it."
Accordingly next morning neither they nor their husbands appeared in the field. The drivers promptly reported the facts, and the overseer sent down to their
cabins to see what was the matter. Word was brought
back that they could 'nt get along wid de niggers, an'
they was gwine to leab. They were at once ordered to
come up and explain themselves; and, in a few moments,
all four made their appearance. They had no complaints to make; they were well-fed and lodged,
promptly-paid, kindly treated.

"We likes you fus-rate, Missah, and we 's be glad to
stay wid you, but dese niggers is all de time a quarrel-
in' an' a fightin' wid us; dey aint like folks at all;
dey 's mean, low-down niggers. We 's nebber been
used to 'sociate wid such; we was n' raised to it, an '
we can't stand it no longer. We 's mighty sorry to leab
you; but we 's a gwine 'way." Thus said the women.
The boys wanted to stay; but if their wives went they

would have to go with them. "Do n't you know that we entered into a contract at the first of the year?"

They said they did.

"Suppose I should refuse to keep my part of it? I owe you now one-half your wages for the last three months. Suppose I should tell you that some of the white folks around here were very mean, and so I would n't pay you?"

They thought he 'd nebber do nuffin o' dat sort.

"Well, then; if I have to keep my side of the contract you 'll have to keep yours. You bargained to work here for a year. If you can prove that I have ill-treated you, you can get off. If you can't prove that, you've got to go to work and keep at it through the year, or go to jail."

"Well, we 's go to jail, den. Dat aint nuffin bad. I 'spec eberbody goes to jail sometimes. I 'spec you been dere you'self, lots o' times, Missah ——."

A house servant was called, furnished a revolver, and told to take the four at once to the agent of the Freedman's Bureau. They repeated to him the same story. They had no complaints to make; but "dey was mighty mean niggers on dat plantation, an' dey would n't wuck dere." The agent talked to them a few moments; then sent the two women off to jail. They went singing camp-meeting tunes, bidding good-by to their friends with great ostentation, and putting the bravest possible face on it. But when they found that their husbands were to occupy a separate cell, their courage forsook them. Meantime their husbands were begging permission to go back to work. After a good lecture to them, the agent finally consented. Thereupon they began begging to have their wives let out.

"We 's make 'em wuck. If dey do n't, we 's whip 'em

good. You juss try us. Please, Missah Cap'en, please do. We's whip 'em mighty hard, an' make 'em wuck."

Finally, on these conditions, the women were released and turned over to their husbands. Whether they have been whipped much or not has not appeared; but it is certain that they have given the planter no further trouble.

The men all claim this privilege to beat their wives, and the women freely concede it. In fact they seem to have less affection for a man, unless he occasionally establishes his superiority by whipping them. The men actually believe that a woman loves her husband all the better for an occasional beating; and certainly the facts would seem to warrant their theory. I have known cases in which the whole force was aroused at night by the noise in some cabin, where a man was beating his wife—she resisting, screaming, threatening, and finally seizing a knife and rushing after him. Next morning I have seen such couples as loving and bright as though their honeymoon was just beginning.

Sometimes, however, their quarrels become serious. I saw one case in which an overseer was aroused in the night by a repentant husband, who said he'd been whipping his wife a little and he was afeard he'd a most done killed her. She was badly bruised, and for a week or more she required medical attention. In another case, on the same plantation, a man's wife in a fit of jealousy attacked his sweetheart. The latter proved the stronger, and absolutely cut the wife's head open with a hoe, so that for weeks she was unable to go into the field. But, in the main, they are surprisingly orderly, and cases of serious violence among them are quite rare.

CHAPTER LII.

Labor Experiments and Prospects.

The officers of a negro regiment at Natchez spent the month of March in mustering it out of the service. First the muster-out rolls gave interminable delays; then every body waited for the mustering officer; then on the paymaster; and, meantime, the camp was inundated by a flood of planters and speculators seeking to contract for hands.

One Surgeon Dayton, late of our volunteer service, son of the late United States Minister to France, had leased a plantation over on Black River. He wanted hands badly, but they would n't leave the Mississippi River. And the truth was, he did n't blame them very greatly. All his neighbors were the old set; mad at him as a Northerner, and mad at the negroes as freedmen. It was n't very pleasant for him and he supposed it would n't be very pleasant for the negroes. But, nevertheless, he must have some hands if he could get them; and he was trying to get an influential sergeant who would be able to carry a dozen or two wherever he went.

Colonel Wallace, late of an Illinois cavalry regiment,* was another. He wanted hands for some plantation in which he was interested, but he had about made up his

---

* Brother to General W. H. L. Wallace, whose death, while gallantly leading his division at Pittsburg Landing, was so widely lamented.

mind that it would cost more than they were worth, to get them.

"Fact is, gentlemen," I heard an officer wearing the United States uniform say to planters, asking about the chances for hands, when the regiment was disbanded; "Fact is, you had better make your bargains with us than with the niggers. We control 'em; and we do'nt mean to take 'em to anybody's plantation without being paid for it." And, in truth, quite a number of officers were bargaining all the time with the negro-seeking planters for their valuable influence. Some insisted on a considerable share of the crop in return for taking a specified number of negroes to the place. Others preferred a fixed salary of two, three, or indeed as high as five or six thousand dollars a year, for their services—not as overseers, for they knew absolutely nothing of cotton culture—but simply in preserving order on the plantations and retaining the confidence of the negro.* After making their own bargain on the most favorable terms they could secure, it became their duty to persuade the negroes that this was the identical place they had been looking for, all the time, in their search for a good home.

In most cases they knew nothing whatever about the homes which they thus recommended; had never seen them, and had never heard of the proprietors until they proved themselves adventurers by making these extravagant offers. In other cases they knew that these men were dishonest and unprincipled; and

* "I told a nigger officer," said a very consequential planter in the vicinity of Jackson, Mississippi, to me in November, 1865, "that I'd give him thirty dollars a month just to stay on my plantation and wear his uniform. The fellow did it, and I'm havin' no trouble with my niggers. They're afraid of the shoulder-straps."

yet they encouraged their confiding subordinates to bind themselves to such men for a year, in remote regions, where there was little hope for protection from the Freedman's Bureau or from civil officers. "Why didn't you warn the sergeant against that man with whom he has contracted?" said the colonel of the regiment, one day to the adjutant. "You had yourself found that the man didn't keep his promises, and couldn't be depended on." The adjutant blushed, stammered, and explained: "I expect to stay in this country myself, and I didn't want to be making enemies of such men!"

This flunkeyism of Northern men, who "expected to stay in this country and didn't want to make enemies," was manifest everywhere. For a genuine toady, commend me to a Northern adventurer, or "runner," in the cotton-growing regions. Through the winter of 1865-'66, the South was full of them, looking for cotton-lands, soliciting custom for Northern business houses, collecting old debts. They never spoke of Rebels, but with great caution called them Confederates. The National armies became, in their mouths, "the Federals." They were always profound admirers of General Lee, the "second Washington of Virginia;" they grew enthusiastic over Stonewall Jackson; and, if it became necessary to speak kindly of any Northern officers, they always, with delicate appreciation of the proprieties, selected McClellan. If they were found out to be Northerners, they were anxious to have it understood that, at any rate, they were not Yankees; and were pretty sure to intimate that if they had any hatred a little more intense than that which good Christians ought to cherish toward the devil, it was evoked by the doings or the presence of these Yankees aforesaid.

Day after day, the camp of the negro regiment was filled with Mississippi or Louisiana planters. It was refreshing to see with what careful consideration and scrupulous politeness they approached the "niggers." Here was no longer "hatred of the upstarts," "war of races," "unconquerable antagonism." The negro was king. Men fawned upon him; took him to the sutler's shop and treated him; carried pockets full of tobacco to bestow upon him; carefully explained to him the varied delights of their respective plantations. Women came too—with coach and coachman—drove into the camp, went out among the negroes, and with sweet smiles and honeyed words sought to persuade them that such and such plantations would be the very home they were looking for. Sambo listened, took the tobacco, drank the whisky, grinned ample return for every smile, and —— cogitated. Scarcely an old planter got a negro, unless by some bargain with the officers. Half of them made no engagements at all; and, in a week after their discharge, the streets of Natchez were full of ragged, hungry negroes who had spent all their money and lost all their clothes; and were anxious to contract for a year's work with the first planter who came along.

Competition had driven the planters who needed hands the worst to offering extravagant wages. Twenty dollars per month, with rations, lodging, etc., was a common offer; and some went as high as twenty-five. Influential sergeants and corporals were offered thirty and forty dollars a month, on condition that they brought a certain number of men with them. In general, the more remote the plantation, the more backward the work upon it; and the less reliable the owner or lessee, the higher were the offered wages. The negroes displayed very little judgment, at last, in making their selections; and, as a rule, the men who made the most big promises, which they never meant to keep, got the most laborers.

About the same time the business of furnishing the labor for sugar and cotton plantations had assumed another phase in New Orleans. A regular system had been organized early in the year, by which agents, white or black, undertook to furnish negroes to the planters who needed them, at so much a head. This gradually degenerated until, in April, hundreds of negroes were within call of these agents, ready to re-enact the *rôle* of the Northern bounty-jumpers. The agent would hire them to a planter, receive his twenty-five dollars a head, and turn them over. The planter would start with them to his plantation. Sometimes they escaped from the boat before it started; in other cases they even went to the plantation, drew their rations for a week, and then ran away. On their return they shared the proceeds of the little operation with the agent. In Vicksburg a similar process of swindling was carried on, but on a smaller scale.

A Missouri cooper, who had managed to make enough money on cotton during the war to secure a plantation, boasted of his better success in securing labor: "I jist went over to Montgomery, Alabama, and from there to Selma. I takes my landlord aside, and persuades him to jine me in a straight drink. Then I told him I was after niggers, and asked him what he thought of my chances. He tole me he had jist six men in the house on the same business already. None of 'em had had any luck, and they was a goin' to Eufala by the Shamrock. All right, my covey, thinks I. So I jist steps down to the Shamrock, bargained awhile with the captain, and finally got the use of her yawl. He was n't agoin' to start till Tuesday mornin' and that was Sunday. I puts my nigger into the yawl, and we pulled down stream all night. Monday mornin' we was in Eufala. I sends my nigger out to talk to the people. They had nothin' to do ; Georgians wanted to hire 'em for their board and clothes; and fifteen dollars a month seemed enormous. Wednesday mornin' the Shamrock got down, and as the Selma niggerhunters stepped off, I stepped on with sixty-five niggers."

He said he had no trouble in getting as many as he wanted, except from the apprehension of the negroes throughout all that region, that any one who proposed to take them away anywhere to labor, really meant to run them over to Cuba and sell them. Several asked him, confidentially, whether Cuba was n't just across the Mississippi River. Even the white men entertained no doubt of his being a negro smuggler. One congratulated him on his remarkable luck, and " calculated that lot would about make his fortune by the time he got them over."

I saw but one successful experiment with white laborers on a cotton plantation. This was in one of the northern parishes of Louisiana, where seventy or eighty Germans, picked up from sponging-houses in New York and elsewhere, had been engaged for the year. At first they worked very badly. The overseer treated them as he had been in the habit of treating the slaves; and, degraded as these Germans were, they would not submit to it. A new overseer was engaged ; and, after a time, matters seemed to go on measurably well. But it was still too early (about the middle of April) to tell how they would succeed during the unhealthy summer months. None of the neighboring planters had any faith in the experiment. These Germans, they said, were not by any means as good as the niggers. If you sought Germans of a better class, they would n't contract with you, unless they saw a chance to become, after a time, the owners of the soil they cultivated.

Against this, and indeed against any subdivision of the great river plantations, the feeling was very strong. That a German should buy a hundred or two acres from the edge of a large plantation, was a thing not to be tolerated. Even sales of entire tracts to newcomers were very unpopular. "Johnson has gone and sold his plantation to a Yankee," exclaimed one. "Is it possible?" was the reply. "Why, I thought Johnson was a better citizen than that. If he had to sell, why did 'nt he hunt up some Southern man who wanted to buy?"

The negroes were all anxious to purchase land. "What 's de use of being free," said one, an old man of sixty, who was begging permission to plant cotton; "What 's de use of being free if you do n't own land enough to be buried in? Might juss as well stay slave all yo' days." "All I wants," said another, explaining what he was going to do with his money, of which he had already saved four or five hundred dollars; "All I wants is to git to own fo' or five acres ob land, dat I can build me a little house on and call my home." In many portions of the Mississippi Valley the feeling against any ownership of the soil by the negroes is so strong, that the man who should sell small tracts to them would be in actual personal danger. Every effort will be made to prevent negroes from acquiring lands; and even the renting of small tracts to them is held to be unpatriotic and unworthy of a good citizen. Through such difficulties is it that the subject-race is called upon to prove, by its prosperity, its fitness for freedom.

"I stops at your plantation de oder day, but I not know tat you had goods of your own to sell mit your niggers. I vill not interfere mit no man's trade."

The speaker was a Jew peddler, who also kept up a little store in Natchez-under-the-hill. He had been peddling down the river on the Louisiana side, and had been driven away from the plantation, whose proprietor he was addressing, by the overseer. Once before, the owner said, the overseer had permitted him to stay all night and trade with the negroes. He had sold, in a few hours, goods to the amount of nearly two hundred dollars, and had received payment in full in greenbacks, from ragged-looking blacks who would never have been suspected of having a penny. Nearly all the negroes had money. Some saved it quite carefully. On this very plantation he had field hands, working at fifteen dollars a month, who had five or six hundred dollars hid away in old stockings. Of course it wouldn't do to look too closely into the means by which they had acquired it. During the war, and especially in the confusion following the surrender, they had great opportunities for trade, and their master's property constituted the stock from which they drew. He had one man who had made several hundred dollars by killing his hogs and selling the pork.

But, with the cunning that seemed natural to them, they would rarely acknowledge the possession of money. "I have had boys come to me with the sorriest stories of their necessities, to get an advance of a few dollars on their month's wages, when I knew that they had as much money in their pockets as I had in mine. The worst of it was, that what they had rightfully belonged to me as much as that in my own pocket-book."

"Vat you tinks about de overflow?" asked the peddler, with an anxious look at the river, which was then rapidly rising.

"Why, what business is it of yours about the overflow? So you can swindle my niggers, what do you care about the overflow?"

"Vy, I wants you to make a pig crop. If tere's an overflow, tere'll pe no monish in te country next fall, and my trade ish gone. But if you makes pig crop, monish ish plenty, and I does pig business."

The planter subsequently explained, that this fellow had sold common unbleached muslins and the cheapest calicoes at from seventy-five cents to a dollar a yard; and that on the trinkets and gew gaws, with which his pack was liberally supplied, his profits were from five to eight hundred per cent.* The negroes bought readily, no matter what price he asked; and for the average plantation hand, the more worthless the article, the greater seemed, often, the desire to purchase it.

There could be no question of the zeal with which, through the exciting spring months, the people in the interior of the cotton States, supported the "President's Policy" of Reconstruction; but it was rarely a zeal according to knowledge.

*I have myself seen earrings that cost fifty cents sold for six dollars

"Just think of the infamous lengths those cursed Radicals are going!" exclaimed a wealthy and by no means illiterate or unpolished Mississippi cotton-planter to me in April; "They've actually turned out Stockton,[54] of Missouri, from the Senate!"

"I thought it was some New Jersey senator," I ventured to suggest.

"Oh, no!" (with great positiveness of manner.) "You got that into your head from having New Jersey and the Stockton name associated. But there's a Missouri family of Stocktons, and its one of the finest in the State. There never was a greater outrage than to turn Stockton out, just to get a party majority."

"But how *can* Mr. Stockton be from Missouri? Haven't they got Mr. Henderson and Gratz Brown there already?"

"Well, what's to hinder them from having three, I 'd like to know, except the infamous usurpation of these Radicals?"

This gentleman owned five large plantations, had an annual income of certainly not less than a hundred thousand dollars before the war, and himself belonged to one of "our first families."

• "Have you heard the news?" said a finely-educated and really very skillful surgeon in one of the inland towns to me one day. "Johnson isn't going to put up with your Radicals any longer. He is going to prorogue Congress at once, to get rid of its meddlesome interference with his policy!" "I have no doubt," he continued, in reply to some incredulous expression of mine; "I have no doubt of it in the world. Why, you can see yourself from Voor*hees'*[55] speech that, if he don't, they're going to impeach him right off. Of course he wouldn't stand that, or wait for it!" Yet this be-

[54] John Potter Stockton, elected Senator from New Jersey in 1865, but denied his seat by the Senate. Re-elected in 1869. [Ed.]

[55] Daniel Wolsey Voorhees, Democratic Congressman from Indiana. [Ed.]

liever in Voor*hees* had been educated in Europe, had traveled nearly over the world, and had the bearing and manners of an intelligent and accomplished gentleman.

"Johnson 'll be the next President, as sure as the Mississippi runs down stream," said a planter, waiting in a bar-room for the ferry-boat. "Why?" "Because he 's got the South with him, sure, to start on. Then he 's got Seward with him, and Seward has had the North in his breeches-pocket for the last six years. I 'd like to know how you are going to beat that combination!"

Sitting in a Natchez parlor, one day, conversing with the hostess, we were interrupted by the entrance of a smart, bright-looking negro girl, clothed in a fashionably-short and fashionably-expanded skirt of common striped bedticking. The child made its little courtesy to the stranger, and timidly stole behind the chair and clung to the skirts of "Missey."

"This is our litle Confederate nigger," explained the lady. "She is the only one I have been able to keep, and I only have her because her parents have n't yet been able to coax her away. You see she wears her old Confederate clothes. When we could get nothing else we were forced to the necessity of ripping up our mattresses to get material for dresses; and we are all too poor yet to buy new things for their every-day wear.

"Did you notice," she continued, patting the woolly head of the child as it lay with its face buried in her lap, "that she called me 'Missey,' just now? All the niggers have been trying to break her of that, but they can't. They tell her to call me Miss Lizzie, but she says 'she may be your Miss Lizzie, but she 's my

Missey.' The other day she made quite a scene in church, by breaking away from the other servants and shouting out, 'I *will* sit with my Missey to-day!' You should have seen everybody's head turning to see who it was, in these sorrowful times, that was still fortunate enough to be called Missey!"

On a Mississippi steamboat, one evening, I encountered an intelligent, substantial-looking Arkansas planter, hirsute, and clad in Confederate gray. The buttons had been removed from his military coat; but I soon discovered that the companion, with whom I was passing an idle evening in talk about planting and politics, was the Rebel General, E. C. Cahell.

He was giving the free-labor experiment a fair trial; and risking upon it pretty nearly all he was worth. He paid his first-class hands a dollar a day, and furnished them lodgings. They supplied themselves with clothing and provisions, which he sold—there being no village, or even store, within six miles of his landing— at a very slight advance on St. Louis prices, barely enough to cover freight and waste. He felt that he was paying very high wages; but he fixed upon this plan in preference to paying them fifteen dollars a month and rations, because a negro seemed to himself to be getting more for his work. "A dollar a day" was short and very easily understood; and the negroes thought it had a big sound.

Thus far he had less trouble with his laborers than he had anticipated. They worked well and seemed contented; but he was by no means certain that his hold upon them was secure enough to give him the slightest guaranty of being able to gather what he was planting. Now and then he found a troublesome negro; but, in the main, they had been unexpectedly open to reason. "The mistake we have generally made in the South has been that we have supposed nigger nature was something different from human nature. But I find that they are just as easily controlled, when sufficient motives are presented, as any other class of people would be." He was getting along without the aid of the Freedman's Bureau; and, indeed, without aid of any sort. He knew of no laws and of no officers; he was off in the woods by himself; and his only resource had been to try and do what was right, and then convince the negroes that he had done so.

On one point he had been closely pressed. His negroes all wanted to plant cotton on their own account, and made a dead-set at him for an acre of land apiece for that purpose. It would never do to tell them the truth—that he was afraid to let them grow any, lest, when picking-time came, they should steal from him to add to their own crops—but he had approached the delicate point diplomatically. "Of course, Jim, it would be all right with you; but then you know there are some of the boys here that *will* steal. They would bring a bad name on the whole of you, and get you all into trouble." And, "nigger nature being very much like human nature," his argument had been successful, and he had been relieved from the embarrassment.

He thought about three-fourths of the good cotton land directly fronting on the Mississippi, so far as his observation extended, was under cultivation and might be relied upon, with a favorable season, for an average crop. Back from the river, through Mississippi, Arkansas, and West Tennessee, he doubted whether one-fourth of the land was under cultivation.

Two or three days later, in another steamboat trip, I encountered a heavy planter, who came to this country originally from Illinois. He owned a fine plantation in Mississippi, fronting on the river, and with the cultivation of this he had always been contented. But this year he regarded as the golden opportunity. The free-labor project had not yet settled down into a steadily-working system. Half these old planters in the interior believed the niggers would n't work, and were doing very little to find out. When all made the discovery that they would work, cotton would come down to nearly its old prices, and there would be no great speculation in it. But this year, the men who " went in " would make the money which the backward ones ought to make, as well as their own. So he had leased, right and left. He had three plantations near his own, in Mississippi, and three more across the river, in Louisiana. On all of them he had plenty of negroes. At that time (3d April) he had a little over seventeen hundred acres of cotton planted. With good weather, in another week, he should have over four thousand.

But this was the last year he would do anything of the sort. He did n't believe there would be so much money in it another year; but, at any rate, he was kept forever running up and down the river, from one place to another, buying supplies and giving directions. He had no peace, day or night; and he meant to make enough this year to be able to retire and have some comfort.

He was trying all the different plans of paying negroes, and, next year, planters would be welcome to his experience. On one place he gave them fifteen dollars per month,* with rations, lodging, and medical attendance. On another he gave twelve dollars per month, and furnished clothing also. On one he gave a fifth of the crop, and supported the negroes; on another, a fourth of the crop, and required them to furnish a part of their own support. But on none would he permit any of the hands to plant a stalk of cotton on their own account. Nobody need tell *him* anything about niggers. He had owned them long enough to know all about them, and there wasn't one in a hundred he would trust to pick cotton for himself (the negro) out of a patch adjacent to the cotton fields of his employer.

He could as yet perceive no marked difference in the work of his hands on the different plantations. None did as much as under the old system, but all did more than was expected. Much depended on the overseer. Where the hands thought he understood his business, and could tell when they were doing their duty, and was, at the same time, disposed to treat them justly, there was no trouble. But some of the old overseers made a good deal of mischief on a plantation. They thought they could knock and cuff niggers about as they used to; and by the time they discovered their mistake, the niggers were leaving, and keeping others from coming in their places.

"One o' my niggers left, the other day, without saying a word to me about it. You couldn't guess why.

* The rate of wages named is that given first-class men. First-class women get, generally, about two-thirds as much. It is rarely the case that over one-third of the men and women on a place can be rated first-class. All the rest receive lower wages, in proportion to their value.

The cussed nigger had been lazy about mending a plow which was badly needed in the field, and the nigger-driver scolded him about it. He said he was a free man, and was n't going to be insulted; so off he started. There's one consolation; he had only been paid half his wages at the end of each month; and so there's a matter of twenty-five or thirty dollars which he lost and I gained by his running away."

This man had but an indifferent education; he had seen little of society or the world; he knew nothing thoroughly, save cotton and the negro. But, coming down, raw, from Illinois, years ago, he had won the good opinions of the heiress to a plantation, and had married,—— it rather than her, as an acquaintance expressed it. Now he was wealthy, and, with a fair season, was sure of not less than five thousand bales of cotton, worth, at only twenty-five cents per pound, half a million dollars, as the profits of this year's operations. How he would spend his money when he got it, it would be difficult to say. Horse-racing and hard drinking were the amusements most congenial to his class. Gambling was pleasant, but his business habits had given him a wholesome dread of it; and, after all, there seemed more probability that he would soon return to cotton, and end his days in worship at its kingly shrine.

CHAPTER LIII.

Concluding Suggestions.

THE President's vetoes of the Freedman's Bureau Bill and the Civil Rights Bill, with his Twenty-second of February speech and subsequent utterances, were received throughout the South-Western Cotton States with an exultation which drove the newspapers* to sad straits. To do justice to the occasion, the leading journal of New Orleans was forced to this:

"In the midst of a storm of passion, beating angrily and furiously against the bulwark of States' rights, when the ambitious and interested partisans who have raised it, attempt madly to ride into power over the ruins of a shattered Constitution; when the bellowing thunder roars on all sides, and the play of the forked lightning serves only to reveal the thick and impenetrable darkness which shrouds our political heavens, no sublimer spectacle can be presented than that of an American President, who, with serene countenance and determined spirit, appears on the arena of bitter and destructive strife, and says, in tones of power to the warring elements: 'Peace! be still!' and instantly the storm is hushed. The growling thunder, though its mutterings are still faintly heard, dies out in the distance. The denunciations of defeated partisans, and of fanatical bloodhounds, cease to spread their alarms over the land. The conflicting winds retire to their mountain cave. The clouds enveloping the concave above us break asunder, and a rainbow of varied dyes, which spans the heavens, gives full assurance of a bright and glorious day for our country."

* It should be remembered, in any estimates of politics at the South, that nearly all the leading Southern journals are still in the hands of the men who, five years ago, in their columns wrote up the rebellion. And, while the men who fought for the rebellion are entirely subdued, the men who wrote for it have seven devils now for every one that formerly possessed them.

The rural journals were less glitteringly general: but they fairly represented the prevailing public sentiment. One of the most outspoken said:*

"The old Tennesseean has shown his blood, and bearded the lion in his lair, 'The Douglass in his hall'—'glory enough for one day'—glorious old man, and let the earth ring his praise to the heavens.

The South and the Government are in the same boat one more time, thank the gods! 'now blow ye winds and crack your cheeks.' If Black Republicanism wishes to find out whether the South is loyal, there is now a beautiful opportunity. If they wish to prove their false assertion, let them now attempt any seditious move, and they will find every blast from Johnson's 'Bugle horn, worth a thousand men;' and before the notes shall die away in the valleys of the South, a soldier from the South will wave the old banner of the Stars and Stripes on the Northern hills; and though we do not desire them to do this, we defy them to do so. We will see then how they like the fit of their own cap.

States reduced to Territories? Indeed a little move in that direction would be of service, we think, in bringing about a full restoration of harmony between the sections. A little taste of their own medicine."

And the enthusiastic writer proceeded to declare, that the fair regions held by the Radical vipers were once more in the hands to which they properly belonged; and that the vipers could, therefore, turn their envenomed fangs upon each other, and with their forked tongues hiss their slimy curses into their own hell-torn, shrieking souls; while the South would, as a meteor shot from the electric realms of air, once more sweep across the skies of the glorious old Republic, and spangle its history with the splendors of her truth, her intellect, and her chivalry.

*Montgomery (Ala.) Ledger.

In spite, however, of such strong writing, and the stronger speaking everywhere prevalent, I was convinced during my visits to New Orleans, and Vicksburg, and the trip northward through the interior, which ended my year's experiences of Southern life, that there was little probability of serious results. Undoubtedly the South would sympathize with the President in any movement against Congress; but it is in no condition to give valuable co-operation. In 1866, as in 1865, the work of reorganization is entirely in the hands of the Government. The South will take—now as at any time since the surrender—whatever it can get.

"I believe in States' Rights, of co'se," said an old gentleman, at Jackson, Mississippi; "but I think my faith is like that described in the Bible: 'The evidence of things not seen, *the substance of things hoped for.*' The person that can see anything of States' Rights now-a-days, has younger eyes than mine." The same old man was very bitter against the "infamous scoundrel," who had written a recent article about the South in the Atlantic Monthly. "There ought to be some law to prevent such libels. You protect individuals against them; why is'nt it more important to protect whole communities?"

All complained of the changed front in the Senate on the Civil Rights Bill. "What business had Dixon to be absent?" exclaimed an officer of Lee's staff. "What if he was sick? If he had been dead, even, they ought to have carried him there and voted him!"

The attitude of Congress was regarded with alarm. Even the unreflecting masses were beginning to suspect that flattery of the President and abuse of Congress would not be sufficient to carry them through the difficulties that beset their political progress.

In most cases, the hostility to the Freedman's Bureau seemed to be general in its nature, not specific. Men regarded it as tyrannical and humiliating that Government hirelings should be sent among them to supervise their relations with their old slaves; but, in practice, they were very glad of the supervision. It was a degrading system, they argued, but, so long as it existed, the negroes could not be controlled except by the favor of the Bureau agents, " and so, of co'se, we have to use them." When the agents were removed from this prevailing respect for their powers, few opportunities were lost to show them the estimation in which they were held.

A steamboat was lying at the New Orleans levee, discharging a quantity of very miscellaneous freight. Among it was what the captain called "a lot of nigger's plunder." The entire worldly effects of a negro family seemed to be on board with little confinement from trunks or boxes. Half a dozen squalling chickens were carried over the gang-plank by the old auntie, in one hand, while in the other was held a squalling picaninny. A bundle of very dirty and ragged bed-clothes, tied up with the bed-cord, came next. There was a bedstead, apparently made with an ax, and a table, on which no other tool could by any chance have been employed. A lot of broken dishes, pots, and kettles followed. Then came an old bureau. The top drawer was gone, the bottom drawer was gone, the middle one had the knobs broken off, the frame remained to show that a looking-glass had once surmounted it, and two of the feet were broken off.

"By the powers, there's the Freedman's Bureau," exclaimed one of the group of Southern spectators standing on the guards. An agent of the Freedman's Bureau, in uniform, was within hearing, and the taunting laugh that rang over the boat seemed especially meant for his ears. To have resented, or noticed it, in that crowd, would have been at least foolish, if not worse. The agent was fortunate to escape with no more pointed expression of the public opinion concerning his office and duties.

Little change in the actual Unionism of the people could be seen since the surrender. In the year that had intervened, they had grown bolder, as they had come to realize the lengths to which they might safely go. They were "loyal" in May, 1865, in the sense of enforced submission to the Government, and they are loyal in the same sense in May, 1866. At neither time has the loyalty of the most had any wider meaning. But scarcely any dream of further opposition to the Government. A "war within the Union," for their rights, seems now to be the universal policy—a war in which they will act as a unit with whatever party at the North favors the fewest possible changes from the old order of things, and leaves them most at liberty to regulate their domestic institutions in their own way.

Nothing but the prevalent sense of the insecurity attending all Southern movements, during the political and social chaos that followed the surrender, prevented a large immigration from the North in the winter of 1865–'66. That the openings which the South presents for Northern capital and industry are unsurpassed, has been sufficiently illustrated. With a capital of a few thousand dollars, and a personal supervision of his work, a Northern farmer, devoting himself to cotton-growing, may count with safety on a net profit of fifty per cent. on his investment. With a good year and a good location he may do much better. Through Tennessee and the same latitudes, east and west, he will find a climate not very greatly different from his own, and a soil adapted to Northern cereals as well as to the Southern staple. The pine forests still embower untold riches; the cypress swamps of the lower Mississippi and its tributaries, only await the advent of Northern lumbermen to be converted into gold-mines; the mineral resources of Northern Georgia and Alabama, 'in spite of the war's developments, are yet as attractive as those that are drawing emigration into the uninhabited wilds across the Rocky Mountains. But capital and labor—especially agricultural labor—demand security.

Along the great highways of travel in the South, I judge investments by Northern men to be nearly as safe as they could be anywhere. The great cotton plantations bordering the Mississippi are largely in the hands of Northern lessees; and few, if any of them have experienced the slightest difficulty from any hostility of the inhabitants. So, along the great lines of railroad, and through regions not too remote from the tide of travel and trade, there are no complaints. It is chiefly in remote sections, far from railroads or mails, and isolated among communities of intense Southern prejudices, that Northern men have had trouble.

Whenever it is desirable to settle in such localities, it should be done in small associations. A dozen families, living near each other, would be abundantly able to protect themselves almost anywhere in the cotton-growing States.

Whoever contemplates going South, in time for the operations of 1867, should not delay his first visit later than November, 1866. Between October and January last, the prices of lands through the South, either for lease or sale, advanced fully fifty per cent. Upland cotton plantations can now be bought, in most localities, in tracts of from one hundred up to five thousand acres, for from eight to twenty dollars per acre; and the richest Mississippi and Red River bottom plantations do not command, in most cases, over forty dollars; the price being generally reckoned only on the open land prepared for the culture of cotton. But purchases should be made and arrangements for labor perfected before the New Year's rush comes on.

I have sought to show something of the actual character of the negroes, as learned from a closer and longer experience than falls to the lot of most tourists. The worst enemies to the enfranchised race, will at least admit that ample prominence has been given to their faults. I shall be glad if any satisfactory data have been furnished for determining their place in the future of the country.

They are not such material as, under ordinary circumstances, one would now choose for the duties of American citizenship. But wherever they have opportunity, they are fitting themselves for it with a zeal and rapidity never equalled by any similar class. Their order and industry are the only guaranty for the speedy return of prosperity to the South. Their devotion to the Union may prove one of the strongest guarantees for the speedy return of loyalty to the South. In any event, there can be no question, in the pending reorganization, as to the policy of seeking to ignore them. The Nation can not longer afford it.

> Better let them build who rear the house of nations,
> Than that Fate should rock it to foundation stone;
> Leave the Earth her storms, the stars their perturbations,
> *Steadfast welfare stays where* JUSTICE *binds her zone.*"

APPENDIX.

A.

[The following is the speech made by Chief-Justice Chase to the negroes at Charleston, under the circumstances narrated on page 83:]

MY FRIENDS—In compliance with the request of General Saxton, your friend and mine, I will say a few words.

He has kindly introduced me as a friend of freedom; and such, since I have taken a man's part in life, I have always been. It has ever been my earnest desire to see every man, of every race and every color, fully secured in the enjoyment of all natural rights, and provided with every legitimate means for the defense and maintenance of those rights.

No man, perhaps, has more deplored the war, from which the country is now emerging, than myself. No one would have made greater sacrifices to avert it. Earnestly desirous, as I always was, of the enfranchisement of every slave in the land, I never dreamed of seeking enfranchisement through war. I expected it through peaceful measures. Never doubting that it would come sometime; fully believing that by a wise and just administration of the National Government, friendly to freedom, but in strict conformity with the National Constitution, the time of its coming might be hastened; I yet would gladly have put aside, if I could, the cup of evil, of which our Nation has drunk so deeply. Not through those seas of blood, and those vast gulfs of cost, would I have willingly sought even the great good of universal emancipation.

But God, in His providence, permitted the madness of slavery-extension and slavery-domination to attempt the dismemberment of the Union by war. And when war came, there came also the idea, gradually growing into settled conviction in the hearts of the people, that slavery, having taken the sword, must perish by the sword. It was quite natural, perhaps, that I, having thought

581

much on the relations of the enslaved masses to the Republic, should be among the first to recognize the fact that the colored people of the South, whether bond or free, were the natural allies of the Nation, [prolonged cheers,] in its struggle with rebellion, and the duty of the National Government to assert their rights, and welcome their aid. A very few months of experience and observation satisfied me that if we would succeed in the struggle we must, as a first and most necessary measure, strike the fetters from the bondsmen. [Cheers.]

Such was my counsel in the Cabinet; and when our honored President, whose martyrdom this Nation now mourns, in common with all lovers of freedom throughout the world, after long forbearance, made up his mind to declare all men in our land free, no one was more ready with his sanction, or more hearty in his approval than myself. [Cheers.]

So, too, when necessarily that other question arose: "Shall we give arms to the black men?" I could not doubt or hesitate. The argument was plain and irresistible: If we make them freemen, and their defense is the defense of the Nation, whose right and duty is it to bear arms, if not theirs? In this great struggle, now for universal freedom not less than for perpetual Union, who ought to take part, if not they? And how can we expect to succeed, if we fail to avail ourselves of the natural helps created for us by the very conditions of the war? When, therefore, the President, after much consideration, resolved to summon black soldiers to battle for the flag, I felt that it was a wise act, only too long delayed. [Cheers.]

And now, who can say that the colored man has not done his full part in the struggle? Who has made sacrifices which he has not made? Who has endured hardships which he has not endured? What ills have any suffered which he has not suffered?

If, then, he has contributed in just measure to the victory, shall he not partake of its fruits? If Union and Freedom have been secured through courage, and fortitude, and zeal, displayed by black as well as white soldiers, shall not the former be benefited in due measure as well as the latter? And since we all know that natural rights can not be made secure except through political rights, shall not the ballot—the freeman's weapon in peace—replace the bayonet—the freeman's weapon in war?

I believe the right of the black man to freedom, and security for freedom, as a result of the war, to be incontestible. I assert it as a simple matter of justice.

In my judgment, the safety of nations, as well as of individuals, stands in justice. It is a true saying, that "he who walketh uprightly walketh surely." The man or the nation that joins hands with justice and truth, and relies steadfastly on God's providence, is sure to issue from every trial safely and triumphantly. Great struggles may have to be gone through; great sacrifices made; great dangers encountered; even great martyrdoms suffered. We have experienced all these. Multitudes of martyrs have perished in this war; the noblest of them all fell but lately by an assassin's hand; but our great cause has thus far triumphed. There may be still perils ahead. Other martyrdoms may be needed. But over all, and through all, the just cause will surely come out triumphant in the end; for a just God is on the throne, and He wills the triumph of justice.

I have said that the battle is over and the victory won. The armies of rebellion are disbanded; peace is coming, and with it the duties of peace. What are these ?

The condition of the country is peculiar. A great race, numbering four millions of souls, has been suddenly enfranchised. All men are now looking to see whether the prophecies of the enemies of that race will be fulfilled or falsified.

The answer to that question, men and women of color, is with you. Your enemies say that you will be disorderly, improvident, lazy; that wages will not tempt you to work; that you will starve rather than labor; that you will become drones and vagabonds. And while your enemies scatter these predictions, many who are not your enemies fear their fulfillment. It remains with you whether they shall be fulfilled or not.

You need not feel much anxiety about what people say of you. Feel rather that, under God, your salvation must come of yourselves. If, caring little about men's sayings, you go straight on in the plain ways of duty; if by honesty, temperance, and industry, by faithfulness in all employments and to all trusts, and by readiness to work for fair wages, you prove yourselves useful men and women; if out of economical savings from each week's earnings you lay up something for yourselves in a wet day; if, as cultivators of the soil, as mechanics, as traders, in this employment or that employment, you do all in your power to increase the products and the resources of your county and State; and if, whatever you do, you make proofs of honesty, sobriety, and good will, you will save yourselves and fulfill the best hopes of your friends.

God forbid that I shall have yet, before I die, to hang my head and say—well, I expected a great deal of this people; that they would bear freedom; that they would be honest, industrious, and orderly; that they would make great progress in learning, in trades, in arts, and, finally, run the race, side by side, with the whites; but I find I was mistaken; they have allowed wretched prejudices and evil passions to grow up among them; they have neglected their opportunities and wasted their means; they have cherished mean envy and low jealousy, where they should have fostered noble emulation and generous rivalry in all good works; they have failed because unwilling to take their lot cheerfully, and persevere courageously in the work of self-improvement.

I may say, with the apostle, "I hope better things of you, though I thus speak." I know the heart of the working-man, for I have known his experience. When a boy on a farm, in Ohio, where then the unbroken forest lay close to our dwelling, I knew what work was. In our rough log cabins we fared as hard and labored as hard as you fare or labor. All we had to go upon—all the capital we had—was good wills to work, patient endurance, and fair opportunity for education, which every white in the country, thank God, could have then; and every black boy, thank God again, can have now. It was on this capital we went to work, and we came to something; [loud cheers, and cries of "That you did!"] and you may go to work on the same capital and come to something also, if you will. I believe you will. You wont spend your time in fretting because this or that white man has a better time than you have, or more advantages; nor will you, I hope, take short cuts to what looks like success, but nine times out of ten will turn out to be failure.

I talk to you frankly and sincerely, as one who has always been your friend. As a friend, I earnestly advise you to lay your foundations well in morality, industry, education, and, above all, religion. Go to work patiently, and labor diligently; if you are soldiers, fight well; if preachers, preach faithfully; if carpenters, shove the plane with might and main; if you till the ground, grow as much cotton as the land will yield; if hired, work honestly for honest wages, until you can afford to hire laborers yourselves, and then pay honest wages. If you act thus, nobody need doubt your future. The result will gloriously surpass your hopes.

Now about the elective franchise. Major Delany has told you that he heard me say, in the Capitol at Washington, that the black man ought to have his vote. If he had happened to hear me twenty years ago in Cincinnati, he would have heard me say the same thing. [Cheers and prolonged applause.]

Matters have been working, since then, toward that result, and have a much better look now than then. If all the people—all the white people, I mean, for the colored people seem pretty well agreed—felt as I do, that it is the interest of all that the rights of all, in suffrage as in other matters, should be equal before the law, you would not have to wait long for equal rights at the ballot-box; no longer than it would take to pass the necessary law. [Cheers.] But very many of the white people do not see things as I do; and I do not know what the National Government proposes to do. I am not now, as you know, in the Cabinet councils; nor am I a politician; nor do I meddle with politics. I can only say this: I believe there is not a member of the Administration who would not be pleased to see suffrage universal; but I can not say, for I do not know, that the Administration is prepared to say that suffrage shall be universal.

What I do know is this; that if you are patient, and patiently claim your rights, and show by your acts that you deserve to be entrusted with suffrage, and inspire a confidence in the public mind that you will use it honestly, and use it too on the side of liberty, and order, and education, and improvement, you will not have to wait very long. I can say this safely on general principles. Common sense tells us that suffrage can not be denied long to large masses of people, who ask it and are not disqualified for its exercise. Believing in your future as I do, I feel sure you will have it sometime; perhaps very soon; perhaps a good while hence. If I had the power it would be very soon. It would, in my judgment, be safe in your hands to-day; and the whole country would be better off if suffrage were now universal.

But whatever may be the action of the white people here in Charleston, or of the Government at Washington, be patient.

That you will have suffrage in the end, is just as sure as it is that you respect yourselves and respect others, and do your best to prove your worthiness of it. Misconduct of any kind will not help you, but patience and perseverance in well-doing will help you mightily. So, too, if the National Government, taking all things into consideration, shall come to a conclusion different from mine, and delay to enroll you as citizens and voters, your best policy, in my judgment, is patience. I counsel no surrender of principle—no abandonment of your just claims; but I counsel patience. What good will fretting and worrying and complaining do? If I were in your place I would just go to work for all good objects, and show by my conduct that the Government, in making a delay, had made a mistake. [Cheers.] If you do so and the mistake is made, it will be the more speedily corrected.

Let me repeat, that I think it best for all men—white men, black men, and brown men, if you make that distinction, that all men of proper age and unconvicted of crime, should have the right of suffrage. It is my firm conviction, that suffrage is not only the best security for freedom, but the most potent agent of amelioration and civilization. He who has that right will usually respect himself more, be more respected, perform more, and more productive work, and do more to increase the wealth and welfare of the community, than he who has it not. Suffrage makes nations great. Hence I am in favor of suffrage for all; but if the Government shall think differently, or if circumstances delay its action, I counsel calmness, patience, industry, self-respect, respect for others, and, with all these, firmness.

Such, in my judgment, is your duty. Ordinarily the simple performance of duty is so blessed of God, that men who live in the doing of it, are the best off, in all respects, even in this world. But if these immediate rewards do not attend its performance, still, if a man carries in his heart the consciousness of doing right, as in the sight God, rendering to each his due, withholding from none his right, contributing all he can to the general improvement, and diffusing happiness to the extent of his power through the sphere of which he is the center, he may go through life as happy as a king, though he may never be a king, and go at last where no wrong finds entrance, nor any error, because there reigns one God and one Father, before whom all his children are equal. [Prolonged cheers.]

B.

[The following is a letter from Rev. Richard Fuller, D. D., of Baltimore, whose visit to his former slaves on St. Helena Island has been described. Dr. Fuller's high position in the Baptist Church, and his prominence in former times as a defender of the divinity of slavery, in the discussions with President Wayland, give weight to his indorsement of the substantial accuracy of what has been said, in the foregoing pages, as to the condition and prospects of the Sea Island negroes. A few sentences of a purely personal nature are omitted:]

"My Dear Sir:—I could add very little to your clear and full statements concerning our visit to St. Helena, and the condition in which we found the negroes. I can only repeat that the freedmen at Port Royal, under General Saxton, seemed to me to present a favorable solution of the question of free labor.

Against my convictions and apprehensions, I was brought to the conclusion, that their former masters might cultivate their fields profitably by these hired servants.

You are mistaken, however, as I think, in speaking of the slaves on these islands as less advanced in intelligence, or morals than the colored people in the interior.

My interest in these people makes me constantly solicitous about their conduct. Never was there a problem more serious or difficult than that which is now before the Nation, as to this race, whose destiny has been confided to the wisdom and honor of our Government. I can only pray that God will give our rulers His aid and blessing in this critical and portentous crisis.

Most sincerely,

RICHARD FULLER."

C.

LETTER FROM CHIEF JUSTICE CHASE TO A COMMITTEE OF COLORED
MEN IN NEW ORLEANS.

New Orleans, June 6, 1865.

Gentlemen—I should hardly feel at liberty to decline the invitation you have tendered me, in behalf of the loyal colored Americans of New Orleans, to speak to them on the subject of their rights and duties as citizens, if I had not quite recently expressed my views at Charleston, in an address, reported with substantial accuracy, and already published in one of the most widely circulated journals of this city. But it seems superfluous to repeat them before another audience.

It is proper to say, however, that these views, having been formed years since, on much reflection, and confirmed, in a new and broader application, by the events of the civil war now happily ended, are not likely to undergo, hereafter, any material change.

That native freemen, of whatever complexion, are citizens of the United States; that all men held as slaves in the States which joined in the rebellion against the United States have become freemen through executive and legislative acts during the war; and that these freemen are now citizens, and consequently entitled to the rights of citizens, are propositions which, in my judgment, can not be successfully controverted.

And it is both natural and right that colored Americans, entitled to the rights of citizens, should claim their exercise. They should persist in this claim respectfully, but firmly, taking care to bring no discredit upon it by their own action. Its justice is already acknowledged by great numbers of their white fellow-citizens, and these numbers constantly increase.

The peculiar conditions, however, under which these rights arise, seem to impose on those who assert them peculiar duties, or rather special obligations to the discharge of common duties. They should strive for distinction by economy, by industry, by sobriety, by patient perseverance in well-doing, by constant improvement of religious instruction, and by the constant practice of Christian virtues. In this way they will surely overcome unjust hostility, and convince even the most prejudiced that the denial to them of any right which citizens may properly exercise is equally unwise and wrong.

Our national experience has demonstrated that public order reposes most securely on the broad base of universal suffrage. It has proved, also, that universal suffrage is the surest guarantee and most powerful stimulus of individual, social and political progress. May it not prove, moreover, in that work of reorganization, which now engages the thoughts of all patriotic men, that universal suffrage is the best reconciler of the most comprehensive lenity with the most perfect public security and the most speedy and certain revival of general prosperity?

Very respectfully, yours,

S. P. CHASE.

Messrs. J. B. ROUDANEZ, L. GOELIS and L. BANKS, Committee.

D.

The Captain-General of Cuba, in a conversation with Chief-Justice Chase, expressed the belief that Coolie labor would be gradually substituted for slave labor, and that slavery itself would come to an end in Cuba within ten years.

THE END.

Revised October 31, 1965

ħarper ✦ ᴄorchbooks

HUMANITIES AND SOCIAL SCIENCES

American Studies: General

THOMAS C. COCHRAN: The Inner Revolution: *Essays on the Social Sciences in History* TB/1140

EDWARD S. CORWIN: American Constitutional History. *Essays edited by Alpheus T. Mason and Gerald Garvey* TB/1136

A. HUNTER DUPREE: Science in the Federal Government: *A History of Policies and Activities to 1940* TB/573

OSCAR HANDLIN, Ed.: This Was America: *As Recorded by European Travelers in the Eighteenth, Nineteenth and Twentieth Centuries. Illus.* TB/1119

MARCUS LEE HANSEN: The Atlantic Migration: 1607-1860. *Edited by Arthur M. Schlesinger; Introduction by Oscar Handlin* TB/1052

MARCUS LEE HANSEN: The Immigrant in American History. *Edited with a Foreword by Arthur M. Schlesinger* TB/1120

JOHN HIGHAM, Ed.: The Reconstruction of American History TB/1068

ROBERT H. JACKSON: The Supreme Court in the American System of Government TB/1106

JOHN F. KENNEDY: A Nation of Immigrants. *Illus. Revised and Enlarged. Introduction by Robert F. Kennedy* TB/1118

RALPH BARTON PERRY: Puritanism and Democracy TB/1138

ARNOLD ROSE: The Negro in America: *The Condensed Version of Gunnar Myrdal's An American Dilemma* TB/3048

MAURICE R. STEIN: The Eclipse of Community: *An Interpretation of American Studies* TB/1128

W. LLOYD WARNER and Associates: Democracy in Jonesville: *A Study in Quality and Inequality* ‖ TB/1129

W. LLOYD WARNER: Social Class in America: *The Evaluation of Status* TB/1013

American Studies: Colonial

BERNARD BAILYN, Ed.: The Apologia of Robert Keayne: *Self-Portrait of a Puritan Merchant* TB/1201

BERNARD BAILYN: The New England Merchants in the Seventeenth Century TB/1149

JOSEPH CHARLES: The Origins of the American Party System TB/1049

LAWRENCE HENRY GIPSON: The Coming of the Revolution: 1763-1775. † *Illus.* TB/3007

LEONARD W. LEVY: Freedom of Speech and Press in Early American History: *Legacy of Suppression* TB/1109

PERRY MILLER: Errand Into the Wilderness TB/1139

PERRY MILLER & T. H. JOHNSON, Eds.: The Puritans: *A Sourcebook of Their Writings*
Vol. I TB/1093; Vol. II TB/1094

KENNETH B. MURDOCK: Literature and Theology in Colonial New England TB/99

WALLACE NOTESTEIN: The English People on the Eve of Colonization: 1603-1630. † *Illus.* TB/3006

LOUIS B. WRIGHT: The Cultural Life of the American Colonies: 1607-1763. † *Illus.* TB/3005

American Studies: From the Revolution to the Civil War

JOHN R. ALDEN: The American Revolution: 1775-1783. † *Illus.* TB/3011

RAY A. BILLINGTON: The Far Western Frontier: 1830-1860. † *Illus.* TB/3012

GEORGE DANGERFIELD: The Awakening of American Nationalism: 1815-1828. † *Illus.* TB/3061

CLEMENT EATON: The Freedom-of-Thought Struggle in the Old South. *Revised and Enlarged. Illus.* TB/1150

CLEMENT EATON: The Growth of Southern Civilization: 1790-1860. † *Illus.* TB/3040

LOUIS FILLER: The Crusade Against Slavery: 1830-1860. † *Illus.* TB/3029

DIXON RYAN FOX: The Decline of Aristocracy in the Politics of New York: 1801-1840. ‡ *Edited by Robert V. Remini* TB/3064

FELIX GILBERT: The Beginnings of American Foreign Policy: *To the Farewell Address* TB/1200

FRANCIS J. GRUND: Aristocracy in America: *Social Class in the Formative Years of the New Nation* TB/1001

ALEXANDER HAMILTON: The Reports of Alexander Hamilton. ‡ *Edited by Jacob E. Cooke* TB/3060

THOMAS JEFFERSON: Notes on the State of Virginia. ‡ *Edited by Thomas P. Abernethy* TB/3052

BERNARD MAYO: Myths and Men: *Patrick Henry, George Washington, Thomas Jefferson* TB/1108

JOHN C. MILLER: Alexander Hamilton and the Growth of the New Nation TB/3057

RICHARD B. MORRIS, Ed.: The Era of the American Revolution TB/1180

R. B. NYE: The Cultural Life of the New Nation: 1776-1801. † *Illus.* TB/3026

---

† The New American Nation Series, edited by Henry Steele Commager and Richard B. Morris.

‡ American Perspectives series, edited by Bernard Wishy and William E. Leuchtenburg.

* The Rise of Modern Europe series, edited by William L. Langer.

‖ Researches in the Social, Cultural, and Behavioral Sciences, edited by Benjamin Nelson.

§ The Library of Religion and Culture, edited by Benjamin Nelson.

ᵘ Not for sale in Canada.

Σ Harper Modern Science Series, edited by James R. Newman.

3

WALLACE K. FERGUSON et al.: Facets of the Renaissance TB/1098

WALLACE K. FERGUSON et al.: The Renaissance: Six Essays. Illus. TB/1084

JOHN NEVILLE FIGGIS: The Divine Right of Kings. Introduction by G. R. Elton TB/1191

JOHN NEVILLE FIGGIS: Political Thought from Gerson to Grotius: 1414-1625: Seven Studies. Introduction by Garrett Mattingly TB/1032

MYRON P. GILMORE: The World of Humanism, 1453-1517.* Illus. TB/3003

FRANCESCO GUICCIARDINI: Maxims and Reflections of a Renaissance Statesman (Ricordi). Trans. by Mario Domandi. Intro. by Nicolai Rubinstein TB/1160

J. H. HEXTER: More's Utopia: The Biography of an Idea New Epilogue by the Author TB/1195

JOHAN HUIZINGA: Erasmus and the Age of Reformation. Illus. TB/19

ULRICH VON HUTTEN et al.: On the Eve of the Reformation: "Letters of Obscure Men." Introduction by Hajo Holborn TB/1124

PAUL O. KRISTELLER: Renaissance Thought: The Classic, Scholastic, and Humanist Strains TB/1048

PAUL O. KRISTELLER: Renaissance Thought II: Papers on Humanism and the Arts TB/1163

NICCOLO MACHIAVELLI: History of Florence and of the Affairs of Italy: from the earliest times to the death of Lorenzo the Magnificent. Introduction by Felix Gilbert TB/1027

ALFRED VON MARTIN: Sociology of the Renaissance. Introduction by Wallace K. Ferguson TB/1099

GARRETT MATTINGLY et al.: Renaissance Profiles. Edited by J. H. Plumb TB/1162

MILLARD MEISS: Painting in Florence and Siena after the Black Death: The Arts, Religion and Society in the Mid-Fourteenth Century. 169 illus. TB/1148

J. E. NEALE: The Age of Catherine de Medici ° TB/1085

ERWIN PANOFSKY: Studies in Iconology: Humanistic Themes in the Art of the Renaissance. 180 illustrations TB/1077

J. H. PARRY: The Establishment of the European Hegemony: 1415-1715: Trade and Exploration in the Age of the Renaissance TB/1045

J. H. PLUMB: The Italian Renaissance: A Concise Survey of Its History and Culture TB/1161

CECIL ROTH: The Jews in the Renaissance. Illus. TB/834

GORDON RUPP: Luther's Progress to the Diet of Worms ° TB/120

FERDINAND SCHEVILL: The Medici. Illus. TB/1010

FERDINAND SCHEVILL: Medieval and Renaissance Florence. Illus. Volume I: Medieval Florence TB/1090 Volume II: The Coming of Humanism and the Age of the Medici TB/1091

G. M. TREVELYAN: England in the Age of Wycliffe, 1368-1520 ° TB/1112

VESPASIANO: Renaissance Princes, Popes, and Prelates: The Vespasiano Memoirs: Lives of Illustrious Men of the XVth Century. Intro. by Myron P. Gilmore TB/1111

History: Modern European

FREDERICK B. ARTZ: Reaction and Revolution, 1815-1832. * Illus. TB/3034

MAX BELOFF: The Age of Absolutism, 1660-1815 TB/1062

ROBERT C. BINKLEY: Realism and Nationalism, 1852-1871. * Illus. TB/3038

ASA BRIGGS: The Making of Modern England, 1784-1867: The Age of Improvement ° TB/1203

CRANE BRINTON: A Decade of Revolution, 1789-1799. * Illus. TB/3018

J. BRONOWSKI & BRUCE MAZLISH: The Western Intellectual Tradition: From Leonardo to Hegel TB/3001

GEOFFREY BRUUN: Europe and the French Imperium, 1799-1814. * Illus. TB/3033

ALAN BULLOCK: Hitler, A Study in Tyranny. ° Illus. TB/1123

E. H. CARR: The Twenty Years' Crisis, 1919-1939: An Introduction to the Study of International Relations ° TB/1122

GORDON A. CRAIG: From Bismarck to Adenauer: Aspects of German Statecraft. Revised Edition TB/1171

WALTER L. DORN: Competition for Empire, 1740-1763. * Illus. TB/3032

CARL J. FRIEDRICH: The Age of the Baroque, 1610-1660. * Illus. TB/3004

RENÉ FUELOEP-MILLER: The Mind and Face of Bolshevism: An Examination of Cultural Life in Soviet Russia. New Epilogue by the Author TB/1188

M. DOROTHY GEORGE: London Life in the Eighteenth Century TB/1182

LEO GERSHOY: From Despotism to Revolution, 1763-1789. * Illus. TB/3017

C. C. GILLISPIE: Genesis and Geology: The Decades before Darwin § TB/51

ALBERT GOODWIN: The French Revolution TB/1064

ALBERT GUERARD: France in the Classical Age: The Life and Death of an Ideal TB/1183

CARLTON J. H. HAYES: A Generation of Materialism, 1871-1900. * Illus. TB/3039

J. H. HEXTER: Reappraisals in History: New Views on History & Society in Early Modern Europe TB/1100

A. R. HUMPHREYS: The Augustan World: Society, Thought, and Letters in 18th Century England ° TB/1105

ALDOUS HUXLEY: The Devils of Loudun: A Study in the Psychology of Power Politics and Mystical Religion in the France of Cardinal Richelieu § ° TB/60

DAN N. JACOBS, Ed.: The New Communist Manifesto & Related Documents. Third edition, revised TB/1078

HANS KOHN: The Mind of Germany: The Education of a Nation TB/1204

HANS KOHN, Ed.: The Mind of Modern Russia: Historical and Political Thought of Russia's Great Age TB/1065

KINGSLEY MARTIN: French Liberal Thought in the Eighteenth Century: A Study of Political Ideas from Bayle to Condorcet TB/1114

SIR LEWIS NAMIER: Personalities and Powers: Selected Essays TB/1186

SIR LEWIS NAMIER: Vanished Supremacies: Essays on European History, 1812-1918 ° TB/1088

JOHN U. NEF: Western Civilization Since the Renaissance: Peace, War, Industry, and the Arts TB/1113

FREDERICK L. NUSSBAUM: The Triumph of Science and Reason, 1660-1685. * Illus. TB/3009

JOHN PLAMENATZ: German Marxism and Russian Communism. ° New Preface by the Author TB/1189

RAYMOND W. POSTGATE, Ed.: Revolution from 1789 to 1906: Selected Documents TB/1063

PENFIELD ROBERTS: The Quest for Security, 1715-1740. * Illus. TB/3016

PRISCILLA ROBERTSON: Revolutions of 1848: A Social History TB/1025

ALBERT SOREL: Europe Under the Old Regime. Translated by Francis H. Herrick TB/1121

N. N. SUKHANOV: The Russian Revolution, 1917: Eyewitness Account. Edited by Joel Carmichael Vol. I TB/1066; Vol. II TB/1067

A. J. P. TAYLOR: The Habsburg Monarch, 1809-1918: A History of the Austrian Empire and Austria-Hungary ° TB/1187

4

JOHN B. WOLF: The Emergence of the Great Powers, 1685-1715. * Illus.　TB/3010

JOHN B. WOLF: France: 1814-1919: *The Rise of a Liberal-Democratic Society*　TB/3019

Intellectual History & History of Ideas

HERSCHEL BAKER: The Image of Man: *A Study of the Idea of Human Dignity in Classical Antiquity, the Middle Ages, and the Renaissance*　TB/1047

R. R. BOLGAR: The Classical Heritage and Its Beneficiaries: *From the Carolingian Age to the End of the Renaissance*　TB/1125

RANDOLPH S. BOURNE: War and the Intellectuals: *Collected Essays, 1915-1919.* ‡ *Edited by Carl Resek*　TB/3043

J. BRONOWSKI & BRUCE MAZLISH: The Western Intellectual Tradition: *From Leonardo to Hegel*　TB/3001

ERNST CASSIRER: The Individual and the Cosmos in Renaissance Philosophy. *Translated with an Introduction by Mario Domandi*　TB/1097

NORMAN COHN: The Pursuit of the Millennium: *Revolutionary Messianism in medieval and Reformation Europe*　TB/1037

G. RACHEL LEVY: Religious Conceptions of the Stone Age and Their Influence upon European Thought. *Illus. Introduction by Henri Frankfort*　TB/106

ARTHUR O. LOVEJOY: The Great Chain of Being: *A Study of the History of an Idea*　TB/1009

PERRY MILLER & T. H. JOHNSON, Editors: The Puritans: *A Sourcebook of Their Writings*
Vol. I TB/1093; Vol. II TB/1094

MILTON C. NAHM: Genius and Creativity: *An Essay in the History of Ideas*　TB/1196

ROBERT PAYNE: Hubris: *A Study of Pride. Foreword by Sir Herbert Read*　TB/1031

RALPH BARTON PERRY: The Thought and Character of William James: *Briefer Version*　TB/1156

BRUNO SNELL: The Discovery of the Mind: *The Greek Origins of European Thought*　TB/1018

PAGET TOYNBEE: Dante Alighieri: *His Life and Works. Edited with intro. by Charles S. Singleton*　TB/1206

ERNEST LEE TUVESON: Millennium and Utopia: *A Study in the Background of the Idea of Progress.* | *New Preface by the Author*　TB/1134

PAUL VALÉRY: The Outlook for Intelligence　TB/2016

PHILIP P. WIENER: Evolution and the Founders of Pragmatism. *Foreword by John Dewey*　TB/1212

Literature, Poetry, The Novel & Criticism

JAMES BAIRD: Ishmael: *The Art of Melville in the Contexts of International Primitivism*　TB/1023

JACQUES BARZUN: The House of Intellect　TB/1051

W. J. BATE: From Classic to Romantic: *Premises of Taste in Eighteenth Century England*　TB/1036

RACHEL BESPALOFF: On the Iliad　TB/2006

R. P. BLACKMUR et al.: Lectures in Criticism. *Introduction by Huntington Cairns*　TB/2003

ABRAHAM CAHAN: The Rise of David Levinsky: *a documentary novel of social mobility in early twentieth century America. Intro. by John Higham*　TB/1028

ERNST R. CURTIUS: European Literature and the Latin Middle Ages　TB/2015

GEORGE ELIOT: Daniel Deronda: *a novel. Introduction by F. R. Leavis*　TB/1039

ETIENNE GILSON: Dante and Philosophy　TB/1089

ALFRED HARBAGE: As They Liked It: *A Study of Shakespeare's Moral Artistry*　TB/1035

STANLEY R. HOPPER, Ed.: Spiritual Problems in Contemporary Literature §　TB/21

A. R. HUMPHREYS: The Augustan World: *Society, Thought and Letters in 18th Century England* º　TB/1105

ALDOUS HUXLEY: Antic Hay & The Giaconda Smile. º *Introduction by Martin Green*　TB/3503

ALDOUS HUXLEY: Brave New World & Brave New World Revisited. º *Introduction by Martin Green*　TB/3501

HENRY JAMES: Roderick Hudson: *a novel. Introduction by Leon Edel*　TB/1016

HENRY JAMES: The Tragic Muse: *a novel. Introduction by Leon Edel*　TB/1017

ARNOLD KETTLE: An Introduction to the English Novel.
Volume I: *Defoe to George Eliot*　TB/1011
Volume II: *Henry James to the Present*　TB/1012

ROGER SHERMAN LOOMIS: The Development of Arthurian Romance　TB/1167

JOHN STUART MILL: On Bentham and Coleridge. *Introduction by F. R. Leavis*　TB/1070

KENNETH B. MURDOCK: Literature and Theology in Colonial New England　TB/99

SAMUEL PEPYS: The Diary of Samuel Pepys. º *Edited by O. F. Morshead. Illus. by Ernest Shepard*　TB/1007

ST.-JOHN PERSE: Seamarks　TB/2002

GEORGE SANTAYANA: Interpretations of Poetry and Religion §　TB/9

C. P. SNOW: Time of Hope: *a novel*　TB/1040

HEINRICH STRAUMANN: American Literature in the Twentieth Century. *Third Edition, Revised*　TB/1168

PAGET TOYNBEE: Dante Alighieri: *His Life and Works. Edited with intro. by Charles S. Singleton*　TB/1206

DOROTHY VAN GHENT: The English Novel: *Form and Function*　TB/1050

E. B. WHITE: One Man's Meat. *Introduction by Walter Blair*　TB/3505

MORTON DAUWEN ZABEL, Editor: Literary Opinion in America　Vol. I TB/3013; Vol. II TB/3014

Myth, Symbol & Folklore

JOSEPH CAMPBELL, Editor: Pagan and Christian Mysteries *Illus.*　TB/2013

MIRCEA ELIADE: Cosmos and History: *The Myth of the Eternal Return* §　TB/2050

C. G. JUNG & C. KERÉNYI: Essays on a Science of Mythology: *The Myths of the Divine Child and the Divine Maiden*　TB/2014

DORA & ERWIN PANOFSKY: Pandora's Box: *The Changing Aspects of a Mythical Symbol. Revised Edition. Illus.*　TB/2021

ERWIN PANOFSKY: Studies in Iconology: *Humanistic Themes in the Art of the Renaissance. 180 illustrations*　TB/1077

JEAN SEZNEC: The Survival of the Pagan Gods: *The Mythological Tradition and its Place in Renaissance Humanism and Art. 108 illustrations*　TB/2004

HELLMUT WILHELM: Change: *Eight Lectures on the I Ching*　TB/2019

HEINRICH ZIMMER: Myths and Symbols in Indian Art and Civilization. *70 illustrations*　TB/2005

Philosophy

G. E. M. ANSCOMBE: An Introduction to Wittgenstein's Tractatus. *Second edition, Revised.* º　TB/1210

HENRI BERGSON: Time and Free Will: *An Essay on the Immediate Data of Consciousness* º　TB/1021

H. J. BLACKHAM: Six Existentialist Thinkers: *Kierke-gaard, Nietzsche, Jaspers, Marcel, Heidegger, Sartre* ° TB/1002

CRANE BRINTON: Nietzsche. *New Preface, Bibliography and Epilogue by the Author* TB/1197

ERNST CASSIRER: The Individual and the Cosmos in Renaissance Philosophy. *Translated with an Introduction by Mario Domandi* TB/1097

ERNST CASSIRER: Rousseau, Kant and Goethe. *Introduction by Peter Gay* TB/1092

FREDERICK COPLESTON: Medieval Philosophy ° TB/376

F. M. CORNFORD: Principium Sapientiae: *A Study of the Origins of Greek Philosophical Thought. Edited by W. K. C. Guthrie* TB/1213

F. M. CORNFORD: From Religion to Philosophy: *A Study in the Origins of Western Speculation* § TB/20

WILFRID DESAN: The Tragic Finale: *An Essay on the Philosophy of Jean-Paul Sartre* TB/1030

PAUL FRIEDLÄNDER: Plato: *An Introduction* TB/2017

ÉTIENNE GILSON: Dante and Philosophy TB/1089

WILLIAM CHASE GREENE: Moira: *Fate, Good, and Evil in Greek Thought* TB/1104

W. K. C. GUTHRIE: The Greek Philosophers: *From Thales to Aristotle* ° TB/1008

F. H. HEINEMANN: Existentialism and the Modern Predicament TB/28

ISAAC HUSIK: A History of Medieval Jewish Philosophy TB/803

EDMUND HUSSERL: Phenomenology and the Crisis of Philosophy. *Translated with an Introduction by Quentin Lauer* TB/1170

IMMANUEL KANT: The Doctrine of Virtue, *being Part II of The Metaphysic of Morals. Trans. with Notes & Intro. by Mary J. Gregor. Foreword by H. J. Paton* TB/110

IMMANUEL KANT: Groundwork of the Metaphysic of Morals. *Trans. & analyzed by H. J. Paton* TB/1159

IMMANUEL KANT: Lectures on Ethics. § *Introduction by Lewis W. Beck* TB/105

QUENTIN LAUER: Phenomenology: *Its Genesis and Prospect* TB/1169

GABRIEL MARCEL: Being and Having: *An Existential Diary. Intro. by James Collins* TB/310

GEORGE A. MORGAN: What Nietzsche Means TB/1198

PHILO SAADYA GAON, & JEHUDA HALEVI: Three Jewish Philosophers. *Ed. by Hans Lewy, Alexander Altmann, & Isaak Heinemann* TB/813

MICHAEL POLANYI: Personal Knowledge: *Towards a Post-Critical Philosophy* TB/1158

WILLARD VAN ORMAN QUINE: Elementary Logic: *Revised Edition* TB/577

WILLARD VAN ORMAN QUINE: From a Logical Point of View: *Logico-Philosophical Essays* TB/566

BERTRAND RUSSELL et al.: The Philosophy of Bertrand Russell. *Edited by Paul Arthur Schilpp*
Vol. I TB/1095; Vol. II TB/1096

L. S. STEBBING: A Modern Introduction to Logic TL/538

ALFRED NORTH WHITEHEAD: Process and Reality: *An Essay in Cosmology* TB/1033

PHILIP P. WIENER: Evolution and the Founders of Pragmatism. *Foreword by John Dewey* TB/1212

WILHELM WINDELBAND: A History of Philosophy
Vol. I: *Greek, Roman, Medieval* TB/38
Vol. II: *Renaissance, Enlightenment, Modern* TB/39

LUDWIG WITTGENSTEIN: The Blue and Brown Books ° TB/1211

Political Science & Government

JEREMY BENTHAM: The Handbook of Political Fallacies: *Introduction by Crane Brinton* TB/1069

KENNETH E. BOULDING: Conflict and Defense: *A General Theory* TB/3024

CRANE BRINTON: English Political Thought in the Nineteenth Century TB/1071

EDWARD S. CORWIN: American Constitutional History: *Essays edited by Alpheus T. Mason and Gerald Garvey* TB/1136

ROBERT DAHL & CHARLES E. LINDBLOM: Politics, Economics, and Welfare: *Planning and Politico-Economic Systems Resolved into Basic Social Processes* TB/3037

JOHN NEVILLE FIGGIS: The Divine Right of Kings. *Introduction by G. R. Elton* TB/1191

JOHN NEVILLE FIGGIS: Political Thought from Gerson to Grotius: 1414-1625: *Seven Studies. Introduction by Garrett Mattingly* TB/1032

F. L. GANSHOF: Feudalism TB/1058

G. P. GOOCH: English Democratic Ideas in Seventeenth Century TB/1006

J. H. HEXTER: More's Utopia: *The Biography of an Idea. New Epilogue by the Author* TB/1195

ROBERT H. JACKSON: The Supreme Court in the American System of Government TB/1106

DAN N. JACOBS, Ed.: The New Communist Manifesto & *Related Documents. Third edition, Revised* TB/1078

DAN N. JACOBS & HANS BAERWALD, Eds.: Chinese Communism: *Selected Documents* TB/3031

ROBERT GREEN MCCLOSKEY: American Conservatism in the Age of Enterprise, 1865-1910 TB/1137

KINGSLEY MARTIN: French Liberal Thought in the Eighteenth Century: *Political Ideas from Bayle to Condorcet* TB/1114

JOHN STUART MILL: On Bentham and Coleridge. *Introduction by F. R. Leavis* TB/1070

JOHN B. MORRALL: Political Thought in Medieval Times TB/1076

JOHN PLAMENATZ: German Marxism and Russian Communism. ° *New Preface by the Author* TB/1189

SIR KARL POPPER: The Open Society and Its Enemies
Vol. I: *The Spell of Plato* TB/1101
Vol. II: *The High Tide of Prophecy: Hegel, Marx, and the Aftermath* TB/1102

HENRI DE SAINT-SIMON: Social Organization, The Science of Man, and Other Writings. *Edited and Translated by Felix Markham* TB/1152

JOSEPH A. SCHUMPETER: Capitalism, Socialism and Democracy TB/3008

CHARLES H. SHINN: Mining Camps: *A Study in American Frontier Government. ‡ Edited by Rodman W. Paul* TB/3062

Psychology

ALFRED ADLER: The Individual Psychology of Alfred Adler. *Edited by Heinz L. and Rowena R. Ansbacher* TB/1154

ALFRED ADLER: Problems of Neurosis. *Introduction by Heinz L. Ansbacher* TB/1145

ANTON T. BOISEN: The Exploration of the Inner World: *A Study of Mental Disorder and Religious Experience* TB/87

HERBERT FINGARETTE: The Self in Transformation: *Psychoanalysis, Philosophy and the Life of the Spirit.* || TB/1177

SIGMUND FREUD: On Creativity and the Unconscious: *Papers on the Psychology of Art, Literature, Love, Religion.* § *Intro. by Benjamin Nelson* TB/45

C. JUDSON HERRICK: The Evolution of Human Nature
TB/545

WILLIAM JAMES: Psychology: *The Briefer Course*. Edited with an Intro. by Gordon Allport TB/1034

C. G. JUNG: Psychological Reflections TB/2001

C. G. JUNG: Symbols of Transformation: *An Analysis of the Prelude to a Case of Schizophrenia. Illus.*
Vol. I: TB/2009; Vol. II TB/2010

C. G. JUNG & C. KERÉNYI: Essays on a Science of Mythology: *The Myths of the Divine Child and the Divine Maiden* TB/2014

JOHN T. MC NEILL: A History of the Cure of Souls
TB/126

KARL MENNINGER: Theory of Psychoanalytic Technique
TB/1144

ERICH NEUMANN: Amor and Psyche: *The Psychic Development of the Feminine* TB/2012

ERICH NEUMANN: The Archetypal World of Henry Moore. *107 illus.* TB/2020

ERICH NEUMANN: The Origins and History of Consciousness Vol. I *Illus.* TB/2007; Vol. II TB/2008

C. P. OBERNDORF: A History of Psychoanalysis in America
TB/1147

RALPH BARTON PERRY: The Thought and Character of William James: *Briefer Version* TB/1156

JEAN PIAGET, BÄRBEL INHELDER, & ALINA SZEMINSKA: The Child's Conception of Geometry ° TB/1146

JOHN H. SCHAAR: Escape from Authority: *The Perspectives of Erich Fromm* TB/1155

Sociology

JACQUES BARZUN: Race: *A Study in Superstition. Revised Edition* TB/1172

BERNARD BERELSON, Ed.: The Behavioral Sciences Today
TB/1127

ABRAHAM CAHAN: The Rise of David Levinsky: *A documentary novel of social mobility in early twentieth century America. Intro. by John Higham* TB/1028

THOMAS C. COCHRAN: The Inner Revolution: *Essays on the Social Sciences in History* TB/1140

ALLISON DAVIS & JOHN DOLLARD: Children of Bondage: *The Personality Development of Negro Youth in the Urban South* || TB/3049

ST. CLAIR DRAKE & HORACE R. CAYTON: Black Metropolis: *A Study of Negro Life in a Northern City. Revised and Enlarged. Intro. by Everett C. Hughes*
Vol. I TB/1086; Vol. II TB/1087

EMILE DURKHEIM et al.: Essays on Sociology and Philosophy: *With Analyses of Durkheim's Life and Work.* || Edited by Kurt H. Wolff TB/1151

LEON FESTINGER, HENRY W. RIECKEN & STANLEY SCHACHTER: When Prophecy Fails: *A Social and Psychological Account of a Modern Group that Predicted the Destruction of the World* || TB/1132

ALVIN W. GOULDNER: Wildcat Strike: *A Study in Worker-Management Relationships* || TB/1176

FRANCIS J. GRUND: Aristocracy in America: *Social Class in the Formative Years of the New Nation* TB/1001

KURT LEWIN: Field Theory in Social Science: *Selected Theoretical Papers.* || *Edited with a Foreword by Dorwin Cartwright* TB/1135

R. M. MACIVER: Social Causation TB/1153

ROBERT K. MERTON, LEONARD BROOM, LEONARD S. COTTRELL, JR., Editors: Sociology Today: *Problems and Prospects* || Vol. I TB/1173; Vol. II TB/1174

TALCOTT PARSONS & EDWARD A. SHILS, Editors: Toward a General Theory of Action: *Theoretical Foundations for the Social Sciences* TB/1083

JOHN H. ROHRER & MUNRO S. EDMONSON, Eds.: The Eighth Generation Grows Up: *Cultures and Personalities of New Orleans Negroes* || TB/3050

ARNOLD ROSE: The Negro in America: *The Condensed Version of Gunnar Myrdal's An American Dilemma*
TB/3048

KURT SAMUELSSON: Religion and Economic Action: *A Critique of Max Weber's The Protestant Ethic and the Spirit of Capitalism.* || ° *Trans. by E. G. French; Ed. with Intro. by D. C. Coleman* TB/1131

PITIRIM A. SOROKIN: Contemporary Sociological Theories. *Through the First Quarter of the 20th Century* TB/3046

MAURICE R. STEIN: The Eclipse of Community: *An Interpretation of American Studies* TB/1128

FERDINAND TÖNNIES: Community and Society: *Gemeinschaft und Gesellschaft. Translated and edited by Charles P. Loomis* TB/1116

W. LLOYD WARNER & Associates: Democracy in Jonesville: *A Study in Quality and Inequality* TB/1129

W. LLOYD WARNER: Social Class in America: *The Evaluation of Status* TB/1013

RELIGION

Ancient & Classical

J. H. BREASTED: Development of Religion and Thought in Ancient Egypt. *Introduction by John A. Wilson*
TB/57

HENRI FRANKFORT: Ancient Egyptian Religion: *An Interpretation* TB/77

G. RACHEL LEVY: Religious Conceptions of the Stone Age and their Influence upon European Thought. *Illus. Introduction by Henri Frankfort* TB/106

MARTIN P. NILSSON: Greek Folk Religion. *Foreword by Arthur Darby Nock* TB/78

ALEXANDRE PIANKOFF: The Shrines of Tut-Ankh-Amon. *Edited by N. Rambova. 117 illus.* TB/2011

H. J. ROSE: Religion in Greece and Rome TB/55

Biblical Thought & Literature

W. F. ALBRIGHT: The Biblical Period from Abraham to Ezra TB/102

C. K. BARRETT, Ed.: The New Testament Background: *Selected Documents* TB/86

C. H. DODD: The Authority of the Bible TB/43

M. S. ENSLIN: Christian Beginnings TB/5

M. S. ENSLIN: The Literature of the Christian Movement
TB/6

JOHN GRAY: Archaeology and the Old Testament World. *Illus.* TB/127

H. H. ROWLEY: The Growth of the Old Testament
TB/107

D. WINTON THOMAS, Ed.: Documents from Old Testament Times TB/85

The Judaic Tradition

LEO BAECK: Judaism and Christianity. *Trans. with Intro. by Walter Kaufmann* TB/823

SALO W. BARON: Modern Nationalism and Religion
TB/818

MARTIN BUBER: Eclipse of God: *Studies in the Relation Between Religion and Philosophy* TB/12

MARTIN BUBER: Moses: *The Revelation and the Covenant* TB/27

MARTIN BUBER: Pointing the Way. *Introduction by Maurice S. Friedman* TB/103

MARTIN BUBER: The Prophetic Faith TB/73

MARTIN BUBER: Two Types of Faith: *the interpenetration of Judaism and Christianity* ° TB/75

Christianity: General

Christianity: Origins & Early Development

Christianity: The Middle Ages and The Reformation

Christianity: The Protestant Tradition

NATURAL SCIENCES AND MATHEMATICS

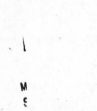